THE MOST DISTRESSFUL COUNTRY

The Green Flag Volume One

ROBERT KEE

QUARTET BOOKS   LONDON

Published by Quartet Books Limited 1976
27 Goodge Street, London W1P 1FD

First published in a single volume (with *The Bold Fenian Men* and *Ourselves Alone*) under the title *The Green Flag* by Weidenfeld and Nicolson Limited, London, 1972

ISBN 0 704 33089 X

To the memory of my father,
Robert Kee (1880–1958),
and of my mother,
Dorothy Frances Kee
(1890–1964)

Printed in Great Britain by litho by The Anchor Press Ltd
and bound by Wm Brendon & Son Ltd
both of Tiptree, Essex

The Most Distressful Country is the first volume of *The Green Flag*, Robert Kee's monumental three-part history of Irish nationalism, unlikely to be superseded as the most comprehensive and lucid study available.

Volume One attempts firstly to answer the crucial question: Who *are* the Irish? From the arrival of the Norman adventurers such as Strongbow in the twelfth century, through the Tudor period of conquest and confiscation, the impact of the French Revolution, the Rebellion of 1798, the campaigns of O'Connell and the Great Famine of 1845–8 and its aftermath, Robert Kee charts the development of the Irish nationalist impulse.

Volumes Two and Three, *The Bold Fenian Men* and *Ourselves Alone*, take the story up to the Home Rule crisis, the so-called War of Independence of 1919–21 and the Irish civil war that followed.

Robert Kee is a well-known and highly regarded author, journalist and TV personality. He has worked on such current affairs programmes as *Panorama*, *This Week* and ITN's daily *First Report*. He has been a special correspondent for the *Sunday Times* and the *Observer*, and was literary editor of the *Spectator*.

Contents

IRELAND

0   50miles
0   80km

Lough Swilly

Rathlin I.

DONEGAL

Derry

LONDONDERRY

Larne

ANTRIM

TYRONE

BELFAST

Bangor

Dungannon

Lisburn

FERMANAGH

LEITRIM

MONAGHAN

ARMAGH

DOWN

Newry

SLIGO

Cavan

CAVAN

Dundalk

LOUTH

MAYO

Westport

Ballaghaderreen

Ballinalee

Drogheda

Tourmakeady

ROSCOMMON

LONGFORD

MEATH

Balbriggan

Tuam

WESTMEATH

Trim

Ashbourne

Athlone

Ashtown

Howth

GALWAY

Galway

OFFALY
(KING'S Co.)

Maynooth

DUBLIN

Clontarf

Dun Laoghaire

KILDARE

Ennistymon

Curragh

Kilcoole

Lahinch

CLARE

Miltown
Malbay

Ennis

LEIX
(QUEEN'S Co.)

WICKLOW

Woodenbridge

Arklow

Limerick

Thurles

Kilkenny

CARLOW

TIPPERARY

KILKENNY

Soloheadbeg

Cashel

LIMERICK

Knocklong

Tipperary

Enniscorthy

WEXFORD

Banna Strand

Ardfert

Kilmallock

Carrick-
on-Suir

Fenit

Tralee

Mitchelstown

Wexford

KERRY

Malloy

Fermoy

WATERFORD

Waterford

Killarney

Clonbanin

Clonmult

Bantry

Macroom

CORK

Midleton

Kilmichael

Cork

Bealnablath

CrossBarry

Bandon

Kinsale

... The study of Irish history does not excite political animosity but leads to the very opposite result. Thoroughly to appreciate the history of this or any country it is necessary to sympathise with all parties ...

> A. G. Richey, from *A Short History of the Irish People*, 1869

A standard to be got for each company ten feet long with a pike in the end, the flag to be of green stuff, about two feet square.

> Military instructions from the Leinster Provincial Committee of the United Irishmen, 19 April 1798

QUESTION: You say that the predisposition to discontent which prevails generally is partly to be attributed to the recollections of ancient times?
ANSWER: I think so. I have heard and I believe that that feeling is kept alive in the minds of the people and is one of the causes ...

> Evidence of Mr George Bennett, K.C., before a *Select Committee appointed to enquire into the Disturbances in Ireland*, given 18 May 1824 (Minutes of Evidence, p. 94)

Preface to Volume One of the Quartet edition

When I finished writing *The Green Flag* in the Spring of 1971 the latest of the ancient troubles of Ireland had already been continuing for nearly two years. It was not part of my scheme then to include any account of them, and it is not now. They are still confused, unresolved and impossible to treat with the historical detachment which I hope is part of the character of this book. What I have tried to do in *The Green Flag* is to unfold as dispassionately as possible a narrative of earlier events (principally from 1789 to 1925) of which some knowledge is indispensable for any understanding of what has happened or may happen in Ireland. Knowledge and understanding do not in themselves provide solutions but there can be no solutions without them. I cannot help hoping that this new edition will, however indirectly, contribute something to an ending of the horror which the events of recent years have brought to the United Kingdom and Ireland.

The present volume, *The Most Distressful Country*, is primarily concerned with Ireland's historic 'wrongs'; and I hope Irish readers will forgive me for often presupposing ignorance of material with which they are familiar. I hope too they may sometimes feel rewarded by finding it viewed in a slightly different light from that to which they are accustomed.

The first inspiration for *The Green Flag* came from a magical valley in Co. Wicklow to whose resident spirit I send across many years gratitude and affection. Among others who gave me help I should like to thank particularly Mrs Ralph Partridge, Sir Nicholas Henderson, the late Dr P. M. Turquet, my wife Cynthia, my son Alexander, Miss Marguerite Foss and Mrs Topsy Levan; also the staffs over many years of the British Museum Reading Room, the British Museum Newspaper Library at Colindale, the London Library, and of the National Library of Ireland.

ROBERT KEE
January 1976

PART ONE

1

Treaty Night

In London, during the night of Monday, 5 December 1921, there occurred one of those sudden changes in the weather which Londoners come to accept as part of their long inconclusive battle against the winter. A week before there had been three days of fog. This was followed by a very cold spell. Then on this Monday night there came a quick rise in temperature so that, according to the newspapers, those who had slept with their windows shut set out next morning unaware of what had happened and arrived at their offices sweating in overcoats and mufflers.[1] Otherwise it must have seemed a night much like any other in the dying year.

But it was during this night that seven centuries of British history came to an end. For at 2.20 a.m., after some last-minute motoring between 10 Downing Street and 22 Hans Place, SW1, where a delegation of men from Ireland had been staying, a document was signed at 10 Downing Street that has come to be known as the Anglo-Irish Treaty. Viewed in the grand perspective of history, England's long attempt to rule all Ireland, begun in the reign of Henry II, was over.

For more than forty years after that night in December 1921 Englishmen gradually allowed themselves to forget that there had ever been an Irish question. Ireland became a country which, if it held English interest at all, held it largely for pleasant amiable reasons. It was – and still is – a beautiful, quiet, rainy country in which, as the Irish Tourist Board once put it with a touch of genius, 'it is easy to take things easy'; a country of good racehorses and stout and an eccentric writer or two, where the Englishman can combine the pleasures of being on unfamiliar ground with the pleasures of feeling thoroughly at home.

But in the late 1960s Britain and the rest of the world were startled by events in Northern Ireland which, violent, unpredictable and sometimes incomprehensible, seemed to most people to strike like a bolt from the blue. But they had not come from the blue. They had come out of Irish history.

Forty odd years before, Englishmen had let themselves think that they had solved the Irish question. Inasmuch as the Anglo-Irish Treaty had removed from England the most complex emotional problem in her long domestic history, this was true. But it had solved the problem for England, not for

Ireland. The chief fault of English government in Ireland had always been not that it had oppressed her but that it had ignored her problems until too late. Now the untied ends of England's 'Treaty' settlement have returned to trouble her.

It is already difficult, fifty years later, to realize what a momentous change, despite its failings, that settlement of 6 December 1921 brought about. In 1921, for more generations than anyone would normally stop to consider, there had been living in Ireland men who thought of themselves as indistinguishably British and Irish and whose lives made the two islands to them one country. Such men would take pride in being 'Irishmen' as Welshmen or men from Yorkshire today take pride in their backgrounds, regarding their love of Ireland as part of a wider loyalty. Others who lived in Ireland shared the experience but with a different emphasis: they thought of themselves as primarily 'Irish', but since 'Irish' was an identity which had so long existed only within the framework of the British Empire, that framework was part of the identity. When such men joined the British Army or Navy, as they did in great numbers, or came to England to build for themselves careers which welded them almost indistinguishably to the people among whom they lived, they developed a more positive wider loyalty without in any way excluding a great love for the country in which they had been born.

Politically England and Ireland had long seemed inextricably entangled. The basic political connection of the two islands through the Crown had until only a very few years before been taken for granted by the vast majority of both Irishmen and Englishmen for many centuries. Until the end of the eighteenth century the two islands had had separate Parliaments under the Crown, but for over a hundred years after that the connection had been closer still, with Ireland sending to a joint British House of Commons roughly one-sixth of that House's representation.

The problems of government in Ireland had preoccupied British, statesmen throughout the nineteenth century. For some fifty years before 6 December 1921, that is to say for the entire adult life of a whole generation of Englishmen, 'the Irish Question' had repeatedly dominated English politics in time of peace. A British Prime Minister, Gladstone, had once described it as 'leading to the utter destruction of the mind of Parliament, to the great enfeebling and impeding of its proper working'.[2]

Now, quite suddenly, on the night of 5–6 December 1921, all this was ended. It was ended by a few strokes of the pen – by the signatures on one side of the British government of the day, and on the other of five men all but one of whom had been quite unheard of a few years before. One had had a price of £10,000 set on his head by the British Government earlier in the year. Another had been educated at Rugby, one of the best known of English public schools.

It is easy to see now that what took place that night was the first crack in the disintegration of the British Empire as it had been known for over a century – a disintegration (transformation is a more comfortable word) which has steadily continued and been so much a part of our own day. But this was a separation far more painful than any of those which were to follow, involving as it did a rupture at the very heart of the Empire itself. The British Empire never recovered from it. Some would say that Ireland has never recovered either.

2
Contradictions of Irish Nationality

In a letter to a friend in February 1918, Eamon de Valera wrote that for seven centuries England had held Ireland 'as Germany holds Belgium to-day, by the right of the sword'.[1] This is the classical language of Irish separatism and can be very misleading.

An Irish nationalism of this sort, which saw England and Ireland as two separate and hostile countries, had itself then only been in existence for a little over a hundred years. From its origin at the end of the eighteenth century until the very year in which Mr de Valera was writing, it had been not so much a normal patriotic faith as an intellectual theory held by idealists who were trying, with little success, to make their theory materialize in practice. Inevitably they used many synthetic and unreal concepts as if they were facts. Chief of these was the notion that England 'held' Ireland by force. Its corollary was that the undoubted ills from which Ireland suffered over the centuries were those inflicted by a strong oppressor over a weak and subject alien people. Both of these notions are a large enough distortion of events to amount to a historical untruth. Between 1845 and 1919, the period during which this view of Irish nationalism laid what foundations it could among the ordinary Irish people, Ireland was in fact 'held' by twelve thousand Catholic Irishmen of the Royal Irish Constabulary, drawn largely from among the younger sons of the suffering peasantry. In these circumstances to talk of Ireland as being 'held' at all in a military sense is patently ridiculous.

It is perhaps a virtue of the British that, often so arrogant when the star of their power was at its zenith, they cheerfully accept almost any interpretation of their former behaviour now that that star has grown dim. They have thus come to accept almost without reserve that what took place in Ireland between the years 1916 and 1922 was a bitter struggle by a small subject nation battling for its independence against British imperialist might in a conflict which the British morally deserved to lose. But perhaps the British like to see it this way because the truth is even more difficult to face. For Britain can take little credit for the way in which she managed that part of herself that was Ireland for seven centuries.

Though the sword indeed played its dreadful part there as savagely as in any other country of Europe, to see Irish history in the plain, uncompromisingly nationalistic terms of Mr de Valera's statement is to miss, together with the truth, much of the poignancy and drama of the strange relationship that persisted between the two islands for so long. It is also the surest way to become bewildered and confused by the very events in which Mr de Valera was then embroiled, as certain obvious facts about these events make plain enough.

For example, the Commander-in-Chief of the Irish forces in the heroic Dublin Rebellion of 1916 was not strictly an Irishman at all, but the son of a Birmingham man. The rebellion itself was unpopular with the great majority of the Irish people at the time, and, after the rebels' surrender, some of the prisoners being marched away through the streets of Dublin by the British were jeered at by the local population. By contrast, one of the British officers who guarded those prisoners was, just over five years later, to be a member of the very Irish delegation which signed the Anglo-Irish treaty on behalf of Ireland.*

The first problem, in fact, is to define an Irishman at all. An English civil servant, Erskine Childers, was one of the most steadfast of all supporters of the Irish republican cause between 1919 and 1922 and was reviled as an Englishman by both English and Irish alike for his pains. He even met his death before a firing squad in the end – and an Irish firing squad at that. One of the bravest of all the many other brave men who died during these years, Cathal Brugha, at first sight an authentic enough Gaelic hero, is on closer examination just plain Charles Burgess, also shot to death by uniformed Irish soldiers for his loyalty to an Irish Republic.

On the other hand Sir Henry Wilson, British Chief of the Imperial General Staff in 1918, was as much an Irishman by his own or Sinn Fein's standards as the members of the Irish Republican Brotherhood who killed him with revolver bullets on the door-step of his home, 36 Eaton Place, SW3 in 1922. And Sir Edward Carson, an equally implacable enemy of Irish independence, was proud to be able to refer to Ireland as 'my country'. Equally an Irishman, by descent at any rate, was the British General Sir Nevile Macready, who on 8 July 1921 walked up the steps of the Dublin Mansion House to negotiate a truce with the leaders of the Irish Republican Army. Many thought then and have thought since that he went unarmed, but, complimenting himself in a peculiarly English sort of way that he knew the Irish too well for that, he put a revolver in the right-hand pocket of his tunic where it can be discerned to this day in the photograph of him taken as he made his way through applauding Dublin crowds to that historic meeting.[2]

The confusing contradictions multiply indefinitely. The leader of the Ulster Volunteers, Carson, was a Dubliner, the leader of the Irish Volunteers

* The Old Rugbeian, Robert Barton.

in the south, MacNeill, an Ulsterman. At the conclusion of the story 'Ulster' is no longer Ulster,* and the most northerly point of Ireland, Malin Head, is in 'Southern Ireland'. But the most serious proof of the complexity of what is still sometimes so simply called the 'War of Independence' can be seen in a study of the judicial executions which took place during and after it. For, between 1919 and 1921, the British Government shot in cold blood or hanged twenty-four Irishmen who had taken up arms for an independent sovereign Irish Republic. Between 1922 and 1923, in the so-called 'Civil War', the new Irish Government executed over three times that number of Irishmen who had taken up arms for exactly the same cause.

Part of the explanation of all this is that the whole struggle was really something of a civil war from the start. But how it came about, and how it was possible for some people to regard it sincerely, however self-consciously or even half-heartedly, as a national struggle, can only be understood if it is seen in the wider context of the Irish history to which it provided such an unexpected climax. For on both sides of this struggle men were sometimes self-consciously, sometimes unconsciously, in the grip of forces other than those of the time in which they lived. For over seven centuries the history of the people who lived in Ireland had been a folk-trauma comparable in human experience perhaps only to that of the Jews. In these years of the twentieth century a haphazard series of events finally exorcized that trauma for ever.

* The historic province of Ulster consists of the nine counties of Antrim, Down, Armagh, Derry, Tyrone, Fermanagh, Donegal, Monaghan and Cavan, and the state of Northern Ireland consists only of the first six of these.

3

Strongbow (1170) to the Ulster Plantation (1609)

There is a fairly close limit in time beyond which it is pointless to go back and try to trace nationality. An Englishman proud of being an Englishman today is himself the product of many warring races. If Mr de Valera in 1918 could identify the Irish who fought the English in our own century with those who fought 'the English' seven centuries earlier, there was no logical reason to stop there. He could have gone back further still and seen the only true Irish as the small dark race called the Firbolg who were in Ireland when the Celts, or Gaels, came to conquer them from the mainland of Europe a few centuries BC.

However, it was the Gaels, bringing from Europe an elegantly ornamental civilization based on a loose tribal structure, who laid a foundation for Irish life and character which was to colour all succeeding influences for some two thousand years. The failure of the Romans to reach Ireland and the survival through the dark ages after the Roman withdrawal from Britain of Celtic civilization in Ireland, christianized by the legendary St Patrick and enriched by trading contacts with the mainland of Europe, ensured that there was left on Ireland a mark of difference from the rest of Britain that even in the latter half of the twentieth century has still not wholly faded.

And yet if one decides to begin with the Gaels as the first 'Irish' and see their High King Brian Boru as the first Irish national hero after his defeat of invading Norsemen at Clontarf in 1014, a problem arises over all the Norsemen who even before that battle had become absorbed into the population of Ireland and all the Norsemen and other 'invaders' who were absorbed soon afterwards.

Seven centuries later the Irish were a too complicated and subtle amalgam of conquered and conquerors for historical racialism to be of much value in explaining events.

It was not in any case 'the English' whom the Gaels, or some of them, fought in the twelfth century. Invaders like Robert Fitzstephen and Richard 2nd Earl of Pembroke, known as Strongbow, who first crossed to Ireland from England in 1169 and 1170 were Norman adventurers, speaking Norman French. They came not in England's interests but their own, in search of land, power and wealth. Moreover, they came at the express invitation of an Irish chief, Dermot MacMurrough, to help him in his quarrel with other Irish chiefs. Such Normans built themselves into the ever-changing pattern of Gaelic tribal alliances in Ireland, and in the process often intermarried with the Irish, adopted their language and customs and became Irish too. It has often been pointed out that many of the names we think of today as most typically Irish – Joyce, Burke, Costello, Prendergast, Fitzgerald, etc. – are in fact the names of these early Norman 'conquerors'.*

For centuries afterwards men who owed a nominal feudal loyalty to the English king continued to settle in Ireland and become, in the medieval phrase, *hiberniores hibernis ipsos* – 'more Irish than the Irish'. Many became indistinguishably Gaelic. The term Old English was later applied to them if their identity had remained in some ways distinct from Gaelic tribal society. But the distinction between the Old English and the other Catholic Irish was, as far as the royal authority was concerned, often only one between the king's rebels and the king's enemies.

The original claim to authority by the English king in Ireland derived from the automatic feudal obligations of his subjects who acquired land there. Henry II had been so alarmed by Strongbow's independent self-aggrandizement in Ireland that he had visited the country almost at once to try and assert these feudal ties, and his royal authority was strengthened by an obscure commission apparently given him by Pope Adrian IV to reform the Irish Church.† But the practical difficulties of medieval communications across a large expanse of sea made the Crown's task of supervision impossible. Over the years the effective authority of the English Crown in Ireland shrank further and further to a small area round Dublin known as the Pale – and was not even always to be found there. The first real sign of any sort of 'national' independent spirit to appear in Ireland came from the Old English themselves – from the Norman Fitzgeralds, who, though nominally the king's deputies, built up for themselves in the second half of the fifteenth and first half of the sixteenth centuries a formidable power which defied the king, and was itself known quasi-regally as that of the House of Kildare.

The Gaelic chiefs themselves had no scruples about submitting to the authority of an English king when this proved tactically necessary. Their one concern was to be left free to pursue their private interests and ambitions by their subtle system of tribal alliances, and to look after their lands with the minimum of outside interference.

* De Jorz, de Burgo, etc. Edmund Curtis's *History of Ireland* (London, 1936), makes this point.

† The medieval historian Giraldus Cambrensis says the Commission was made in the form of the Papal Bull *Laudabiliter* of 1155. The authenticity of this Bull has been doubted. It does not exist in the Papal Archives. However, there is other evidence that Adrian IV made some sort of grant of Ireland to Henry II. (See Curtis, *History of Ireland*, pp. 56–7.)

In 1541 Henry VIII, having finally succeeded in breaking the power of the House of Kildare, determined to turn nominal feudal ties into effective administrative ones. He had himself proclaimed in Dublin 'King of this land of Ireland as united, annexed and knit for ever to the Imperial Crown of the Realm of England'. So many of the Gaelic chiefs attended the ceremony that the bill was read over to them in Irish and they expressed their 'liberal consents'. Five years later the Earls of Tyrone, Desmond and Thomond with the Fitzpatrick, O'Connor, O'Murphy, O'Carrol, MacGeoghan and other native chiefs wrote to the king in Latin: 'We call God to witness that we acknowledge no other king or lord on earth except your Majesty.'[1]

As it happened, this sort of talk was no longer to do them any good. The new Tudor state was out to replace not only the independent power of Old English nobles but also the power of Gaelic tribal organization by the authority of a central administration. A peaceful system of submission was offered to the Gaelic chiefs by which they could surrender their lands to the king and immediately receive them back again, 'regranted'. In this way they acknowledged that their only title to the land they held was through the king.

Some accepted willingly. But such a system, assuming, as it did, acceptance of English laws of succession, clashed directly with Gaelic tradition. By Gaelic, or Brehon law, land was the property of the tribe, and the chief, who was elected, held his title only for life. In cases where the chiefs themselves were ready enough to accept the new English laws, the lesser Irish whose interests were thus disregarded often refused to asquiesce so obligingly. Sometimes the situation was reversed. A native chief, defying the new attempt at control of his affairs, would take to arms to resist it and at the same time try to strengthen his position with his lesser chiefs by forcing them into a closer obedience than was traditional. In such cases, as one historian has put it, 'the lesser chiefs ... sought only to maintain their local independence and hailed the English as deliverers'.[2] One way or another, violent conflict between the new system and the interests it challenged was inevitable. And where the principle of 'surrender and re-grant' broke down it was replaced by the Tudors with conquest and confiscation. But this was not a conflict between one nation and another. It was a conflict between an old system of government and a new one, and men of Gaelic and Old English origin were to be found motivated by self-interest on both sides.

When resistance was encountered, whether from Old English or Gaelic Irish, the Tudors dealt with it with a ferocity which, in the words of the great historian Lecky, 'has seldom been exceeded in the pages of history'.[3] The fiercest of the great Gaelic chiefs to challenge the new system was Shane O'Neill, and if any chief had been thinking in modern terms of national leadership it would have been he. But 'no Irish chiefs had learnt to look beyond the limits of his tribe',[4] and the battle which finally brought about Shane O'Neill's downfall was fought not against the English but against another Gaelic chief, the O'Donnell.

If this war, like all Ireland's wars, was a civil war and not a national one, it brought, as all were to do, terrible suffering to the people who lived in Ireland. An eye-witness description by the poet Spenser of a contemporary scene from these Tudor wars, was from one cause or another, to become all too representative of the experience of the common people of Ireland for the next three centuries: 'Out of every corner of the woods and glens', writes Spenser, 'they came creeping forth upon their hands, for their legs could not bear them. They looked like anatomies of death; they spoke like ghosts crying out of their graves . . .'[5] And the English sixteenth-century historian, Fynes Morison, who witnessed the campaigns in Ulster, also uncannily pre-echoes scenes of later centuries when he writes of the multitudes of dead 'with their mouths all coloured green by eating nettles, docks and all things they could rend above ground'.[6]

The lands of those, of whatever origin, who resisted the new centralization process were confiscated and planted where possible with settlers from England or Scotland. The first of such plantations had actually been carried out with settlers from the Pale in the reign of the Catholic sovereigns Philip and Mary in the counties Leix and Offaly, then re-named King's and Queen's Counties.* However, plantations often failed to take root and where this happened those who had been dispossessed drifted back on to their former lands without any precise legal status. It was this lack of any right to be on the land on any other terms than those of mere sufferance, in contrast with a certain sense of post-feudal mutual obligation which characterized relations between landlord and occupier elsewhere in Europe, that was to determine the condition of the Irish peasant for three centuries.

The most successful of all 'plantations' was completed in the reign of James I, principally in six of the nine counties of Ulster. These had been the lands of Hugh O'Neill, Earl of Tyrone. He was the last of those great Gaelic chiefs who, though acknowledging in theory the sovereignty of the English monarchy, tried to resist the new Tudor administrative machine. Despite help from Spain, O'Neill was defeated decisively at the battle of Kinsale in 1601. Finally, in 1607 he abandoned all hope of recovering his former position and sailed from Ireland for ever with his ally the Earl of Tyrconnell. The event became nostalgically enshrined in Irish folk-memory as 'the Flight of the Earls'. Their lands were confiscated and 'planted' with new settlers.

With these Ulster plantations a profoundly significant addition was made to the Irish population. For the new inhabitants of Ireland were Protestants.

* Although Mary was a Catholic she pursued the policy of establishing the central government's authority with the same purpose as Protestant Tudors.

The Reformation itself had not made much impression on Ireland. This was partly because the Gaelic population was often physically inaccessible and largely intellectually inaccessible behind the language barrier, and partly because at a time when Ireland could so easily provide a base for England's Catholic enemy Spain, it was important not to antagonize the Old English unnecessarily by forcing on them an unwelcome change of faith. So the new Protestant inhabitants of Ireland set about their lives among other Irish, who, whether Gaelic, Gaelicized or Old English, were largely Catholics. Very few of the old families, Gaelic or Old English, changed to the new Protestant faith, although among those that were eventually to do so were names of both types: the O'Briens, for instance, already Earls of Thomond and later of Inchiquin from among the Gaelic Irish, and the Butlers, ancient Earls of Ormond, from among the Old English. But racial origins in themselves were now becoming less and less important. This was an age in which religion determined political thinking. With the Protestant plantations, a cleavage between two sections of the Irish population was established which, though it was to make no distinction between who was an Irishman and who was not, set a pattern for the social and political development of Ireland for many centuries.

By the early seventeenth century, the people who lived in Ireland were a people of mixed racial origins and differing interests and could hardly be said to form any single distinct nation. Certainly Gaelic language and traditions surviving from an older form of society and often acquired by those to whom they had not been native gave the majority of them a very distinctive character. But even for these there was no single political or constitutional identity. The monarch of England was universally accepted as the monarch of Ireland. The only dispute was about the effectiveness with which he was to wield his power. Neither in groups nor as a whole did this mixed people want to assert a political national independence. All that could be said was that a tradition had been established by which the stretch of water between Ireland and the rest of Britain induced a remarkable independence of spirit in whoever crossed it.

Certainly, too, the deliberate winding-up of formal Gaelic tribal society had left a deep confused nostalgia among the majority of the population. In fact, Gaelic society, even in the days of its High Kings, had never been more than a loose association of tribal kingdoms, sharing common laws, customs and a language under the High King's symbolic leadership. By the very nature of its individualistic organization it could never have been nor could have aspired to be a nation state, and clearly the Gaelic chiefs had no patriotic objections to the *theory* of submission to an English king. O'Neill himself, the Earl of Tyrone, had been brought up in London as an Elizabethan gentleman. He fought for his own local, if considerable, self-interest and ambition. But he did leave behind a very powerful legend of resentment for myth to work on, a legend about individual resistance to central authority and particularly to the new ownership of land.

In that beautiful country of mountain, bog and fern the legend would have lingered a long time in any case, preserved and ornamented as it was in a Gaelic language of its own. But the subsequent repetition of great personal suffering by the majority of the people of Ireland for the next three centuries kept this resentful nostalgia very much alive. As late as 1824, a Catholic priest from County Cork told a Parliamentary Committee how the peasantry among whom he lived still talked frequently of the days of Elizabeth and Tyrone, having, he said, 'recollections of the liberty and what they conceive the privileges they enjoyed formerly compared with their present degraded state'.[7] And a writer early in the twentieth century met a shepherd near Luggala in the Wicklow Hills dreaming of Ireland before the battle of Kinsale.[8]

But this was an emotional rather than a political legacy. Politically important for the future was the fact that the Gaelic resistance to central authority had had no coordinated national expression. The difficulty of effectively coordinating such feeling was to bedevil the efforts of those trying to create Irish nationalism until well into the twentieth century.

4

Great Rebellion (1641)
to Penal Laws (1703)

In 1641 a great rebellion broke out in Ireland. It began simply as an attempt on the part of the dispossessed Gaelic Irish of Ulster to recover their confiscated lands. But it was not just the dispossessed Gaelic Irish of Ulster who felt they had a grievance. For years, all Catholics in Ireland had been agitating for the redress of grievances. These were embodied principally in their status as 'recusants', or citizens who refused to acknowledge the Crown's spiritual as well as temporal supremacy over the Pope. Particularly this penalized recusant status gave those Catholics who still held land (and Catholics at this date still held two-thirds of the cultivable land of Ireland) a feeling of uneasiness and insecurity about their rights to that land; for the monarch, who proclaimed himself the source of all land ownership, held in his hands the ultimate weapon of dispossession for uncooperative subjects.

In 1641 the Puritan Parliament of England actually went so far as to decree the absolute suppression of the Catholic religion in Ireland. But by then the rebellion which had begun as a local Gaelic uprising for the return of lost lands in the North had become an alliance of all Catholics in Ireland, whatever their origin, determined to preserve their religion and defend their rights and property under the monarchy and within the Constitution. Gaelic Irish and Old English joined together to form what later historians called 'The Confederation of Kilkenny'.

The history of this 'confederation' was confused. The alliance between its Gaelic Irish and Old English wings was not always easy.* There was a further complication in that it became in time a third force in Charles I's own war against his Parliament. But the effect of the rebellion's final suppression by the Parliamentary forces under Cromwell in 1652 was devastatingly clear. The terrible suffering which Cromwell inflicted in the name of God on all Catholic rebels in Ireland, regardless of racial origin, forged for them

* The attractive leader of the Gaelic wing was Owen Roe O'Neill, nephew of the great Hugh O'Neill, Earl of Tyrone, who had fled abroad in 1607. Owen Roe O'Neill arrived in Ireland from Spain in 1642.

something very like a single identity and strengthened still further the cleavage between them and the other (Protestant) part of Ireland's population. Fynes Morison, the Elizabethan historian, had once drawn a distinction between 'the Irish in general' and 'the mere Irish' (by which he meant the Gael or Gaelicized).[1] 'The Irish of English race' was how the Old English had been referred to officially a generation before Cromwell's war.* From the time of Cromwell onwards, native Irish and Old English Catholics became increasingly indistinguishable.

The eleven years of fighting in the civil war that began with the rebellion of 1641 cost the lives of about one-third of the Catholic Irish, and many of those who were neither killed nor transported by slave-dealers to the West Indies were sentenced in their own country to a life of social ignomy and handicap. Most of the best land of Ireland was now confiscated from its owners and divided among more new Protestant settlers and adventurers, many of them Cromwellian soldiers who were in this way compensated for arrears of pay. Whereas, even after the plantation of Ulster in James I's time, two-thirds of the cultivable land of Ireland had remained in the hands of Catholics, now, after Cromwell's settlement, rather more than three-quarters of the cultivable land was to be found in the hands of the small minority of Protestants.

But though down the retrospect of history it is reasonable enough to give to these people who fought and suffered and died at this time a common identity as 'the Irish', the Protestants who had been settled in Ireland could, by now, also reasonably be called 'Irish' too. And there is one all-important fact about the Catholics which was later often forgotten. Both the Gaelic and the Old English elements in the rebellion constantly proclaimed their loyalty to the Crown – indeed it was exactly this which accounted for much of the Republican Cromwell's savagery. The first leader of the Ulster Gaelic rebels to take the field, Sir Phelim O'Neill, had insisted in his opening call to arms that the rebellion was in no way directed against the king. And even before the Old English had properly joined the rebellion the leaders of the Gaelic Irish had introduced an oath of association which contained the words: 'I further swear that I will bear faith and allegiance to our sovereign lord King Charles, his heirs and successors, and that I will defend him and them as far as I may, with my life power and estate . . .'.[2] The confederation fought under the slogan: *'Pro Deo, Pro Rege, Pro Hibernia Unanimis'* – 'One for God, King and Ireland'. And by 'King' they meant the man who was king of both England and Ireland simultaneously. A separatist nationalism was no part of their outlook; they were fighting only for what they regarded as their rights under the British Crown. Patriotic love of Ire-

* e.g., at a council meeting at Southampton in 1625. (Aidan Clarke, *The Old English in Ireland, 1625–1642*, London, 1966, p. 33.)

land was, and was long to remain, wholly compatible with loyalty to a British monarch.

The restoration of the monarchy in 1660 indeed automatically raised Irish Catholic hopes that Cromwell's settlements would be reversed and that they would get back their family lands. But Charles II owed his restoration more to the wily compromise he had worked out with Protestant parliamentarians than to the individual loyalties of Catholics. He could hardly afford to alienate the interests of his new Protestant supporters in the Irish House of Commons. And although Catholics were able to enjoy a more tolerant religious atmosphere, there was no change in the law in so far as the land was concerned and the Restoration Act of Settlement with minor modifications virtually confirmed the land settlement of Cromwell.

It was when Charles's Catholic brother James II succeeded him as King of England and Ireland in 1685 that the moment of the Catholics in Ireland seemed at last to have arrived. A Catholic was appointed Viceroy; Catholics were placed in key administrative positions and a new Catholic-dominated Parliament in Ireland actually passed an Act reversing the Cromwellian land settlement, ousting the new Protestant occupiers (though not without compensation) and returning the land confiscated by Cromwell to its former owners.*

This Act, like the rebellion of 1641 itself, had a traumatic effect on later generations. For though it never had time to come into force, the idea that the Catholics might one day try to reassert their ancient titles to land taken from them, and long held by Protestants, was the nightmare that seemed to justify the Protestant Irish in their assumption of total ascendancy in Irish society. Two hundred years later one of the Land Commissioners of 1841 was to report:

> The Repeal of the Irish Act of Settlement by the Parliament of James II gave the Protestant proprietors a fright from which they have not properly recovered even to this day.... They seem to think that they only garrison their estates, and therefore they look upon the occupiers – I cannot call them tenants – as persons ready to eject them on a favourable opportunity.[3]

What prevented the Irish Catholic Parliament's reversal of the land settlement from coming into force was the military defeat of James II by the English Parliament's new Protestant champion, William of Orange. This took place at the battles of the Boyne and Aughrim in 1690 and 1691, and these defeats were followed by the capitulation of James's army under the Catholic Irish General, Patrick Sarsfield, after William's siege of Limerick.

The words 'Remember the Boyne' are still periodically chalked up on the

---

* The separate existence of an Irish Parliament and its constitutional relations with that of England are discussed below, on pp. 29–31.

walls of Belfast today, and 12 July,* the anniversary of this victory which took place over 280 years ago, is still celebrated in Northern Ireland as if it had some real significance for the present. And so, in the curious political anomaly that is Northern Ireland, it has. For the Boyne and other disasters suffered by the Catholics of Ireland between 1689 and 1692 marked the beginning of a long period, fading slowly in intensity over the centuries but not yet in the North wholly ended, in which to be Catholic in Ireland meant automatically to be the under-dog. To be Protestant meant, whatever one's status, and by no individual effort of one's own, to be automatically superior. Ireland became a place where, as the Protestant historian Lecky was to put it, 'many who would never have sought ascendancy if it had not been established, wished to preserve the privileges they had inherited, and the most worthless Protestant, if he had nothing else to boast of, at least found it pleasing to think that he was a member of a dominant race'.[4]

'After Aughrim's great disaster . . .' runs an Irish song commemorating the significance of this and the other defeats of the period for the majority of the people of Ireland. Indeed, they now joined Kinsale and the Flight of the Earls as further ingredients of popular myth. And yet in view of the separatist slant that was to be given to this myth in the twentieth century it must be remembered that at Aughrim James's troops were rallied by appeals to their religion, not to their race,[5] and that this and the other disasters of the time were suffered by Irishmen fighting for a man who had ascended the throne as an English king and whom they wanted as their king too.

The Catholic Irish soldiers who fought for James II were allowed under the Treaty of Limerick to leave for France and large numbers of them did so. For over a hundred years these 'Wild Geese' and their later followers and descendants were to be found fighting under the banners of the Irish Brigade in the armies of France on every major battlefield of Europe. They at least became members of a separate race, though not an Irish one. Some drifted into the service of other foreign states besides France, and within a generation or two Irish families were to be found dispersed throughout Europe speaking French or Spanish or German or Russian as their first language.† Sarsfield himself, a personification of the merged Catholic Irish people, descended as he was from Gaelic chieftains on one side and an Old English Catholic family on the other, was killed in 1693 at the battle of Landen in Flanders with, so it is said, the words: 'Would it were for Ireland!' on his lips.

In Ireland itself the Irish Protestants now proceeded to turn their victory

* By the new style calendar introduced in 1752. Before this date 1 July was the day of celebration.

† Among the many descendants of the 'Wild Geese' who achieved international fame or notoriety in later times were Macmahon, the French general of the war of 1870, and Taafe, the Prime Minister of the Austro-Hungarian Empire.

to personal advantage. Still more confiscations directly transferred an even greater proportion of the land into the hands of the Protestant minority. In 1688 the Catholic share of the land had been just under a quarter, or twenty-two per cent. In 1703, after the Williamite settlement, it was only fifteen per cent.[6] Moreover, in the course of the next two decades a body of severely discriminatory legislation was passed against all Catholics in Ireland, which apart from inflicting crippling social handicaps reduced the proportion of land held by Catholics further still.

This new legislation is known in history as the 'penal laws'. The injustice and inhumanity of these laws (there was actually one curious legislative proposal to castrate Catholic priests) is here less relevant than their effect on the country's social future. For many years they excluded Catholics from all public life and much normal private social activity. They made any form of Catholic education illegal. Most important of all was the effect they had on the system of land ownership and tenure. They made it illegal for Catholics to buy land, obtain a mortgage on it, rent it at a reasonable profit or even inherit it normally. When a Catholic land-owner died his estate could not descend to his elder son by the normal law of primogeniture, but had to be divided equally among all his sons. On the other hand, if any of the sons were to turn Protestant he automatically inherited the whole estate over the heads of any elder brothers. Similarly, if the wife of a Catholic turned Protestant she automatically acquired part of her husband's estate. While a Catholic was legally allowed to rent land on a lease not exceeding thirty-one years, if he made a profit of more than one-third of his rent he might lose the lease to the first Protestant who could inform against him. In this way not only did the penal laws prevent Catholics from acquiring land by purchase or lease, they also saw to it that such land as was still left in the hands of the Catholic majority after all the confiscations dwindled with the years. By the mid-eighteenth century the fourteen per cent of the land of Ireland still held by Catholics after the Williamite settlement of 1703 had been halved to seven per cent.

By dealing these and other social and economic blows at the old Catholic landed class and their tenants, the penal laws isolated the vast majority of the people of Ireland in an inferior identity. They became segregated from the rest of society and the normal processes of law. Both the Lord Chancellor and the Lord Chief Justice in fact declared at one time that 'the law does not presume any such person to exist as an Irish Roman Catholic'.*

* Catholics could not now join the army or navy, vote or be elected to Parliament or enjoy any offices of state, and those who had previously been able to lead the lives of country gentlemen found themselves subject to the penalty of whipping for keeping a sporting gun or a horse worth more than £5. The Catholic priesthood had to leave the country and were liable to be hanged, drawn and quartered if they returned. A system of registering ordinary Catholic priests was at first introduced, but the terms proved almost impossible for a priest to reconcile with his conscience. Mass had to be celebrated in bog or forest as an outlawed conspiracy. The only education for

This division between Protestant and Catholic which was to shape for so long the whole character of Irish society heightened an even more fundamental and obvious division common to every society: the division between rich and poor. Certainly some Catholic gentry did manage to avoid submergence into the lowest classes, clinging to what land they could by good luck or ingenious circumvention of the law. Others switched interests and even sometimes made fortunes in trade. But, in general, Catholicism and all the older traditions of Ireland, including the Gaelic language, now coloured poverty with a special identity, making the poor, more even than in most countries, a nation of their own.

Catholic children which did not involve their exposure to Protestant proselytism was in illicit schools in hedgerows and byways. The degree to which these laws were strictly applied varied greatly. In time many came to be tacitly circumvented or were allowed to fall into abeyance.

5

Majority Living (1703–1880)

Since long before Henry VIII had become King of Ireland as well as England, Ireland had had her own Parliament under the Crown. Here, as in the English Parliament, grants of money and supplies were made to the Crown in return for consideration of the interests of those inhabitants who made them. But use of this Irish Parliament by the Old English as an instrument for establishing independent strength in Ireland had led to its powers being curbed considerably and by the mid-seventeenth century it was partly *de jure* and wholly *de facto* subservient to the Parliament of England.

The later English Parliament took advantage of this constitutional subservience to see that local economic interests in the Kingdom of Ireland should present no threat to those in the Kingdom of England. Irish trading and manufacturing opportunities were severely restricted to protect England's own trade and manufactures. For instance, in 1699 the export of woollen goods from Ireland — one of the island's principal manufactures at the time — was totally forbidden to everywhere but England where English import duties were themselves prohibitive. This and earlier restrictive measures had the most profound effect not just on the trading class but on the majority of the population. For them, who were in any case precariously placed on the land, the land now became virtually the only source of livelihood available.

On the land, without any surviving vestige of a feudal link between peasant and landlord that elsewhere involved at least some unwritten status, the Irish peasant lived on sufferance, paying the highest possible rent that could be extracted from him. He had neither rights against extortionate rent, nor against arbitrary eviction whether paying rent or not, nor rights to any improvements he might carry out. In fact, to carry out improvements at all was undesirable because to do so only raised the value of the land and thus the rent. All this, to a people among whom there were dim folk-memories of a Gaelic system in which the common people had certain rights of common ownership in the soil, and whose landlord was an elected chief, was doubly painful.

Only in North-West Ulster where tenants had been 'planted' with the landlords on confiscated land were they awarded a certain status. What came to be known as the 'Ulster custom' prevailed there – a custom which gave certain basic rights to a tenant such as security of tenure provided he paid the rent, and a financial interest in such improvements as he might make to his land. But even in Ulster the once privileged status of tenants often became partially obscured by the passage of time and excessive competition for land there led to excessive rents and caused distress.

The Protestant Dean Swift described in 1720 the condition of the Irish tenant of his day as being worse than that of English beggars.[1]

The landlords, he said, 'by unmeasurable screwing and racking their rents all over the kingdom, have already reduced the poor people to a worse condition than the peasants in France, or the vassals in Germany or Poland'.[2] 'Whoever travels this country,' he declared, 'and observes the face of nature, or the faces and habits and dwellings of the natives will hardly think himself in a land where law, religion, or common humanity is professed.'[3] Swift's contemporary, the Protestant Bishop of Derry, wrote of a journey he made through Ireland in 1723: 'Never did I behold even in Picardy, Westphalia or Scotland such dismal marks of hunger and want as appeared in the countenances of the poor creatures I met on the road.'[4] And another Protestant bishop, the philosopher Berkeley, asked in his publication *The Querist:* 'whether there be upon earth any Christian or civilised people so beggarly wretched and destitute as the common Irish', and he repeated the question in a new edition in 1750.[5]

A gentleman living in Dublin in 1764 sent a friend near Dover an account of the conditions of the Irish peasantry in which he drew attention to the numbers of middlemen exploiting the desperate need for land, saying that holdings were being sold by private tender to the highest bidder, 'in small parcels of £20 or £30 a year at third, fourth and fifth hand from the first proprietor'. The condition of the lower class of farmer, he wrote, was 'little better than a state of slavery'.[6]

The Viceroy himself wrote in 1770: 'I hoped to be excused for representing to His Majesty the miserable situation of the lower ranks of his subjects in this kingdom. What from the rapaciousness of their unfeeling landlords and the restrictions on their trade, they are amongst the most wretched people on earth.'[7] In 1787, even the Protestant Attorney-General Fitzgibbon described the poor of Munster as 'being in a state of oppression, abject poverty, sloth, dirt and misery not to be equalled in any part of the world'.[8] As for the sloth, a Frenchman who travelled through Ireland in the 1790s, and found himself shocked by the nakedness of the poor and by their huts which did not seem made for human beings at all, remarked shrewdly that they might well have been industrious and hard-working had there been any hope of work improving their lot. But if they produced more the landlord only put up the rent. 'When reduced to starvation, is it not better to do nothing if the most assiduous labour can do nothing to prevent it?' The excessive drinking to which the peasantry were given was simply a form of Lethe and their apathy and indifference 'no more than the habit of despair'.[9]

Descriptions of the living conditions of the Irish peasantry vary astonishingly little over the whole vast period that spans the defeat of James II and the land reforms of Gladstone. Yet to paint only a tragic and bleak picture of the lives of the Irish common people over such a great expanse of time is to miss the real poignancy of their suffering. Some years were, in the course of nature, less rigorous than others, and in any case the everyday poetry of these people's language, their love of music, their simple gifts of resourcefulness, charm and wit always coloured a natural easy-going and tenacious love of life, if life could only somehow be supported. 'As we went along', an eye-witness was to write of conditions during the Great Famine of the next century, 'our wonder was not that people died but that they lived: and I have no doubt whatever that in any other country the mortality would have been far greater: that many lives have been prolonged, perhaps saved, by the long apprenticeship to want in which the Irish peasant has been trained, and by that lovely touching charity which prompts him to share his scanty meal with his starving neighbour.'*

Nor did the Irish people always accept their condition docilely. Another witness of the next century also gives a glimpse of something more than their misfortune, when he describes before the government's Devon Commission a typical 'agrarian crime' of the period in which twenty of a landlord's cows had been driven up on to the top of a cliff and then 'clifted', or thrown over. A financial reward was offered for the apprehension of the culprit and the whole village then came forward to claim it, having persuaded a convenient small boy to confess. The Devon Commission witness commented: 'They were a very desperate people at this period with all this degree of courtesy, hospitality and cleverness among them.'[10]

Their desperation had in fact long expressed itself at the one level at which it could find an outlet – crudely and locally, in the form of intimidation and violence on the land. After the confiscations and massacres of Cromwell, the more enterprising and desperate of the persecuted had taken to the hills in marauding bands of 'Tories' and 'Rapparees'. Now, under the permanent social persecution which crystallized as the land system of Ireland at the time of the penal laws and long outlasted them, the Irish poor resorted to primitive self-help in the one obvious form that was available. A rough justice of the common people's own making took the place of the law which gave them so little.

* W. E. Forster, from the transactions of the Central Relief Committee of the Society of Friends, quoted in Gavan Duffy, *Fours Years of Irish History* (p. 431). Nearly forty years later Forster was to become a Chief Secretary for Ireland in Gladstone's government, and to earn the nickname 'Buckshot' for carrying out the planned humanitarianism of arming the Royal Irish Constabulary with buckshot rather than ball cartridges.

Lawlessness was no more a natural trait of the Irish common people's character (as has occasionally been suggested) than it is of any other social grouping, the majority of whom are always instinctively law-abiding. It was just that in Ireland for nearly two centuries there were two different sets of law in existence: the one, established by a society and government which did nothing to alleviate the common people's plight; and the other seeking to supply the deficiency, administered by the secret societies with which Ireland became riddled.

Both sets of law had their disadvantages and inconveniences; both could be inexorable and powerful. The punishments exacted by the secret societies were more often than not exacted from the persons and property of the peasantry themselves – on incoming occupiers of land from which a man had been evicted, or simply on unfortunates who out of land hunger were paying extortionate rents when a secret decree had gone out against doing so. Nevertheless, when the mass of people looked at the two sets of law available, the one clandestine and crude, the other official and aloof, the former at least had the advantage that it proclaimed itself to be on their side.

A prototype of this sort of violence which was to dominate Irish life for so long had first made an appearance in Ireland as early as 1711. Bands of armed men, with blackened faces and wearing white shirts over their clothes for easier mutual recognition at night, started to roam the countryside mutilating cattle and carrying out other reprisals for the tyranny and rapacity of harsh landlords or the subservience of those who played along with them. Threatening letters to landlords and others appeared signed by a mysterious 'Captain Eaver'.[11] But that there was no fundamental political outlook in such outbreaks, no purpose so constructively serious as that of overthrowing the government, was soon proved in a most convincing fashion. For both in 1715 and in 1745 when at least some stirring might have been expected in Ireland in favour of a Catholic Pretender to the throne of Great Britain and Ireland, nothing of the sort occurred. The country remained loyal and quiet. And this lack of sophisticated wider political purpose, this concentration on local day to day conditions, was long to remain a consistent feature of Irish agrarian violence, and be the bane of those who later sought to mobilize it for nationalism.

It was in 1760 that the Whiteboy movement, as it came generally to be called, broke out on a large scale. Bodies of armed men, numbering anything from half a dozen or so to five hundred, again took to riding about the countryside at night with white shirts over their clothes, tearing down fences which enclosed land for pasturage rather than tillage, punishing those who collected tithes for the Protestant Church, preventing the payment of extortionate rents, intimidating would-be tenants from taking land from which another had been evicted, and generally asserting the existence of a rough and ready justice to redress the grievances of the poor. For the next hundred years and more, similar organizations, with names that vary with the years and the locality, conducted similar operations with similar objectives and a surprisingly similar degree of cruel detail.

Thus men assembling by night with white shirts over their clothes later called themselves Rightboys, and in the early 1800s Thrashers. They are Rockites and Ribbonmen in the 1820s and subsequent years. 'Ribbonmen' in fact tended to become the generic term for the secret-society phenomenon in the nineteenth century, as 'Whiteboys' had done in the eighteenth, but there were also groups calling themselves Whitefeet, Blackfeet, the Lady Clares, the Terry Alts and other names. Finally, there was a curious survival of Ribbonism which functioned under the more respectable official cover of the Land League in the late 1870s and early 1880s.*

All were secret, oathbound organizations of a rather primitive nature in which the swearing of the oath (often forcibly exacted) was an important part of the ritual. Their leaders were shadowy men whose names, though occasionally found in police reports, reach the history books only in the form in which they struck awe and terror into the countryside, the 'Captains' Rock, Right, Starlight and Moonlight of whom there would usually be a number operating under the same pseudonym at any given time.† The methods by which they practised their rough justice hardly vary across two centuries: the ham-stringing of cattle, the levelling of houses, the burning of ricks and barns, the firing of shots through windows, the delivery of threatening letters and many other violations of the government's law which were to become a commonplace in constabulary reports from Ireland. Even the actual physical details of the savage tortures inflicted on offenders against the code, such as the branding of flesh, the lacerations with wool cards, and the particular addiction to cutting off small pieces of the ear, are all found over and over again in records that run from the early eighteenth century to the 1880s.

'Wool-carding', for instance, the drawing of a steel tooth comb through the flesh of the victim, had become frequent in the early nineteenth century and had even given its name to a secret society of the time: the Carders. But by 1832 a contemporary witness was able to say that it had 'not been used at all latterly'.[12] However, nearly fifty years later in Land League days in 1880 a man named Costello was dragged from his bed at 1.30 a.m. by about twenty men, who made him swear he would not fence in some grazing land then in

* These secret societies should not be confused with the simple 'factions' such as the Shanavists, Caravats, Ruskavallas and others who were little more than rival gangs disturbing the peace with often lethal 'faction fights' at fairs and elsewhere. A most important late eighteenth-century peasant secret society, the Defenders, though its details often followed the familiar pattern of agrarian societies, was in fact somewhat different in character from all others, expressing political and national aims of a crude but positive nature. It is examined at length below on pp. 44–5, and 57–6.

† Sometimes it was 'General' Rock.

common use and then 'drew a wool card down his hip lacerating his flesh'.[13] Mutilation of the ears, frequent in the eighteenth century, survived not only into the time of the Land League but even into the twentieth century.

At times these secret societies held certain areas of Ireland largely at their mercy. The warning to children: 'The fairies will get you' once carried sinister undertones. In Tipperary in 1762 parties of more than five hundred men were described as doing 'whatever mischief they please by night under sanction of being fairies as they call themselves', and it was said that no one dared take the place of a dismissed servant or shepherd in the county unless 'he had more interest with the fairies'.[14] In parts of County Cork in 1824 the gentry had their houses permanently barricaded and posted sentries on them during the daytime. Some houses were dark almost all day long because the barricades, being bullet-proof and of considerable thickness, were so heavy that it was too much of a business to move them daily; and sometimes for the same reason there was only one sitting-room where light was admissible at all in daytime and then not even through all the windows.[15]

All this activity was either wholly unpolitical or politically very crude. Even when, as happened from time to time, attempts were made to enlist it for political purposes it tended to remain most stubbornly what it had always been: the simplest form of war that the poor can wage against the rich or those who play the rich man's game.

When, for instance, the first Whiteboys were executed in 1762 – for being present at the burning down of the cabin of a peasant who would not combine with them – they declared categorically, when past all hope of reprieve, that 'in all these tumults it never entered into their thoughts to do anything against the King and government'.[16] And a government commission which reported on the disturbances in the *London Gazette* of May 1762 confirmed that 'no marks of disaffection to His Majesty's person or government appeared in any of those people'.[17] An Irish gentleman on a tour of Ireland in 1764 who met with a band of Whiteboys in arms between Waterford and Carrick-on-Suir, was told by them that they were not motivated by 'any disposition to rebel against their King or the peace of their country', but only by their resentment of their everyday conditions.[18] When on the occasion of the revolt of the American colonies in 1775, the Catholic gentry expressed their loyalty to the Crown in fulsome terms, they probably, as they claimed, expressed the *political* thinking of all their co-religionists quite truthfully when they wrote: 'We humbly presume to lay at his (Majesty's) feet two millions of loyal, faithful and affectionate hearts and hands, unarmed indeed, but zealous, ready and desirous to exert themselves strenuously in defence of his Majesty's most sacred person and government.' Their address described Irish Catholic loyalty as 'a loyalty which we may justly say is and always was as the dial to the sun, true, though not shone upon'.[19] Many years later, in 1832, a witness of the very considerable agrarian tumults that occurred in Ireland in the second and third decades of the nineteenth century stated: 'I never knew a single instance of hostility or combination against the government.'[20]

By that date a most important further development had taken place in Irish society: the Penal Laws preventing Catholics from owning, leasing and inheriting land had been repealed in 1778 and 1782, and Catholics were land-owners again on a quite considerable scale. All contemporary witnesses including Daniel O'Connell agree that not only were attacks directed proportionately as much against Catholic as Protestant land-owners but also that the Catholic gentry were equally active in putting disturbances down.[21] In the sphere that mattered most to the Irish peasantry, that of their economic status on the land, members of their own religion and blood were to be found in the nineteenth century increasingly on the other side of the fence, or the landlord's wall, with the Protestant. Thus non-political in character, these Whiteboy and other organizations were not predominantly sectarian in motive. Most of the activists were, of course, Catholics simply because most of the poor who were trying to live off the land were Catholics, and this common basis of identity often proved a useful rallying cry. But in the eighteenth century in the Presbyterian North, where, in spite of the 'Ulster custom', there were harsh landlords prepared to exploit land hunger by the excessive raising of rents as elsewhere in Ireland, secret societies known as Oakboys and Steelboys developed as Protestant counterparts of the Whiteboys.

For nearly two centuries such secret societies regularly absorbed much of the natural political energy of the Irish masses. The spirit of protest and concern remained focused there at a primitive level, just below that of the higher public politics which were a normal part of this as of any other organized society.

6

Minority Politics, Eighteenth Century

For much of the eighteenth century, after the defeat of James II and the Catholic Irish, the public political life of Ireland had flowed placidly and steadily, almost, it seemed, dissociated altogether from the currents in the depths below. This public political life was confined by the Penal Laws to the Irish Protestant minority and, in an era before the reform of Parliament and the widening of the franchise, even to a minority of them. But in the second half of the eighteenth century, this small oligarchic Irish political world developed an exciting dynamic of its own which was to have an influence on the whole subsequent course of Irish history.

An 'Irishman' by the eighteenth century meant simply anyone who had by now taken root in Ireland. The rigorous Protestant ascendancy established by the victories of William of Orange and confirmed by the Penal Laws was an Irish one. Ireland alone gave it personality and coherence. It is true that in the main it consisted of those who had become Irish more recently than the rest of the population, but even this was not wholly the case. Any Catholic, by changing his religion, automatically became eligible for the ruling class. And though only about four thousand such converts were actually registered in the eighteenth century, many of them were ancient Gaelic or Gaelicized nobility re-seeking their inborn sense of superiority in the terms of a new society. Among the names to be hated most of all as symbols of oppression over the next two hundred years, the vast majority were those of Irishmen. Some were the most Irish of all, with long-blended Norman and Gaelic blood in their veins.*

This mixed Irish Protestant ascendancy of the eighteenth century eventually asserted their Irishness in a pattern made familiar by the past. Emphasizing their nominal loyalty to the joint Crown of the two Kingdoms, they gradually developed a spirit of independence towards the English Government.

* For example, in the late eighteenth century, the Lord Chancellor John Fitzgibbon, Earl of Clare, and in the nineteenth century those Burkes who, having turned Protestant and been created Earls of Clanrickarde long before, were responsible for some of the harshest evictions.

Colonists throughout history have felt an ambivalence towards their mother country like that with which all adolescents regard their parents, seeking somehow to reconcile an affection for the ties which bind them with impatience at the restraint these place on freedom of action. Nowhere was this colonists' ambivalence ever more intensely felt than in Ireland where even geography conspired to emphasize it by making the two islands quite separate and yet not too far apart.

Early in the eighteenth century the spirit of Irish colonists' independence began to be vigorously expressed in the writings of two men. One was William Molyneux, a scientist and a member of Trinity College, Dublin, who clearly put forward a political theory that the Irish colonists' Parliament alone had the right to legislate for Ireland; the other was Jonathan Swift, the Irish-born Protestant Dean of St Patrick's, Dublin, who emphasized his allegiance to the king not as King of England but as King of Ireland and told his fellow Irishmen to burn 'everything English except their coal'. Both men attacked the unfairness of the commercial restrictions on Irish manufacture and trade which had been imposed by the English Parliament in the interests of English manufacturers and traders, and claimed that such legislation was an interference with ancient Irish colonists' rights.

The exact constitutional status and power of the Irish Parliament had in fact always been vague. In the late Middle Ages the Old English had consistently used the Irish Parliament to assert their own interests against the King's Government, and it was to curb such use of it that an Act passed by Sir Richard Poynings, a Viceroy of the day, had made the Irish Parliament's right to legislate subject to previous approval of Bills by the English Government. But with this important proviso, the Crown in the Irish Parliament was still theoretically regarded in matters that were of Irish concern as being the sovereign authority for Ireland. It was where matters of Irish concern were of English concern as well, as for instance in commerce and trade, that these had usually been judged to be the affair of the English Parliament. But in attacking the unfairness of all the restrictive commercial measures both Molyneux and Swift claimed that the English Parliament had usurped the Irish Parliament's sovereign rights and had no right to legislate for Ireland.

In fact, whatever the original constitutional theory of the Irish Parliament's rights may have been, practice had long established its virtual insignificance. Of the hundred and six years between 1586 and 1692 the Irish Parliament had only sat for fifteen. In 1719 the English Parliament finally tried to forestall further constitutional ambiguity or awkward insistence on Irish Parliamentary sovereignty with a so-called Declaratory Act, which categorically stated that the English Parliament had a full right to legislate for Ireland if it wanted to.

But the ideas first put forward by Molyneux and Swift slowly began to find wider acceptance. By the second half of the eighteenth century, the

'Protestant nation' of Ireland, as it was called by one of its political leaders, the lawyer Henry Flood, had already established its Irish social individuality in the life and architecture of its capital. Dublin had become in the eighteenth century one of the finest and most sophisticated cities in Europe, and many streets and squares still stand in Dublin today as monuments to that 'nation's' elegance. It was inevitable that such a Protestant nation, irked by commercial restrictions from England, should in the end stake political claims to dignify its social individuality – just as it was inevitable that the American colonists under similar provocation should do the same.

The links of sympathy between Ireland and America were obvious. In the first place there was a physical bond. During the eighteenth century Presbyterians had emigrated in large numbers from Ulster to the American colonies in times of agricultural distress and in protest against the disabilities imposed on them by law as Nonconformists. These emigrants were now some of the fieriest spirits among the American colonists. Secondly, the growing commercial and political aspirations in both countries were very similar.

By 1760 Protestant Ireland was developing a general unwillingness to recognize the dependence of the Irish Parliament on the British Parliament. 'To be uneasy in their present state', wrote a contemporary, 'and to express among themselves this uneasiness is the turn and fashion of the upper sort of the people, and is caught from them downwards.'[1]

But a most important practical consideration seemed to make the Irish Parliament's subservience a permanent reality. The machinery of government in Ireland was theoretically a replica of that in England. That is to say, a Viceroy with the title of Lord Lieutenant, worked through the Irish Parliament with Irish Ministers of the Crown and against such opposition as presented itself, as in England. The Irish Protestant Earl of Charlemont, in defining his view of his country's (i.e. Ireland's) Constitution in 1760, spoke optimistically of this machinery as a 'distinct' executive of the Kingdom of Ireland. But, given the facts of eighteenth-century political life, it could not really be distinct at all, however attractive to Irish Protestant self-esteem the theory might be.

In the eighteenth century the system by which a small number of individuals could influence up to the point of total control the result in a number of constituencies was common to both the English and Irish Parliaments.* The person who thus controlled the constituency could ensure, in return for suitable rewards by those with patronage at their disposal, that the vote of his constituency's representative went whichever way the patron thought was the right one.

The eighteenth-century political system was thus often a battle of patronage rather than of votes. This practice which the twentieth century sees as

* The so-called rotten or pocket boroughs often had only one or two voters.

corrupt can also be seen less pejoratively as simply the machinery by which the political system happened to function at that time. But certainly the system was very much more corrupt, or mechanical, in Ireland than in England.

According to the contemporary Irish historian, Plowden, a moderate and objective man, 128 of the 300 members of the Irish House of Commons could by the most generous estimate be reckoned to have been freely chosen by such electorate as there was. The remaining 172 seats – a comfortable majority – were the property of less than a hundred individuals, some thirty of whom controlled a sufficient number to provide a majority of the House. In these circumstances it was obviously very easy for the Crown to deploy its powerful patronage to effect. As many as one-third of the entire House were in fact direct pensioners or placemen of the Crown. In England only one-ninth of the House of Commons were reckoned Crown placemen or pensioners and there such members had to submit themselves for re-election on receipt of their benefits – which was not the case in Ireland.

In both countries Ministers of the Crown worked through Parliament with a majority secured as far as possible by the Crown's patronage. But in Ireland, since so many of the seats were in the control of such a small number of individuals, the Crown, with easily the largest single source of patronage at its disposal, could command the support of most of these controllers and thus count on an almost automatic majority in the House.* And, since Crown patronage in Ireland and in England emanated from a single source in England, whoever controlled the source in England – that is to say, the English Government of the day – controlled Ireland as well.

After Henry Flood, the early leader of 'the Protestant Nation' in the Irish House of Commons, had been induced to join the administration for seven years, another lawyer, Henry Grattan, emerged as the most effective orator of a so-called Protestant 'Patriot' party in Parliament.

When the clash with the American colonists came, the loyalty of the Irish Protestants to the Crown was full of ambiguous undertones which the Patriots exploited and which the administration was shrewd enough to see must be kept to undertones by concession. Both sides played the situation skilfully. The successes of the American colonists considerably strengthened the hands of the Irish Protestants in their own restiveness, drawing attention both to what could happen if colonists were pushed too far and to the value in the circumstances of the Irish loyalty to the Crown. Reciprocally, the American colonists' successes made the English Government readier for concession in Ireland to avoid a second imperial disaster.

The formation of 'Irish Volunteers', originally to defend Ireland against

* Where these individuals gave the support of the seats they controlled to the Crown they were known as Undertakers because they 'undertook' to get the government's business through the House.

possible French invasion after regular troops had been withdrawn for the American war, began in 1778. These companies of Volunteers in their various uniforms of brilliant scarlet, blue, orange and green had at first been raised locally by private subscription, but before long welded themselves into something like a national force, well armed – partly, though with some misgivings, by the government – and even in possession of artillery. They were all imbued with the now widespread public theory that the Irish Parliament should by right have full legislative sovereignty under the Crown of Ireland and that this had been usurped in times past by the English Parliament. The point of their existence now subtly altered. Instead of simply being there to defend the coastline, these Volunteers became a fashionable and extremely effective expression of the Protestants' political aspirations. Their very presence enormously strengthened the hand of men like Grattan, and Charlemont and other leading Protestant 'Patriots' in their attempts in Parliament to get the commercial restrictions rescinded and the Irish claim to legislative independence acknowledged. By the end of 1778 the Volunteers numbered some forty thousand men.*

With that force behind them, the independent minority in Parliament concentrated first on attacking the commercial restrictions. Within a year they had brought the administration to abandon the entire system of restrictive commercial legislation. Ireland obtained complete freedom to trade in anything with anybody.

But the basic loyalty to the Crown underlying the new spirit of independence was well demonstrated in 1779 when a motion in the Irish Parliament to give Ireland complete legislative independence of England was withdrawn out of deference to the government's feelings on the arrival of the news of military disasters from America.

In 1780 Grattan for the first time tried to get the Irish House of Commons to vote an Irish Declaration of Independence. He was then unsuccessful, owing to the Crown's effective control of the majority in Parliament, through the system of patronage. By the end of the following year, however, the Volunteers outside Parliament had become much stronger. They were said now to number some eighty thousand men, and early in 1782 a convention of democratically elected Volunteer delegates was held at Dungannon, a sort of parliament outside Parliament, backed by potential physical force for the first but by no means the last time in Irish history. This Volunteer convention unanimously resolved that 'a claim of any body of men, other than the King, Lords and Commons of Ireland, to bind this kingdom is unconstitutional, illegal and a grievance'. Before the end of the year the government

---

* All were Protestants at this stage. Catholics' offers to raise companies were initially rejected, but wealthy Catholics did contribute liberally to the funds from the start. Although still technically disqualified from bearing arms, Catholics eventually joined the Volunteers in considerable numbers.

yielded to the implied armed threat and Grattan was able to persuade the Irish Parliament to pass his Declaration of Independence unanimously.

This Declaration of Independence was accepted by the English Government. There were then repealed: both that Act of George I which categorically affirmed the English Parliament's right to legislate for Ireland and also that part of Poyning's law which proclaimed that the Irish Parliament must first submit its legislation to the English Parliament for approval. To complete the apparent triumph, in 1783 Flood, who had now rejoined the opposition, insisted on ramming the Protestant Irish victory home by pressing the English Government for a specific Act of Renunciation of English legislative rights in Ireland.* This was eventually agreed to and the Act declared, in words to be much quoted thereafter in Irish history, that the 'right claimed by the people of Ireland, to be bound only by laws enacted by His Majesty and the Parliament of the Kingdom in all cases whatever – shall be, and it is hereby declared to be, established and ascertained for ever, and shall at no time hereafter be questioned or questionable'.

Thus there came into existence for nineteen years what is usually known as Grattan's Parliament, though in it Grattan himself never took office. The Irish Protestants had won for 'Ireland' in the abstract an explicitly free and sovereign constitution, complicated only by a limitation which seemed neither a complication nor a limitation at the time: namely, the inalienable identity of the Irish Crown with that of England.

This connection of two independent 'nations' – one Irish, one English – under a joint Crown and within one British Empire had always been a cardinal principle of Grattan's political thought. He saw in the very connection itself a sort of guarantee of the purity of the Irish independence achieved. The society of Ireland had, he said, asserted 'her liberty according to the form of the British Constitution, her inheritance to be enjoyed in perpetual connection with the British Empire.... Connected by freedom as well as by allegiance, the two nations, Great Britain and Ireland, form a constitutional confederacy as well as an Empire.' And the emotional tie, now that it was, nominally, no more than that, was unashamedly acknowledged: '... the people of this kingdom have never expressed a desire to share the freedom of England without declaring a determination to share her fate likewise, standing or falling with the British nation.'[2]

The concept of a totally independent country under a joint British Crown was a fine inspiring one for men like Grattan. Ironically, it might have made good political sense in terms of the twentieth century. Constitutional monarchy, as evolved in the framework of a reformed Parliament and a widened franchise, would have permitted a true sovereign independence for Ireland under a joint Crown. Later constitutional practice has made it quite

* Since his position as opposition leader had been taken over by Grattan, he made a bid to reassert himself by putting forward more strongly radical views.

possible for the same monarch to have different faces in different situations. But in Grattan's time, with Parliament still unreformed, the nominal independence inevitably remained nominal only. For the old flaw in the status of the Irish Parliament survived legislative independence intact. The actual government of the 'King of Ireland' was still carried on by an Irish executive who were dependent in the end not so much on what happened in Ireland as on the power to influence the Irish Parliament made available to them in the form of Crown patronage by changing English ministers.

In an unreformed Irish Parliament, with such power at their disposal, the Irish ministers were a permanent professional department of the British Government. Certainly they had to work through the Irish Parliament and certainly the will of that Parliament was now technically sovereign. But that will could still be manipulated freely by English-controlled influence and patronage. Moreover, in the period after 1782 the government in London made a deliberate practice of extending their parliamentary influence in Ireland by the sale of honours, places and pensions. The only way to get round this and make 'Irish legislative independence' into something more than a nominal phrase was, as Grattan and the Patriots saw, to reform the whole parliamentary system and make seats in Parliament dependent on the true will of the electorate.

On the issue of legislative independence itself, the true will of the electorate and of the Irish House of Commons had been able to assert itself. But this was only because behind it there had been really effective pressure in the threat of armed force from the Volunteers. On that occasion the system tactfully allowed itself to lose face in order to maintain power. But there was not to be the same unanimity among Irish Protestants on the new issue of reform. Moreover, there was a further important question which now had to be confronted squarely if the new independent Ireland were really to be a country at all in anything but theory. All the talk about 'Ireland' and 'Irish legislative independence' had proceeded as if 'the Irish' were the Irish Protestants. But of course they were only a small minority of the Irish. The vast majority of the population were Catholics. And yet all Catholics were still excluded from the entire political system.

These two issues of parliamentary reform and Catholic Emancipation now dominated the Irish Parliament's life until the end of the century.

The Patriots' argument for reform was clear enough. If Ireland were to be in practice as well as in theory a genuinely distinct country, confederate with Britain, then obviously she must have control over her own affairs. This could only be achieved by such a reform of the parliamentary system as would make two-thirds of the seats in the Irish Parliament no longer the property of a few men who could always be bought by the English Government.

But apart from this national constitutional argument there was more down-to-earth pressure for reform. Those Protestants who were not part of the small oligarchy involved in the system of patronage and the rotten borough, were beginning to clamour on their own account for the power from which it permanently excluded them.

A similar clamour was also arising from similar classes in England for a reform of the English Parliament. But the clamour in Ireland was more acute. For not only was the Irish Parliament much more exclusive and corrupt, but it owed its present proud and independent 'national' status to the pressure through the Volunteers of this very Protestant yeomanry and middle class which was still virtually unrepresented in it.

The argument for Catholic emancipation was equally clear. If Ireland were to be truly an independent nation under the Crown, then the three-quarters of the nation who were Catholics would have to be eligible for the same rights in their identity as Irishmen as the quarter who were Protestant. Again, the admission of Catholics to political life was also an issue in England. But again a far greater urgency applied in Ireland, where Catholic Emancipation meant not, as in England, political recognition for a small minority, but for the vast majority of the country.

In 1778 the first Catholic Relief Bill had been passed enabling Catholics to start buying property again. Edmund Burke had written to an Irish Protestant: 'You are now beginning to have a country. . . . I am persuaded that when that thing called a country is once found in Ireland, quite other things will be done than were done when the zeal of men was turned to the safety of a party.'[3] (By which he meant the Protestant party.) Now, in 1782 that country had been found and the Volunteers who had done most to find it were not only chafing for representation but had to some extent at least shown themselves ready for new thinking about Catholics. At Dungannon, referring to the recent changes in the land laws, they had resolved, with only two dissentient voices in an assembly of 143 delegates, that 'as men and as Irishmen, as Christians and as Protestants, we rejoice in the relaxation of the penal laws against our Roman Catholic fellow-subjects, and . . . conceive the measure to be fraught with the happiest consequences to the union and the prosperity of the inhabitants of Ireland'.[4] Grattan had taken tolerance further in the Irish House of Commons with the words, 'the question is now whether we shall be a Protestant settlement or an Irish nation . . . for so long as we exclude Catholics from natural liberty and the common rights of man we are not a people'.[5] In this year 1782 a further Relief Act was passed admitting Catholics fully to exactly the same rights of property and leasehold in land as Protestants.

All the same there was still so much disagreement, even among the old Patriot party, on the issue of admitting Catholics to *political rights* that Reform assumed more convenient priority. Both Charlemont and Flood, for instance, were opposed to admitting Catholics to full political rights. Charlemont even believed that Catholics could not safely be admitted to political power for a hundred years. On the issue of Reform, on the other hand, all those at least who had led the parliamentary struggle for independence were agreed on the desirability of the goal.

The only difficulty was how to achieve it – how those two-thirds of the House of Commons who depended one way or another on the government for place and patronage were to be brought to abandon the whole structure of their personal advantage and aggrandizement.

The logic of the situation was certainly that the instrument of force present in the Volunteers, which had been so useful in the background when legislative independence was won, might be used again. But some of the old leaders of the Patriot party were squeamish at the prospect of putting extra-parliamentary pressure on that very independent Parliament which they had created. Thus the concentration of the drive for Reform was nothing like so great as it had been for legislative independence.

Flood, most radical of the leaders on the issue of reform, believed in using the Volunteers, sitting as they were by 1783 in a democratically elected Convention of the whole country in Dublin, as the necessary external pressure on Parliament. It is difficult in retrospect not to think that he was tactically right in wanting to apply the same method again. But Charlemont and even Grattan himself, whose pleasure in the more nebulous ties of the connection somewhat clouded his daring, disapproved of unconstitutional threats to the new sovereign legislature by a sort of alternative legislative assembly of armed men. When Flood, ostentatiously wearing Volunteer uniform, brought a Reform Bill from the Convention to put before the House of Commons it was overwhelmingly rejected. Even Flood himself was not so radical as to try and push the Volunteers' pressure to its logical extreme in face of this defeat and resort to force, though in Belfast the Volunteers had their artillery ready with round shot and grape shot and five hundred of them waited hourly for the order which never came, to march on the Dublin Parliament. The Convention disbanded. And though the Volunteers continued nominally in being for many years as a nostalgic association, and a few companies were to develop a very special character several years later, their effective political power as a body was now really dispersed for ever.

A century or so later lofty nostalgia was often evoked by politicians on behalf of 'Grattan's Parliament' or 'the old house on College Green'. The constitution of 1782 came to be thought of by many as compatible with the highest aspirations of Irish 'nationality'. But though it may have been good politics, such talk was poor history. For, once the independence of the Irish Parliament had been technically granted, the English government's hold over it was actually tightened by its systematic ever-increasing outlay of Crown patronage in Ireland.

That the constitution of 1782 was in practice a sham, and Ireland's claim to enjoy full independence within the Empire a romantic illusion, eventually became clear enough even to Grattan himself. On 2 February 1790 he castigated the Ministers of the Irish Crown in the Irish House of Commons in a speech which not only demonstrates the simple mechanism by which the 'independent' legislature was officially undermined, but also already carried significant if gentlemanly echoes of the great revolution that had begun in France the year before. Grattan declaimed, of the Irish ministers:

We charge them publicly in the face of their country, with making corrupt agreements for the sale of peerages, for doing which we say they are impeachable; we charge them with corrupt agreements for the disposal of the money arising from the sale, to purchase for the servants of the Castle, seats in the assembly of the people, for doing which we say they are impeachable; we charge them with committing these offences, not in one, not in two, but in many instances, for which complication of offences we say they are impeachable; guilty of a systematic endeavour to undermine the constitution in violation of the laws of the land . . .[6]

The only answer Grattan got from the Ministers was that the disposal of Crown patronage was a matter of the royal prerogative and therefore above debate. In the latter days of this Parliament Grattan was driven to refer to the 'base condition of our connection and allegiance' which the corrupt structure of Parliament necessitated – though he never wavered from his deep emotional conviction that an honourable British connection was the only conceivable framework for true Irish independence. But the falsity of Ireland's 'national' position had been faced earlier with even bleaker frankness by another member of the Irish House of Commons who was emotionally just as loyal to the principle of the connection as Grattan himself.

'Boast', said Sir Laurence Parsons, in the Irish House of Commons in 1790,

Boast of the prosperity of your country as you may, and after all I ask: what is it but a secondary kingdom? An inferior member of a great Empire without any movement or orbit of its own. . . . We may pride ourselves that we are a great kingdom, but the fact is that we are barely known beyond the boundaries of our shores. Who out of Ireland ever hears of Ireland? Who respects us? Where are our ambassadors? What treaties do we enter into? With what nation do we make peace or war? Are we not a mere cipher in all these, and are not these what give a nation consequence and fame? All these are sacrificed to the connection with England. . . . A suburb to England we are sunk in her shade. True we are an independent kingdom; we have an imperial Crown distinct from England; but it is a metaphysical distinction, a mere sport for speculative men. . . . It is asked why, after all the acquisitions of 1782, there should be discontent? To this I say that when the country is well-governed the people ought to be satisfied but not before. . . . It has been the object of English ministers ever since to countervail what we obtained at that period, and substitute a surreptitious and clandestine influence for the open power which the English legislature was then obliged to relinquish . . .

All this was undeniably true. What then of the future? Parsons outlined it with prophetic clarity:

Those concessions on the part of the English Parliament I grant were as ample as they well could be for they were everything short of separation. Let ministers then beware of what conclusions they may teach the people if they teach them this, that the attainment of everything short of separation will not attain for them the good government. . . . Where, or when, or how is all this to end? Is the Minister of England himself sure that he sees the end? Can he be sure that this system, which has been forming for the coercion of Ireland, may not ultimately cause the dissolution of the Empire?[7]

A friend of Sir Laurence Parsons at this time was a young Protestant middle-class lawyer, already showing a slightly erratic interest in politics, whose name was Theobald Wolfe Tone. Meanwhile, in France, a country with which Ireland had long been associated by ties less explicit but in some ways as strong as those which bound her to England, an event was taking place which was gradually shaking all existing political thought everywhere to its foundations.

PART TWO

1

Ireland and the French Revolution

The French Revolution had a remarkable message for all peoples, to the effect that an apparently deadlocked society was not necessarily deadlocked at all, and that a new order of society based on the theory of the people's participation rather than just on their acceptance of their lot was a practical possibility. This excited the minds of political thinkers all over the world, particularly in Britain, and most particularly of all in Ireland, where even more acutely than elsewhere in the British Isles, an urgent need for the reform of the political system along more popular lines was already being widely felt and discussed.

To the more independent-minded, even among the aristocracy and gentry, the deadlock of a Parliament in which a few individuals controlled the majority of the representatives, whose support the English Ministry could always secure by extending the Crown's patronage, made nonsense of the nominal legislative independence won in 1782. Grattan, himself the most enthusiastic and loyal architect of that independence, had become increasingly disillusioned, and had already used the term 'a creeping union' to describe the relationship between the two countries.[1] As for the commercial and professional middle classes, who by their self-organization and external pressure in the hey-day of the Volunteers had helped to win the independence of '82, they found that the goal of parliamentary reform and thus their own share and influence still eluded them; whereas in France they saw their class in the seats of power overnight. Now therefore in Ireland, merchants, lawyers and doctors, often wealthy and almost always Protestants, banded together to provide most of the intellectual leaders of a new radical movement.

At the same time, the peasantry, the vast majority of the common people of Ireland, lived in conditions a good deal harder than those suffered by the peasantry of France. An English traveller through Tipperary in 1790 found his mind 'filled with melancholy on contemplating these poor creatures who drag on a miserable existence under an accumulation of woes that it is hard to think human nature can sustain. . . .'[2] Their situation was 'not better than a beast of burden,'³ and the last straw in the burden was the tithe, a tax in the form of about one-tenth of the peasant's produce which he was by law compelled to pay for the upkeep of a Protestant Church to which he did not belong.

A folk memory of the outlawry of the peasant's own religion, of the legal oppression of himself and his fellows simply for being the sort of people they were, went back well over a hundred years in aggravation of all this. Every Catholic's legal position had in fact improved out of all recognition in the recent past with the Catholic Relief Acts of 1778 and 1782. But folk memories are inordinately long when any grievances at all remain, and to the average Irish peasant everyday life was itself grievance enough. There were in any case still some legal humiliations to which all Catholics were subject. Under the surviving penal laws Catholics of every class were still prevented from voting, sitting in Parliament or occupying any of the offices of state. It was the Catholic middle class and gentry who felt the deprivation of this and all it symbolized most directly, but reaction to the anachronism was one which could and did usefully unite many radical men of every type and class, while to the peasantry it provided an obvious symbol of their total grievance.

Parliamentary reform, Catholic Emancipation and the need to improve the lot of the peasantry particularly with regard to the injustice of tithe – these were the political thoughts circulating in Ireland at the moment when all political thought received a sudden stimulus from the sensational developments in France.

The politically articulate among the reformers in Irish society had few direct contacts with the peasantry. And though an acknowledgement of the peasantry's condition was fairly widespread among all classes, people interested in reform and change inevitably concentrated on those issues that seemed closest and most real to them. Reformist and radical circles in Belfast and Dublin concerned themselves with Parliamentary reform or Catholic relief and sometimes the two together, persuading themselves that once the system of government was reformed at source and made more representative, the necessary change in the condition of the peasantry would follow automatically.

As a result, the stimulus which the French Revolution gave to the hopes of the peasantry worked in isolation from the rest of society at first. In the years just before the French Revolution, secret societies had been particularly active in the South and West of Ireland. There, in 1786 and 1787, a society known as Rightboys had been accumulating large numbers of adherents by oath-taking ceremonies in Catholic chapels, each chapel when sworn sending on representatives to swear in the next. The oaths taken were to obey the laws of 'Captain Right', and not to pay more than a certain amount of rent per acre of land. Apart from this regulation of rent their objects were the raising of the price of labour and the abolition of hearth and other taxes and, in particular, tithes. Before long Captain Right's boys had spread over the whole of Munster and were sometimes to be met with openly in parties of five hundred or so at a time. They were usually unarmed, but busied themselves with the infliction of savage punishments on any peasant who refused to join them, dragging him from his bed in the middle of the night and burying him alive in a grave lined with thorns, or setting him naked on horseback tied to a saddle of thorns and perhaps sawing his ears off as well.[4]

Meanwhile, similar secret society activity, but with one important difference, was developing simultaneously in the North.

In North-East Ulster the mainly Protestant tenantry had, ever since the great plantation of the seventeenth century, benefitted from the so-called 'Ulster custom', which allowed fairly extensive rights to tenants, such as freedom from eviction, so long as they paid their rents, and compensation on departure for any improvements they might have made to their land. They were thus on the whole a good deal more prosperous than the Catholics in the South. (Catholics in North-East Ulster were chiefly labourers without any land at all.) Nevertheless, throughout the eighteenth century the Presbyterian tenantry in the North had suffered not only from certain social and civil penalties inflicted on them as nonconformists, but also, like any other tenantry in Ireland, from the rapaciousness of landlords and middlemen. Rents, as elsewhere in Ireland, were determined solely by the inexorable law of supply and demand. And under pressure of these high rents and nonconformist civic disadvantages, many Presbyterians in the eighteenth century, better able to afford emigration than the peasantry of the South, had left for America.

In 1779 and 1782 by the Catholic Relief Acts, Catholics were again permitted to purchase and hold leases on land on an equal footing with Protestants. Many of them moved on to land in Ulster left vacant by the Presbyterian emigrants. Such Catholics, long acclimatized to a lower standard of living, were prepared to bid the price of land up to heights to which Presbyterians refused to go. But for years agrarian secret societies among the Presbyterians, with names like 'Oakboys' and 'Steelboys', had fought successfully to keep the price of land down. In 1763, for instance, the 'Hearts of Oak boys', who forced land-owners to promise on oath not to raise rents above seven shillings an acre, had been described as 'absolute masters' of Armagh, Cavan and other counties. At Belturbet in Cavan they had entered the town, headed by a man on horseback in soldier's clothes, with drums beating, horns blowing and a fife playing, and flying red and white colours, and compelled several gentlemen to take their oath, threatening to remove their wives and daughters if they refused.[5] It was this spirit of local solidarity which the new eager Catholic tenants in Ulster now threatened to undermine, introducing as they did a new element of undisciplined competition for land. And the Protestant secret societies began to array themselves against the Catholics just as effectively as they had already arrayed themselves against the landlords.

It was around 1785 that this specifically anti-Catholic form of secret society first made its appearance in the North. It was known simply as 'the Protestant Boys', sometimes expressively as 'the Wreckers', but most often as 'the Peep o' Day Boys', because it was at dawn that its members took to appearing at the houses of Catholics and burning them or otherwise terrorizing their occupants into removing to some other part of Ireland. The Catholics in these districts soon formed a rival protection society, which, while assuming the traditional pattern of former agrarian secret societies, also had a new emphasis in that it was formed for the defence of Catholics solely as Catholics and against Protestants. Its members called themselves, appropriately enough, the Defenders.

At first these Defenders did exist simply for local defence against a real threat from the Ulster Protestants. But as they were driven from their homes in Ulster into neighbouring counties like Meath and Louth, where Catholics were in a majority, the Defenders continued and developed their organization on the assumption that the whole Catholic peasant identity in Ireland required defence on principle, and that the best form of defence was often attack. It was on just such an organization on the brink of a crude political attitude, primitive and ill-coordinated and yet expressing incoherently the everyday grievances and resentments of over a century, that the French Revolution inevitably worked a powerful influence.

For a hundred years close ties between France and Catholic Ireland had made Ireland sensitive to anything that happened there. Ever since the Wild Geese had flown to France after the Treaty of Limerick,* adventurous Catholics, frustrated by the penal laws, had been crossing the seas to put on the uniform of France, fight in her armies and become her citizens. French boats arriving at lonely points off the southern and south-western Irish coasts to take off these recruits, or to carry priests to and from their training or the sons of gentry to and from their education or simply smuggling out wool and smuggling in claret and brandy, had been a permanent feature of popular Irish life. If the people of France felt overcome by a sudden sense of emancipation it was inevitable that the people of Ireland should be strongly affected by it too, particularly when one of the first acts of the Revolution in France had been to abolish tithes. A powerful democratic influence at work in both countries was Tom Paine's *Rights of Man*, which was being so generally distributed in Ireland in 1791 that people were hired to read it to those who could not read themselves.[6]

The earliest oaths of the Defenders' societies began with a straightforward expression of allegiance to the king and his successors, together with general

* See above, p. 18.

expressions of mutual aid and support. The idea was plainly much influenced by Freemasonry, which had enjoyed a great revival in the North of Ireland at the time of the Volunteers some years before,[7] and from which many of the forms of the Defenders' Society were copied. The rules of a local Defender Committee in County Louth in 1789 declared that no Defender was 'to strike another upon any account' or to come to the monthly meeting drunk. There was to be 'no swearing or speaking loud', and secrecy about membership and passwords was strictly enjoined.[8] But it was soon clear that the Defenders were determined, even when not under direct pressure, to be something more than a mere Masonic brotherhood of Catholics.

In this County Louth Defender Committee's oath of April 1789, some months even before the outbreak of the French Revolution, there is already a significant variation in the phrasing of the oath which, in Masonic tradition, expresses allegiance to the king. For, after swearing to be true to one another, and to obey the committee in all things that are lawful, the Louth Defenders swear that 'as in our former oath we are bound to his Majesty King George III and his successors, so for this present year 1789 we promise faithfully the same obedience and also while we live subject to the same government . . .'[9] As an experienced Defender organizer was later to remark, this form of the oath was very useful in getting those with loyalist misgivings to join the society for, as he put it, 'if the King's head were off tomorrow we were no longer under his government'.[10]

The Catholic Irish peasantry had traditionally drawn strength from looking back to better times in the past. They were natural conservatives and the idea of anything but allegiance to the traditional form of monarchical government had never been heard in Ireland. There was also another important conservative factor at work. Though the Revolution in France attracted the Irish peasantry with its abolition of tithes and its general appeal for emancipation of the suffering common man, and though a certain amount of fashionable free-thinking had been discernible among the Rightboys, yet the anti-clerical character which the Revolution assumed in France was generally confusing to a people who had for so long seen in their religion the only popular symbol of their identity.

With such confusing trends at work among the peasantry, and the interests of the peasantry in any case uncoordinated with those of the middle class, the organization of the potentially revolutionary forces in Ireland into a successful revolution on the French model could never have been an easy task. Even so, it must be said of the men into whose hands the manipulation of the new revolutionary spirit now fell, that though they proved themselves men of great courage and integrity, they hardly showed that outstanding political and organizational ability which the occasion demanded.

2

Wolfe Tone
and Samuel Neilson

At the beginning of the French Revolution there had been many members of the ruling class in Ireland with a poor opinion of the way things were done in their country and who thought that they should be changed. 'If', the lord lieutenant wrote some years later, 'the French Revolution had taken a humane and genial turn, and had not degenerated into such a rapid succession of tyranny upon tyranny, the speculative minds among the educated and superior classes of this kingdom would have hearkened eagerly to democratic novelties.'[1] But the course of the French Revolution, with its ruthlessness and its radical republicanism, antagonized conservative democrats and left even Patriot reformers like Grattan and Sir Laurence Parsons helpless between their wish for political freedom and their refusal to try and achieve it by endangering the whole equilibrium of society. Leadership of the new spirit fell more and more into the hands of men who had no inhibitions about being as radical and, in the long run, if needs be as republican and violent as the revolutionaries across the water.

The names of these men are, with the exception of a very few – notably Wolfe Tone – largely forgotten today even in Ireland. One of them, a few nights before his death on the scaffold, wrote in a letter from prison to his family: '... justice will yet be done to my memory, and my fate be mentioned rather with pride than with shame ... if I did not expect the arrival of this justice to my memory, I should be indeed afflicted at the nominal ignominy of my death.'[2] His death was in fact to be peculiarly ignominious, for by some clumsiness on the part of the executioner he was hauled up on the rope for nearly a minute before being lowered again to the platform for his final drop.[3] He has a small street named after him in Cork but otherwise his name, John Sheares, has little popular appeal in modern republican Ireland. Thomas Emmet, Samuel Neilson, William MacNeven, Arthur O'Connor, Oliver Bond, Thomas Russell, Napper Tandy, John Lawless, John and Henry Sheares, Beauchamp Bagenal Harvey – these are some of the names who deserve to share with Wolfe Tone and the romantic Lord Edward Fitzgerald the fame of founding the separatist republican movement.

Among them Napper Tandy alone has become popularly known, though few who sing the opening verse of the 'Wearing of the Green' probably have any idea who he was or what he did.*

Most of these men were of considerable bourgeois standing in society – Fitzgerald was an aristocrat – and all but one were Protestants. Of them all Wolfe Tone is the best known, being usually described as 'leader' of the Society of United Irishmen which finally in 1798 tried to carry out a republican revolution in Ireland. Tone was in fact out of Ireland during almost the whole time in which the movement took on its characteristically violent and conspiratorial form. His contribution to events lay in the persistent and effective personal pressure he put on the French Government to give military aid to Irish conspirators with whom he was largely out of touch and in many cases unacquainted. He shares with Lord Edward Fitzgerald the honour of being the most celebrated figure of the rebellion, partly because like Fitzgerald he suffered a brave and pathetic death in the course of 1798, partly because as a shadowy figure behind the scenes, in league with the enemy, he took on a legendary quality for his opponents even in his own lifetime, and partly because he left behind him memoirs of considerable shrewdness and charm, in which he now shines through history by contrast with some of the other revolutionary figures.

The first Tone to settle in Ireland more than a century before had been a soldier of Oliver Cromwell's. Both by antecedence and upbringing Tone could hardly have had fewer connections with Gaelic Ireland, nor would this have seemed to him at any stage of his career a matter of the slightest relevance. His father, a respectable Protestant, had succeeded to the leasehold of a farm near Naas in County Kildare and later moved to Dublin to become a coachbuilder. His mother, whose name was Lamport, was the daughter of a sea captain in the East India trade. Tone himself, after a good Protestant schooling in the city, was sent to Trinity College where he studied logic. His real wish was to be a soldier, and he longed to be allowed to join the British Army then fighting the colonists in America. But his father insisted that he should complete his education, and he took his degree. At Trinity Tone enjoyed himself and always retained 'a most sincere affection' for his old university to the end of his life, though it was a pillar of that establishment which he came to oppose. An attractive and spirited young man who loved the material pleasures of life, particularly eating and drinking in good company, Tone is, in his account of his early activities in Ireland, always more a student prince of politics than any sort of national hero in the making.

* Oh, I met with Napper Tandy and he took me by the hand,
  And he says how's poor oul' Ireland and how does she stand?
  'Tis the most distressful country that ever yet was seen
  For they're hanging men and women for the wearing of the green.

Tone married at the age of twenty-two and tried to take his responsibilities seriously by going to London to study law. But in this, by his own admission, he had little success, finding the rest of life more enjoyable than the law itself. He did, however, apply himself seriously to one political scheme: a plan for establishing a British colony in Captain Cook's newly discovered islands in the South Seas, in order, as he wrote, to 'put a bridle on Spain in time of peace and annoy her grievously in time of war'.[4] It was an odd political debut for one usually thought of as first practitioner of the principle that England's difficulty was Ireland's opportunity. He actually went round to Downing Street and handed in a copy of this plan personally to the porter there, but Pitt, the Prime Minister, did not even acknowledge it. He took the affront in reasonably good part and his next move was to try and volunteer with his brother for the East India Company's military service. But calling at their offices one day in September he found that no ships were sailing until the following March, so he gave up the idea and returned to Dublin on 23 December 1788.[5]

Called to the Irish bar early in 1789 Tone's interests again turned instinctively to politics. The two fashionable progressive issues of parliamentary reform and Catholic Emancipation made an obvious appeal to a young man of his spirit. He joined a political club, the Whig club, which had been founded by Grattan and Charlemont to obtain a reform of Parliament, made friends with Sir Lawrence Parsons and other 'patriot' members of the opposition, and even entertained some hopes of sitting in Parliament himself. But before long he was playing with political ideas that were a good deal more progressive and shocking altogether.

His first important publication in fact was a pamphlet written when the British Government was on the point of breaking off relations with Spain, and this time he took up a very different attitude from that which had taken him to Downing Street. He now suggested that Ireland as an independent nation would not in fact necessarily be bound to go to war with Spain at all, even if Britain did. Hanging about the Dublin bookshops on the first day of this pamphlet's publication, Tone was delighted to hear bishops and other Establishment figures express their outrage and indignation at its seditious contents. But his political ideas were still immature, for soon afterwards he was once again advocating his old South Sea colony scheme for thwarting Spain on Britain's behalf. This time he not only got an acknowledgement from the government but approbation from the Foreign Secretary, Grenville.[6] However, an improvement in relations between Britain and Spain soon made both points of view irrelevant. In any case the shock waves were by now beginning to be felt of that great developing political event in France which finally directed Tone's thinking towards the separatist and eventually republican lines for which he became famous.

Tone later wrote that the Revolution 'changed in an instant the politics of Ireland' and that within twelve months when its implications for monarchy and aristocracy had become clear it had divided political thinkers clearly into 'aristocrats' and 'democrats'.[7] Given the compressive tendencies of hindsight – Tone himself was, after all, still toying with his Imperial South Sea project in the summer of 1790, because he 'had nothing better to do'[8] – this is a fair enough definition of the Revolution's effect on Ireland.

To one group of Irishmen in particular the Revolution had acted like a clarion call and in the light of later Irish history this makes a strange paradox. Protestant Ulster, and particularly Belfast, from which most of the anti-British American colonists had come, had long been a centre of popular republican ideas. Presbyterianism, with its dislike of bishops, was in any case a religion cast in a republican mould. In Belfast in the early 1790s the remnants of the old Volunteers of ten years before still survived to a much more positive extent than in Dublin. They were now proud companies of radical political thinkers sticking devotedly to the great cause of reform which had received such a setback when Flood failed to force it through the Irish Parliament, wearing his Volunteer uniform, in 1783. On that occasion the Belfast Volunteers had been prepared to march on Dublin, and something of the same spirit still survived, much stimulated by recent events in France.

A close friend of Tone's, a twenty-three-year-old officer in the British Army called Thomas Russell who had served in India and who had spent the summer of 1790 on half-pay with Tone and his wife at their 'little box of a house' by the sea at Irishtown, was posted to join his regiment in Belfast in the autumn. Russell, who had a radical turn of mind himself, was soon in touch with the surviving groups of Volunteers there who elected him to one of their political clubs. He discovered that political thought in these clubs and among the Volunteers was being actively directed and influenced by a secret committee headed by the thirty-year-old son of a Presbyterian clergyman, one Samuel Neilson. Neilson more than any other single figure can be said to be the founder of the society soon to be known as the United Irishmen.

Russell wrote to Tone in the summer of 1791 to tell him of his new friends. It seemed that, in one most important respect, the thought of some of these clubs was developing on parallel lines to some recent discussions he and Tone had been having earlier. These had concerned the possibility of getting Protestant Dissenters to overcome their prejudices against Catholics and to unite with Catholics to realize a joint strength for Ireland in the cause of change and reform. There was nothing particularly original in such an idea. It had been put forward years before in the hey-day of volunteering by the *Volunteer Journal*, which had proclaimed for a while: 'When the men of Ireland forget their destructive religious prejudices, and embrace each other with the warmth of genuine religious philanthropy, then, and not until then, will they eradicate the baneful English influence, and destroy the aristocratic tyrants of the land.'⁹ But though there had been a certain amount of such thinking among the more radical Volunteers it was not on the whole typical of the Protestant attitude of the day. And, in any case, the objective of the Volunteers on that occasion – legislative independence – had been won without the need fully to resolve ancient prejudices.

To apply the principle of united effort to the new issue of reform was logical and reasonable enough. Russell, writing to Tone, asked him to draw up a suitable declaration for his new friends in the North, and on 14 July 1791, the second anniversary of the storming of the Bastille, Tone sent three resolutions 'suited to this day' to Belfast for adoption.

These were: (1) that English influence in Ireland was the great grievance of the country; (2) that the most effective way to reform it was by a reform of Parliament; and (3) that no reform could be any use unless it included the Catholics.¹⁰ In a covering letter to his new contacts in Belfast he added: 'I have not said one word that looks like a wish for separation, though I give it to you and your friends as my most decided opinion that such an event would be a regeneration of their country.'¹¹

It was the third of Tone's open resolutions – the key one, that a union of all the people of Ireland, Protestant and Catholic, was indispensable to achieve reform – that was treading on the most dangerous ground in the North. For some years clashes between Peep o' Day Boys and Defenders there had been growing more and more ugly, and it was in many ways the worst possible time to try and put forward such an otherwise intelligent proposition. Tone himself admitted to his diary that this last resolution 'in concession to prejudices, was rather insinuated than asserted'. But only three days later he was told by Neilson that in spite of his care it had had to be dropped altogether. The news made him note bitterly that in that case he would devote himself solely to the Catholic cause from then on because clearly the people in the North who were nominally most anxious for reform were really just seeking 'rather a monopoly than an extension of liberty ... contrary to all justice and expediency'.¹²

Tone was in fact always too excited by the desirability of a union between Catholics and Dissenters to pay lasting attention to the practical obstacles to it with which he was constantly presented. He, and many United Irishmen later, fell too easily into the assumption that the reconciliation could be brought about almost as easily as it could be wished for.

In any case encouraging evidence had appeared in Dublin itself, quite independently of Tone and his new friends in Belfast, that similar ideas to theirs were stirring in other radical minds. As early as June 1791 – even before Tone had sent his heads of proposals to Belfast – a broadsheet had been circulated in Dublin which outlined proposals for a future separatist nationalism with a prophetic touch.

It is proposed at this juncture [the broadsheet ran] that a SOCIETY shall be instituted in this City, having much of the secrecy and somewhat of the ceremonial attached to Freemasonry ... Let one benevolent, beneficent conspiracy arise, one Plot of Patriots, pledged by solemn adjuration to each other in the service of the people ... let its name be the Irish Brotherhood ... What are the rights of Roman Catholics, and what are the immediate duties of Protestants regarding these rights? Is the independence of Ireland nominal or real, a barren right or a fact regulative of national conduct and influencing national character? ... Is there any middle state between the extremes of union with Britain and total separation, in which the rights of the people can be established and rest in security? ... By the Brotherhood are these questions and such as these to be determined.[13]

Tone's own thoughts concentrated more and more on the absurdity of Protestants trying to think and act as Irish patriots while at the same time regarding Catholics, the vast majority of the people of Ireland, as somehow not involved with them in Irish patriotism. In September of this year, 1791, he published under the pseudonym of 'A Northern Whig' a well-reasoned pamphlet entitled *An Argument on behalf of the Catholics of Ireland*. It was addressed to the Presbyterians of the North, urging them to 'forget all former feuds, to consolidate the entire strength of the whole nation and to form for the future but one people'.[14]

This pamphlet attracted immediate approval and interest in its author by an organization called the Catholic Committee, a respectable and hitherto conservative body of Catholic gentry founded in the middle of the eighteenth century to represent Catholic views with the minimum of offence to the Establishment. Stimulated, like every organisation in Ireland, by the French Revolution, the Catholic Committee had recently been showing new life under the guidance of a middle-class Catholic radical named John Keogh, who soon split the Committee in two and assumed leadership of the radical half which from then on was the only part that effectively counted. It was natural that Keogh should want to get in touch with Tone at once and he did so. But the pamphlet excited an equally immediate response from the quarter to which it was directly addressed, namely, the Protestants of the North.

For Tone's argument was exactly the sort of message that Neilson and the more sophisticated radicals of his secret committee in the North had been trying to get across to the ordinary Presbyterian members of the various Volunteer bodies and clubs there. Neilson and his friends invited Tone to Belfast in the following month. He met the secret committee formally for the first time at dinner at four o'clock on 14 October and there helped argue out the final resolutions of a new and quite open reforming organization to be officially launched under the name of the Society of United Irishmen.

Tone found that the political temperature of Belfast had risen noticeably since his first proposals had had to be watered down in the summer. The secret committee in their turn were delighted to hear from him and his friend Russell of developments within the Catholic Committee. But there were plenty of indications that the desirable Union was still more easily wished for than achieved.

For instance, at this very inaugural secret meeting which Tone attended it had to be agreed that the North was 'not yet ripe to follow' to the full the lead they were being given.[15]

Some days later Tone found himself engaged in an argument after dinner in which individuals took up the relative positions of Peep o' Day Boys and Defenders. The Peep o' Day Boys, wrote Tone, were 'ashamed of their own positions'.[16] At another dinner some days later there was another 'furious battle, which lasted two hours, on the Catholic question, as usual neither party convinced'.[17] A dissenting clergyman of some prominence, the Reverend William Bruce, was particularly anti-Catholic. Tone noted that almost all the company were of the same opinion, citing the prevalent fear that the Catholics might revive their claims to ancient estates. Bruce declared that thirty-nine out of forty Protestants were opposed to the liberation of the Catholics.[18] It was an ill-omened start to a movement whose chief tactic was to try and gain strength by bringing Catholics and Dissenters together.

But on this first visit to the North, Tone also heard a lot that he found stimulating and reassuring. Walking in the Belfast Mall with Russell and an American named Digges, one of the inner circle of the Belfast club, Tone asked Digges whether he thought Ireland could exist independent of England and was told yes, decidedly. Nothing could be done, said Digges, until all the religious sects were united and England engaged in a foreign war, but 'if Ireland were free . . . she would in arts, commerce and manufactures spring up like an air balloon and leave England behind at an immense distance'. There was, continued Digges, 'no computing the rapidity with which she would rise'. 'Digges'. wrote Tone in his diary, 'promised to detail all this, and much more, on paper.'[19]

The important immediate result for Ireland of Tone's visit was that the first open meeting of the United Irishmen took place in Belfast on 18 October 1791. The agreed resolutions were unanimously adopted: namely, that a union of Irishmen of all religious persuasions was required to counteract the weight of English influence in the country and secure a reform of Parliament.

Returning to Dublin ten days later after a good deal of convivial hospitality, Tone got in touch with a prominent Dublin radical and former stalwart of the Volunteers of 1782 named Napper Tandy whom he had been commissioned to contact by the Belfast secret committee. Tandy found the approach much to his liking. On 9 November 1791 a similar club of United Irishmen to that in Belfast was founded in the capital and Tandy took charge of it from the start. Signing the Dublin Society's declaration at its inaugural meeting Tandy wrote:

In the present great era of reform when unjust governments are falling in every quarter of Europe ... we think it our duty as Irishmen to come forward and state what we feel to be our heavy grievance, and what we believe to be its effectual remedy. We have no National Government. We are ruled by Englishmen and the servants of Englishmen whose object is the interest of another country, whose instrument is corruption, whose strength is the weakness of Ireland, and these men have the whole power and patronage of the country as means to subdue the honesty and the spirit of her representatives in the legislature.[20]

There was nothing in this with which Grattan and other members of the Whig club would not theoretically agree, though the very radical nature of the language might suggest eventual extremes which would be too much for them. Even the simple open affirmation which all members of the United Irish Society were called upon to make – at this stage no oath was required – was constitutional, and technically inoffensive:

I, A.B., in the presence of God, do pledge myself to my country that I will use all my abilities and influence in the attainment of an adequate and impartial representation of the Irish nation in Parliament, and as a means of absolute and immediate necessity in the attainment of this chief good of Ireland, I will endeavour as much as lies in my ability, to forward a brotherhood of affection, an identity of interests, a communion of rights, and a union of power among Irishmen of all religious persuasions ... the freedom of this country.[21]

Contrary to the proposal in the Dublin broadsheet earlier in the year, the society was an open one and as yet adopted none of the paraphernalia of Freemasonry. The United Irishmen did not become a secret society until three years later, when its character changed altogether. Now it set itself up as little more than a radical reform club or debating society, though already convinced republicans like Tandy in Dublin and Neilson in Belfast held secret designs in reserve.

Before the end of 1791 Tandy issued a circular letter signed by himself in which he declared: 'The object of this institution is to make a United Society of the Irish Nation; to make all Irishmen Citizens, all Citizens Irishmen ...' And he added that for a century past there had been tranquillity 'but to most of our dear countrymen it has been the tranquillity of a dungeon'.[22] In other words the Irish patriotic principles which had so often been so eloquently invoked by the Protestant gentry and middle classes on their own behalf were now taken to their logical conclusion in a patriotism which all Irishmen might invoke equally. A new comprehensive Irish patriotism was on offer to all.

3

United Irishmen
and Defenders

Tone himself almost at once ceased to play any active part in the Society of United Irishmen. He concerned himself more and more with the agitation for Catholic rights by Keogh's Catholic Committee of which he became a salaried official in the course of 1792. In his own words he sank 'into obscurity'[1] in the affairs of the United Irishmen which were conducted by men like Napper Tandy and William Drennan, a doctor, who probably wrote the Dublin broadsheet of the summer and certainly coined for Ireland the phrase 'the Emerald Isle'. Other active members of the Society at this stage were two young lawyer brothers from Cork, Henry and John Sheares, and a wealthy Wexford land-owner named Beauchamp Bagenal Harvey. All of them, like Tone, were Protestants, though Catholics did in fact join the Society in considerable numbers.

However, Tone kept up his personal links with Neilson and the branch of the United Irishmen in Belfast, and visited them twice during the summer of 1792. Each time he was again confronted by the gap between United Irish aspirations and the realities of the situation in Ireland.

He went to Belfast, for instance, to celebrate the third anniversary of the storming of the Bastille, an occasion on which he was to address some of the Northern Volunteer corps. '... Expect sharp opposition to-morrow,' he wrote in his diary the day before. 'Some of the country corps no better than Peep o' Day Boys ...' Neilson, returning to his hotel that evening, and passing a half-open door behind which he heard a voice he recognized, pushed it open to discover one of the Volunteer Captains haranguing against the Catholics.[2]

Soon afterwards Tone journeyed from Belfast to the small town of Rathfriland to investigate personally the scenes of recent clashes between Peep o' Day Boys and Defenders. Several people had been killed on both sides. Great offence was being taken by the Protestants at the Catholics 'marching about in military array and firing shots at unseasonable times'.[3] Tone claimed to find that the Protestants were universally the aggressors, and that on the whole the Catholics seemed not to 'do anything worse than meet in large bodies and fire powder; foolish certainly but not wicked'.[4] Some days later a gentleman of Sligo gave Tone 'a most melancholy account' of the depression and insult under which Catholics of that town were labouring. '... Every Protestant rascal breaks their heads and windows for his amusement ... the Catholic spirit quite broken.'[5]

On a third visit to Belfast, in August 1792, travelling to Rathfriland again with John Keogh of the Catholic Committee, he found that the landlord in the inn would not even give them rooms there when he knew who they were. And that day he saw some 150 Peep o' Day Boys exercising within a quarter of a mile of the town. The boisterous optimism with which he countered such evidence is revealed by a diary entry he made only three days later, on 14 August, after visiting the shipyards with an industrialist member of the United Irishmen named Henry Joy McCracken:

> Walk out and see McCracken's new ship, the Hibernia. Hibernia has an English Crown on her shield. We all roar at him. ... The Co. Down getting better everyday on the Catholic question. Two of the new companies applied to be admitted in the Union regiment * ... were refused membership on the ground of their holding Peep O' Day principles. *Bon* ... Lurgan† green as usual. Something will come out of all this. Agree to talk the matter over to-morrow when we are all cool. Huzza: Generally drunk. Vive la Nation! ... Generally very drunk. Bed. God knows how.[6]

Tone's optimistic frivolity was far more damaging to his constructive political thought than his drinking, which was probably no more than any spirited young man of his background engaged in. He was not an alcoholic but he was a chronic optimist. Finding that a new Volunteer corps which had been raised in Ballinahinch had actually been raised on Peep o' Day principles, he pondered less the long-term implications of such an incident than the short-term success of one McClockey who, temporarily at any rate, converted them to the principles of the United Irish Society and was chosen lieutenant of the company in return. 'All well,' wrote Tone cheerfully, '... Both parties now in high affection with each other, who were before ready to cut each other's throats.'[7]

In Dublin in November 1792, together with Tandy, Tone set about the formation of a new corps of city Volunteers, devoted to United Irish principles. They were to wear a uniform with buttons embossed with the Irish harp without the Crown above, and similar to that of the National Guard of Paris, after whom it was to be called.

'Is that quite wise?' commented Tone in his diary. 'Who cares?'[8]

He had to note that there was not all that much enthusiasm for the idea, and indeed owing to the lack of sufficient support for such a republican manifestation this National Guard never paraded in public.[9] Tone, however,

---

* i.e., the United Irishmen.
† A town in County Armagh.

took comfort from the fact that it was becoming fashionable for Dubliners to address each other as 'Citizen' in the French fashion, and that 'trifling as it is, it is a symptom'.[10] An even more encouraging symptom was that on the anniversary of William of Orange's birthday the remnants of the old Dublin Volunteers had not paraded as usual round his statue on College Green, but had simply held a normal parade wearing 'national' green cockades instead of the traditional orange ones. 'This is striking proof', wrote Tone optimistically, 'of the change of men's sentiments when "Our Glorious Deliverer" is neglected. This is the first time the day has passed uncommemorated since the institution of the Volunteers. Huzza! Union and the people for ever!'[11]

However, the Dublin Volunteers by this time numbered no more than 250 men,[12] and the Great Deliverer's birthday was hardly neglected by others, as *The Times* newspaper recorded. After 'a splendid appearance' at noon of the nobility and other persons of distinction to compliment the lord lieutenant on the anniversary, the lord lieutenant himself, attended by the nobility and gentry and escorted by a squadron of horse, went in procession round King William's statue. Guns in the Phoenix Park fired a salute which was answered by volleys from regiments of the garrison drawn up on College Green, and at night there were bonfires, illuminations 'and other demonstrations of joy'.[13] If Tone's concept of an Irish Union* was to progress beyond the Huzzas of his own diary, or the parochial deliberations of intellectual societies in Dublin and Belfast, this formidable establishment and the automatic respect it commanded had somehow to be assaulted.

In fact, Tone in his capacity as an official of the Catholic Committee was already on the point of breaching one bastion in the Establishment's position. He and Keogh, besides making intensive propaganda for the Catholic cause, had, in this year 1792, succeeded in bringing about a Convention of elected Catholic delegates sitting in Dublin, the first representative body of Catholics to meet in Ireland since the Parliament of James II over a century before. And together Tone and Keogh played an important part in applying pressure which in 1793 helped lead to the admission of Catholics to the vote on exactly the same terms as Protestants.

The passing of this further Catholic Relief Act in 1793 was in itself testimony to the sycophancy and impotence of the so-called independent Irish Parliament. For the year before, this Parliament had overwhelmingly rejected exactly the same measure, because the government in England had not been in favour of it. Now, in 1793, the English Government under Pitt was prepared to accept the measure and it was passed on 9 April. Also,

---

* Anyone studying the years preceding the Parliamentary Union of 1801 will be struck by the extent to which the terms 'the Union' and 'the Irish Union' were then in current usage to express a sense very different from that which eventually became so familiar. Throughout these years 'the Union' is constantly used to mean that union of all Irishmen, independent of Britain, at which the United Irishmen were aiming.

early in 1793 occurred an event of the greatest importance which was to colour the attitudes of both government and would-be reformers in Ireland for many years to come. This was the outbreak in February 1793 of war between England and France.

On the outbreak of war, the English Prime Minister's immediate concern over Ireland was to prevent the country from becoming a seat of disaffection which France could exploit. And in this respect the recently passed Catholic Relief Act was distinctly helpful. Tone had more than once noted with some apprehension that the Catholics might not be interested in any political aim beyond their own sectarian Emancipation. Once when Grattan had said to him that he thought of the Catholic question only as a means of advancing the general good, Tone had commented: 'Right! But do the Catholics consider it so? The devil a bit except one or two of them.'[14]

Pitt did not grant full Emancipation and there was, as Tone pointed out, a ludicrous inconsistency in granting the vote to the peasant Catholic forty-shilling freeholder and yet continuing to disallow Catholic gentry to sit in Parliament.* So that some grounds for resentment remained. But the Act was undoubtedly a major concession encouraging Catholics to look no further than their own sectarian interests when contemplating political goals.

Meanwhile, almost entirely dissociated from the middle-class reformers represented in the Society of United Irishmen and the Catholic Committee, the peasantry had been stirring on its own account. For the first time in Irish history the Irish common people had begun to take something like primitive political action of their own. In Louth and Meath, counties adjacent to Ulster where Catholics were in the majority, the Defenders were assuming a more and more aggressive role. Their activities were still very like those of the agrarian secret societies already so long a feature of Irish rural life, and for many who took part in the raiding of gentlemen's houses for arms and horses there can have been little distinction in their minds between these and the familiar Whiteboy raids of the past. However, the vague political innuendoes in the Defender oath for those who chose to see them, and the general revolutionary infection of the time, gave a rather more generalized attitude to protests which in the past had been limited and localized. In the South, where the Defender Society as such had not yet superimposed itself on the old Whiteboy system as it was soon to do, raids when they occurred were described as simple Whiteboy activities, as for instance on the night of 17 September 1792 when arms, horses, bridles and saddles were taken from

* 'During the whole progress of the Catholic question', Tone wrote, 'a favourite and plausible topic with their enemies was the ignorance and bigotry of the multitude ... If the Catholics deserved what has been granted, they deserved what has been withheld; if they did not deserve what has been withheld, what has been granted should have been refused.' (op. cit., i, p. 100.)

houses near Cork.[15] 'But in other parts of Ireland a new organized pattern of such activity under the banner of the Defenders was becoming unmistakable.

Defenders, acting more and more on the principle that attack was the best form of defence, had started appearing in armed bodies in Louth in April 1792 and by the end of the year they had spread to Meath, Cavan, Monaghan and other predominantly Catholic counties adjacent to the Protestant areas of Ulster, and had attacked some forty houses for arms in County Louth alone, mostly successfully. In the last week of December they assembled in very large numbers first at Dunleer and then at Dundalk, armed with guns and pitchforks. Their exact purpose was not clear, but it was thought that they would possibly try to liberate a large number of convicts then collected in that area from all over the North on their way to transportation. There were no military available to deal with them, but *The Times* reported that 'the respectable inhabitants of the town, principally Roman Catholics, went among them, and having conferred with them for some time they dispersed'.[16]

On 9 January 1793 *The Times* again referred to 'those infatuated and deluded people', the Defenders, being involved in an engagement with troops at Carrickmacross. The 'insurrection' was reported to be spreading, and the insurgents' aims were variously described as sometimes the abolition of tithes, sometimes the lowering of rents. '. . . In Louth,' said *The Times,* 'the first object seems to be to get arms and ammunition.'[17] There was another engagement with the military later in January, this time at Kells, in County Meath, and eighteen Defenders were killed.[18]

A correspondent from the Bishop of Meath's palace at Ardbracken wrote in February 1793: 'Not a night passes that the Defenders do not assemble and break open houses in some part or other of this country', and he recounted how 150 of them on foot and horseback with a drum and three sledges had raided Lord Maxwell's house, where, however, 'they had behaved with some degree of politeness'. After taking three double-barrelled guns, two muskets and two cases of pistols, his Lordship, who was particularly fond of one of the cases of pistols, asked if he could buy it back from them. The Defenders complimented him on his taste and returned it to him, refusing the money. 'This house', wrote the correspondent, 'now looks more like a Bastille than a Bishop's Palace, from the quantity of bolts, bars and cross barricades on the doors and windows of the house and offices.'[19]

On 22 February 1793 *The Times* drew attention to what was different about this outbreak of disturbances from previous Whiteboy activities. 'The disturbances in Ireland', it wrote – much too sweepingly in fact – 'are not on account of any complaint of grievances. They arise from the pure wantonness of a set of desperadoes called Defenders . . . encouraged and abetted by a secret Junto, that like the French Jacobins, wish to throw all government into confusion . . .'[20]

Retribution of course was not long in catching up with such a primitively organized movement, and the Defenders were soon being hanged in droves. In the months of March and April 1793 alone, sixty-eight Defenders were reported by *The Times* as being sentenced to death while a further seventy-seven were sentenced to transportation for administering or taking the Defender oath. But the cheapness with which the Defenders regarded life right up to the final bloodbath of 1798 was always the most impressive tribute to the desperation with which they pursued their confused cause. And though the sentence of capital punishment was at this period a particularly savage one, including as it did the phrase '. . . but being yet alive, should be cut down, but being alive their bowels be taken out and burned before their faces',[21] it seems to have had surprisingly little force as a deterrent. More than two years later an Irish government official was writing to the English Prime Minister: 'Defenderism puzzles me more and more; but it certainly grows more alarming daily, as the effect of the executions seems to be at an end and there is an enthusiasm defying punishment.'[22]

The intensity of Defender activity varied from time to time, but as a crudely organized secret system, controlled apparently by a shadowy and probably rather ineffectual central committee, it was throughout the 1790s superimposing itself on all already existing secret society organizations in Catholic Ireland, giving them for the first time some appearance of uniformity and at least a primitive political tinge. Where any particular grievance was uppermost the Defenders now organized crude protest. Their significance lay in the fact that they were expressing, however incoherently, for the first time in Irish history, something like a national resentment of the long general grievance of the Irish common people's everyday suffering.

Soon after the outbreak of war between England and France, Pitt began to balance his conciliatory approach to Irish Catholics with strictly defensive measures. At almost the same time as the Catholic Relief Act, an Act went through the Irish Parliament creating an Irish militia whose rank and file were to be drawn by ballot from among the peasantry. The government's refusal at first to allow substitutes for those drawn for this militia led to widespread resistance which was organized by the Defenders. By June 1793 reports of anti-militia riots were coming in from all over Ireland.

The Times reported from Sligo: 'The abstracts of the Militia Act which have been lately circulated through this country operated like electric fire on the weak understanding of the poor uninformed multitude.'[23] Reports, possibly exaggerated, spoke of bands of six or seven thousand men roving the Sligo countryside, and it was noted that two Catholic country gentlemen in particular, one actually a delegate to the recent Catholic Convention in Dublin, had been treated with uncommon cruelty when their houses had been raided by the Defenders for arms. Nineteen Defenders were killed and several prisoners taken at a battle at Boyle in County Roscommon; eight more were killed at Manor Hamilton in County Leitrim, and a further large anti-militia assembly was reported from Baltinglass in County Wicklow, all within a few days.

In July 1793 the most serious engagement of all took place just outside the town of Wexford, where fifty of the recruited militia under a Major Valloton confronted some two thousand Defenders, armed with guns, scythes and picks. The Defenders demanded the return of two men taken prisoner a few days earlier. While a parley was taking place between the two sides the Major was suddenly struck down and killed, whereupon the militia fired, killing some eighty Defenders and putting the rest to flight. The leader of the Defenders, a young farmer of twenty-two named John Moore, whose legs were broken by the militia's first volley, fought on his stumps until his men fled. He himself was then shot out of hand. Five prisoners taken were executed two days later.

Grievances over the enrolment of the militia were largely met by government concessions which allowed voluntary enlistment as well as conscription by ballot, and at the same time permitted substitutes to be found for those upon whom the ballot fell. But one significant feature had emerged from these events: the loyal behaviour of those militia whom the Defenders had engaged in the Wexford incident. For it was to be by the Catholic militia itself, drawn from exactly the same class as the Defenders, that the Defenders were eventually to be crushed.

The Defender system, which continued to grow dramatically after the particular grievance of the militia had abated, was almost as much of a puzzle to the radical middle-class members of the Society of United Irishmen and the Catholic Committee as it was to the government. Certainly they seem to have known little about the Defenders for a long time, though a Committee of the (Irish) House of Lords which reported in 1793 claimed that there was a liaison between the leaders of the Catholic Committee and the Defenders.[24] However, the experiences suffered by the Catholic gentry at the Defenders' hands makes this improbable, and the allegation seems to have been based solely on the fact that the Catholic Committee had subscribed funds for some of the unfortunate peasants facing trial. The Catholic Committee, besides refuting the House of Lords committee's charge, issued a strong condemnation of the Defenders on their own account, describing them, like *The Times*, as 'deluded people', expressing their 'utmost detestation and abhorrence of such illegal and criminal proceedings' and calling upon 'these unhappy men ... to desist from such unwarrantable acts of violence ... and to return to their obedience to the laws and the laudable pursuits of honest industry'.[25] The Catholic Bishops in Dublin also issued a strong condemnation of Defenderism.

Tone described the Defenders contemptuously as 'rabble',[26] though he had some correspondence with them. Nevertheless, for middle-class Protestant radicals already thinking in terms of a republican attempt at revolution, the Defenders were clearly a force of great significance about whom it was necessary to become better informed. Napper Tandy, in the summer of 1793, met some Defender leaders at Castlebellingham in County Louth and took the Defender oath, but he was betrayed by an informer and fled for his life, first to America and then to France. Such knowledge of the Defenders as was held in middle-class reforming and radical circles at this time was later summed up by the United Irishman, Thomas Emmet, as follows: 'The Defenders were bound together by oaths obviously drawn up by illiterate men, different in different places, but all promising secrecy and specifying whatever grievance was, in each place, most felt and understood. ... The views of these men were in general far from distinct.'[27] There was, he continued, some sort of 'national notion that . . . something ought to be done for Ireland' but nothing more precise than that, except that arms would be necessary and therefore had to be procured.

Meanwhile, in Dublin and Belfast, the Society of United Irishmen, that more sophisticated and articulate body which also held the notion that 'something ought to be done for Ireland', was making singularly little progress. In Dublin it had continued to issue stirring addresses to the Irish nation and particularly to the remnants of the Volunteers.

'Citizen Soldiers to Arms!' it had proclaimed in December 1792, desperately trying to animate the old Volunteering spirit with the new principles of revolutionary France on behalf of parliamentary reform. 'Fourteen long years are elapsed since the rise of your associations, and in 1782 did you imagine that in 1792 this nation would still remain unrepresented . . .?'[28]

While the Catholic Convention was still sitting in Dublin the Society of United Irishmen made its theoretical position clear:

'The Catholic cause is subordinate to our cause and included in it, for as United Irishmen we adhere to no sect but to society. . . . In the sincerity of our souls do we desire catholic emancipation, but were it obtained tomorrow, to-morrow we would go on, as we do to-day, in the pursuit of that reform as well as our own.'[29] And on 25 January 1793 with a cry of 'Ireland! O! Ireland!' the society put forward its plan for reform which consisted of universal male adult suffrage with annual parliaments.

In spirit the society resembled very much those democratic clubs and societies which had become so much a feature of the radical scene in England: the London Corresponding Society, the Constitutional Society and the 'Friends of the People' to the last of which a member of the Irish House of Commons, Lord Edward Fitzgerald, younger son of the Duke of Leinster, already belonged. There was even in England a society of United Englishmen. What aggravated an otherwise similar situation in Ireland to such a dangerous pitch for the government was the combination of such activity with a French threat of invasion and such a significant quantity of open peasant unrest. The Society of United Irishmen itself was at this time hardly one to give the government much concern. But in the prevailing circumstances they could not afford to take any chances with it. Not long after the outbreak of war early in 1793, all the remaining Volunteer corps in Ireland were suppressed. And in Dublin the government had already begun a long and successful tradition of informers when they started receiving inside information of the proceedings of the Dublin Society of United Irishmen within six weeks of its foundation.[30]* Their informer's news was reassuring. He reported that the affairs of the society were in fact at a low ebb, and attendance had sunk to around thirty. Its most energetic and uncompromising leader, Napper Tandy, was in exile; another official, Hamilton Rowan, had been found guilty of seditious libel and was in prison. Tone himself was preoccupied with agitation for full Catholic Emancipation.

Thomas Emmet, a barrister who was already a member of the society and in a later phase was to become one of its principal leaders, wrote of this period: 'The expectations of the reformers had been blasted, their plans had been defeated, and decisive means had been taken by government to prevent their being resumed. It became necessary to wait for new events, from which might be found new plans. Nor did such events seem distant, for now the French arms were again emblazoning their cause with success and hiding in the splendour of their victories the atrocities of their government.'[31]

* From a linen merchant, Thomas Collins.

4

French Contacts

With France successful in arms all over Europe, and England emerging as her chief enemy, the war sharpened all attitudes in Ireland to extremes.

The French, in spite of, indeed partly because of, the presence of large numbers of *émigré* Irish families in Paris, were not particularly up to date in their information about Ireland. But they had begun to show a new interest in her since the very beginning of the Revolution. An agent sent to Dublin in 1789, discerning new trends, had reported in 1790: 'A few years more and the Irish may form a nation which they have not been for 600 years.'[1] In December 1792 another agent, impressed presumably by the renewed activities of the old Volunteer companies in Ulster and by contacts with the United Irishmen in Dublin and Belfast, had reported dramatically if prematurely that under the guidance of six or seven daring conspirators an Irish revolution was being prepared and France might find a powerful ally in Ireland in the coming struggle.[2] In the following year, 1793, another special emissary from France appeared, this time with an introduction to the now notoriously radical Irish aristocrat, Lord Edward Fitzgerald.

Fitzgerald, who was twenty-nine, had been for many years an officer in the British Army, and had served with heroism in action against the American colonists. He was now one of those Irishmen who were most sympathetic to the French revolutionary cause. From Paris he had written enthusiastic letters to his mother dated '1st Year of the Republic', signing himself 'le citoyen Edouard Fitzgerald'.[3] In November 1792 he had attended a dinner in Paris to celebrate the great French victory at Jemappes and had there proposed a toast that the Marseillaise might 'soon become the favourite music of every army'. This was too much for the British Army and shortly afterwards he was dismissed from its service. The following January, 1793, Fitzgerald shocked the Irish House of Commons by declaring that the lord lieutenant and the majority of the House were the worst subjects the king had. He must have seemed a natural contact for the French. In fact, Fitzgerald, who was not then a member of the United Irishmen, passed the new agent on to the society but they would have nothing to do with him. Next year, however, the French sent another agent to Ireland whose mission was to have much more widespread repercussions.

This new agent was an Anglican clergyman of Irish descent named Jackson who had lived in France professing radical views for the past three years. He now came to Dublin as a secret emissary of the French Committee of Public Safety. He was an inexpert choice, and displayed little skill for the subtlety and security demanded by his new profession. However, his mission to Ireland became a sensation for he was accompanied throughout it by an old friend from London, a solicitor called Cockayne, now acting, unknown to Jackson, as a counter-spy for the British Government. Cockayne reported to London everything that happened, though he found his assignment a considerable strain, complaining to his masters that Jackson would never let him go to bed before 2 a.m. without at least three bottles of claret, whereas he was used to no more than a pint of wine. '. . . Besides,' he added, 'the expense is enormous.'[4] It may have been this that caused Cockayne to turn out little more competent as a counter-agent than the man on whom he was keeping watch. Though Jackson himself was arrested, little hard evidence of treason had been acquired against those with whom he had been in contact. The government had to admit to themselves that Cockayne would 'not speak positively to the different conversations of these persons, but only caught the substance by hints and accidental words'.[5] And when after nearly a year's delay Jackson was eventually brought to trial in 1794 the nature of Cockayne's evidence must have proved exasperating to the Crown. Asked if he had heard a certain conversation he replied:

'Yes.'
'Did you understand it?'
'Yes, in part.'
'How do you mean, in part?'
'They were at one corner of the room and I in another with a book in my hand and I did not hear enough to hear what they said.'[6]

The two men whose conversation he had in part overheard were Jackson himself and Wolfe Tone.

Tone was at this time disillusioned both with the incomplete nature of the Catholic Relief Act of 1793 and with the Catholics themselves for not pressing for total Emancipation more forcefully. He was reluctantly coming to the conclusion that the only hope of making his theory of a united Irish nation materialize was revolution. He was not by nature a violent or bloodthirsty man and had, for instance, deprecated in his diary the need for Louis XVI's execution. But now a fellow lawyer, Leonard Macnally, introduced Jackson to him as an emissary from the Committee of Public Safety who held out the hope that if the state of Ireland were properly known in France she would be prepared to help the Irish win their independence. Tone replied that 'it would be a most severe and grievous remedy for our abuses' but that he saw no other.[7]

The day after the meeting with Jackson, Tone rashly committed to paper his view on the state of Ireland and the likelihood of the country's favourable response to a French invasion. He showed the paper to Jackson. It was a typically optimistic document inspired more by a regard for the facts as they might have been than as they were. 'In a word,' summarized Tone, 'from reason, reflection, interest, prejudice, the spirit of change, the misery of the great bulk of the nation, and above all the hatred of the English name, resulting from the tyranny of near seven centuries, there seems little doubt that an invasion in sufficient force would be supported by the people. There is scarcely an army in the country, and the militia, the bulk of whom are Catholics, would to a moral certainty refuse to act, if they saw such a force as they could look to for support.'[8] The resolute performance of the militia against the Defenders at Wexford was something he appeared to ignore.

Though the desirability of sending someone back to France to urge Tone's point of view in person was also discussed, Tone made it clear that he himself could not go because of family ties. However, even by this degree of contact with the French agent, he was most seriously compromised. And a few days later a copy of his paper came into the government's hands. As Tone himself put it, his situation was 'a very critical one'.[9]

The immediate effect of Jackson's arrest was to cause the flight of some of those United Irishmen with whom he had been in contact. Hamilton Rowan, for instance, escaped from the prison where he was serving his sentence for libel and where Jackson had been able to visit him, and fled romantically by horseback and fishing vessel to France. But the effect of Jackson's arrest on another United Irishman, Macnally, the lawyer who had introduced Jackson to Tone and others, was of greater importance. For Macnally, scared by the treasonable implications of his own association with Jackson, agreed in return for immunity from prosecution and certain sums of money, to turn informer for the government. For many years he was to remain one of the government's most valuable sources of information, high as he was in the councils of the United Irishmen and other radicals, and quite unsuspected of perfidy, even defending them consistently in court on charges of the very treason from which he had been made immune. Tone himself entered into a compact with the government of a more honourable, though still rather curious sort. Making use of his aristocratic friends' influence with the government he agreed that he was in an awkward spot and declared that he would neither fly the country nor give evidence against anyone else, and would stand trial if necessary. But he added that if the government decided not to prosecute him he would voluntarily undertake to exile himself to America. The bargain was agreed to, though Tone kept his part of it in leisurely enough fashion, not leaving for America until Jackson's trial had ended a year later and, thereafter, it might be argued, breaking the spirit of the agreement if not the letter.[10]

Jackson himself, the first important contact between revolutionary

France and the potential revolutionary forces in Ireland, died a most dramatic death. The case against him was amply proved. Before the pronouncement of the inevitable sentence a legal argument took place in court about whether or not the indictment was to be read in full, as requested by Macnally, his defence counsel. The judge drew attention to the prisoner's apparent ill state of health and said that in view of it he 'would not wish to increase his labour by waiting. But do as you please . . .'.[11] During the course of the long ensuing argument between Macnally and the Attorney General it was noticed that the prisoner had grown very faint, and the court ordered the windows to be opened so that he could get some fresh air. Later still it was noticed that 'the prisoner having sunk upon his chair appeared to be in a state of extreme debility'. And when the judge came to pronounce sentence he declared:

'If the prisoner is in a state of insensibility it is impossible that I can pronounce the judgement of the court on him ... humanity and common-sense would require that he should be in a state of sensibility.'

A doctor, called to remedy this unsatisfactory state of affairs, himself pronounced of the prisoner that 'there was every apprehension that he would go off immediately'. A juryman, who was a chemist, then stepped down from the box and declared the prisoner 'verging to eternity with every symptom of death about him'. The slumped figure was about to be carried from the court when the Sheriff finally pronounced him dead. An inquest was ordered and the body left in the dock until nine o'clock next morning when a surgeon found nearly a pint of 'some acrid and mortal matter ... a metallic poison' in his stomach, which had been the cause of death. It is said that on entering court on the last day Jackson had whispered to Macnally a cryptic suicide line from Otway's *Venice Preserved* – 'We have deceived the Senate' – and certainly in his pocket was found a verse from the Psalms which read 'O keep my Soul and deliver me. Let me be not ashamed, for I put my trust in thee.'

Jackson's arrest and subsequent trial and suicide mark a watershed in the series of events which were to reach their bloody climax in 1798. Immediately on his arrest, the hitherto legal and constitutional Society of United Irishmen was suppressed. At the same time, would-be reformers had to face the fact that every attempt at achieving parliamentary reform by constitutional means, such as those initiated by Grattan and his friends, seemed permanently doomed to founder hopelessly in the Irish House of Commons.

To confirm this sense of hopelessness there had taken place, just before the trial itself, a curious political incident. After a political change in England by which a Whig element joined forces with Pitt's administration, a new viceroy, Lord Fitzwilliam, was appointed to Ireland. Fitzwilliam was prepared to recommend total Catholic Emancipation to the Irish House of Commons. But as a result not so much of this attitude – though it caused difficulties enough for Pitt with the king and the Irish executive – but of Fitzwilliam's attempt at some parliamentary reforming from within by dismantling the hereditary grip held on the Irish parliamentary system by one of the leading Irish families, the Beresfords, the new Viceroy was recalled. Tone himself in February 1795 accompanied a last desperate delegation of the Catholic Committee to London to try and prevent the recall. Six weeks after Fitzwilliam's departure and ten days after Jackson's death, he kept his compact with the government and sailed from Belfast for America.

Before leaving he learnt of the existence of a new secret organization which had come into being in Belfast in 1794 when the old open Society of United Irishmen was suppressed. Its existence was until then as unknown to him as it was to the government. Its nucleus was one of the Belfast United Irish societies which had somehow escaped the government's attention and had continued to meet in secret. Merged together with some members of another political club as a secret society they had decided to resume the former name of United Irishmen, but to replace the old test of membership by an oath which left room for republican sentiments. Samuel Neilson was once again one of the prime movers of the organization, which consisted in its early days principally of mechanics, petty shop-keepers and farmers, though as it grew it embraced members higher and higher up in the middle-class social scale. At a meeting on 10 May 1795, seventy-two secretly elected delegates met in Belfast to coordinate a planned system of district, county and eventually provincial and national committees, though at that time the organization in fact extended little further than the two Ulster counties of Antrim and Down. After business the chairman asked every delegate what he stood for and got the answer: 'A republican government and separation from England.'[12]

Tone was asked by Neilson to pass information about the growing strength of this new organization on to the French Government through its Minister in Philadelphia, the port to which he was sailing. A most important part of the new United Irishmen's secret plans to which Tone had been introduced was their intention of contacting and coordinating their efforts with the Defenders.

5

Defenders and Orangemen

Jackson's trial, apart from anything else, had had the effect of publicizing the serious interest the French now had in Ireland. Fitzwilliam's recall and the denial of total emancipation, though of little practical relevance to the peasantry, made for a hardening of their emotional attitudes.

The Defender organization had in any case continued to be active through-out 1794 and was now spreading over the whole of Ireland. In March, at Kinsale, County Cork, a body of Defenders was dispersed with ten killed – again significantly by the (Catholic) Carlow militia.[1] There were as many as 185 Defenders under arrest in Cork gaol that month alone, while on the North-East circuit some three hundred more were awaiting trial at Trim, Dundalk and Drogheda.[2] On 21 May an engagement was reported from County Cavan in which between one hundred and two hundred Defenders were killed.[3] And in the same month seventy were killed in Ballina, County Mayo.[4] By the summer of 1795, when the new secret society of United Irish-men was still only just completing its skeleton organization, there were already thirteen different Irish counties from which armed bodies of Defenders, usually numbering hundreds and sometimes thousands at a time, were being reported.[5]

In several counties the Defenders, who held their own primitive courts, were sufficiently strong to intimidate juries in the normal courts of law and secure acquittals against all the evidence. In return the government embarked for the first time on its own course of rough justice by rounding up the peasantry in those parts of the country where the Defender movement was strong and transporting them without trial into the navy.

Lord Camden, the new Viceroy who replaced Fitzwilliam, commented on the way in which blacksmiths everywhere were being organized by the De-fenders to make pikes.[6] But the structure of the Defender system, though widespread, seems to have been a very loose one, varying from county to county with different oaths and recognition signs. Objectives too were still often local: the lowering of rent or the increase of wages. Nevertheless, per-vading always what was often no more than old-fashioned Whiteboy activity were the new fashions of French liberty and the doctrines of Tom Paine – 'the whiskey of infidelity and treason' as the Solicitor General once described them.[7] Indeed, the vague feeling that 'something ought to be done for Ireland', and that the opportunity would come when the French landed, was spreading very like some cloudy intoxication.

Such feelings were actively encouraged by Defender organizers who moved from county to county, often with only the most rudimentary regard for security. Known as 'committee men', they received a shilling for each new Defender they enrolled, a fact which may well have accounted for the rashness and eagerness of their approach. Public houses were a favourite place for the transaction. 'Where are you going?' a man might be asked.

'To the Defender maker,' would come the reply, as readily as if he were off to the shoemaker.[8]

The new recruit might be asked to swear, as in one Defender oath of 1795, 'to be true to the present United States of France and Ireland and every other kingdom now in Christianity'.[9] He would follow this with a number of equally solemn expressions of Masonic brotherly obligation. At other times the old ambiguous formula of swearing loyalty to the king '... whilst I live under the same government...' still did service. After a glass of punch, perhaps,[10] and the oath on the prayer book, the new Defender would be instructed in a strange sort of catechism.

'What is your designs?'
'On freedom.'
'Where is your designs?'
'The foundation of it is grounded upon a rock.'
'What is the password?'
'Eliphismatis.'[11]

(Asked in court the meaning of the word 'eliphismatis' one sworn Defender said he didn't know but that it was Latin. Counsel dismissed it as mere 'trash of enigmatical or rather nonsensical import'.)

Another similar Defender catechism ran:

'Are you a Christian?'
'I am.'
'By what?'
'By baptism ...'
'Are you consecrated?'
'I am.'
'By what?'
'To the National Convention – to equal all nations – to dethrone all Kings, and plant the tree of liberty on our Irish land – whilst the French Defenders will protect our cause and the Irish Defenders pull down the British laws ...'[12]

There would be instruction in recognition signs: 'Two hands joined backwards on top of the head and pretend to yawn, then draw the hands down upon the knee or on the table. Answer by drawing the right hand over the forehead and return it to the back of the left hand.' A less complicated form of greeting seems to have been, on shaking hands, to press the thumb of the right hand on the back of the other's – 'and not be afraid to hurt the person' – coupled with pronunciation of the magic password 'Eliphismatis'.[13]

There would be talk of the need to get arms to help the French, and if, as frequently happened, through the action of an informer, the novitiate soon afterwards fell into the hands of the law, he would be tried with full solemnity for associating '... with several false traitors associated under the name of Defenders, to aid, assist and adhere to persons exercising the powers of government in France in case they should invade Ireland'.[14]

Yet the crude nature of many of the Defenders' proceedings make it clear that in so far as it was a national conspiracy it was a very clumsy one and ill-organized. Such practical projects as came to light involving anything more than arming in preparation for a French landing seem to have been of the most primitive sort. In 1793 a society called the Philanthropic Society, which later merged with the Defenders, had a theoretical plan to take Dublin Castle, the seat of government, by sending in a hundred of its members disguised in the scarlet coats of soldiers, but nothing came of it.[15] When, early in 1794, Jackson finally came up for trial, the same society had a plan to kidnap Cockayne the British counter-spy, the night before the trial opened – but this plan too came to nothing.[16] The next year some Dublin Defenders had a plan to take the powder magazine in the Phoenix Park and seize Dublin Castle, and 'to put all the nobility to death there',[17] but again nothing happened. The carelessness endemic in many Defender proceedings is revealed by one ardent Defender who failed to prevent his wife being seen hiding sixty musket balls 'in a dirt hole' and who himself openly asked his lodging-house keeper if he could let him have a room where a society could meet.[18]

Some of the Defender oaths were of the wildest sort and often contained ominous portents for the future. Thus, as early as February 1795, a group of Defenders declared that they would have no king, would recover their estates, 'sweep clean the Protestants, kill the Lord Lieutenant and leave none alive'.[19] The gap which was later to prove so fatal between the semi-literate mass Defender movement and the more sophisticated world of the Belfast and Dublin radicals is here well illustrated by the fact that while Defenders were taking this oath the Lord Lieutenant was still Lord Fitzwilliam, the centre of sophisticated Catholic hopes. Indeed, the crude sectarian spirit of the Defenders, which though little more at first than a defensive mark of identity was the very opposite of the goal at which the United Irishmen were aiming, was on the increase. At least one Protestant Defender in 1795 who had been passing himself off as a Catholic among his colleagues turned informer on hearing that 'as soon as the harvest was in' the Defenders would rise against the Protestants and put them all to death.[20]

This sectarian element in the Defender system was heightened and developed by the continual feuding between Defenders and Peep o' Day Boys which was now more than ever a feature of the North. The tension in these areas, growing as it did from economic competition, had understandably been aggravated by the recent political progress of the Catholics. Catholic forty-shilling freeholders had been admitted to the vote in 1793. Now total Emancipation itself, raising Catholics to full equal status with Protestants, had become a burning issue of the day and at one time looked like becoming a reality at any moment. The Protestants felt themselves more than ever threatened.

The new outbreak of feuding in the North reached its climax in September 1795 at the so-called Battle of the Diamond, a piece of ground near the town of Armagh. A large party of Defenders attacked a party of Peep o' Day Boys there and got the worst of it, leaving twenty or thirty corpses on the field. The incident, which in itself constituted nothing new, is a historical landmark since it led the Peep o' Day Boys to reorganize under a name which was to play an increasingly significant role in the future of Ireland: the Orange Society – the colour orange having long been a popular symbol with which to celebrate the victory of William of Orange over James II a century before.

For the time being the Orangemen remained a crude organization, successors to the Peep o' Day Boys, turning Catholics out of their homes with great brutality that often ended in murder. An alternative was to affix to the doors of Catholics such threats as 'To Hell – or Connaught' or 'Go to Hell – Connaught won't receive you – fire and faggot. Will Thresham and John Thrustout.'[21] Those Catholics thus 'papered', as it was called, seeing the barbarous punishments inflicted on those who did not obey, usually took the hint and left for Connaught. At the end of 1795, at a famous meeting of northern magistrates, all but one of whom were Protestants, the Orangemen were described by Lord Gosford, Governor of Armagh, as 'a lawless banditti' carrying out a ferocious persecution of Roman Catholics simply because they professed that faith. Sending the unanimous resolutions of his magistrates, condemning the Orangemen, to the Chief Secretary, Gosford wrote: 'Of late no night passes that houses are not destroyed, and scarce a week that some dreadful murders are not committed. Nothing can exceed the animosity between Protestant and Catholic at this moment in this county...'[22]

But though the Defenders in other parts of Ireland were inflamed by news of these atrocities, the driving force behind their own organization still remained the poverty which so often went together with their religion, rather than their religion for its own sake. Catholicism was the mark of their identity. Their increasingly sectarian spirit denoted not proselytizing zeal but assertion of rights for that identity. They continued to be strongly condemned by the Catholic Church, and some of the worst Defender outrages were committed against Catholic magistrates. Where the Defenders were opposed by members of their own class and religion, as in the various county militias, they found themselves regarded not primarily as Catholics but as rebellious trash, and as such were fought and defeated.

In 1795 a Kildare schoolmaster called Laurence O'Connor was tried for administering a Defender oath 'to be loyal to all brother Defenders and the French'. The judge declared astonishingly before passing the inevitable death sentence that 'there was no country in Europe where a poor man had more advantages than in Ireland'. The prisoner was asked if he had anything to say. After listing the grievances of the poor, chief of which were the fantastically high rents, O'Connor concluded that 'prosecutions were not the means of bringing about peace in the country; but if the rich would alleviate the sufferings of the poor, they would hear no more of risings or Defenders, and the country would rest in peace and happiness'.[23]

The man's head, which was severed from his body 'with no great dexterity',[24] ended up on a seven-foot spike outside the gaol at Naas. His words were echoed a few months later by a very different sort of Irishman, Lord Edward Fitzgerald, who, speaking almost for the last time in the Irish House of Commons in February 1796, attacked the Insurrection Act which the government then introduced in an attempt to break the Defenders and tranquillize the country. Nothing, said Lord Edward, would in fact tranquillize the country but the sincere endeavour of the government to redress the grievances of the people. If that was done the people would return to their allegiance.[25]

This Insurrection Act, which was passed in March 1796, was the first of the severe measures by which the government now set about trying to counteract the danger which the Defenders presented. Though the severity of these government measures was to increase steadily over the next two years and finally reach a brutal crescendo which did much to provoke the very rebellion they were designed to prevent, it is important to understand the extreme gravity of the situation as the government now saw it. It was not just a question of establishing public order in conditions of growing anarchy. The kingdoms of Ireland and of Great Britain were at war with France, whose armies in Europe, particularly in the years 1795 and 1796, were sweeping all before them. The final logical step for France was the defeat of her one unbeaten enemy, Britain, by an invasion of England, either direct, or through Ireland.

England itself was at this time full of radical clubs, founded originally to promote a return of Parliament, but in many cases now imbued with French republican principles of an extreme sort. Many of them were arming themselves with pikes and drilling. In Sheffield alone in 1797 there were forty to fifty such small clubs; and in every important town in the north of England the picture was similar.[26] In London the Constitutional Society and the London Corresponding Society carried on near-treasonable activity, run by a secret committee of five persons. By 1797 there were more than seventy United Corresponding Societies in Great Britain. Yet the government knew that in England, in the event of French invasion, the probability was overwhelming that the majority of the British people, for all their grievances, would stand firmly and patriotically behind the government.

In Ireland the situation was very different. In the Defenders, a massive though ill-coordinated and unsophisticated conspiracy already existed, which for all its political incoherence linked a hazy pro-French republicanism to real everyday grievances, and was daily acquiring more supporters throughout the country. And this was the country open to French invasion from Atlantic ports much less easily supervised by the British Navy than those in the Channel. The government's chief force for dealing with the danger, apart from the normal processes of law, was the militia, which apart from a proportion of Protestant officers and other officers of the Catholic gentry consisted almost entirely of those very Catholic peasants and artisans who were filling the ranks of the Defenders. The Defenders were already making a bid to seduce the militia from their allegiance, and numbers were known to be taking the Defender oaths. The crime of O'Connor, the executed schoolmaster, had been that of administering a Defender oath to a private of the North Mayo militia.

The government's situation was in fact even worse than the Defender disturbances and their seduction of the militia made it seem. For the Defenders were not the only potential rebels they had to face. In the North, though not yet widely organized into any effective military conspiracy, a ready-made traditional body of radical middle-class Protestant opinion was profoundly disaffected. Disappointed for the last ten years or more in their efforts to give Parliament that broader base which would include themselves, these northern radicals had been strengthened in their natural republican instincts by the successful republican progress of the French. Here – and to a much smaller extent in the Protestant radical circles of Dublin – organized in the Society of United Irishmen was that sophisticated political approach noticeably lacking in the clumsy but much more powerful organization of the Defenders. If the two hitherto distinct forces were to come together no force of government would be able to stop them. And in August 1796 Camden, the Viceroy, wrote to the British Home Minister, Portland, that the recent endeavours of the Belfast Clubs to form a junction with the Defenders had 'been attended with much success'.[27]

We have the word of the members of the Directory of United Irishmen that they themselves had no military organization, 'until the latter end of 1796'.[28] Even then, for a time its only existence was in Ulster. But plans at least for eventual revolution had begun to be formed earlier in the year. Ever since the formation of the new secret United Irish Society its members had for obvious reasons wanted to make contact with the Defenders. In 1795 and early in 1796 the northern United Irishmen sent emissaries among the Defender leaders in Meath, Dublin and elsewhere to explain the advantages of a proper unified organization with coherent political aims. The Defenders also sent deputations to Belfast.

As a result of these meetings an agreement was reached by which the Defenders undertook to incorporate their societies within the 'Union' and to take the United Irish oath. From then on United Irish organizers appeared more and more among the Defenders, explaining the political advantages of their ideas. In particular, they spread alarm about the outrages of the Orangemen in the North and made inflammatory suggestions that it was the Orangemen's intention to deal similarly with Catholics throughout Ireland. The rumour was spread that the Orangemen had entered into a solemn league and covenant 'to wade up to their knees in Papist blood'. The United Irish leaders wrote later: 'To the Armagh persecution is the Union of Irishmen most exceedingly indebted.'[29] On a short-term view they were correct, though their exploitation of it had much to do with their failure in the end. Catholics did in fact begin to think that they had no alternative but to join 'the Union'. But by inciting Catholics to join a non-sectarian organization with threats of sectarianism from another quarter, the United Irish agents were playing with fire. Inevitably they turned the higher political principles of 'the Union' into something of secondary importance, and themselves encouraged a crude sectarian hate.

Evidence of these successful overtures to the Defenders by the United Irishmen caused the government great concern, particularly as the United Irishmen were simultaneously known to be strengthening their links with France.

6

Bantry Bay

The leaders of the United Irishmen always had some reservations about seeking aid from France. This was due partly to a natural pride which made them want to achieve independence by their own efforts, and partly to a practical fear that the French might dominate Ireland once they arrived. Wolfe Tone himself wrote that he would never be accessory to 'subjecting my country to the control of France merely to get rid of that of England. We are able enough to take care of ourselves, if we were once afloat, or if we are not, we deserve to sink.'[1]

The matter of pride was resolved by what, in the circumstances, may seem a curious reference to historical precedent : namely, the acceptance of foreign intervention from William of Orange over a century before. 'We were of the opinion,' wrote one of the United Irish leaders, 'that if the people were justified in calling for foreign aid to rescue the liberties and constitution from James's government it was infinitely more justifiable in us to call in foreign aid.'[2] The statement shows the deeply Protestant radical cast of mind of even the most sophisticated leaders of the United Irishmen.

The danger of domination implicit in acceptance of French aid was dealt with by asking the French only for a suitably limited number of troops in any expedition.

By 1796 it had been accepted by the United Irishmen that French help was required. This very acceptance did much to harden the separatist and republican strain in United Irish political thinking, for the only *quid pro quo* the Irish could offer the French for their support was a guarantee of the total separation of the two islands in the future.

The first local societies in Ulster had been agitating for some mission to the French since 1795. However, since Tone had then only just set sail for his exile in America, under a definite obligation to press the Irish cause on the French minister in Philadelphia, it was decided at first merely to send Tone a letter stressing the increased discontent in Ireland since he had left and the progress being made by the new organization of United Irishmen. Tone received this letter in America towards the end of November 1795 at a crucial psychological moment.

He had arrived there in August after a six weeks' voyage during which he narrowly escaped being press-ganged by three British naval frigates which stopped his ship off Newfoundland – a fairly routine procedure of the day. Most of the crew and fifty or so of Tone's fellow passengers were taken off and he himself had already been ordered into one of the boats when the screams of his wife and sister softened a British officer's heart.[3] On arrival in Philadelphia itself he met with what seemed to him only a lukewarm response from the French Minister there. In fact we know that the Minister wrote to his government warmly commending Tone and his project of French intervention in Ireland.[4] But, waiting in America, Tone grew despondent. Far from being the single-minded driving force of the United Irishmen, as he has sometimes been supposed, he was making preparations to settle down for good as a farmer on a 180-acre farm near Princeton when in November 1795 the letter from Belfast arrived, signed by his old friends Keogh and Russell. He changed his plans and on 1 January 1796 set sail from New York for France where he landed a month and a day later at Le Havre. He carried letters of introduction from the French Minister in Philadelphia, but came, as he admitted a few months afterwards, more to discharge a duty than with much expectation of success.[5]

Tone's day-to-day record of his next few months in France is of the greatest interest not only for its vivid picture of life in Paris in the hey-day of the Directory, but also because of his most realistic and convincingly unheroic account of the way in which the French came to mount their great expedition to Ireland of 1796. Tone, acting with something of the quiet forcefulness of a good journalist trying to see those people who matter, eventually penetrated to the top of the French government hierarchy. He clearly impressed those he met there. But he was long kept in the dark as to whether or not the expedition he urged so strongly both verbally and in written memoranda was really being seriously considered. The French Directory had many other preoccupations besides an expedition to Ireland and Tone often became depressed and felt he was getting nowhere. As late as 2 May 1796 he wrote: '... I am utterly ignorant whether there is any design to attempt the expedition or not; I put it twice to Carnot (the Minister for War) and could extract no answer. My belief is, that as yet, there is no one step taken in the business, and that, in fact, the expedition will not be undertaken ...'[6]

Tone began to think again of retiring to the backwoods of America. Carnot had told him to work through a young General named Clarke, the son of an Irish Catholic *émigré*, whose ideas about Ireland seemed far astray. Clarke even asked Tone if Fitzgibbon, the Lord Chancellor, might not prove useful to them. 'Anyone who knows Ireland,' commented Tone, 'will readily believe that I did not find it easy to make a serious answer to this question.'[7] Clarke earned further scorn from Tone later when, apparently thinking that Ireland was still devoted to the House of Stuart, he suggested that a new Pretender might be found.*[8] Tone even began to suspect Clarke of being a traitor, for he worked out that he was remotely related by marriage to Fitzgibbon himself.

But in fact the French were taking the idea of an expedition to Ireland quite seriously and Clarke was a faithful enough bureaucrat in the service of Carnot.[9] Tone had impressed the French with his sincerity and ability but, as Clarke explained to an agent whom he decided to send to Ireland for further information, it was several months since Tone had left Ireland and things might have changed considerably in that time. Moreover, he said, Tone urged the Irish cause so earnestly that the French could not help feeling he might be heightening the picture a little, though without any conscious intention to deceive.[10]

During the summer of 1796 the French began seriously to plan an expedition to Ireland to be led by the brilliant young General Hoche, then second in repute only to Bonaparte. In July, Tone, sitting in his hotel studying a French cavalry manual (for he was about to be given the rank of colonel in the French Army), received a summons to Carnot's War Ministry in the Luxemburg Palace. He waited in an office there for two hours when the door opened, and a handsome young man in a brown coat and yellow pantaloons entered and said:

'*Vous êtes le citoyen Smith?*' ('Smith' was the *nom de guerre* under which Tone had been living since his arrival in France in an ineffectual attempt to avoid the attention of Pitt's spies.)

The young man had a sabre cut right down his forehead, eyebrow and one side of his nose, which did not, however, disfigure him. Tone thought he was an official of the War Ministry.

'*Oui, citoyen, je m'appelle Smith.*'

'*Vous vous appelez, aussi, je crois, Wolfe Tone?*'

'*Oui, citoyen, c'est mon véritable nom.*'

'*Eh bien,*' replied the stranger. '*Je suis le Général Hoche.*'[11]

That evening Tone dined with Hoche, Carnot, Clarke and others. ('Very well served without being luxurious.' Two courses, dessert and coffee.) During dinner it was made unmistakably clear that preparations for a strong expedition to Ireland were under way. It was to consist of ten to fifteen thousand men with great quantities of arms, ammunition and stores.

Yet the French continued to keep Tone in the dark about some of their contacts with Ireland. Less than a fortnight later, by which time Tone had received his commission as a colonel in the French Army, he was discussing future arrangements with Hoche, when the conversation took a strange turn.

* Clarke was an exception among *émigrés* descended from the Wild Geese in not emigrating from France after the Revolution. Most of the old Irish Brigade, aristocratic and monarchical by temperament, did so. There was actually a project for merging the Brigade with the British Army. Some Irish Brigade French officers even went on a recruiting visit to Ireland for this very purpose but met with a poor response.

Hoche suddenly asked him if he knew a man called Arthur O'Connor, and a little later what he thought of Lord Edward Fitzgerald.

O'Connor was the thirty-six-year-old youngest son of a rich Protestant land-owner in County Cork.[12] He had sat in the Irish House of Commons since 1790 and had at first shown no radical tendencies whatever. He had actually spoken against a bill intended to reduce the number of government pensioners in 1791 – a year in which he was High Sheriff of Cork – and had been quite silent when the Catholic Relief Bills came before the House in 1792 and 1793. But he had visited France just before war broke out, had been deeply impressed by the Revolution, and had come back an ardent republican. He acted out his conversion in the Irish House of Commons, where in 1795 he spoke out vigorously in favour of Grattan's bill for total Catholic Emancipation.

O'Connor had good contacts with the Whig opposition in England, though he concealed from them the extreme, treasonable position he soon reached. He was also a close friend of that other wealthy convert to republican radicalism in Ireland, Lord Edward Fitzgerald, from whom there was by this time no need to conceal anything. For both O'Connor and Fitzgerald, if not themselves already technically members of the United Irishmen, were by now in close contact with them and assuming among them positions of leadership. O'Connor also seems to have been in the inner councils of the Defenders in the south, and certainly before the year was out his brother Roger was one of the chief nominal organizers of that society.[13]

To Hoche's question, which Tone assumed to have been put on the strength of O'Connor's speech in the Irish House of Commons of 1795, Tone replied that he did know O'Connor, thought highly of his talents, principles and patriotism, and hoped that he would undoubtedly join them. He made a mental note if he ever met O'Connor to tell him that he seemed to be well thought of in France. But really Hoche had made rather a fool of Tone, being in close personal contact with O'Connor at the time.

Two months earlier, while Tone still imagined himself to be struggling alone in an attempt to get the French to mount an expedition to Ireland, Lord Edward Fitzgerald had gone to Hamburg and opened his own line of approach to the French. He had soon afterwards gone back to Ireland and returned to the Continent a month later, in June 1796, with Arthur O'Connor. He and O'Connor then started detailed negotiations with the French Directory.

O'Connor, who took the lead, presented a rosy picture of the state of revolutionary affairs in Ireland. He emphasized the extent to which secret societies had now sworn Irishmen both North and South into a conspiracy for a separate republic and that the country was ripe for insurrection. The militia, he said, would go with the people. Cork, Waterford and even Dublin could easily be captured. And a successful insurrection in Ireland would knock England out of the war. All that was needed was guns, artillery, officers and a few troops. 'We only want your help in the first moment,' O'Connor continued. 'In two months we should have 100,000 men under arms; we ask your assistance only because we know it is your own clear interest to give it, and only on condition that you leave us absolute masters to frame our government as we please.'[14]

But when the French, taking him at his word, suggested that perhaps the rising could then take place before the landing, O'Connor emphasized the severity of the measures the government were taking to disarm the people under the Insurrection Act and entered a certain caution about the militia. Although, he said, the great majority of them were certainly in favour of revolution they were scattered about the country, they had had no munitions and their officers were anti-revolutionary. The Irish leaders, he insisted, were resolved that the arrival of French aid must be the signal for the rising.[15]

In September 1796, when the French plans were progressing and Tone had joined Hoche at his headquarters at Rennes, convenient for the port of Brest, Hoche one day in conversation with Tone referred obscurely to 'somebody here who wished to see me, but I did not press him for an explanation and he did not offer it'.[16] In fact this person was none other than Arthur O'Connor who had actually been in conference with Hoche close by. But for some reason best known to the French, Tone was left in ignorance of what he called his 'invisible cooperators' right up to the time he sailed. He took his exclusion from the full secret amiably enough, remarking to himself that at least it divided the responsibility and didn't leave the whole thing 'resting on my single assertion'.[17]

In view of this September check-up between the French and the actual revolutionary leadership in Ireland it is strange that final coordination between them turned out so imperfect. For when Hoche's expedition finally sailed for Ireland on 16 December, neither O'Connor nor Fitzgerald seem to have known.[18]

Bad luck was to play a very large part in the events that followed, but the misunderstanding and lack of closer cooperation between the two sides was remarkable. The French had definitely told the United Irish societies of Belfast to expect an expedition shortly.[19] But then there had arrived another message saying that the expedition had been postponed.[20] The efficient channels of communication so necessary between the two major parties in such a hazardous enterprise were clearly inadequate. Equally dangerous was the fact that Fitzgerald and O'Connor had conveyed a false picture of the revolutionary organization in Ireland. It was nothing like so well coordinated or under their control as they had represented.

In the first place, incorporation of the vast and fragmented Defender organization within the United Irish system was often more nominal than real. Second, even among the United Irish societies of the North themselves there was a good deal of independence and autonomy. It was during this winter that the final Executive Directory of the United Irishmen took shape, consisting of O'Connor, Fitzgerald, Thomas Emmet, the barrister, Dr William MacNeven, a doctor of medicine, and Oliver Bond, a wealthy wool merchant. But the degree of authority the Directory held over the subordinate societies is problematical. Signs of insubordination from local committees in Ulster itself were not infrequent.

At the secret meeting of the Down County Committee on 13 October 1796, for instance, the 'Reporter' from the Ulster provincial committee told the members that foreign aid was expected immediately and that the United Irishmen were to hold themselves in readiness. Whereupon 'a person at the meeting desired to know what they should rise with?'

The Reporter answered:

'With pikes and guns and with any other weapons they could in any way get,' reassuring them further that 'the United Business was going well in England and Scotland.'[21]

In December 1796 a lower committee poured cold water on much of the big talk that was going on, complaining indignantly of a County Committee report which, it said, was 'unworthy of men who are fit to represent a county and an insult to our understandings'. They were being rushed into things, they continued. It was impossible to hide registered arms as they were ordered to '... We are called upon to learn to march well, as if a knowledge of military tactics could be acquired in a closet or by night.' And, warning against any rash attempt at rebellion, they added: '... although we are well aware that oppression greatly abounds and abuses exist, yet it is evident that a few counties in Ulster would be unable by force of arms to accomplish an object of such magnitude until our principles are more generally known and understood.'[22]

The truth was that for all Tone's fine words to the French Government about an Ireland ripe for liberation, and all the more up-to-date enthusiastic confirmation provided by O'Connor and Fitzgerald, no sort of properly coordinated rebellious system, let alone a revolutionary system, covered the whole of Ireland.

If, however, the United Irish conspiracy, for all its vast potential, was an amateurish affair at this stage – and indeed largely remained so to the end – the other participants in the situation, the French and British governments, were professionals.

The British government had at its disposal a militia of eighteen thousand men (though as a largely Catholic body its loyalty was open to doubt); about fifteen thousand regular troops most of them also Catholic Irish troops but well-trained and disciplined; and finally, a new force of yeomanry raised late in 1796 officered by local gentry and predominantly Protestant, though where the units were Catholic they outdid the Protestants in keenness and loyalty. On the legal side the government had the benefit of the Insurrection Act which greatly assisted the military's natural impatience in its search for arms, and in November 1796 a further impediment to over-nice procedure was removed by the suspension of Habeas Corpus.

The French, too, were poised for action. Tone, who now held the rank of a General in the French Army, had spent the last weeks before setting sail from Brest in a state of some anxiety, first for his family who were somewhere on the high seas on their month-long journey between America and France, and secondly for his friends Neilson and Russell who he learned had been arrested and imprisoned in Ireland. His mind, he wrote, was 'sixty times more troubled than the ocean on which I am going'.[23] To add to his troubles Hoche disappeared from Brest altogether for two days to pursue an affair with a local girl.[24] However, by 16 December everyone was ready. Hoche issued an order of the day:

Jaloux de rendre à la liberté un peuple digne d'elle, et mûr pour une révolution, le Directoire nous envoie en Irlande, a l'effet d'y faciliter la révolution que d'excellents Républicains viennent d'y entreprendre ...

A sharp injunction followed to avoid rape and pillage and to treat the Irish as allies rather than enemies. The weather, wrote Tone, was delicious, the sun as warm and bright as May. All were in high spirits, and the French troops – about fourteen thousand of them altogether – 'as gay as if they were going to a ball'.[25] The fleet of forty-three sail must indeed have presented, as Hoche's biographer maintained, 'a most majestic spectacle'. '*Aussi fière que la flotte romaine,*' he expanded, '*qui, commandé par Scipion, portait la ruine de Carthage, l'escadre est rassemblée, les voiles deployées – il part.*'[26]

It was in trouble at once.

On the passage out of Brest during the night one of the French ships struck a rock and all but thirty-seven of the 550 troops aboard were drowned. The next day a violent storm partially dispersed the fleet and drove another ship of the line ashore with the loss of a thousand men. The flagship, the *Fraternité*, with the Admiral and Hoche himself aboard, parted company with the main body, and, after a series of appalling adventures in the course of which it once found itself undetected in the middle of the English fleet, finally succeeded in returning to France three weeks later. Meanwhile fog, succeeding the storm, brought further confusion to the rest of the fleet. By 21 December, however, all but eight or nine had reassembled off the southwest coast of Ireland and were making their way into Bantry Bay, a magnificent piece of water, twenty-six miles long, seven miles broad and with a draught of forty fathoms in the middle. A head wind was blowing strongly against them and their progress was extremely slow. They cast anchor off Bear Island, half-way up the Bay, some time after six on the evening of 21 December 1796.

A heavy gale blew throughout the night so that when Tone woke next morning he found the mountains on the northern shore covered with snow. He also found that twenty of the thirty-four ships which had arrived had been blown out to sea again. Though there had been absolutely no sign that the enemy was yet aware of their existence, spirits on board the French fleet, which was now reduced to less than half its strength, were low. Tone himself, now so close to his native land that he felt he could have thrown a biscuit on to the shore, was still uncertain whether in this gale he would ever set foot on it again. He was surprised to find that he felt no emotion at all. 'I expected I should have been, at returning in these circumstances after an absence of more than a year, violently affected,' he wrote. 'Yet I look to it as if it were the coast of Japan.'27 He added that if they did not take some action soon the enemy would have collected a superior force and they would be in serious trouble.

It was in fact only on the evening of the previous day that a messenger, riding desperately hard over the snow-covered roads between Bantry and Cork, and covering over forty miles on a single horse in four hours, had managed to bring to the government news of the appalling danger that now threatened. That the French were in strength was clear, although their precise numbers were unknown and it could not even be said for certain whether this was the main force or only a diversion. The only troops able to oppose them at once were some four hundred men of the Galway militia stationed at Bantry, together with the local yeomanry, who were mobilized by the principal local land-owner, a Mr Richard White, later rewarded with the title of Lord Bantry for his part in these events. Only about three thousand men stood between Bantry and Cork altogether, and the British General Dalrymple wrote to Pelham, the Chief Secretary for Ireland, that he could not possibly concentrate more than eight thousand before the French reached Cork. Even then he could not hope for anything better than a holding action while he fell back on main positions on the River Blackwater near Kilworth and Fermoy.

If the French had indeed arrived in Bantry Bay with the fourteen thousand troops with which they had set out, the future history of Ireland might have been very different. But the French had arrived not only with less than half their troops, but without their commander. The continuing gale prevented them both from landing where they were and also from making any further progress to more sheltered waters up the Bay. Grouchy, the military second-in-command of the expedition, was determined to try and land at almost all costs, but when on Christmas Day the storm grew even worse and the French ships were making almost no progress towards Bantry (about fifty yards in eight hours, Tone says) the naval second-in-command, Admiral Bouvet, decided he could no longer be responsible for his ships under such conditions and gave orders to cut cables and make for the open sea before the gale.

His signals were either not received or else not properly understood, so that the other ships which remained at anchor during the night found on the following day that they were now without even secondary commanders on land or sea, for both Bouvet and Grouchy had been aboard the same frigate and, mistakenly imagining themselves to have been followed by the rest of the fleet, were already far out to sea on their way back to Brest. For those ships still in the Bay which just managed to hold their anchors the weather worsened. Visibility came down to barely more than a ship's length, which added to the confusion. Finally, one by one the great ships found it impossible to hold on any longer and, cutting their cables, ran down the Bay and out to sea again. Tone's ship, the *Indomptable*, weighed anchor on the 28th, or rather, having had considerable difficulty in pulling up one anchor, cut the other and put to sea followed by about eight or nine others. Tone noted that he didn't wonder at all at Xerxes whipping the sea; he felt like doing the same. Even this small squadron was now dispersed and after failing to rendezvous as agreed at the mouth of the Shannon, where they had hoped to make some last-minute desperate attempt on that part of Ireland, they returned one by one to France which Tone himself reached again on the first day of 1797.

Some ships remained in the Bay a few days longer and as late as 31 December there was even an alarm on shore when some boats were seen to put off from a French ship with the intention, it was supposed, of landing. The Galway militia drew themselves up in their full strength on the beach, thus hoping to deceive the French into thinking there were greater numbers in reserve behind them. But it was a false alarm. The French were merely boarding an American ship in the Bay and soon afterwards returned to their own ship. Three days later they had all left Bantry Bay for good. The only Frenchmen who had actually set foot on Irish soil were an officer who landed from an open boat on Bear Island and was taken prisoner, some patrols which had reconnoitred Whiddy Island off Bantry itself and others who had collected some sheep off an island in the Shannon. Tone noted reasonably in his diary that England had not had such an escape since the days of the Spanish Armada.

Yet perhaps the most significant feature of the incident lay after all in the behaviour not of the elements, but of man. For in the ten days that the French had lain in the Bay, molested only by the weather, the Catholic peasantry of the district, far from rising in disaffected multitudes to greet their liberators, had displayed a remarkable lack of enthusiasm for them. Although the French patrols which landed on Whiddy Island met with a civil enough reception, being informed, as was no more than the truth, that they had been expected for some months,[28] all government reports agreed that the loyal spirit of the peasantry in general was exemplary. 'Their good will, zeal and activity exceeds all description,' wrote General Dalrymple to the King.[29] In

Limerick the peasants were boiling their potatoes for the soldiers.[30] And a correspondent from Mayo wrote revealingly that the local inhabitants had associated the French with the Protestants of the North, who, they understood, had invited the French over. Since their chief memory of the Protestants of the North was of Orangemen and Peep o' Day Boys, they had consequently transferred part of their hatred to the enemy 'who, they are persuaded, are coming with their northern allies to drive them from their habitations and properties'.[31] No comment could reveal more plainly the deep confusion of Irish radical emotions at that time.

In the North the United Irishmen showed no particular disappointment over the failure of the French at Bantry. This was hardly surprising since they had had so very little precise information about their arrival from the start. The net result was on the whole probably encouraging for the Bantry expedition at least proved beyond doubt that the French were in earnest. Activity in the North intensified ahead of the next French attempt. And before long a vast new invasion fleet for Ireland was indeed being assembled at Texel by France's new ally, the Dutch Republic, with Tone once more in attendance.

Though the rebellious preparations in the North still remained largely a matter of individual local societies drilling and organizing – a central military committee for the whole of Ireland did not come into existence until 1798 – yet these local preparations were now being conducted on such a scale as to cause the government the greatest concern. Nightly drillings, the cutting down of trees to make pike handles, raids on gentlemen's houses for arms, the seduction of the militia by the United Irish oath – all this was now commonplace and continuous in Ulster in the early months of 1797.

After the fright the government had received at Bantry and with another French invasion in the offing it was inevitable that they should resort to the harshest policies. Backed by the Insurrection Act, and equipped with specific instructions to disarm the North, the British commander, General Lake, set about his task with vigour, and by March 1797 most of Ulster was virtually under martial law. But something more than normal military firmness was required to deal effectively with the situation. Political concessions – which meant some measure of parliamentary reform – would, according to one of the United Irish leaders, still have prevented rebellion as late as the middle of 1797.[32] However, parliamentary reform did not enter into the government's calculations and certainly was of no concern to the military. As the population of the North grew more and more skilful at concealing their arms, only the sternest methods of repression seemed to offer any chance of success. A vicious spiral of terror soon began which led within a year to the worst display of savagery Britain had witnessed since the wars of Cromwell.

7

United Irishmen in Trouble

For all General Lake's zeal in Ulster during the early spring of 1797, the situation there continued to worsen. Virtually all 'the lower order of the people', as Lake himself told the government in March, and most of the middle classes were by now determined Republicans, imbued with French principles and set on revolution.[1] And in case the government should think that this was just the sort of sweeping militarist conclusion any general in charge might be expected to form, he emphasized that he had been talking to a lot of men who were still keen on parliamentary reform but were now scared out of their wits because the tenants and labourers they had first introduced to the idea had now got completely out of control. Magistrates from many different localities confirmed the situation. One wrote from Newry in the same month that nearly the whole population round about had been sworn into the United Irishmen and that every tree in his neighbourhood had been cut down for the making of pike handles.[2] 'The game is nearly up in Ulster,' he concluded. The French were expected again by I May.

In County Monaghan, on the pretext of planting potatoes, gangs of several hundred men roamed the countryside, carrying the white flags which were the characteristic emblem of the Defender corps among the United Irishmen and singing republican songs.[3] Part of the country near Omagh in County Tyrone was wholly in the hands of the United Irishmen. A hundred men, well-armed and officered, openly paraded the streets of Dromore. 'The insurgents', as the local clergyman already called them, were going about in great gangs, swearing, plundering, burning, maiming. 'Yesternight', he wrote, 'the hills between this and Clogher exhibited a striking scene. The summits topped with bonfires – bugle horns sounding and guns occasionally firing, no doubt as signals to the marauding parties who were employed seeking for weapons in the neighbourhood.... The populace are now so powerful and desperate, that for any individual to attempt resistance would be both imprudent and romantic ...'[4]

At Ballyclare in County Antrim a large leaden statue of Neptune which had stood in a mill-dam for over a hundred years was spirited away by the United Irishmen during the night to be recast into bullets.[5] Engagements with the troops were soon taking place; fourteen United Irishmen were killed and ten taken prisoner in a skirmish near Dundalk in May.

The United Irish leaders, who were high-minded, educated men, later protested strongly that they had never countenanced the use of murder or terror to enforce support. It is reasonable to believe them. But the nature of their control over the multitude of lower committees, with their cruel peasant tradition derived from the agrarian secret societies, was so tenuous that the leaders clearly often had very little idea of what was going on at the popular level. The many magistrates' accounts of murder and terror must certainly also be believed. 'You can have no idea', wrote a magistrate from Donegal, 'of the terror that pervades the whole country.'[6] Another correspondent from Antrim wrote: '. . . they are all uniting and threatening anyone who will not join them; the Murphys are in a dreadful situation, dare not stir out at night, particularly Sam.'[7]

Counter-terror seemed the only answer. It did not immediately become official policy, but brutality and excesses by troops not much interested in distinguishing between the guilty and the innocent became increasingly frequent, and the search for arms was conducted with ever increasing ruthlessness. It was this ruthlessness which, one way and another, was to determine the whole future course of events.

It is easy enough to read into what now took place the interpretation placed on events by later nationalists, and to see the undoubtedly brutal troops who acted against the ill-organized peasantry and others as 'British' troops putting down 'the Irish'. But the terms are very misleading, for the troops though British were also mainly Irish and of Catholic labouring stock. In the rebellion that was about to break out, the fighting was between groups of Irish subjects wishing desperately to overthrow or at least protest against the established form of government by which they did so badly, and other Irish subjects remaining loyal to that establishment. A small caucus of intellectuals and political aspirants gave the rebels an ambitious separatist political theory, which the masses apprehended only dimly and with little coherence.

The burning of cabins by troops in Ulster in the course of their searches for arms rapidly became normal practice, both as a punishment and a warning to others. The wounding and killing of the cabins' inhabitants also soon became an inevitable part of the process and, in this too, the difficult business of distinguishing between guilty and innocent went increasingly by default. A captain of the Dublin militia carrying out searches for arms in the County of Down in June 1797 found a sort of competition in brutality going on between a notorious Welsh yeomanry regiment known as the Ancient Britons and the local yeomen of the district. He described how he made his way to the scene of one disturbance by the smoke and flames of burning houses and by the dead bodies of boys and old men killed by the Ancient Britons, though there had been no opposition at all. The only shooting had come from the yeomanry themselves though '. . . I declare there was nothing to fire at, old men, women and children excepted'.[8]

General Lake, like all high military commanders in such situations, stood by his men as charges of brutality and outrage piled up against them. 'Considering their powers and provocations,' he said, they had acted well and he had tried on all occasions 'to prevent as much as possible any act of violence on the part of the troops.'[9] But a more humane British general in Ireland, Sir John Moore, referring to what happened in the North of Ireland in 1797 wrote that 'undoubtedly enormities had been committed entirely disgraceful to the military as well as prejudicial to their discipline'.[10] In March of the following year a newly appointed Commander-in-Chief, Sir Ralph Abercromby, resigned soon after his appointment because the government would not support him in his efforts to improve the army's conduct. In a private letter to relatives he wrote of the 'violence and oppression' which had been employed in Ireland for more than twelve months, adding that within that time 'every crime, every cruelty that could be committed by Cossacks or Calmucks has been transacted here'.[11] Before he resigned he explained to his subordinate Sir John Moore the attitude of the government which, he said, wanted the Commander-in-Chief and the army to take the responsibility of acting 'with a violence which they did not choose to define, and for which they would give no public authority'.[12] With the one slightly embarrassing hitch of Abercromby's own resignation, this formula in fact worked well enough from the government's point of view over the whole period in question.

In March and in May 1797 the government made successive proclamations in Ulster, demanding the surrender of all arms within a certain period, coupled with offers of pardon and 'protection' if these were complied with. In the first proclamation General Lake had exhorted the people 'instantly' to 'rescue themselves from the severity of military authority'.[13] Arms, he added, would be paid for. In the orders given to him he was allowed, rather naïvely, 'the greatest latitude, relying at the same time on your prudence and discernment in the exercise of it, so that the peaceable and well-affected may be protected . . .'.[14] The combination of toughness with pardon was soon working so successfully and so many former United Irishmen began to come in to surrender their arms and take the oath of allegiance that the time limit on the second proclamation was extended. How much sincerity was involved in such oaths of allegiance is obviously questionable. A government informer, who was the United Irishmen's chief legal adviser in the North, afterwards declared that many people took the oath after the first proclamation as a mere cloak of protection for themselves, and that most of them on that occasion did not deliver up their arms.[15] As late as June a loyalist making the journey between Belfast and Dublin said he found almost everyone he met among the people on his journey an open well-wisher to the

United Irishmen's cause and expecting an early rising *en masse* with French support.[16] But the back of the movement in the North was slowly being broken. Neilson's radical newspaper, the *Northern Star*, which had achieved very wide popularity, was suppressed. And even though many arms were being held back the surrender of them under the military counter-terror was soon on a very considerable scale. By August 1797 the government had been successful enough in Ulster to be able to restore civil law there.

An important force in achieving this success, but one which also considerably aggravated the savagery, had been the participation on the government side of the Orangemen, the former Peep o' Day Boys, either in independent groups or incorporated in units of yeomanry. The Orangemen needed to be handled by the government with great delicacy and care. In 1795 authorities had not hesitated to describe them as the 'lawless banditti' they undoubtedly then were.[17] As late as mid 1796 the government had been criticizing the 'supine' and 'partial' conduct of magistrates in Armagh who favoured the Orangemen as opposed to the Defenders in the continuous disorderly feuding between the two. But threatened now by foreign invasion and a secret society whose avowed aim was to unite all Catholics and Protestants in support of the invader, the government would have been unrealistic not to make use of this other secret society whose principle was to keep Catholics and Protestants at enmity. A magistrate writing to the government in May 1797 summed it up: 'The enemies of our Establishment have reduced us to the necessity of making "divide" a justifiable measure.'[18] Already, in the course of 1796, an officially more respectable, propertied element, including some of the previously partial magistrates, had taken over the machinery of the Orange Society, disavowing its vicious sectarian trend and converting this, so they claimed, into no more than an emotionally charged loyalty to the establishment.

That the Orangemen were still emotionally charged is beyond doubt. It was the Orangemen in the yeomanry who in 1797 were responsible for the worst excesses of that year in Ulster, and the terror they spread throughout the countryside was duly amplified by the United Irishmen to rally the masses throughout Ireland in a Union, if not of political principle, as had originally been intended, at least of self-defence.

The wearing of some piece of green clothing had become a symbol of identification with the United Irish cause, and it was taken to be such whether so intended or not. One lady's maid in a loyalist party travelling from the North to Dublin, inadvertently wearing a green ribbon in her bonnet, was so pursued by waiters at the inns crying 'Success to your colours, ma'am!' that her employer made her remove it in a great hurry.[19] The Orangemen invariably made the wearing of green a cause for provocation and reprisals, and there were many incidents recorded of women having green articles of clothing torn from them and being humiliated for the effrontery of displaying them. The Frenchman De Latocnaye touring Armagh in 1797 met a party of Orangemen on the road with Orange cockades in their hats, and shortly afterwards went into some of the peasants' cabins which he had visited on an earlier tour. He found the inhabitants cowed and frightened and not nearly so pleased to see, him as they had been before. Eventually an old woman said to him: 'You are come, sir, perhaps from some distant place – perhaps your umbrella on account of the string of it may bring you into trouble.' Realizing that the string of his umbrella was indeed a greenish colour, he laughed at first but on second thoughts, remembering the Orangemen on the road, cut it off.[20]

One loyalist eye-witness of the Orangemen's activity about this time wrote to the government: 'Were I to enumerate the robberies, murders and shameful outrages committed on the Catholics of this place, by those Orange Boys, headed by officers in full yeomanry uniforms, it would be an endless business . . .'[21] A slightly less squeamish government supporter who conceded that the excursions of the yeomanry, when headed by their officers, had at first had a happy effect 'in bringing in arms and returning the country to its allegiance', nevertheless deplored that, without officers, they should be 'permitted at their pleasure day after day, and what is worse, night after night, to scour whole tracts of country, destroy houses, furniture, etc., and stab and cut in a most cruel manner numbers that, from either private resentment or any other cause, they may take a dislike to . . .'.[22]

The hitherto local feud between Peep o' Day Boys and Defenders was turning to something on a national scale. Catholics fled from Ulster into other parts of Ireland where the Defender societies were widely organized, carrying tales of the terror with them. The ground was being prepared for the crude and desperate rebellion that was to take place in the South in the following year.

So successful, however, were the various measures in Ulster in 1797 and so soon did it become apparent that the whole movement there was in danger of disintegration, that the Ulster Directory of the United Irishmen even put forward a desperate project to start the rebellion without waiting for French help any longer. But the proposal was over-ridden by the recently formed Leinster Directory in Dublin, dominated by an Executive consisting of Arthur O'Connor, Lord Edward Fitzgerald, Thomas Emmet, Oliver Bond and W. J. MacNeven – the latter incidentally being the only Catholic in the group.

The decision not to act at this moment brought accusations of cowardice against the Leinster Directory, but dependence on French help had long been regarded as an indispensable part of United Irish plans. MacNeven even paid a secret visit to France in June 1797 to make sure it was coming. It was coming all right, but not yet, and it was this further failure of the French to arrive this year that proved virtually the last straw for the Protestant

Republican movement in Ulster. It was already strained almost to breaking point by the vigorous severity of the government's measures. Now, with the chances of French help and ultimate successes receding fast, the offers of pardon became more and more attractive. And the heart began to go out of the Republican movement in the North.

In any case, the old rivalry between Protestant and Catholic, continually kept alive by the spilling of fresh blood, proved far more durable than any new theoretical alliance. As early as May 1797 it had been noted by the government that the Protestants of Armagh, who had for some time been deluded by the United Irishmen, were renouncing the societies and returning to their loyalty.[23] The wishful thinking about reconciliation between Presbyterians and Catholics which Tone and others had indulged in so easily in spite of so much deep-seated evidence to the contrary, was now revealed for what it was. Under the first serious strains, the divisions which the United Irishmen had partially papered over re-appeared.

In 1798 a clergyman wrote to the old Earl of Charlemont, who had been proud President of the Volunteers in the great days of the late seventies and early eighties, and confirmed what had been taking place:

Your old Ballymascanlan (Co. Louth) Volunteers [he said] who six months ago were all United Irishmen, are now complete Orangemen, which is more congenial with their feelings.... In speaking of the astonishing increase of Orangemen, I forgot to mention the most wonderful part of it, that immense numbers of them are in Belfast.

When rebellion did break out in Ireland in this May of 1798 the contribution of the North – the centre of the conspiracy the year before – was to be negligible.

8

New French Preparations

The failure of the French to arrive in 1797 had a profoundly depressing effect on the North. But the French, as in the year before, had been serious enough in their intentions. As at Bantry they were once again thwarted by the elements. This time the first stage of their expedition had been mounted on behalf of France by her new ally, the Dutch Republic. 'They venture no less than the whole of their army and navy,' wrote Tone, who by July 1797 was assisting with the preparations at the North Sea port, the Texel.[1] He was much impressed by the scale of the preparations and the condition of the Dutch fleet, which he considered superior to that of the French the year before. But even as late as this he had reservations about accepting any help at all from the French and their allies. In a conversation with Hoche on 1 July he had raised the whole question of the amount of control the French might want to claim for themselves in Ireland, saying that he feared it would be greater than the Irish might want to allow them.[2] Tone cited Bonaparte's proclamation to the Government of Genoa published in that day's *Gazette*, which he thought 'most grossly improper and indecent as touching on the indispensable rights of the people'. He added that in Italy such dictation might pass, but never in Ireland where they understood their rights too well to submit to such treatment.

'I understand you,' said Hoche. 'But you may be at ease in that respect; Bonaparte has been my scholar, but he shall never be my master.'

Tone was not wholly reassured for he rightly discounted some of this as jealousy of Bonaparte.

Perhaps it was reservations and hypothetical fears, together with natural personal anxieties about his own fate and that of his family, which produced in Tone the same curious apathy he had noted in himself the year before when anchored in Bantry Bay. He even used the same image to describe it. For, with fifteen sail of the line, ten frigates and sloops, and twenty-seven transports all ready and waiting for a fair wind for Ireland he wrote: 'For our expedition I think no more of it than if it were destined for Japan.'[3]

It was not in fact destined for anywhere at all. Once more and at an even more critical moment than the year before the elements came to England's rescue. This time the wind blew not too hard but in the wrong direction.

For weeks, while the British fleet had been largely paralysed by mutinies at the Nore and at Spithead, the Dutch had not been ready. Now at last the great fleet lay ready at the Texel but no wind blew which would enable it to put to sea. 'Eighteen days aboard and we have not had eighteen minutes of fair wind,' wrote Tone, in whom desperate impatience alternated with apathy and despair. 'Hell! Hell! Hell! Allah! Allah! Allah!'[4]

On 30 July 1797 the wind seemed set fair at last, and the ships were just about to get under way when it suddenly changed again and left them. A few days later messages arrived from Ireland bringing news of the loss of confidence in Ulster and the despair that was setting in with the continuing success of Lake's disarming measures and the continuing failure of the French to arrive. A month later, Tone's hopes and those of all revolutionaries in Ireland received a severe blow. Hoche, the one man in France who was as enthusiastic about the expedition to Ireland as the Irish themselves, died suddenly of consumption. The blow was capped by an even greater one in October when the Dutch fleet ventured out of Texel roads for the first time, and was totally defeated by the British in a bloody battle off Camperdown.

In December Tone had his first meeting with Bonaparte whom he found 'perfectly civil' though not very well informed about Ireland whose population he believed to be only two millions, less than half its actual figure.[5] It was extremely difficult to assess what the great man's attitude to Ireland was going to be and how important he would consider it, although early in January 1798 Tone took some encouragement from the fact that Bonaparte told him personally that he was assigned with the rank of Adjutant General to the Army of England.[6]

Another French expedition was indeed collected for Ireland in 1798. It was to be the only one of the three mounted in three successive years actually to land there.

Paradoxically it was not until after the real strength of the United Irishmen had begun to disintegrate in the North that they began to organize themselves on something like a national scale. Only right at the end of 1797 were delegates secretly elected to a National Directory for the first time. The head of the society became in fact more and more active as its control over its limbs became less and less coordinated.

But the cause of the political revolutionaries appears much more desperate in retrospect at this point than it must have seemed to the conspirators themselves at the time. In the first place, although the French expeditions had failed to materialize, news arrived in February 1798 that the third was being prepared.[7] France was now unquestionably the greatest military power in Europe. Secondly, the huge uncoordinated bodies of the Defenders in the three other provinces of Leinster, Munster and Connaught were still largely untouched by the government's measures. It was among the Defenders with their promising contacts with the militia that the United Irishmen who had nominally incorporated them within their system made increasing efforts to stimulate enthusiasm and exert control. The new National Directory centred on Dublin sent emissaries throughout Ireland spreading tales of the Orange terror in the North. They embroidered them with extravagant details such as the Orangemen's 'oath of extermination' and generally promoted the idea that on top of all the grievances which the Defenders were combined to protest against was now the threat of a general massacre of all Catholics in Ireland.

Lord Edward Fitzgerald was now the chief organizer of the United Irishmen's military efforts. His experience in action with the British Army in America made him a plausible focus for the hopes of the new revolutionary patriotism. The peasantry retained from their inherited Gaelic traditions a mystical respect for aristocratic chieftains, and this plumpish, brave and energetic, if not particularly subtle, aristocrat fitted the bill very well. There was even talk among the ignorant rebels later at Wexford that he was to be their king. A song called the Shan Van Vocht (the name of the legendary poor old crippled woman who is Ireland) relates him to the excitement of the time:

Oh the French are on the sea
Says the Shan Van Vocht,
The French are on the sea,
Says the Shan Van Vocht ...

And where will they have their camp?
Says the Shan Van Vocht,
Where will they have their camp?
Says the Shan Van Vocht.
On the Curragh of Kildare,
The boys will all be there,
With their pikes in good repair
Says the Shan Van Vocht.

To the Curragh of Kildare
The boys they will repair
And Lord Edward will be there,
Says the Shan Van Vocht ...

The military organization of the United Irishmen, such as it was, had been superimposed on their pyramid-like political structure late in 1796 and early in 1797.[8] The secretaries of the lowest-level committees were made sergeants. Groups of five committees sent delegates to a higher committee with the rank of captain, and ten of those committees sent delegates to a still higher committee with the rank of colonel. All these ranks were elected. Colonels had to submit to the Executive the names of three men to be considered by them for the rank of general. Each member of a society who could afford to was supposed to provide himself with a musket, bayonet and ammunition, while the rest were to provide themselves with pikes and, if possible, a pair of pistols. Hence the incessant raids for arms on gentlemen's houses, although the leaders, probably sincerely but certainly unrealistically, always claimed that they disapproved of these.

Fitzgerald himself seems to have recognized that his organization existed more effectively in theory than in practice. In a conversation in November 1797 with someone who had expressed doubts about the ability of the United Irishmen to stand against the king's troops, he had replied that this would not be altogether necessary in view of the French help that was expected. Some of the United Irishmen, he replied, would be incorporated in the French army where they would learn discipline soon enough, but by far the greater part would be engaged in harassing ammunition trains, cutting off foraging parties, and generally making the king's troops feel themselves in enemy country, while the actual battles would be left to the French.[9]

Nevertheless, it was Fitzgerald's chief concern to extend as much discipline and control as he could over the ranks of the Defenders incorporated within the United Irishmen. And in this winter and spring of 1797-8, while United Irishmen from Dublin worked up enthusiasm for the cause among the Defenders with their tales of impending terror and massacre, some such extension was nominally achieved. By February 1798 Fitzgerald's secret returns showed him that theoretically he had some 280,000 men he could call on – 170,000 of them from counties outside Ulster.[10] Once again a dispute took place, this time within the Supreme Directory of the United Irishmen itself, as to whether or not to take the field before the French came. Fitzgerald himself was personally in favour of this, but the belief that a French invasion was imminent was running so strongly that it hardly seemed like hesitation to delay a little longer. The latest messenger from France had spoken of the invasion taking place by the middle of May at the latest. The British Government too was receiving, through its intelligence, news of extensive invasion preparations at four Channel ports.

Tone himself, apart from Bonaparte's assurance that he was assigned to the Army of England under the command of a general of Irish descent named Kilmaine, had been told almost nothing about the actual preparations. A friend of his, Edward Lewins, who had been sent to France in 1797 by the United Irishmen to act as permanent diplomatic representative there, was informed on 1 April 1798 by the President of the French Directory that the timing and placing of the newest French expedition could not be divulged because it was a State secret. Lewins was, however, reassured that there would never be any question of France making peace with England on terms which did not include the independence of Ireland.*[11]

On 4 April Tone set off for the third time in three years to an invasion headquarters, this time making for Rouen, the headquarters of the Army of England. But before then news had reached him of two successive blows which had struck the United Irishmen at home. The first was the arrest at the end of February of Arthur O'Connor at Margate while trying to embark clandestinely for France – presumably to coordinate final arrangements between the new expedition and the rebels. The second was far worse. In fact, Tone described it in his diary as 'the most terrible blow which the cause of liberty in Ireland has yet sustained'.[12] This was no less than the arrest on 12 March 1798 of the entire Leinster Provincial Committee of the United Irishmen, containing as it did most of the members of the Supreme National Directory. Lord Edward Fitzgerald alone escaped.

It was not only intelligence of the French that the British Government had been getting. Their penetration of the Society of United Irishmen itself by informers at a reasonably high level had long been extensive. Among the principal informers, apart from the lawyer Macnally, was a former member of the Ulster Provincial Committee, a young Protestant gentleman named Samuel Turner, who had provided the information for the arrest of Arthur O'Connor at Margate. Thanks to such informers the government had in fact long been aware of the identity of most of the leaders of the United Irishmen.

It is a curious reflection on the contradictory nature of the political morality of the time that they had not felt able to arrest any of them earlier. For while prepared passively to condone, in the interests of the State, barbarities when practised on the peasantry in the course of a relentless hunt for arms, the government could not bring itself while the civil law still applied throughout most of Ireland to arrest political opponents without bringing them to trial. The normal processes of the law were, of course, always open to them, but for this sufficient evidence had to be available to make conviction certain. It was a condition of service made by most top-level informers, out of an understandable instinct of self-preservation, that they should not have to come forward in open court to give evidence. The government also had an interest in their not doing so, since even if the informer survived retaliation, he would be of little use as an informer in the future. And there was still a great deal of information they wanted. Whereas the United Irishmen's own knowledge of its associated Defender corps was vague enough, the government's view of the relationship was wrapped in mystery. All they knew was

* Both Tone and Lewins had had to spend a great deal of their time in Paris coping with the sort of jealousy invariably found among any groups of political exiles. Napper Tandy, claiming great military expertise on the strength of his membership of the old Volunteers corps, seems to have been the chief source of this. But of the Irishmen in Paris at this time, clearly it was Tone and Lewins whom the French trusted. Indeed, this fact was probably the main cause of the jealousy.

that considerable bodies of the discontented peasantry, organized as Defenders, were now affiliated to the United Irishmen's political conspiracy. And they had to assume there was still much to discover before they could have the situation under control.

However, early in March 1798, soon after O'Connor's arrest red-handed at Margate, a new informer of great importance approached the government with information on which, in the mounting tension, it was decided to take action against the whole Directory. This new informer was a young silk-merchant named Thomas Reynolds, a colonel in the United Irishmen's military organization and a friend of Fitzgerald himself. He now revealed to the government that the Leinster Provincial Committee of the United Irishmen, including as it did members of the Supreme National Directory, would be meeting in the house of the woollen merchant Oliver Bond on 12 March. Out of last-minute personal loyalty Reynolds seems to have warned Fitzgerald to keep away. Fifteen members of the Directory were taken that day, including Emmet, Bond and MacNeven.

Fitzgerald remained at large, but only for another few weeks. He spent this time in feverish last-minute organization of military revolt. But before it could break out he was caught in the house of a rich Dublin leather merchant, betrayed by yet another informer named Magan. Lying on a bed at the moment the police entered the room, he fought furiously, stabbing an officer many times with a knife and inflicting wounds which proved fatal. Fitzgerald himself was shot through the shoulder in the struggle but the wound was not thought to be serious at first. He died from it in prison six weeks later. His arrest took place on the very day his uniform as commander-in-chief of the rebel army, with its coat, jacket and trousers of dark green edged with red, together with a conical military cap, was delivered to his hiding place from the tailor.[13]

9

Repression, 1798

Military technique in Ulster had not been confined to the burning of houses and the periodical slaughter of guilty and innocent. It also included torture, though the methods were more or less the standard military punishments of the day. These involved picketting, or the suspension of a man by one arm with one pointed stake below his feet on which alone he could rest his weight, and, much more commonly, flogging, both applied as inducements to the victims to supply information. A clergyman living near Ballymena in County Antrim reported to his patron as early as May 1797 that the soldiers were not hesitating to strip men, tie them to a tree and flog them with bits and bridles.[1] In June 1797 he himself saw 'a country fellow' given seventy lashes, which was all he could take without fainting, and which would have rendered him useless for further information. A few days later, he watched an old man of over seventy stripped naked and given forty lashes while being held down by two soldiers.[2] A Belfast doctor confirmed that this sort of procedure was general when he wrote in October 1797: 'Many are the military outrages which have been committed in the north, such as inflictions of military punishment on poor people in no way subject to martial law.'[3]

But what had happened in the North was nothing to the severity with which the military – regulars, yeomanry and militia -- soon applied their systems of punishments to suspects in Leinster, particularly after the arrests of the leading United Irish conspirators at Bond's house. The advanced state of the conspiracy was now openly revealed and the government set out to break it by the harshest methods possible.

The army's official view of what constituted harsh methods can be gauged from its own standard of punishment at the time. Thus, in the previous year, when a number of militia and dragoons in a camp at Bandon near Cork were found to have taken the local Defender oath, they were given sentences which, when other than death, consisted of from 500 to 999 lashes. Only between 200 and 425 of these were in fact administered – the remainder being remitted on the culprit's agreement to serve abroad for the rest of his life. General Coote, no sentimentalist, who witnessed this particular flogging, described it in a letter to the lord lieutenant as 'a dreadful business'.[4] A man who as a boy of ten witnessed floggings of his neighbours by the army in 1798 described how one of them had begged to be shot while his flesh was being torn to shreds and how another, before he had received a hundred lashes, had cried out: 'I'm a-cutting through.' There had been a very heavy shower of rain at the time, he remembered.[5] Numerous accounts of such floggings which were now to play a most important part in Irish history confirm their bestiality with descriptions of flesh torn in lumps from the body by the cat o' nine tails, and the baring of bones and even internal organs.

On 30 March 1798, many districts in Leinster were officially proclaimed as areas in which the military could thenceforth live at free quarters and search for arms. Discipline among the militia and the yeomanry was poor at the best of times. General Sir John Moore had already noted in his diary in January 1798 that the system of proclaiming areas simply meant 'to let loose the military, who were encouraged in acts of great violence against all who were supposed to be disaffected'.[6] Now, in April and the first weeks of May 1798, there were virtually no restraints at all on the troops living at free quarters in the proclaimed districts. Their one task was to obtain the surrender of arms and procure information as to the identities of local sergeants, captains and colonels of the United Irishmen.

Other forms of torture besides flogging were introduced. All were applied fairly indiscriminately to both guilty and innocent since torture itself was the speediest method of distinguishing between the two. So-called 'half-hanging' became common: the pulling of a rope tight round the victim's neck from which it was slackened every time he lost consciousness. A fiercely loyal Protestant of New Ross in County Wexford described with some disapproval how about this time he began to hear of 'very many punishments put in execution in the barracks yard to exort confessions of guilt'.[7] One man, named Driscol, a hermit-like figure who was taken in a wood outside the town with two Roman Catholic prayer-books in his pocket on which he was suspected of swearing United Irishmen, was half-strangled three times and flogged four times during confinement 'but to no purpose'.[8] In other districts, the torment of the pitch-cap was introduced. This was a brown paper cap filled with molten pitch which was jammed on to the head of the victim and, after it had been allowed to set a little, was then set fire to. As the frantic wearer tried to tear it off, burning pitch fell into his eyes and down his face and the cap itself could usually only be removed with the accompaniment of much hair and scalp as well. The practice was inspired by a recent fashion of cropping the hair short adopted in imitation of the French republicans. A song, 'Croppies Lie Down', popular among the Orange yeomanry, acquired a sinister ring for all who either rashly or just unwittingly adopted the fashion.

> Oh, Croppies ye'd better be quiet and still
> Ye shan't have your liberty, do what ye will,
> As long as salt water is found in the deep

Our foot on the neck of the Croppy we'll keep.
Remember the steel of Sir Phelim O'Neill
Who slaughtered our fathers in Catholic zeal
And down, down, Croppies, lie down . . .

But it was the floggings which inspired the greatest terror and which proved the most effective method of obtaining quick information and a surrender of arms. After the proclamation of 30 March, the wooden triangle, on which the victim was spreadeagled, seems first to have been set up in the town of Athy in County Kildare. A captain of the United Irishmen wrote many years later an account of the terror which first-hand news of this immediately inspired in his own town of Carlow, some ten miles away.

There was no ceremony used in choosing victims, the first to hand done well enough. . . . They were stripped naked, tied to the triangle and their flesh cut without mercy and though some men stood the torture to the last gasp sooner than become informers, others did not, and to make matters worse, one single informer in the town was sufficient to destroy all the United Irishmen in it.[9]

General Sir John Moore came across one of these routine flogging sessions a few weeks later. The High Sheriff of Tipperary, a man named Fitzgerald, was at work. Already, by his severity he had most effectively broken the United Irish movement altogether in that county.

We found a great stir in Clogheen, [wrote Moore, who arrived there about ten o'clock on a hot fine morning]. A man tied up and being flogged, the sides of the streets filled with country people on their knees and hats off. . . . The rule was to flog each person till he told the truth and gave the names of other rebels. These were then sent for and underwent a similar operation. Undoubtedly several persons were thus punished who richly deserved it. The number flogged was considerable. It lasted all forenoon. That some were innocent is I fear equally certain.[10]

A loyalist Quaker lady, a schoolteacher, already experiencing the 'unchecked robbery' which free quarters meant in her village of Ballitore, in County Kildare, now heard her once peaceful village street ring with the shrieks of those who were being flogged and the cries of their loved ones looking on. Guards were placed at every entrance to the village to prevent people entering or leaving. 'The torture,' she wrote later, 'was excessive, and the victims were long in recovering.'[11]

It is, however, necessary to remember that this whole system of torture was being carried out on the Irish population largely by Irish soldiers, a great proportion of them Catholics of the poorest class in the militia, who were ready enough to do their duty against their fellow-countrymen as unworthy rebels. Of all the troops available for the government in Ireland before and during the coming rebellion, over four-fifths were Irish.*

* On 8 December 1797 Sir John Moore listed 76,791 men as available to the government in Ireland out of whom 11,193 were English or Scots (Maurice Moore (ed.), *Diary of Sir John Moore*, vol. ii, p. 270). Additional English and Scots troops were not brought into Ireland in any quantity until after the rebellion was over.

Soon the terror of the floggings, the burning of houses, of pitch-capping, half-hanging and indiscriminate shooting was so great that all over Leinster people started sleeping out in the fields at night for safety. 'No one slept in his own house,' wrote a man who himself soon became a rebel though he had never been a United Irishman. 'The very whistling of the birds seemed to report the approach of an enemy.'[12] And although he was then writing some thirty years after the event he added that the memory of the wailings of the women and the cries of the children still awoke in his mind, even at that distance of time, feelings of deep horror.

On 29 May 1798 a Lady Sunderlin living in Sackville Street, Dublin, wrote to her friend, Mrs Roper, in Berkhamsted: 'Our long threatened rebellion has at length broken out in various parts about Dublin.'[13]

She made no mention of any other part of Ireland. She was safe, she said, and the rebellion appeared to be premature. The rebels were out in very great numbers, but wherever they had been engaged they had been defeated with great loss. The Lord Mayor's butler had been arrested as a United Irishman and the servants in the country were said to be letting the Defenders into their masters' houses.

Lady Sunderlin's account was fairly accurate. The rebellion which had now indeed erupted was to prove a haphazard, desperate and pathetically unco-ordinated affair.

After the arrests at Bond's house on 12 March the United Irishmen claimed that they had filled the vacancies on the Leinster Committee immediately and, five days later, on St Patrick's Day, they confidently announced in a handbill that the organization of the capital was 'perfect'.[14] A new National Directory had in fact been set up under the leadership of a young Protestant barrister of some brilliance, named John Sheares. Though born into the Establishment (his father had been a member of the Irish House of Commons) he had been deeply impressed by the French Revolution and had become a member of the Society of United Irishmen in its open and legal days. His respectability in fact was to prove a source of distress and embarrassment to the judge who was eventually to sentence him and his brother Henry to death for high treason, for he knew their parents well.[15]

The Sheares brothers were arrested only five weeks after the arrest of the previous Directory at Bond's, and two days after Lord Edward Fitzgerald himself had been caught. They had been working together with Fitzgerald and with Samuel Neilson on details of a plan to take Dublin, which involved the capture of the military barracks at Loughlinstown, theoretically undermined from within by the swearing in of many of the troops there as United Irishmen. The government had been watching them all the time. A young captain of the King's County militia, whom they had mistakenly and most rashly assumed to be sympathetic to their plans, simply because in earlier times he had expressed himself as a radical, was daily giving in a detailed report of all their preparations. This captain, whose name was Armstrong, has gone down in legend among the execrable informers of Irish history, but he was hardly an informer in any dishonourable sense and his first utterance on cross-examination at the Sheares' trial was the proud statement that he was an Irishman.[16] He made just as sincere though less flamboyant a claim to patriotic motives as the Sheares themselves, in whose house was found a premature address to the people, beginning: 'The National Flag, the Sacred Green, is at this moment flying over the Ruins of Despotism ...'[17]

The control of the original Directory over the United Irishmen's unwieldy component parts had been inadequate enough. That of the Sheares brothers was even more so. Whatever powerful mystique Fitzgerald himself might have been able to substitute for effective organization disappeared with his arrest on 19 May. By 21 May the Sheares brothers were in gaol. Whoever replaced them must have been going blindly through the motions of setting off the rebellion planned for 23 May. Matters had gone too far to be stopped. Among the peasantry the tension could hardly be contained any longer. The basic sense of injustice which had first driven them into the Defender organizations was now inflamed to desperation by the military terror. At the same time, this had very nearly broken their spirit. They were at a point where the alternatives of total despair or a desperate gesture were perilously close together.

William Farrel, a United Irish captain from Carlow, gives a vivid account of the way in which the local attempt at rebellion in that town finally came about. It may serve as an individual representative example of the experience of many localities in and about the Irish midlands at this time. Everything was expected from the great men in Dublin, but when it came to fighting 'everyone wished most earnestly to see it done but none cared to do the job himself'.[18] Government posters had been up in Carlow town for several days, demanding the surrender of arms and threatening the full rigour of martial law at free quarters if they were not forthcoming. Only ten miles from Athy and its flogging triangle everyone now knew what that meant. In the absence of any word from 'the great men behind the curtain in Dublin' the United Irishmen of Carlow themselves debated as to whether to surrender the arms or not. Farrel himself was in favour of doing so, but the majority were not, and on 24 May orders came down from Dublin to rise.

The United Irishmen's military organizer in the district was a man named Heydon, actually a member of a local yeomanry corps. After alerting as many sympathizers in the town as he could, he rode off to raise the countryside. He found the country people reluctant to move, saying that they were 'heart-sick of the business and would much rather give it up and have peace'.[19]

They implored him not to lead them into the town unless he could guarantee that he could take it with the support he had there anyway. With a wild optimism which was often typical of future Irish conspiracies, Heydon replied that he had nearly all the yeomanry with him, nearly all the militia and a considerable number of the Ninth Dragoons who were stationed in the town. All the country people would have to do would be to march into the town at a given signal, raise a great shout and all would be over.

As evening came on it began to be whispered in Carlow town that the country people were coming in and that boats were ready on the River Barrow to ferry other contingents of rebels over from the neighbouring Queen's County. Farrel himself stole out of the town to check on this last report, but finding it to be false became even more determined to have nothing to do with what he was now convinced must be a disastrous rising. In the darkness, though, about a thousand of the Carlow men were already gathering. A famous ballad written many years later immortalizes another Farrel of this time, a man of at least more ballad-worthy mettle:

'Oh, then, tell me Sean O'Farrel, tell me where you hurry so?'
'Hush my boucal, hush and listen' – and his cheeks were all aglow –
'I bear orders from the Captain; get you ready quick and soon
For the pikes must be together by the rising of the Moon.'

'Oh then, tell me Sean O'Farrel, where the gathering is to be?'
'In the old spot, by the river, right well known to you and me.
One word more: for token signal whistle up the marching tune
With your pike upon your shoulder by the rising of the Moon.'

Out from many a mud-walled cabin, eyes were watching through the
    night:
Many a manly heart was throbbing for that blessed warning light;
Murmurs passed along the valley, like the banshee's lonely croon;
And a thousand pikes were flashing by the rising of the Moon.

Down along yon singing river, that dark mass of men was seen;
High about their shining weapons floats their own beloved green;
Death to every foe and traitor! Forward strike the marching tune,
And hurrah, my boys, for Freedom! 'Tis the Rising of the Moon.

The rebels started moving towards Carlow at two o'clock in the morning of 25 May. A Catholic parish priest called O'Neill whose house they passed came out and went on his knees imploring them to turn back. They pressed on. But a little later doubts seem to have beset them and they were only rallied by a man called Murray with a blunderbuss who threatened to blow out the brains of the first man to turn back. One contemporary says that a man was shot as an example, thus giving timely warning to the garrison of their approach.[20] Heydon repeated his assurances that the town was as good as won. They marched into Carlow through one of the four main gates without opposition and halted when they came to the potato market. There they raised the great shout which was to deliver the town into their hands. It died away into the silence of the night.

They had hardly time to sense panic before the first shot rang out. The yeomanry, the militia and the Ninth Dragoons had indeed been waiting for them and now opened a murderous fire. They flew, wrote Farrel long afterwards, 'like frightened birds'.[21] But there was virtually nowhere to fly to for they had been neatly trapped. Those who escaped the firing from the ends of the streets and from the windows of the houses managed to force their way into a cluster of poor peasant cabins on the edge of the town. The soldiers poured volley after volley into the cabins, setting them alight. Those who tried to escape the flames were bayonetted or shot or immediately hanged from signposts and gateways. Between four and five hundred people may have died altogether. The government troops had no losses at all. It was a massacre. Many bodies were thrown, when daylight came, into a sand-pit called 'the croppy hole'.

Heydon, who had vainly tried to rally his panic-stricken followers for a time, had eventually decided to escape as best he could. He succeeded in doing this by putting on his yeomanry uniform and mingling with his former comrades. He made his way out into the country but was caught three miles from Carlow and hanged the next day from a lamp-iron, going to his death, as Farrel who witnessed it declared, 'seemingly as unconcerned as if he was going to some place of amusement'. The rope broke, and after lying insensible on the ground for a few moments he had to go through the business of mounting the ladder and being 'turned off' all over again. This time the rope held.

Retribution was only just beginning. The triangle was now set up in the barrack square at Carlow and scenes of incredible brutality took place as men were stripped and flogged and their flesh cut to shreds by the cat o' nine tails in attempts to extract information from them. Some who refused to talk were finally hanged, naked, bleeding and insensible as they were. Gordon, the loyalist historian, reckons that some two hundred people were executed in Carlow by hanging or shooting, as a result of courts-martial. alone.[22]

A dozen or more such 'risings' of ill-organized groups of peasantry armed with many pikes and some firearms took place in the counties round Dublin between 23 and 25 May. Sometimes these amounted to little more than demonstrations. Mary Leadbeater, the Quaker lady who had heard her village street ringing with the cries of those flogged by the soldiers, was now to have experience of the rebels.[23] After the withdrawal of the military to deal with the situation nearer Dublin, certain people in the village who had been lying low suddenly appeared in the streets dressed in green, and in the afternoon about two or three hundred men came in from the surrounding country armed with pikes, knives and pitchforks and carrying poles with green flags flying. They were accompanied by young girls wearing green ribbons and carrying pikes and were headed by a man riding a white horse. A number of the rebels crowded into her kitchen demanding food and drink, but otherwise behaved quite respectfully. She was cutting bread for them a little apprehensively when a small elderly man relieved her of the task telling her not to worry and that they would be 'out in a shot'. She told them that she felt unable to wear anything green since as a Quaker she could not join any party.

'What?' they asked her, 'not the strongest?'

'None at all,' she replied.

Among them she noticed a young farmer named Horan whom she had seen unhappily getting a 'protection' slip from an officer only a few days before. His whole face was now quite changed and radiant with excitement.

The man on the white horse did what he could to prevent bloodshed and 'showed as much courage as humility'. But at least one yeoman who had been taken prisoner by the rebels was piked and shot. They took a number of horses which they galloped about unmercifully, making her feel glad that she had lent hers to a yeomanry officer and thus could not give it to a rebel who demanded it from her with a drawn sword. Her other bad moment was when one rebel, brandishing a pistol, demanded her husband, though another persuaded him to leave her alone.

The real horror of these Quakers' experience only took place when the loyalist military descended on the village a few days later. The rebels had by then wisely fled, leaving only peaceable loyalists behind. Nevertheless, for two hours the village was delivered over to what Mary Leadbeater called 'the unbridled licence of a furious soldiery'. Houses were burned, windows smashed, and one soldier on learning that she had given food and drink to the rebels placed a musket against her breast and seemed about to shoot her when he changed his mind and simply swept pans and jugs off the kitchen table with his musket and broke the kitchen window. Another soldier lolling in one of her chairs boasted of having just burned a man in a barrel. She saw the grisly remains in the village a little later.

Outside, terrible scenes were being enacted. The village blacksmith, who had actually been acquitted of the charge of making pikes by a court-martial a few days before, was taken out and shot. The village carpenter who had hidden himself in terror with his family in the graveyard was unearthed there and quickly done to death. The widow of a yeoman who had actually been killed fighting on the loyalist side in a battle against rebels at Kilcullen had her house sacked while her brother, her son, and her servant were all murdered. The local doctor, himself a yeoman, a much loved man who had taken control of the village when the army left, and had had his horse and all his instruments taken by undisciplined rebels with whom he finally made terms, was now given a peremptory court-martial in the course of which he was several times slashed by dragoons' sabres and finally clumsily shot. 'Such', wrote the Quaker lady, 'are the horrors of civil war.'

It was the sort of pattern that was repeating itself in these days in many of the counties round Dublin. Only at one point, at Prosperous in County Kildare, where some twenty-eight men of the Cork militia were trapped in a burning barracks and slaughtered either in the flames or on the ends of pikes as they jumped from the blazing windows, did the rebels have any-thing that might be called a victory. The leader of the rebels on this occasion was a Catholic lieutenant of yeomanry named Esmond, who after his victory went back to his unit and nonchalantly reappeared there, as if nothing had happened, to take part on the loyalist side in the defence of Naas. He was recognized by a soldier who had escaped from Prosperous, sent to Dublin and hanged.

At all the other points the rebels were finally routed with great slaughter, though at a few points they first inflicted some casualties on the troops, and the scale of the rebel movements in Kildare caused Dublin Castle consider-able anxiety for a time. The rebels' own casualties were said to be enormous, running, so the army claimed, into several hundred after each battle. It seems likely that the majority of these rebel casualties took place after the battle itself was over. William Farrel, the United Irishman of Carlow, described how, after the events there, 'any person seen flying through the country could be shot on the spot, without any ceremony, and no more thought of it than shooting a sparrow'.[24] Lord Cornwallis, who became both viceroy, replacing Camden, and commander-in-chief after some weeks of rebellion, wrote to the British Prime Minister that the numbers of enemy given as destroyed were 'greatly exaggerated', adding that he was sure anyone found in a brown coat (i.e. civilian clothes) within miles of the action was 'butchered without discrimination'.[25] Though this was perhaps to be expected in the circumstances from the loosely disciplined units of yeomanry, particularly where they were composed of Orangemen, it is clear that the same barbaric ferocity was displayed by the Catholic militia itself, of whom Cornwallis indeed wrote that they were 'ferocious and cruel in the extreme when any poor wretches either with or without arms came within their power'.[26] 'In short,' he added, 'murder appears to be their favourite pastime.' Burnings of houses, floggings and summary executions now began to take place on a far greater and more violent scale even than before.

Even before the inevitable retribution had made itself felt in its full horror, such desperate heart as the local rebel leaders had managed to put into their disordered bands in Kildare and the neighbouring counties was showing signs of disappearing. An assembly of some two thousand rebels, under the leadership of a man named Perkins, surrendered their arms on the Curragh of Kildare on condition that Perkins himself should be delivered up and the rest of them be allowed to return home unmolested, which they did, 'dispersing homewards in all directions with shouts of joy, and leaving thirteen cart-loads of pikes behind'.[27] A few days later an attempt by another large collection of rebels to repeat this performance foundered when somebody discharged his firearm by mistake and the military seized the excuse to massacre several hundred of them.

A fight on the hill of Tara, ancient seat of the High Kings of Ireland, which resulted in the death of some 350 rebels for the loss of relatively few loyalist troops, was remarkable for the effective part played in the action on the loyalist side by the Catholic Lord Fingall and his Catholic yeomanry.[28] Not that there was any real fear of Catholics, simply as Catholics, being favourable to the rebels. A few days after the desultory rebellion had erupted a loyal address, signed by the entire Roman Catholic college of Maynooth, four Catholic peers and some two thousand other members of the gentry, was presented to the lord lieutenant. This ran:

> We, the undersigned, his Majesty's most loyal subjects, the Roman Catholics of Ireland, think it necessary at this moment publicly to declare our firm attachment to His Majesty's person, and to the constitution under which we have the happiness to live. . . . We cannot avoid expressing to Your Excellency our regret at seeing, amid the géneral delusion, many, particularly of the lower orders, of our own religious persuasion engaged in unlawful associations and practices.[29]

Nevertheless, some doubts about the possible delusion of the Catholic militia were understandable, for they themselves were drawn from the lower orders. The Defenders had made a good deal of nominal progress in seducing the militia from their allegiance the previous year. Courts-martial in the summer of 1797 alone had shown that soldiers from at least eleven different county militias had taken the Defender oath and that the 2nd Fencible Dragoons stationed near Cork were also seriously tainted.[30] And though the deterrent effect of the savage punishments meted out to the culprits can hardly have been nil, it was natural for the government to be apprehensive when rebellion finally broke out.* However, from the start the militia showed remarkable loyalty, earning rebuke only for the very ferocity they displayed against those of their own class they met as rebels.

'You will have observed,' a correspondent wrote to the Chief Secretary, Pelham, after a week of the '98 rebellion, 'that our militia, even the King's County regiment, have all behaved very well,' though he added that there had been 'instances of disaffection among the yeomanry'.[31]

Lord Castlereagh, who substituted for Pelham during the latter's ill-health, and was eventually to replace him as Chief Secretary, wrote, referring to the militia's regrettable excesses among the civilian population, that they were 'in many instances defective in subordination, but in none have they

---

* As late as July 1798, twelve privates of the Westmeath militia were tried and sentenced for taking the United Irish oath. Report of Secret Committee of House of Commons (Dublin 1798), 297.

shown the smallest disposition to fraternize, but on the contrary, pursue the insurgents with the rancour unfortunately connected with the nature of the struggle'.[32]

It might of course have been argued that the real test of the militia's loyalty could not be made until the French had landed. But there was no sign whatsoever of the French. Tone, who had spent most of the month before the outbreak of the rebellion 'deliciously with my family at Paris',[33] was now back with the Army of England at Le Havre, but he was soon doing his best to get sent to India to join his brother Will, recognizing, as he said, 'that there is no more question or appearance here of an attempt on England than of one on the Moon'.[34] On that same day about three o'clock in the morning Lady Louisa Connolly, sister of Lord Edward Fitzgerald, watched about two hundred rebels force their way through her gates at Castletown in County Kildare and pass quietly across her front lawn.[35] Writing about it soon afterwards she said they did not seem to know what they were fighting for. To the North, South and West, she reported, everything was perfectly quiet. Yet to the South, unknown to her as yet, the most serious threat the rebels were to mount was already under way.

10

Rebellion in Wexford

Dublin itself, which had remained firmly under government control, assumed proudly for a time something of a siege mentality. A United Irish attempt to undermine the city from within by getting the lamplighters to withhold their services was summarily countered by sending them to work with, as the Bishop of Dromore wrote gleefully to his wife in England, 'a bayonet in the breach'.[1] Men of sixty and seventy put on uniforms and joined any corps that would have them.[2] A young yeomanry captain arriving in the capital on 4 June, the day after Fitzgerald's death from his wounds in prison, found 'every man in the city a soldier'.[3] The law courts were shut and all business was at a standstill. The Castle was barricaded and gunners stood on the alert outside it with lighted matches ready beside their guns. The same was true of St Stephen's Green – then on the outermost limits of the city. Express messengers were arriving every moment with accounts of what was happening to the rebels and the army. Communication with Cork and Limerick had been cut off for several days and had only just been re-opened.

The next day, this particular captain was to join his yeomanry unit in the Queen's County, where 11,500 men were said to have been sworn into the United Irishmen, although, as he wrote in his letter, 'by flogging and co. such information had been gained as to enable the officers and magistrates of the county to get possession of many of the Captains and to break in upon their organization'.[4] However, news from the South was bad. Wexford Town and most of that county were in rebel hands and 'matters seemed to wear a serious aspect'.

An organization of the Defenders had existed in County Wexford for many years. In 1793 they had fought the celebrated battle outside the town of Wexford itself over the raising of the new militia.* But since then they had not been particularly active. In 1797 some United Irish emissaries had been in the county, circulating what seemed increasingly plausible rumours among the peasantry that the Orangemen were about to rise and murder all Papists. But beyond strengthening an already natural sense of Catholic peasant solidarity, they do not seem to have created anything like a really active conspiracy. Wexford was in no sense the county where anyone expecting rebellion

* See above, p. 60.

in this year would have expected it to appear particularly menacing. The number of sworn United Irishmen in the county – as distinct from Defenders – was only around three hundred.[5] And yet it was only in Wexford, so feebly organized, that the rebellion in fact took on any menacing proportions at all.

The explanation of this lies partly in accident – the cause of much important history – and partly in a number of special factors local to the county. One such local factor was this very absence of serious rebellious organization, and the consequent lack of concern on the part of the government until almost the last moment. The number of militia or regular troops garrisoning the county was small. As a result, when the government happened to find a note of Fitzgerald's which mentioned the port of Wexford as possibly suitable for French disembarkation, a last-minute alarm was raised about the state of the county. The task of searching for arms was left to the local yeomanry, who were mainly Protestants, and by their amateur nature less concerned with the niceties of disciplined behaviour even than other troops. Here another special local factor operated. For the Protestants of Wexford had long been more sectarian in their outlook than those of most other counties of Leinster. In the days of the original Volunteers it had been the one county in Ireland not to permit Catholics to enrol in the corps.[6] And in 1798 itself a private attempt to raise a yeomanry corps composed largely of Catholics had collapsed because of official disapproval.[7] Thus when the Protestant yeomanry now began their forays round the country in a last-minute search for arms they employed a sectarian viciousness which much aggravated the sense of apprehension and terror already there. In 1797 only 16 out of 142 parishes had been 'proclaimed' as Defender-tainted areas subject to special military regulations. As late as 9 April 1798 Lord Mountnorris, one of the most influential Protestant landowners of the county, who for some time had been sucessfully exhorting the people to give up arms and make declarations of allegiance to the government, forwarded one such declaration to the government signed by a local priest and 757 of his flock from the small Wexford parish of Boulavogue.[8]

The chief signatory of this declaration of 9 April was a curate named Father John Murphy. Since he was soon to take a prominent part in the insurrection, there has been an assumption by some commentators, chiefly Protestant, that the declaration represented merely deception on the part of a cunning priesthood and peasantry. But other commentators, usually Catholic, maintain that this and other similar declarations were genuine and made in good faith at the time; and this in fact seems more probable. The completely haphazard nature of the insurrection in Wexford when it did break out, with its lack of considered strategy or design, and its precarious and largely aimless gyrations round the country as it gathered force, suggests not artifice and cunning but an act of desperation undertaken at the last moment in the belief that neither declarations of allegiance nor written 'protections' were any longer of use against the burnings, floggings, shootings and general depredations of the military. Certainly a Protestant clergyman, the Reverend James Gordon, who lived in the heart of the affected area at the time and afterwards wrote an intelligent and balanced history of the whole rebellion, thought that but for the floggings and half-hangings and other 'acts of severity' the rebellion there might possibly never have broken out at all.[9]

To supplement the yeomanry and make matters worse, the troops the government sent to Wexford were the North Cork militia who, though predominantly Catholic, were the very troops popularly credited with the invention of the pitch-cap method of torture. One of their sergeants named Heppenstal had acquired the nickname of 'the walking gallows' for his peculiar skill in half-hanging men over his shoulder. And the Reverend James Gordon, emphasizing the fear which gripped the people of Wexford in these last days of May 1798, tells of a man who having subscribed for a pike which he had not yet received and which he was therefore unable to surrender, actually dropped dead from fright.[10]

The yeomanry and the North Cork militia were already at work in Wexford when the rebellion broke out in the counties round Dublin. The sense of terror naturally rose accordingly. News of the sadistic slaughter at Carlow must have travelled fast to the adjoining county. Certainly news of the shooting of twenty-eight prisoners at Carnew in Wicklow and the killing of others at Dunlavin in the same county reached Wexford, where the country people were already sleeping out in the fields at night in fear, on 26 May.

The day before, a party of men had been cutting turf near Boulavogue, the very parish which had sent in its massive declaration of allegiance to the Crown six weeks before. The curate, Father John Murphy, was with the men on the top of a bank when a troop of yeoman cavalry came galloping up to them. After wheeling round they came galloping back again and again drew up in front of them in menacing fashion.[11] Murphy, who had been playing an important part in getting the people to surrender their arms in return for 'protections', decided that the situation was too menacing for them to remain at work and recommended them to return home.

The Arms Proclamation in Wexford had allowed a period of fourteen days for the surrender of arms. But the local magistrates and troops had shown no inclination to wait that long but had begun floggings and other tortures immediately.

An eye-witness of the Boulavogue incident said of the mood of the time: 'A portion of the men in this district had now become spiritless. They saw that a Proclamation issued with all the formality and apparent binding of an Act of Parliament was despised and made no account of ... Their arms in a great measure surrendered, they became silent, sullen and resolved to meet their fate with such arms as they were in possession of.'[12] He adds that even now such thoughts were not generally entertained but were only being put forward as far as he knew by individuals in this one locality.

Murphy, who was constantly being asked for advice, was himself becoming more and more desperate. On the evening of the next day, 26 May, accompanied by a number of men in similar mood, some of whom were carrying arms, he had just visited the house of a neighbouring farmer when he encountered a troop of cavalry similar to that on the day before. The cavalry either fired a volley and demanded the surrender of the group's arms, or simply made the demand. In either case they were met with shots and a shower of stones. While the main body of the cavalry then withdrew with some circumspection, the lieutenant in charge, named Bookey, and one other man pressed through the crowd and set fire to the farm. The thatch caught alight easily, for Ireland was experiencing an unusually long period of hot dry weather that summer.

About ten minutes later, attempting to rejoin the main body of his men, Bookey and his companion found themselves surrounded by Murphy's group. Someone stabbed Bookey with a pike on the side of his neck. He fell from his horse and was grimly finished off on the ground. His horse, which had also received a pike thrust in the flank, plunged so violently in its agony that it wrenched the pike from the pikeman's hand and galloped all the way into the nearest village, trailing the ugly weapon behind it.* In the words of an eye-witness of this event: 'The first blow of the insurrection in Wexford was now struck and they immediately proceeded to rouse their neighbours – a thing easily done, as scarcely any of them had slept in their houses on that, or the preceding night.'[13]

The next day, as a reprisal, houses were in flames all over the countryside. Bookey's cavalry unit burned over 170 on that day by their own admission, including Father Murphy's chapel at Boulavogue.[14] They also slaughtered a number of people who seemed as if they were collecting in a rebel body on Kiltomas Hill. The group with Father Murphy, gathering strength to about a thousand men, camped on Oulart Hill. They had only about forty to fifty firearms among them and virtually no commander. Father Murphy and the only other man with any sense of leadership, a sergeant of the local yeomanry named Roache who had joined them, were principally occupied in trying to decide what to do next and in preventing desertion. However, when they were attacked by a detachment of about 110 men of the North Cork militia, the rebels courageously held their ground and finally drove the troops from the hill, killing many of them for the loss of only about six of their own men.

As when the situation was reversed, most of the slaughter seems to have

* The detail book of the yeomanry unit involved merely records that Bookey, on meeting Murphy's party, ordered them to deliver their arms but was received with shots and a shower of stones which knocked him from his horse. The fuller account is the later record of an eye-witness.

taken place after the battle was over. The defeated men of the North Cork militia, being Catholics, presented Catholic prayer books to prove it and called out for mercy but received none, or none at least from the rebel pikes. One of the last to die, when asked his name, replied in Irish: "Thady Illutha'. But since the Wexford rebels did not understand Irish they had to have this translated for them as Thady, the Unfortunate. Whereupon they appropriately ran the man through with a pike. He did not die immediately but struggled helplessly, calling for mercy for some time.[15]

Flushed with this victory at Oulart Hill, and equipped now with a valuable addition of arms from the slaughtered militia, the rebels went on a round-about march through the countryside and finally attacked the town of Enniscorthy. A clergyman who watched their assault through a telescope noticed a man on a bright bay horse who seemed to be some sort of leader. He was wearing a scarlet coat which glittered in the sun and had probably been taken from one of the officers of the North Cork killed the day before, but he was without boots. 'Yet,' noted the clergyman, 'he rode along the rising ground with some address, and the mass of the people moved in whatever direction he waved or pointed a drawn sword by the gleam of which I could observe with my glass that it was a long sabre.' He could also discern two or three white standards and one green flag.[16] After a three-hour fight the rebels took Enniscorthy, virtually burning it to the ground in the process. They then set up what was to be their most permanent base camp in the rebellion on a prominence beside the town called Vinegar Hill.

On the Sunday morning on which Enniscorthy was taken the young Catholic farmer, Thomas Cloney, who had found even the whistling of the birds so sinister* and who had himself never been either a United Irishman or a Defender, still knew nothing of this startling course of events though he lived not far away. He and his neighbours were simply filled with gloomy forebodings for their own safety in anticipation of the fury of the soldiers then known to be rampaging round the countryside. They had been listening for some time to the sounds of battle from Enniscorthy when a roughly-dressed horseman galloped up crying 'Victory! Victory!'[5] His neighbours immediately recovered sufficient spirit at least to search the houses of the neighbouring yeomanry and commit a certain number of 'excesses'.

Two days later, large bodies of rebels rode up to Cloney's house on two separate occasions to urge him to join them. He finally agreed to do so on the principle that this part of the country was now a prey to the military whether it resisted or not, so he might as well resist. He rode off to Vinegar Hill. There he found some thousands of people in a state of total disorder and confusion, relating their sufferings at the hands of the military to each other and calling blood-thirstily for revenge. The only concept of future strategy seemed to be that they should march off towards whichever place seemed

* See above, p. 100.

most likely next to find itself at the mercy of the troops. But there was such difficulty in determining which this would be, each man putting forward the claims of his own district as paramount, that no final decision could be reached. Revenge was more easily come by, and had indeed already begun.

Vinegar Hill was topped by the remains of a windmill on which a green flag had been planted. Inside this mill some thirty-five Protestants from Enniscorthy, suspected in the most general and haphazard way of Orange sympathies, had been collected and on the very Tuesday of Cloney's arrival some fourteen or fifteen of them were clumsily put to death by an execution squad of rebels armed with pikes and guns, lined up in front of the windmill door and commanded by a man with a drawn sword named Martin.[17] One of their victims, severely wounded, was found next morning insensible but still alive by his wife, just as an old man with a scythe was going round the silent forms finishing off those that showed any signs of life.[18]

Another man, a glazier of Enniscorthy called Davies, had even greater luck. The Protestant clergyman, Gordon, relates how, after hiding in a privy for four days 'during which he had no other sustenance than the raw body of a cock, which had by accident alighted on the seat, he fled from this loathesome abode', but was found, taken to Vinegar Hill, shot through the body, piked in the head and thrown into a grave where he remained covered with earth and stones for twelve hours.[19] His faithful dog discovered him, scraped away the earth and revived him by licking his face. The man came to, dreaming that pikemen were about to stab him again and moaning the name of a local Catholic priest whom he hoped might save him. This priest, one Father Roche, happened to have become one of the rebel leaders, and the pikemen, who were indeed in the offing, were so impressed by what seemed their victim's conversion to Catholicism in near-miraculous circumstances that they took him to a house where he recovered.

A Protestant lady, a Mrs White, who bravely came to Vinegar Hill in search of a 'protection' from this same Father Roche for herself and her family, also described the scene there. The camp

... presented a dreadful scene of confusion and uproar. ... Great numbers of women were in the camp. Some men were employed in killing cattle, and boiling them in pieces in large copper brewing-pans; others were drinking, cursing and swearing; many of them were playing on various musical instruments, which they had acquired by plunder in the adjacent Protestant houses ...[20]

Besides musical instruments the rebels also brought Wilton carpets and fine sheets to Vinegar Hill, and to other such hill camps which became a standard feature of their movements round the Wexford countryside during the next few weeks.[21] However, they had few tents and mostly lay out in the open at nights in the astonishingly fine weather which they took as a favourable omen, saying that it would not rain again until final victory was theirs.[22]

Mrs White got her protection. 'No man to molest this house, or its in-habitants, on pain of death.' However, while she was still on the hill trying to obtain it '. . . the pikemen would often show us their pikes all stained with blood, and boast of having murdered our friends and neighbours'.[23] Though there is plenty of evidence that such vengeance – which was to be repeated elsewhere – was deplored by all the more intelligent and sensitive rebels like Cloney himself, it was difficult to restrain because it was the one form of posi-tive action easily available to the mob in the general frustration. The dis-cipline which the senior officers were able to maintain among the rebels was always tenuous. Otherwise, quite apart from humanitarian considerations, it would clearly have been in their interest to have employed the energies wasted on such brutalities in some more strictly military design.

The lack of almost any coherent strategic plan, or indeed of any true leadership, was to be the rebels' undoing. Their determination and bravery in the field, already displayed effectively enough at their first two victories at Oulart Hill and Enniscorthy, was to prove remarkable on many sub-sequent occasions, stemming as it did from the sense of desperation with which they had finally taken up arms. But their discipline even in battle was poor. The Reverend James Gordon wrote: 'As they were not, like regular troops, under any real command of officers, but acted spontaneously, each according to the impulse of his own mind, they were watched in battle one of another, each fearing to be left behind in case of retreat, which was gener-ally swift and sudden.'[24] For the same reason, they were reluctant to take part in actions at night when it was less easy to tell what was going on and who was doing what. Cloney, the young farmer, although he had no previous military or organizational experience, soon found himself in a position of authority among the rebels. He described them as often 'ungovernable'. Since it was everyone's ambition to get hold of a firearm, in which few in fact had any experience, and since there was a good deal of drunkenness, they were constantly letting off their guns and exposing themselves and their com-rades to danger.[25]

The rebels' clothes were usually those of the ordinary Wexford farmer or labourer of the day: felt flowerpot hats, swallow-tailed coats, corduroy knee-breeches, stockings and shoes with a buckle. Sometimes they carried raw wheat in their pockets as an iron ration. This, it is said, was often to be seen in the following year sprouting from the crude and nameless graves.[26] Some of the captains, colonels and generals wore a sort of uniform; Roache, the yeomanry sergeant who went over to the rebels before the battle of Ennis-corthy, and became a general, is described by an eye-witness as wearing ordinary clothes except for 'two most enormous epaulettes and a silk sash and a belt in which he carried a large pair of horse pistols'.[27] He carried a sword by his side. The same witness says that the only proper uniform he ever saw was worn by a shoe-black named Monk who was a United Irish captain. This consisted of a light horseman's jacket of green, with silver lace cross banded in front; pantaloons to match with silver seams; and a green helmet cap, with a white ostrich feather on top. The lower ranks wore white bands round their hats, while those with some authority had a green ribbon either with a gold harp surrounded by the words *Erin Go Bragh* ('Ireland for Ever'), or the words Liberty and Equality. Whenever they could, they decorated themselves with green feathers and green handkerchiefs. They carried flags and standards in profusion – generally green, but where enough green material could not be found any colour except orange did service. Their total numbers always seem to have been exaggerated by the loyalists, partly probably through natural apprehension, and partly because in military reports exaggeration of the enemy's numbers is equally convenient both in victory and defeat. Probably the total number of rebels who took arms in the entire Wexford insurrection did not exceed thirty thousand men, and may have been much less.[28]

The confusion and indecision to which the rebels on Vinegar Hill had immediately succumbed was temporarily resolved by the arrival there of emissaries from the loyalists in the town of Wexford. These were two Catholic gentlemen who had been imprisoned by the authorities for suspected United Irish sympathies, but had now been sent on parole to entreat the rebels to disperse. The entreaty had no other effect than to put the idea of capturing Wexford into the rebels' heads.

If there had been any sort of overall coordinated rebel plan, it would undoubtedly have involved an attempt to link up with the rebels in Kildare and the other counties near Dublin. In this case, the Wexford rebels would have marched north, rather than southwards to Wexford town, for already the town of Gorey on the northern route had been abandoned in anticipatory panic by the loyalists. In preparation indeed for the rebels' arrival, the middle-class Catholics of Gorey had been apprehensively forming themselves into guard companies to protect the houses of their Protestant neighbours. If the rebels had marched straight to Gorey, Arklow still further north would have been threatened and possibly also abandoned, whereupon the road into Wicklow and Dublin itself would have lain open. But this was no strategically designed rebellion. In fact, several days later, after further victories in the south, the rebels did eventually move northwards with some of their forces, but by that time the loyalist troops had had time to make their dispositions.

Before that, however, the rebels drawn quixotically towards Wexford had established another camp on a hill called Three Rocks just outside the town itself. There they spent the night, and in the stillness of the summer darkness the calls of rebel stragglers trying to find the men of their own locality could be heard clearly by the loyalists' outposts down below.[29] The next morning, on this site of Three Rocks, the rebels defeated and killed or captured some seventy men of the Meath militia and shortly afterwards entered Wexford itself from which the garrison had hastily withdrawn.

A genteel Protestant lady, a Mrs Brownrigg, who in panic had just taken passage with her family for Wales on a ship in the harbour, watched them pouring down in great hordes into the town. The captain of her ship promptly declared himself a United Irishman and prepared to land her again. Coming ashore, she was filled with terror to find the streets crowded with rebels shouting and firing their guns. She and her family took refuge in a Catholic friend's house where, however, they expected to be murdered hourly. The rebels held a sort of parade twice a day outside the house with fifes, fiddles and drums. 'It was,' she wrote in her diary, 'a kind of regular tumult, and everyone was giving his opinion.'[30]

A Quaker family, the Goffs, who lived in the country just outside Wexford, had heard the morning thunder of the cannon from Three Rocks and soon afterwards had their first contact with the rebels. These came in search of two Goff cousins who had been with the defeated militia in the battle and had taken refuge in the house. But the cousins managed to escape and the worst that happened to the Goffs that day was that two of their Catholic servants were made to join the rebel force and given pikes – 'the first we had seen'.[31] Mrs Goff, on hearing of this, was deeply shocked and insisted that 'she could not allow anything of the kind to be brought into the house'. Whereupon the offensive weapons were always left outside the door at nights when the servants returned home from their work with the rebel army. Some 250 other Protestants, however – men, women and children – were taken from all over the neighbourhood and confined as prisoners in a barn at Scullabogue House, about a mile and a half away, where a grisly fate awaited them.

The Goffs, who were respected by the country people like most of the Quakers in Ireland, suffered only from a continual massing of rebels on their lawn, asking for food. Large tubs of butter-milk and water were placed outside the door and the servants frequently had to stay up all night baking bread while the women of the house made their hands bleed cutting up bread and cheese.[32] The men were so impatient that they sometimes carried away whole loaves of bread and cheeses on the ends of their pikes. And though some of the pikemen had such savage tales to tell of their prowess that one of the girls wept as she was handing round the food, there were always others who rebuked such manners and won the Goff family's admiration and respect.

The absence of resolute stratagem and decision, which had so far marked the triumphant progress of the rebels round County Wexford, was now theoretically remedied by the appointment of a most curious commander-in-chief. This was Beauchamp Bagenal Harvey, a Protestant land-owner with the then considerable income of some £3,000 a year. A sophisticated radical by temperament, he had been a United Irishman in the early days of the society, while it was still open and legal, but seems to have had no connection with it in its later clandestine phase, though his radical sympathies clearly remained unchanged. He had made no secret of them and had been arrested as a precaution by the authorities in Wexford on the outbreak of the rebellion. He was immediately released by the insurgents when they entered the town, and accepted the post of commander-in-chief, hoping, it seems, that he might at least be able to bring some sort of order into their confused ranks, though he had no military experience whatsoever. Another Protestant gentleman of radical political inclinations, Matthew Keogh, who had at one time been a captain in the British Army, was put in charge of the town of Wexford itself by the rebels. Whether or not as a result of these appointments, some signs of stratagem now appeared in the rebel army – numbering by this time perhaps some sixteen thousand men. It split into three columns, one moving westwards under its new commander-in-chief to the important town of New Ross, whose capture would open the way to the large bodies of Defenders known to exist in Kilkenny and Waterford. Another column moved north to the town of Bunclody (or Newtownbarry) in an attempt to penetrate into County Wicklow. A third moved north-west towards Gorey and Arklow and the road to Dublin.

On 5 June one of the three decisive battles of the rebellion in Wexford took place at New Ross. The rebel army of about three thousand men, under Bagenal Harvey, had already delayed in camp for three days on the nearby hill of Carrickbyrne, behind which it had spent some time trying out artillery captured from the military at Three Rocks and elsewhere. Now, on the 5th it finally attacked in force, driving before it, in antique Irish military style, herds of cattle which most successfully overran the loyal outposts and enabled the rebels themselves to penetrate into the heart of the town. There the battle raged backwards and forwards through the streets for thirteen hours. An officer of the garrison, writing next day, said the rebel attack was as severe as could possibly have been made by men fighting with such primitive weapons, and that they gave proofs of 'very extraordinary courage and enthusiasm'.[33] Thomas Cloney, who now held a position of command over some five hundred men, described it as a battle fought entirely without tactics on both sides: '... two confused masses of men, struggling alternately to drive the other back by force alone'.[34]

The rebels, who suffered from some desertions before the assault, were, as Cloney admits, unamenable to discipline throughout, and the initial attack, which had been intended simply to be a shock assault, turned into a tumultuous uncontrolled advance of everyone who felt like joining in. Once in the town the rebels displayed a fatal tendency to be distracted by liquor. Cloney has a particular rebuke for one small group who made a cask of port their base in an entrenched position just outside the town, from which they occasionally sallied forth to inquire, 'How goes the day, boys?' before safely retreating again to their source of courage. He singles out for praise a woodcutter's daughter named Doyle, who was always in the thick of the fight, distinguishing herself particularly by cutting off with a small billhook the cross belts of twenty-eight fallen dragoons and distributing their cartridge boxes to her friends. Cloney also pays tribute to the fighting qualities of his enemies in the Clare militia, almost all of whom must have been Catholics and who held their positions against him throughout the day. A young United Irish colonel, who led the first rebel assault, was John Kelly, a blacksmith from Killan. He was to become the hero of a popular ballad in later times when these bloody events acquired the rather fusty veneer appropriate to the drawing-room heroics of purely political warfare.

After thirteen hours, in which they had more than once looked like gaining the town, the rebels withdrew. Their losses were heavy, though probably nowhere near the figure of two thousand which some loyalist writers suggest. Among those killed on the rebel side was a Mr John Boxwell, a Protestant gentleman of some property. Among the hundred or so loyalist troops killed was Lord Mountjoy who, as Luke Gardiner twenty years before, had carried through the Irish House of Commons the first Catholic Relief Bill, permitting Catholics once again to own land.

On the same day as the battle of New Ross a massacre of Protestant prisoners took place in the barn at Scullabogue. It is thought that rebels flying from the battle with news of slaughter and defeat helped to work up a hysterical frenzy against them. The barn was set on fire and men, women and children inside it burned to death while others were executed on the lawn with pikes. Dinah Goff, the fourteen-year-old daughter of the local Quaker family, heard the screams and smelled the appalling stench a mile and a half away. The number said to have perished varies in different accounts but was possibly around two hundred.

Again, given the crude simplicity of the average Irish peasant of the day, it is not difficult to see how such atrocities came about. For weeks they had either experienced at first hand, or heard from those who had, examples of the most brutal physical cruelty on the part of the military. These were quite enough to sustain all the wild rumours of Orange atrocities and plots to annihilate all Catholics. What was surprising was not that such massacres occurred but that they did not occur more often. The crude state of mind of the average rebel is well illustrated by evidence from the various trials which eventually followed massacres such as that at Scullabogue. One of those responsible for the murders there, on hearing the cries and lamentations of the bereaved in a nearby village, came up to one of the women and threatened her that if he heard any more they would all go the way of their husbands. A few days later he solemnly gave the same woman a pass to have herself baptized a Catholic, for, he said, 'they must all be of one religion, it was that they were fighting for'.[35]

The other two rebel columns met with no more final success than the one which, under Harvey, had tried to take New Ross. But the Arklow column rambling in the general direction of Dublin gave the government at least one fright, at Tuberneering, before it was turned back. Here, as whenever they fought at all, the rebels fought with courage and tenacity, and, though displaying a typical characteristic of inexperienced troops in frequently firing too high, they made good tactical use of hedges and other natural cover. They decisively defeated a body of the king's troops, killing or taking prisoner over a hundred of them, largely through the skilful exploitation of a good ambush position. What, however, was even more typical of the rebels was their delay after their victory of several days spent looting and drinking before pressing on to attack the key town of Arklow on 9 June.

Yet when they did finally attack, they not only disposed themselves skilfully but fought with almost absurd dash and bravado. One young Irish loyalist who fought at Arklow thus described them:

... about 4 o'clock all of us at our posts I first saw in a moment thousands appear on the top of ditches forming one great and regular circular line from the Gorey road through the fields quite round to the Sand Banks near the sea as thick as they could stand. They all put their hats on their pikes and gave most dreadful yells. I could clearly distinguish their leaders riding through their ranks with flags flying . . .[36]

Among these leaders was Father Michael Murphy, who two months before, like his namesake Father John from Boulavogue, had been prepared to swear allegiance to the Crown.

Grape shot among the rebels 'tumbled them by twenties'. But the gaps in their ranks were immediately re-filled and they came on like madmen.

Another of the king's soldiers at Arklow also describes the rebels coming at him with green flags flying and how one of their officers galloped ahead waving his hat and shouting: 'Blood and wounds, my boys! Come on, the town is ours!'[37] until, turning a corner into the mouth of a cannon, he and his horse were sent sprawling into the dust by a volley of muskets and bayonets and a final bullet in the head finished him off. The priest, Michael Murphy, was killed within thirty yards of the loyalist lines.

Bravery was not enough. The rebel tactics in anything like an open battle were unsubtle, their marksmanship inaccurate and their weapons inferior. Though they had some cannon of their own at Arklow, captured from the North Antrim militia at Tuberneering, it seems to have fired too high for much of the time, since the rebels had no artillerymen of their own and had to force prisoners taken with the guns to operate them, which they seem to have done to minimum effect. By eight o'clock in the evening the loyalist army still stood their ground, though there had already been some talk of their retreat. But the rebels, now short of ammunition, themselves withdrew, with what one of them afterwards described as 'a sulky reluctance'.[38] The battle, regarded by the contemporary historian Gordon as the most important in the whole rebellion, was over.

A third strong rebel column, consisting of about 2,500 men, had set out for Bunclody (Newtownbarry) in County Wicklow under the command of another redoubtable priest, called Father Kearns. He was a man so physically enormous that when, years before, in the course of a visit to France during the Terror he had been hanged from a lamp-post, the lamp-iron had bent under his weight and he had been saved from strangulation by his toes touching the pavement. His strength was, however, of little avail at Newtownbarry. There his followers drove the King's County militia from the town, then abandoned themselves to plunder and drunkenness on such a scale that they proved an easy prey to the counter-attack which expelled them with much slaughter.

Meanwhile, such coherent leadership as Beauchamp Bagenal Harvey had temporarily represented had collapsed. His bizarre command had only lasted a few days. Returning to his camp on Carrickbyrne Hill after the battle of New Ross he was appalled to hear the news of what had happened at Scullabogue. He immediately issued an edict from his headquarters which reveals the true state of that army over which he was trying to exercise discipline. After laying down that all 'loiterers' found still at home should be brought to join the army on pain of death, and equally threatening death to all officers who deserted their men, all who left their respective quarters when 'halted by their commander-in-chief ... unless they shall have leave from their officers for doing so' and all who did not turn in plunder to headquarters, he finally dealt with the appalling event that had taken place that day, declaring that 'any person or persons who shall take upon them to kill or murder any person or prisoner, burn any house, or commit any plunder, without special written orders from the commander-in-chief, shall suffer death'.[39] Though it could be maintained that this order came late in the day and that the event at Scullabogue might have been foreseen, at least one body of Protestant prisoners had reason to be grateful for it. It seems certain that twenty-one Protestants would have been massacred at Gorey after the battle of Arklow but for the arrival in time there of the order from Carrickbyrne. Since there was, however, nothing in the order about applying the torture of the pitch-cap to prisoners, this was proceeded with – a significant enough comment in itself on the motive of revenge behind such atrocities. Even at this simple level, however, the lust for vengeance was by no means always indulged. On one occasion, when a Quaker found a group of rebels about to flog a man suspected of being an informer they agreed to desist, declaring that 'though they had received very grievous treatment they ought not to return evil for evil'.[40] And the clergyman who had watched the battle for Enniscorthy through his spy-glass later commented: 'In justice

I must allow that the rebels often displayed humanity and generosity deserving of praise and admiration.'[41]

Whether on account of the excessive humanitarianism of his edict or simply because he had lost the battle of New Ross the day before, the rebels now deposed Harvey from his rank of military commander-in-chief, and his place was taken by Father Roche, who had been the victor at Tuberneering. Harvey continued to head the rather tenuous apparatus of rebel civic government which had its seat in Wexford town, but he was becoming a desperate man. Only two days after his deposition, when a fellow-Protestant wrote to him beseeching a 'protection', Harvey replied:

I from my heart wish to protect all property; I can scarce protect myself. ... I took my present situation in hopes of doing good and preventing mischief and had my advice been taken by those in power the present mischief would never have arisen. ... God knows where the business will end, but end how it will the good men of both parties will inevitably be ruined.[42]

And according to Mrs Brownrigg, the genteel Protestant lady who had failed to escape from Wexford town, he told her that 'he had no real command and that they were a set of savages exceeding all descriptions'.[43]

In the short run, there could now only be one end to the rebellion: inexorable destruction of the rebel forces by loyalist troops. This took place in the course of a few weeks. After one particularly frightful scene of last-minute massacre on the wooden bridge at Wexford, in the course of which perhaps a hundred Protestants were either shot or piked and tossed writhing from the ends of pikes into the waters of the River Slaney below, the rebels withdrew from the town to face a concerted government attack on their main camp at Vinegar Hill on 21 June. It was a strong position, with what a loyalist eye-witness described as the rebels' 'green flag of defiance' flying from the remains of the old windmill.[44] Another witness recounts how the rebels themselves began the battle while the Crown forces under General Lake were still waiting for reinforcements. Lake then fired eighty or ninety 'bomb-shells' into their ranks, carrying 'death in a variety of awful forms to the terrified and wondering multitude' who, according to this witness, were soon crying out, 'We can stand anything but those guns which fire twice.'[45] An assault was then ordered and after a two-hour climb, during which the rebels kept up a smart but irregular fire on the attackers, the summit was stormed with shouts of 'Long Live King George!' and 'Down with Republicanism!' The rebel standard was seized and trampled underfoot. The cannon were drawn up and brought into action and as the rebels retreated down the hill they 'fell like mown grass'.[46] A considerable number of rebels escaped owing to a gap in the Crown forces' ring of encirclement, but it was the beginning of the end.

11

Collapse of United Irishmen

Of those rebels who escaped from Vinegar Hill on 21 June 1798, one sizeable body, which included Father John Murphy, made its way into County Kilkenny, hoping to find fresh support there. But though they won a short engagement at Goresbridge and actually occupied the mining town of Castlecomer in that county for a few hours, there was small sign of the Kilkenny Defenders or anyone else rising to join them, and they even found themselves plundered and preyed on by the local inhabitants. They had no alternative but to withdraw again, and suffered a particularly bloody final rout when their base camp on Kilcomney Hill was stormed by government troops on 26 June. An officer in one of the yeomanry units, who helped to defeat them, has described how the remnants of this rebel force then made their way in disorder into Meath, Westmeath and Louth, 'harassed beyond all example' and leaving behind them a trail of half-eaten sheep and bullocks from which they often did not even have time to strip the skin or remove the entrails.[1] 'The people in the counties they marched into', he wrote, 'refused to join them as they saw their cause was desperate.'[2]

The rest of the Wexford rebels were soon in an equally hopeless situation. They disintegrated into bands of varying sizes, mainly making their way northwards as best they could and taking refuge principally in the mountainous country of County Wicklow, under two powerful local leaders, Joseph Holt (a radical Protestant farmer) and Michael Dwyer (a Catholic). One group operated for a shorter time in Kildare under the leadership of William Aylmer, the twenty-two-year-old son of a Protestant gentleman of some property in that county. Though the latter force was quite soon suppressed and Aylmer himself came in to surrender on the promise that his life would be spared,* the bands in Wicklow were much more difficult to dislodge, and long presented a considerable nuisance to the government with their constant raids on houses for arms and occasional sorties against government troops. (Dwyer did not surrender until 1803.) Yet they presented no serious threat to the political stability of Ireland. All signs of that had disappeared within six weeks of the rebellion's outbreak. By 1 July Cornwallis, the lord

---

* He subsequently had an adventurous military career with Bolivar in South America.

lieutenant, was writing to one of his generals that there was not the least need for all the English regiments they were sending.[3] The Buckinghamshire and Warwickshire militias which had already arrived were quite enough, provided there was no French invasion. Cornwallis added significantly: 'The violence of our friends, and their folly in endeavouring to make it a religious war, added to the ferocity of our troops who delight in murder, most powerfully counteract all pleas of conciliation.'

The behaviour of his own troops was now to present Cornwallis with almost as much of a problem as the rebels had done. It was his policy to issue written certificates of pardon (popularly known as 'Cornys') to all rank and file among the rebels who were prepared to surrender within fourteen days and accept them. But as Sir John Moore, engaged in mopping up operations in Wicklow, observed: 'They would have done this sooner had it not been for the violence and atrocity of the yeomen, who shot many after they had received protections and burned houses and committed the most unpardonable acts.'[4] The whole mopping up procedure, in fact, was if anything an even bloodier business than anything that had taken place during or before the rebellion itself.

The officer who pursued the fugitives from Kilcomney Hill into Meath and beyond reported that the king's troops 'never gave quarter in the rebellion ... hundreds and thousands of wretches were butchered while unarmed on their knees begging mercy; and it is difficult to say whether [regular] soldiers, yeomen or militia men took most delight in their bloody work'.[5] In such actions as he saw, all the male inhabitants of any house in which the rebels took refuge were put to death and the German contingent in the king's army, Hessians commanded by a Count Hompech, won fame for their rape and slaughter of women.* The same officer reckons that altogether 25,000 rebels and peaceable inhabitants were killed in this way, 'by the lowest calculation', and the Protestant historian, Gordon, in trying to assess the total number of people killed on both sides in the whole rebellion and reaching the tentative figure of 50,000, says he 'has reason to think that more men than fell in battle were killed in cold blood'.[6]

The more humane members of the government were appalled by what happened as the rebellion disintegrated. Cornwallis, the lord lieutenant and commander-in-chief, applied his strictures equally to foreigners, the militia and the yeomanry. Of the latter he wrote that they had 'saved the country, but ... now take the lead in rapine and murder'.[7]

At least for the leaders of the rebellion certain formalities of retribution were reserved, though these were often, in accordance with the custom of

---

* The government has been so universally reviled in nationalist historical tradition for its use of German troops in the rebellion of 1798 that it is interesting to note that Wolfe Tone himself had envisaged the use of German troops in Ireland as part of an invading army. (See Tone (ed.), *Tone*, ii, p. 235.)

the day, barbarous enough. Father John Murphy, taken soon after the rout at Kilcomney, was hanged at Tullow, his body burned in a tar barrel and his head set upon a spike in one of the main streets. In Wexford itself, courts-martial began their work immediately after the liberation of the town. Bagenal Harvey, the earnest intellectual radical of many years' standing, with long face and expressive eyes, who had so recently been sporting a pair of silver epaulettes on his ordinary clothes,[8] was now ignominiously hauled out of a cave on the Saltee islands in which he had taken refuge and given the inevitable death sentence. He pleaded in extenuation of treason the fact that he had hoped by his leadership to save lives and property. But this, as smaller fry were to find, was a dangerously double-edged plea, being accepted as often as not as conclusive proof of a rebel's authority and influence rather than of his humanity. Harvey can hardly have expected to be spared. He, together with Matthew Keogh, the rebel Wexford town governor who had once been a British Army officer, and Father Roche were all hanged on 1 July off Wexford Bridge, a place of grisly and vengeful associations which, when the loyalist army moved in ten days earlier, had been covered in human blood from the massacre of Protestants the previous day, its rails everywhere indented with bullet holes and vicious pike thrusts.[9] The bodies of Harvey, Keogh and Roche were thrown into the River Slaney below and their heads impaled upon pikes over the court-house where they remained for several weeks.[10]

There was one rather remarkable exception to the general blood-letting. It illustrates the vast gap between those who planned the theory of the rebellion and those who gave it its crude unsophisticated reality. For in prison in Dublin were some seventy of the political élite of the United Irishmen, including all the members of the Leinster Executive taken in March at Oliver Bond's house and elsewhere, and among them Arthur O'Connor, Thomas Emmet, William MacNeven, Samuel Neilson and other leaders of the movement. Few had as yet been tried, but the execution of one man had already taken place and that of Bond himself was due shortly. The fate of the others against whom the government had massive evidence would in the course of time have been inevitable. However, seeing that the rebellion had wholly collapsed and hoping to avert all further bloodshed as well as their own, O'Connor, Emmet and MacNeven agreed, with the concurrence of the other prisoners, to divulge to the government all they knew of the origins of the United Irish movement. The conditions were, first, that they should not be obliged to name any individuals and, second, that they should thereafter be allowed to exile themselves to a country of their own choice outside the United Kingdom. The compact was agreed to by the government, and though there were to be mutual recriminations of breaches of faith over details, in its essentials it was kept. Bond himself was saved from the gallows just in time (though he died almost immediately afterwards of a heart attack).

The other prisoners were never brought to trial, but after a prolonged period of relaxed imprisonment in Fort George in Scotland (the cause of accusations of bad faith against the government on the part of the prisoners, who had anticipated immediate release) they were allowed in 1802, at the time of the Peace of Amiens, to go to France. From there, some, including Emmet and MacNeven, subsequently moved to America. Emmet became State Attorney of New York, MacNeven a distinguished American physician. O'Connor became a general in the French Army.

For those who had actually taken up arms and who may often not even have heard of their would-be political leaders, a very different sort of fate was in store, even if they did manage to escape the gallows or the unlicensed butchery that now raged in Ireland. Some were handed over, by government arrangement, as slaves to the King of Prussia; others, often after severe floggings, were transported to the fleet or to the new penal colonies in New South Wales.

The disclosures made to the British Government by the imprisoned conspirators revealed little it did not already know by means of its excellent informer network. But the government was at least enabled to make the information public for propaganda purposes, without jeopardizing its sources. The amount of light people like O'Connor and Emmet were able to throw on the primitive mass movement which had provided the main source of energy for the rebellion was of course minimal. Even such revelations as they could make about their connections with the Defenders were sketchy and vague in the extreme, for the simple reason that these connections themselves had always been sketchy and vague. The account of their negotiations with the French was much more explicit, though the details were already largely known to the government through its spies.

The United Irishmen's wary attitude to French help was emphasized by MacNeven, who declared that, 'faithful to the principle of Irish independence', the amount of French help the executive had worked for had been 'what they deemed just sufficient to liberate their country, but incompetent to subdue it'.[11] They also made other statements which throw a useful light on the nature of that Irish republican separatism which they now bequeathed as an idea to posterity. Thus, in MacNeven's evidence there is a sudden almost inspired glance into the future, and to one Irish crisis 123 years later in particular, when he says in his public examination before the House of Lords:

'... I am now and always have been of the opinion, that if we were an independent republic, and Britain ceased to be formidable to us, our interest would require an intimate connexion with her.'[12]

The unsectarian nature of republican theory as opposed to the rebel practice was spelt out by MacNeven who, when asked if it had not been the intention to establish the Roman Catholic Church in Ireland, replied that he would as soon establish Mahomedanism.[13]

Emmet, also before the Lords, faced up frankly enough to this gap between the theory and reality of the new Irish nationalism. Of the issue of Parliamentary Reform, which had after all been the mainspring of the whole United Irish movement, he said: 'I don't think the common people ever think of it, until it is inculcated into them that a reform would cause a removal of those grievances which they actually do feel.'[14] And as far as the poor were concerned, he put Catholic Emancipation, which by now meant little more than the fight for Catholics to sit in Parliament and occupy high offices of state, into the same category. He said he didn't think it mattered 'a feather' to the common people, or that they ever thought of it.[15] Asked by the Speaker if it were not so that 'the object next their hearts was a separation and a republic', Emmet replied: 'Pardon me, the object next their hearts was a redress of their grievances.' He said that if such an object could be accomplished peaceably, 'they would prefer it infinitely to a revolution and a republic'. This remains a sound enough definition of Irish 'nationalism' as it was to be found among the bulk of the Irish population for the next century and more.

Much heroic phrase and ballad-making later went to enshrine the memorable events of 1798 as a classic example of a small subject nation's struggle for freedom. But though often punctuated by heroism, these events can be seen on any objective reading to have grown out of a much more complex and subtle social situation than any plain heroic confrontation of nationalities. Perhaps the ballad of 1798 that best expresses the true mood of confusion and desperation in that pathetic year is one which significantly does not even mention the United Irishmen at all, but is entitled 'The Banished Defender'.

> ... For the sake of my religion I was forced to leave my native home,
> I've been a bold defender and a member of the Church of Rome,
> ... They swore I was a traitor and a leader of the Papist band,
> For which I'm in cold irons, a convict in Van Diemen's Land.
>
> Right well I do remember when I was taken in New Ross
> The day after the battle as the Green Mount Ferry I did cross,
> The guards they did surround me and my bundle searched upon the spot,
> And there they found my green coat, my pike, two pistols and some shot.
>
> The reason that they banished me, the truth I mean to tell you here,
> Because I was head leader of Father Murphy's Shelmaliers,
> And for being a Roman Catholic I was trampled on by Harry's breed,
> For fighting in defence of my God, my country and my creed.
>
> Transubstantiation is the faith that we depend upon
> Look and you will find it in the sixth Chapter of St John ...

And yet somewhere in the desperation that had made that simple Irish-man take up arms, driven either by the need for social self-justification or simple self-defence, there had developed through the organization of the Defenders a crude and confused notion of an independent Irish patriotism. Not only Tone and his friends, in the sophisticated style of the political theorist, but also the semi-literate Defender had learnt, in these years, to think of themselves for the first time as somehow fighting for their country when they opposed its established order.

On the Saturday after the battle of Arklow fifteen rebel prisoners were, so a contemporary writer records, 'all hanged together out of the same tree'. They were made to hang each other. Before this dance of death took place a young bandsman of the militia who was watching called out to the rebels: 'For decency's sake, for religion's sake, and for your precious souls' sake, reflect properly on your awful passage into eternity and be reconciled to your Saviour.'

Whereupon one of the rebels called back to him:

'You be damned! I die in a good cause: I die fighting for my country and shall go to heaven; and you will go to hell for fighting against it.'[16]

In this simple answer a new emerging patriotism in Ireland seems plain enough. Yet a confusing element, and one which these men had no time left to ponder, though it was to confuse other Irishmen for generations, was that the bandsman (probably as firm a believer in transubstantiation as any Defender) considered that in supporting the established order he was fighting for his country too.

On 8 July 1798, some six weeks only after the outbreak of the rebellion, Cornwallis had summed up the military situation for the benefit of the British minister, Portland. The only rebel forces still in arms were, he wrote, (1) in Wicklow, where parties of five thousand or so, armed mainly with pikes, were at large; (2) on the northern boundaries of Wexford (where die-hard deserters from the militia had taken to the woods); and (3) in Kildare and on the borders of Meath and County Dublin – the latter being small parties which burned and murdered and then retired to the shelter of the bogs. By the end of July he could report that the rebellion in Kildare was over. And by the middle of August, in spite of the continued existence of the Wicklow bands under Holt and Dwyer, he could report temporarily that the county now had 'a quiet and settled appearance'.[17] In fact, things were settling back into that fairly normal state of armed peasant lawlessness which Ireland had more or less taken for granted for half a century and which was to continue to pass for normality for almost a century more.

The absence of serious repercussions of the rebellion in other parts of Ireland had been one of its most curious and fortunate aspects for the government. On the day of Vinegar Hill, a small rising of sorts had taken place between Bandon and Clonakilty in County Cork, but, though it was to inspire a heroic monument of a pikeman in Clonakilty a hundred years later, the real event was concerned more with the rescue of some prisoners than any serious attempt to coordinate with the Wexford rebels, and, as Cornwallis remarked, the rescue of prisoners by bodies of Whiteboys or Defenders was 'a practice not unusual in this country'.[18]

As already seen, the calculated attempt by the force who escaped from Vinegar Hill to raise the country in Kilkenny was an ignominious failure. What Cornwallis called 'an appearance of insurrection'[19] in Tipperary, taking place in July, well after the main rebellion was over, was quickly crushed, and again significant, if of anything, of a return to normal unrest. In only one other part of Ireland, apart from Leinster, had there been any attempt at serious rebellion and that had been remarkable not for the fact that it took place but that it took place so half-heartedly and ineffectually. For it was, after all, in the North, in Ulster, that the whole concept of an Irish republican rebellion to be brought about by a union of Irishmen of every class and creed had first been planned.

'The quiet of the North is to me unaccountable,' the government Under-Secretary Cooke had written on 2 June,[20] as the full momentum of the Wexford rebellion began to reveal itself. And Wolfe Tone in France, where details of the events in Ireland only arrived late, wrote incredulously as the news at last began to pour in: 'In all this business I do not see one syllable about the North, which astonishes me more than I can express. Are they afraid? Have they changed their opinions? What can be the cause of their passive submission, at this moment, so little suited to their former zeal and energy?'[21]

In two respects the United Irishmen had always lived in a world of illusion. First, they had too gladly assumed that the union of Catholic and Protestant which their theory proclaimed was automatically achieved by proclaiming it. Second, their actual mechanism of conspiracy was similarly less effective in practice than in theory.

With the arrests at Oliver Bond's house in March, coordination between any National Executive in Dublin and the Provincial Committee in Ulster clearly became much more difficult, while between the higher and lower committees in Ulster itself coordination seems to have broken down altogether. A United Irishman, who later escaped to America, wrote, in his account of 'the Republican Army' of Down during May 1798:

In that month several communications from the Executive relative to the Insurrection had been communicated. Special orders with respect to the Counties had been given in the Commissions to the Adjutant Generals – these Orders on account of the supineness of the Adjutant Generals were not universally communicated, but in your county they were diffused and their good effect was lost by the ignorance or supineness of the subaltern officers . . .[22]

Also, he said, the procedure for filling gaps in the ranks after an arrest was inadequate, so that such arrests 'threw the whole battalion into disorder, and in the moment of embodying [i.e.mobilizing] proved of infinite disadvantage, for instead of the force meeting at any point in collected or organized bodies, they met more by accident than by design – and they were in no better order than a mere country mob . . .'[23]

There was also little effective coordination between various county committees. In the end, the two strongest counties, Antrim and Down, conducted risings not only independent of what was happening in Wexford, but also independent of each other. The leaders of these only took up their commands at the very last moment. The originally designated leader in County Antrim, theoretically 'commander-in-chief' for all Ulster, actually resigned on 1 June, the day after the rebels in the South had taken Wexford, but before anything had happened in the North at all. His place was taken by Henry Joy McCracken, a Presbyterian cotton manufacturer who had helped found the first open society of United Irishmen with Neilson, Russell and Tone many years before, and at whose ship bearing the Crown above the Irish harp on its insignia they had once all jeered in such carefree fashion.*

In County Down, the designated leader was arrested on 5 June, also before he had taken the field, and his post was filled haphazardly by a prosperous Episcopalian draper, Henry Monro, only a day before the rising in that county finally broke out.

This sort of confusion did not augur well for the future, and in both Antrim and Down the risings ended quickly in disaster. McCracken's men in Antrim, after capturing Randalstown and looking for a while as if they might take Antrim town, were eventually driven out and bloodily dispersed. The dead and wounded were left on the streets for two days and were then cleared away together in carts and dumped into sand-pits near the lake. A land agent who watched one such cartload arriving at the pits heard an officer of the yeomanry ask the driver:

'Where the devil did these rascals come from?'

A feeble voice from the cart itself replied:

'I come frae Ballybofey.'

The entire load was buried together.[24]

Well might the historian Lecky, writing innocently long before the horrors of the twentieth century, comment on the events of this year in Ireland: 'In reading such narratives we seem transported from the close of the eighteenth century to distant and darker ages, in which the first conditions of civilized society had not yet been attained and to which its maxims and reasonings are unapplicable.'[25]

Three days after the defeat at Antrim, the Down rebels under Monro took the field. Arrayed on a hill-top like the Wexford rebels, armed mainly with

* See above, p. 55.

pikes and wearing their Sunday clothes with green ribbons and cockades in their hats, while some of the leaders wore green coats of military cut with yellow facings, and, like the Wexford rebels, depleted by wayward desertions on the eve of battle, they were routed by the king's troops after a fierce fight at Ballinahinch on 12 June.[26] There were a few other, uncoordinated appearances of rebels in arms (sometimes carrying only pitchforks) at different points in the counties of Down and Antrim, with skirmishes at Saintfield and Ballymena, but with the battle at Ballinahinch the rising in the North, for so long the great hope of Irish revolutionaries and the dread of the government, was over. It had given far less trouble than the simple protest of the desperate Wexford peasantry into whose heads the idea of a republican rebellion had barely entered a few short weeks before.

As in the South, great slaughter and savagery followed the northern rebels' defeat. In the town of Antrim after the battle there, a Quaker described the men of the Monaghan and Tipperary militia who cleared it as acting 'with great cruelty, neither distinguishing friends nor enemies.... Numbers who were not in any way concerned lost their lives, for the soldiers showed pity to none ...'[27] And when this awful ordeal of liberation was over, 'people were to be seen here and there saluting their neighbours, like those who survived a pestilence or an earthquake, as if they were glad to see each other alive after the recent calamity ...'[28] Both McCracken and Monro were soon taken and executed.

This almost unbelievably ineffectual performance by rebel Ulster, birth-place of the whole United Irish movement, must be explained by something more than mere haphazard organization and incompetence. To a large extent, certainly, the heart had already gone out of the movement in Ulster in 1797, when the severity of the government's military measures, coupled with conditional offers of pardon, had proved so effective. Another factor already operating then had been disillusionment with the French. France's increasingly unidealistic and cynical attitude to small nations like the Swiss and Genovese, together with their repeated inability to put in an effective appearance in Ireland, combined to make many republicans abandon hope of French support altogether, and without French support republican hope itself easily seemed unrealistic. But the most important factor of all in deter-mining the northern débâcle was the large-scale reversion to the standard Protestant–Catholic rivalry which had persisted as one of the ever-present factors of life in the North.

The rebellion in the South had, in a most acute form, laid bare that deep division between Dissenter and Catholic which the United Irishmen had so long done their best to paper over in the interests of new political strength. It had already been noted by observers that where Protestant United Irish-men in the North had been persuaded to give up the conspiracy, either by force or cajolement or a mixture of the two, they reverted easily to their former sectarian attitudes, and going to the other extreme tended to express their old radicalism in the new Orange Society. Now, the insurrection in the South had revealed from the start an almost exclusively Catholic character. Worse than that, it had revealed a distinctly anti-Protestant bias. News of some of the massacres of Protestants on Vinegar Hill and of the murders in the barn at Scullabogue had reached the North before either McCracken's or Monro's forces took to arms in Antrim and Down. Many of those old radical volunteer corps who had shocked Neilson and Tone in the early days with their 'Peep o' Day Boy' principles, but who had eventually been persuaded to sink these in the new principles of the United Irishmen, must now have felt that if Vinegar Hill and Scullabogue were what the United Irishmen stood for, then they were on the wrong side after all.

It is significant that even in those rebel forces in the North which did take the field there, dissension was reported between the regiments of the Defenders and those of the United Irishmen with whom they nominally associated. A song of the time which celebrates an unsuccessful attempt to take Glenarm Castle in Antrim expresses Defender resentment in terms which cast an odd light on the idealistic patriotic cause in which they were supposed to be united:

> Treachery, treachery, damnable treachery!
> Put the poor Catholics all in the front,
> The Protestants next was the way they were fixed
> And the black-mouthed Dissenters they skulked at the rump.

This was all a far cry from those edifying principles of united brotherhood for which the United Irishmen had nominally taken up arms, and on which Tone and others had relied to establish a new sense of Irish nationality and their country's independence.

12

The French Landing

A significant postscript to the rebellion was still to come. It revealed once again how little any coherent idea of nationality was as yet an indigenous Irish political force. It also brought to a sombre end the adventures of Wolfe Tone.

For all the United Irishmen's chronic optimism, they had generally regarded French military help as essential to a successful revolution in Ireland. All their other hopes had been built on it. And the failure of the French to appear in 1797 or in the early months of 1798 had done much to weaken such revolutionary enthusiasm as existed in a movement that in any case always contained more desperation than political consciousness. When the rebels finally did chaotically take the field, uncoordinated as they were with their own leaders, they had no contacts at all with the French. The men of Wexford thought of the French chiefly to revile them for leaving them in the lurch.

Tone himself had spent the early part of the summer with the immobile French invasion fleet at Le Havre, increasingly despondent. Now, in August 1798, such rebellion as had been able to gain momentum was crushed, and the slaughter of the rebels was proceeding so methodically that at least one gaoler felt the need to invent for himself a gallows which would hang thirty at a time.* It may therefore seem the final disastrous absurdity that at this, of all moments, the French should send another expedition to Ireland, and one which this time succeeded at last in landing on Irish soil.

Yet the idea of the expedition was in many ways a credit to the French. If the state of Irish national feeling had been as positive as Tone, O'Connor and others had repeatedly represented it, the plan would not have been unreasonable. For the events of May and June, though terrible and disappointing, could be expected to have inflamed the Irish national spirit still further. It was true that the resolution with which the Catholic militia had fought rebels of their own class and creed in the king's name had been disconcerting, yet even Tone, when insisting that the militia would come over to a man, had always made the arrival of a French force a necessary proviso.

* 'I hate this dribble drabble work', he told an English militia officer in Kilkenny, meaning hanging in ones and twos. (*Diary of Captain Hodges*. BM Add. MSS. 40,166.)

All the French did now was to put to a final test the theories of militant Irish nationality to which they had been converted.

Bonaparte, who after the death of Hoche had inherited the notion of an invasion of Ireland as part of the Directory's strategic outlook, had been at best non-committal about it when he met Tone in January 1798. But for the next few weeks at least most serious preparations were continued for a major assault on the British Isles. And though Kent and Sussex were clearly in Bonaparte's mind more than Ireland, it is unlikely that, had that assault been launched, some part of it would not have been concerned with Ireland if only as a diversion. In any case, even a descent on Kent and Sussex might have been expected to have important repercussions in Ireland. The preparations were on a vast scale. The whole of the Channel coast from Antwerp to Cherbourg had been turned into a vast naval area, and other work was proceeding in the Atlantic ports of Brest and La Rochelle.

Why then, knowing as the French did at this time that a rebellion of sorts was about to break out in Ireland, did they not strike immediately in support of it?

The answer is that just before the rebellion's haphazard outbreak, the French Directory, for whom Ireland was always only one factor in a vastly complex strategic situation, had been persuaded by Bonaparte to change their strategy altogether. An inspection of the Channel in February had convinced Bonaparte that France was not within sight of that mastery of the sea which he considered essential for a successful invasion.[1] He persuaded the Directory to switch their attention towards the East. An Army of the Orient was created in April, drawing its strength from the former Army of England, and late in May, as the Irish rebellion lumbered into the open, Bonaparte himself sailed for Egypt.

But, having completed this major readjustment of strategy, the Directory remained honourably true, at least in spirit, to their recent assurances to Tone and Lewins. In July they finally issued the orders containing plans 'to bring help to the Irish who have taken up arms to shake off the yoke of British domination'.[2] Three small separate expeditions were to carry troops, arms and ammunition to the help of the Irish simultaneously by different routes: some light vessels with émigré Irishmen on board were to sail from the Channel ports, another expedition was to leave from Rochefort (by La Rochelle) and a third – the largest, with about three thousand men – from Brest. The overall command of this 'Army of Ireland' was given to General Hardy, and of the naval arrangements to Admiral Bompard stationed at Brest. The instructions ended with an exhortation to do everything to encourage Irish morale by keeping up a hate for the name of England, and at the same time to preserve a discipline which would be a model to the Irish troops who, it must not be forgotten, were 'their persecuted brothers fighting in a common cause'.[3] No expedition, concluded the orders, could have greater influence on the political situation in Europe. Command of that part of the expedition which was to sail from Rochefort was given to a general named Humbert.

Humbert was a true son of the Revolution. Then a man of thirty, of peasant stock, he had risen from the ranks and had fought in Europe, in the Vendée and at Quiberon Bay. He had taken part in Hoche's Bantry Bay expedition of 1796, sailing in the ship *Les Droits de l'Homme* which was intercepted by the British on the return journey and wrecked with the loss of some 1,200 of its 1,800 men. In 1797 Humbert had put up to the Directory ideas for what would now be called commando-type expeditions to be landed in Scotland or Cornwall, and he may have been disappointed not to have been given overall command of the new expedition to Ireland. In any case, he seemed determined to seize the major share of whatever glory was to be had from the enterprise. Held up in port like the other two parts of the expedition for lack of cash, due to the bureaucratic delays of the French Treasury, Humbert succeeded in raising the money himself from local sources, and on 6 August 1798 set sail for Ireland independently with his three frigates, and just over a thousand officers and men, together with some five thousand stand of extra arms and a number of spare French uniforms.

Though audacious, his action was not as absurd as hindsight may make it seem. He knew that the other forces of the invasion were about to follow him to the north-west corner of Ireland. He knew that the force which was sailing from the Channel ports was specially designed to bring extra supplies to those Irish whom his own arrival should bring out in insurrection. Above all he assumed, and this was the premise on which the whole concept of the enterprise was based (for Tone and his friends had done their work well), that the Irish people, though they might have suffered a terrible setback two months earlier, must be only waiting for the chance to rise *en masse* again. After experience of the *chouannerie* in the Vendée his military thinking was particularly attuned to the idea of fast-moving commando-type forays behind the enemy lines. And personally he was a very brave man. In any case, the omens seemed on his side. For Humbert's expedition began with a brilliantly successful evasion of a large British squadron that was patrolling for the French ships just outside Rochefort.

Sixteen days later, on 22 August 1798, at about two o'clock in the afternoon, three men o' war flying the British flag appeared in the Bay of Killala, a small town in County Mayo which was the seat of both a Protestant and a Catholic bishopric. Two sons of the Protestant bishop were among those who eagerly pushed off in small boats to examine the new arrivals. One British Army officer who had himself only just arrived in Killala to take over command of the garrison there rowed out to offer them a catch of fish he had made on his way from Sligo. He arrived on board to find himself surrounded by Frenchmen and made their prisoner. By the ruse of flying the British flag, Humbert's expedition had achieved total surprise.[4]

The French, who on the last few days of their voyage had experienced rough weather and had been unable to get in at their first choice of landing point, Donegal Bay, must have had the disastrous anticlimax of Bantry Bay two years earlier very much in their minds. This small force of about a thousand men now disembarked immediately with efficiency and speed, hidden from the town of Killala itself by a chain of hills and the indentation of the bay.

The Protestant bishop was giving a dinner-party that fine summer evening for three or four visiting clergymen and some officers from Ballina. They were on the point of rising from their wine to join the ladies when a terrified messenger entered the room to say that three hundred Frenchmen were within a mile of the town. After a brief and not particularly heroic stand in the streets by the local yeomanry, the French themselves were in the house, headed by their general, a man of good height and shape, in the full vigour of life but with 'a small sleepy eye ... the eye of a cat preparing to spring on its prey'.[5] The bishop, though a liberal-minded man, could not help noticing that Humbert's 'education and manners were indicative of a person sprung from the lowest orders of society', but conceded that he knew how to assume the deportment of a gentleman when he wanted to. Humbert immediately made clear that the French intended to behave with total correctness, in accordance with his orders. Later, the bishop was to pay a glowing tribute to the impeccable discipline with which the French conducted themselves throughout the whole of their stay.[6]

The next morning a green flag was hoisted over the castle gate, bearing the inscription *'Erin go Bragh'*, or 'Ireland for Ever'. The moment that the United Irishmen and the Defenders had awaited with such desperate hope for so long, and which the government had so long dreaded, had come at last. A French Army was on Irish soil, calling upon the Irish to rise.

Humbert issued a proclamation headed 'LIBERTY, EQUALITY, FRATERNITY, UNION!'

Irishmen, you have not forgot Bantry Bay – you know what efforts France has made to assist you. Her affections for you, her desire for avenging your wrongs, and assuring your independence, can never be impaired.

After several unsuccessful attempts, behold Frenchmen arrived amongst you.

They come to support your courage, to share your dangers, to join their arms, and to mix their blood with yours in the sacred cause of liberty. They are the forerunners of other Frenchmen whom you shall soon infold in your arms ...

We swear the most inviolable respect for your properties, your laws and all your religious opinions. Be free; be masters in your own country. We look for no other conquest than that of your own liberty – no other success than yours.

The moment of breaking your chains has arrived. . . . Can there be any Irish-man base enough to separate himself at such a juncture from the grand interests of his country? If such there be, brave friends, let him be chased from the country he betrays, and let his property become the reward of those generous men who know how to fight and die.

Irishmen . . . recollect America, free from the moment she wished to be so.

The contest between you and your oppressors cannot be long.

Union! Liberty! the Irish Republic! – such is our shout. Let us march. Our hearts are devoted to you; our glory is in your happiness.[7]

A measure of the sort of response that Humbert had hoped for is shown by his treatment of the first two officer prisoners he took. One of these, a Lieutenant Sills, was sent on board his ships to be conveyed to France because he was an officer in an English regiment, the Leicester Fencibles. The other, a Captain Kirkwood of the local yeomanry unit, he released on parole because he was an Irishman. Indeed, on the very evening of his arrival Humbert made a vain attempt to get the bishop himself to join the Irish Republic, offering him a post in the Directory of Connaught which he was about to form and telling him that such powerful other forces would soon be on their way from French ports that Ireland would be free within a month.[8]

The French, as they admitted afterwards, had been led by the Irish in France to expect that 'a numerous and well-disciplined army, headed by the gentry and chief land-owners, would join them'.[9] Their hopes of the peasantry had, of course, been even higher, but these too were to be no less seriously disappointed.

It may be asked, as the Bishop of Killala asked himself, why the French should have landed in this particular north-west corner of Ireland at all, where so far there had been virtually no suspicion of disloyalty among the population. But they had received many assurances, such as one from MacNeven in the previous year in which he declared with typical over-optimism that . . . 'Even in the places where the United Irish system has not been fully adopted, the cooperation of the poor and middle classes can be counted on.'[10] Moreover, in June 1798, Lewins, urging the Directory to take action, had given them details which may well have been accurate of the disposition of loyalist troops in Ireland and the fact that in the north-west these were thinly distributed. He had added assurances similar to MacNeven's about the Irish patriotism of the greater part of the militia and the *yeomanry* as well (Lewins's italics).

The reality of Humbert's reception was very different from what he had been led to expect. Certainly the peasantry turned out to welcome him rap-turously on the roadside. And when on the very first day the French started distributing arms and uniforms in the castle yard at Killala, there was no shortage of customers. The bishop estimated they arrived in thousands to take part in the share-out. But campaign-toughened French republicans fresh from chasing the Pope out of Italy, were rather astonished to hear them say that they had come to take arms for France and the blessed Virgin. About a thousand were given complete blue uniforms, including helmets edged with spotted brown paper to make them look like leopard skins. A French naval officer stood on a barrel thumping the helmets down on to peasant heads to make them fit. Some 5,500 muskets were also distributed. Swords and pistols were reserved for rebel officers.

The distribution of the muskets togethei with ball and powder proved rash, for the peasantry were not naturally disciplined soldiers. In the course of experimentation with the new weapons Humbert himself narrowly escaped death from a clumsy recruit whose gun went off accidentally in the yard, sending a bullet past the general's ear as he stood at a window, to lodge in the ceiling just behind him. The French soon refused to hand out any more ammunition until the peasantry agreed to cease using it for shooting at ravens.[11]

Although the Irish who rallied to Humbert were occasionally, like the rebels in Wexford, to give proof of great quixotic courage and bravado, they proved a military disappointment. Their rapaciousness and lack of discipline appalled their French commander and he more than once had to deal with them severely. One senior officer later told the bishop that he would never trust himself to such a horde of savages again.[12] It seemed particularly inappropriate to the French, too, that these Irish should consider themselves as fighting primarily for their religion. As one officer remarked: 'God help these simpletons. If they knew how little we care about the Pope or his religion they would not be so hot in expecting help from us. . . . We have just sent Mr Pope away from Italy, and who knows but that we may find him in this country?'[13]

He also commented that if it were up to him he would pick one-third of them and shoot the rest.

Humbert had been led to expect something like a national revolutionary organization at work in Ireland. He found only an ignorant, neglected peasantry. In them, a sometimes desperate sense of being on their own in society could be momentarily excited into a spirit of revolt, but at the same time their long hard training in individual survival at all costs made them individualists to the end.

The size of the French force was in any case hardly large enough to inspire any but the most foolhardy or dedicated to chance their new arms, particularly after the terrible retribution that had so recently overtaken those who took to arms in Wexford. When Humbert sent his first dispatch to the French Admiralty a few days later, he reported, in spite of the eager acceptance of arms and uniforms, that 'The Irish have until this day hung back.

The County of Mayo has never been disturbed and this must account for the slowness of our approach which in other parts would have been very different.'[14]

By then, in fact, about six hundred Irish had already been in battle with him, but they had fled at the first cannon shot, though, he wrote, 'I expected as much and their panic in no way deranged my operations.'[15] The final words of that sentence were no boast. By contrast with the rest of his news, this disappointing showing of the Irish seemed insignificant. For the dispatch also contained accurate details of a sensational success of French arms.

Leaving about a fifth of his small army behind at Killala as a garrison, Humbert quickly moved south, and within a week had met and totally defeated a much superior British force under General Lake at Castlebar. Lake lost more than fifty of his men killed and the rest fled in panic, some of them falling back as far as Athlone, a distance of sixty-three miles said to have been covered in twenty-seven hours. The battle has gone down to history as 'the races of Castlebar'.

Humbert immediately set up a Provisional Government, making its President a young Catholic Irish gentleman named John Moore, and 'in the name of the Irish Republic' required everyone between the ages of sixteen and forty inclusive to rally at once to the French camp and march *en masse* 'against the common enemy, the Tyrant of Ireland – the English; whose destruction is the only way of ensuring the independence and happiness of ancient Hibernia'.[16] He also incidentally declared traitors to their country all those who having received arms did not rejoin the army within twenty-four hours.

At the same time Humbert sent for the two hundred Frenchmen he had left to garrison Killala. The bishop and the Protestant citizens of that town now had only three French officers between themselves and the rough Irish levies Humbert had armed. Everything the Protestants had heard about the recent massacres in Wexford was naturally very much in their minds. But it is to the credit of the trio of French officers that nothing of the sort occurred in Mayo. They acted quickly as soon as any signs of unmilitary personal vengeance appeared among their Irish followers, and in this, on the bishop's evidence, had the support of some Irish officers among the rebels who, like their less successful counterparts in Wexford, wished to prevent any degradation of their cause. Sixty Protestants imprisoned in Ballina as alleged Orangemen had the narrowest escape. They were released on the immediate intervention of one of the three Frenchmen. Otherwise, though it proved impossible to prevent looting of Protestant houses which took place on a considerable scale, there was not a single attempt to kill Protestants in cold blood during the entire month in which Connaught – or more accurately the country round Killala – was under the nominal government of the 'Irish Republic'. Creditable as this was, both to the French and certain Irish rebel captains, it is difficult not to conclude that it was due as much to the absence so far of any government terror of the sort that had inspired such a desperate desire for revenge in Wexford.

In his dispatches after Castlebar Humbert wrote confidently to the French Directory that he hoped to link with Irish insurgents either in the North or in Roscommon, and then march on Dublin. At the same time he recommended a suitable anchorage for the fleet that was to follow him. But the Bishop of Killala noted in his diary that in spite of the early success the French officers with him were soon considering themselves a forlorn hope with little more than nuisance value and little other future than surrender. In fact, their fate still very much depended on whether or not the two eventualities for which Humbert was hoping took place: the rising of substantial bodies of rebels in Ireland and the arrival of the planned reinforcements from France.

From Castlebar he marched North again with his army – only just over eight hundred men now, for his losses at Castlebar had been proportionately high – in the direction of Sligo which he seemed to intend to seize as a suitable harbour for the eventual arrival of Bompard's fleet. But on coming into contact with a small British force close by he wrongly supposed it to be the vanguard of a much larger army and turned away eastwards into County Leitrim where he had hopes of being joined by a considerable body of rebels. Unpleasantly harassed, though from a respectful distance, by troops under Lake, the general he had defeated at Castlebar, Humbert knew now that Cornwallis himself, the lord lieutenant and commander-in-chief, was moving towards him with a great new army of some twenty thousand men against which even his hardened veterans of the Army of Italy, now of the Army of Ireland, could have little chance. As there was still no word of any of the other expeditions from France, his one hope lay with a major rising of Irish rebels. News of an important rising near Granard in Leitrim now came in, reported to the French as a success.

Humbert ordered an immediate march in the direction of Granard, telling his men that they would be in Dublin in two days.[17] At Cloon they were met by a rebel chief, armed, according to one of the French officers, from head to foot and looking like one of the knights errant of the thirteenth century.[18] He asked them to wait for a day while he mustered ten thousand men. But the very next day Humbert received a terrible blow. As his third-in-command put it, 'He was astonished to learn that the insurgents, informed of the state of our forces, and judging them too weak to resist Lord Cornwallis ... no longer wanted to swell our ranks and make common cause with us. The fear of seeing their women and children murdered, if they abandoned their homesteads, was another reason for deciding to play for safety and run no further risks.'[19]

In fact, the rising at Granard had been bloodily repulsed by the military, and equally disastrous failure met an attempted simultaneous rising in County Westmeath. So much for all the assurances Tone and the United Irishmen had been giving the French for so long. They had been given honestly enough. But they had been based on a concept of how they thought things ought to have been rather than of how they were. The only evidence Humbert had had of the national rising promised to the Directory had been utterly insignificant. The crude levies of peasantry who had presented themselves at Killala had fought bravely when they had fought at all, but they were unpredictable and ungovernable and in the long run more an embarrassment than an asset. More relevant had been the ninety-odd men of the Longford and Kilkenny militias who had deserted to the French after Castlebar. The Bishop of Killala had watched them come into his yard after the battle with their coats turned. But after all the French had been told about the state of mind of the militia such members were pitifully few.

With the collapse of all hopes of serious help from the Irish, and still no sign of the other expeditions from France, it was inevitably only a short time before Humbert was cornered. On 8 September 1798 he found himself trapped by Cornwallis at Ballinamuck and, after a short battle in which the French put up little more than a token fight, he surrendered. The French prisoners, consisting of 884 officers and men, were treated with the greatest respect by their captors, and their week's journey across Ireland to Dublin by mail coach and canal, during which they played cards, sang the Marseillaise and attended dances, had something of a triumphant progress about it. One of the officers of Humbert's escort was reported as saying that Humbert had little but contempt for the allies he had come to liberate, and complained that on the very first day of his landing they had immediately relieved him of £50 and his watch.[20] On arrival in Dublin, they were given a banquet in their honour before being put on a ship to England from which they were soon afterwards returned to France.*

A starker fate awaited the Irish. One French officer has recorded how, at least at Ballinamuck, some three hundred of them had 'fought bravely to the last and were cut to pieces, selling their lives dearly'.[21] The usual indiscriminate slaughter overtook most of those who fled. A fortnight later, a detachment of the loyalist army consisting of some Highlanders and the Queen's County, Downshire and Kerry militias (the latter under the command of Maurice Fitzgerald, the Knight of Kerry), marched inexorably

* Humbert afterwards took part in the suppression of Toussaint l'Ouverture's revolt on Haiti, but later fell out with Napoleon and found exile in the United States. There he took part in the War of 1812 in which, at New Orleans, he was opposed by a man who had also faced him at Ballinamuck, General Pakenham. He engaged in the Mexican rebellion against Spain of 1815, but after its failure returned to New Orleans where he died in 1823, 'passing the closing years of his life in comparative obscurity, and earning a modest competence as a teacher of French and fencing'. (V. Gribayedoff, *The French Invasion of Ireland in '98*, p. 182.)

against Killala itself. The town had remained throughout this fortnight in the hands of three French officers and the Irish rebels, a further 750 of whom had actually come to offer their services to the French *after* the battle of Ballinamuck. ('A great crowd of clowns came in this day, armed with pikes ...' was how the bishop reported their arrival.) There were in fact about nine hundred rebels in the town of Killala as the loyalist army approached it along the road from Ballina on 22 September.[22] Some of these rebels ran away before any battle could take place, but others were soon 'running on death with as little appearance of reflection or concern as if they were hastening to a show'.[23] They posted themselves behind the low stone walls on either side of the road and awaited the assault of their fellow countrymen wearing the king's uniform.

They stood bravely for about twenty minutes, firing too high as usual, and then broke and ran. Some four hundred of them were killed during the fighting, and in the usual savage mopping-up operations that followed. The always fair-minded bishop commented of his deliverers: 'Their rapacity differed in no respect from that of the rebels, except that they seized upon things with somewhat less of ceremony or excuse, and that his Majesty's soldiers were incomparably superior to the Irish traitors in dexterity at stealing.'[24]

Though Cornwallis issued 'protections' for those 'deluded' people who had served the French as rank and file, there followed the usual savage courts-martial for those who had served in any position of authority. Some ninety death sentences were carried out, and among the victims were Wolfe Tone's brother, Matthew, and another Irishman who had accompanied the expedition, Bartholomew Teeling. They had been taken wearing French officer's uniform but, in spite of the plea of their commander Humbert that they were entitled to be treated as prisoners under the laws of war, they were shown no mercy. As a passionate loyalist of the day remarked with approval in the context of loyalist severity throughout the rebellion as a whole: 'Where the sword of civil war is drawn, the laws are silent.'[25]

But the year still held a few more surprises. For, unaware of what had happened to Humbert, except for the news of his early successes, two other components of the multiple French expedition to Ireland had already set sail.

The first had left Dunkirk on 4 September, four days before Humbert's surrender at Ballinamuck. This new expedition was a minute one, consisting solely of one of the fastest sailing corvettes in the French navy, the yellow-painted *Anacreon*, with some 180 men on board and a large supply of arms, including artillery, and saddles and bridles for Irish cavalry. The whole expedition in fact was prepared on the assumption that Ireland had risen in revolt. There were also a number of *émigré* Irishmen on board, including the remarkable Napper Tandy, now boasting the rank of a French general, while the overall command was held by a French American called Rey.[26]

They landed on Rutland Island off County Donegal at midday on 16 September, with Tandy one of the first ashore. Appeals to the population were immediately distributed. One of these, signed by Rey, was headed: 'Liberty or Death! Northern Army of Avengers. Headquarters, the first year of Irish Liberty.'

It began: 'United Irishmen . . .' and declared that the French, with Napper Tandy at their head, sworn to lead them on to victory or die, had come 'to break your fetters, and restore you to the blessings of liberty. . . . The Trumpet calls . . .' Another proclamation, similarly headed, and signed by Tandy himself, told the people that it was their duty 'to strike on their blood-cemented thrones the murderers of your friends' and 'to wage a war of extermination against your oppressors, the war of liberty against tyranny, and liberty shall triumph'.[27]

The number of Irish who could then read English in that part of Donegal must have been very few. In any case, the local population had fled to the mountains and showed no inclination to join the invaders at all.[28] Tandy and his allies who, as they told the local postmaster, had come expressly 'to try the pulse of the people', were shattered by the disappointment; their discomfort was completed by news of the fate of Humbert's army at Ballina-muck. After a meal, which they asked for politely, and paid for, they returned to their ship and sailed away again. Tandy, who was fond of drink, had to be carried on board and was in such a state that he made water on the shoulders of those carrying him.[29]

Their ship, the *Anacreon*, had an encounter with an armed merchantman off the Orkneys on the way back, in the course of which Tandy sat on deck drinking brandy with eight-pound cannon balls in his pockets, ready to leap overboard and drown himself if necessary rather than submit to capture.[30] But the French were victorious, and after escaping all pursuing British warships the corvette reached Hamburg. From there, however, the British Government managed to secure Tandy's extradition. He was brought to England, kept in prison a long time, but finally reprieved, partly thanks to the intercession of the lord lieutenant, Cornwallis, who stressed 'the incapacity of this old man to do further mischief'.[31] Tandy was eventually returned to France in 1802, during the short Peace of Amiens, and died soon afterwards.

Long before this, the British Government had at last caught up with the most attractive personality of all among the early United Irishmen, Wolfe Tone. Tone had set off for Ireland on the last instalment of the French invasion just two days before Tandy and co. made their dismal landfall on Rutland Island. The fleet which Tone accompanied was the largest to set sail for Ireland since the expedition to Bantry Bay nearly two years before. It was, however, considerably smaller than that, being composed of only ten ships altogether: of which only one was a ship of the line, appropriately named the *Hoche* of 74 guns with Admiral Bompard, General Hardy and Tone himself on board. The rest of the fleet consisted of eight heavy frigates of between 24 guns and 12 guns, and one fast schooner.[32] They carried some three thousand men in all and quantities of stores. It was at least better than the 'corporal's guard', which Tone had always said he was ready to go to Ireland with if necessary, and it was still not known what had happened to Humbert.

At 5.30 on the morning of 12 October, after a twenty-three day voyage, the French were intercepted off the northern coast of Donegal by a British squadron under Sir John Warren which, though numerically smaller, was much more heavily gunned, including as it did six ships of the line.[33] Seeing that a battle was inevitable, and defeat more than likely, the French tried to persuade Tone to leave the *Hoche* and escape to France in the fast sailing schooner. But, as one would expect from his character, he refused to go and commanded a battery on board during the fight.[34] An action began about 7.30 a.m. The *Hoche* suffered the handicap of being without her main top-mast which had been carried away in the rough weather of the previous days. Castlereagh's uncle, Sir James Stewart, watched the battle from Horn Head.[35] It took place too far out to sea for him to be quite certain of the outcome, but he thought it had gone favourably for the British. In fact, the *Hoche* put up a gallant defence, but after four hours struck her colours. The other nine ships all tried to make their escape back to France but six were eventually taken and found to be 'full of troops and stores'.[36]

Three weeks later, when several hundred prisoners were being landed from Lough Swilly to which the *Hoche* had been brought for repair, one of the first men to step out of one of the boats in the uniform of a French officer was Tone himself. The British Government had known he was on board the *Hoche*, but he seems to have made no attempt to conceal his identity. Recognizing a loyalist bystander on the shore, who had been at Trinity with him, he spoke to him at once.[37] He was taken to Dublin in irons, an insult to the French uniform which he much resented, and on Saturday, 10 November, appeared in court in that uniform: 'a large and fiercely cocked hat with broad gold lace and the tricoloured cockade, a blue uniform coat, with gold and embroidered collar and two large epaulettes, blue pantaloons with gold-laced garters at the knees, and short boots bound at the top with gold lace'.[38]

The result of the trial was a foregone conclusion. Tone admitted the charge of acting hostilely to the king, though he refused to use the word guilty himself, simply saying that he had admitted the charge 'and consequently the appellation by which I am technically described'.[39] He delivered a rather high-flown but dignified address to the court, which he was made to abbreviate because of its inflammatory irrelevance, but he concluded with the words:

Success is all in this life; and, unfavoured of her, virtue becomes vicious in the ephemeral estimation of those who attach every merit to posterity. In the glorious race of patriotism, I have pursued the path chalked out by Washington in America and Kosciusco in Poland. Like the latter I have failed to emancipate my country; and unlike both I have forfeited my life. I have done my duty, and I have no doubt the Court will do theirs. I have only to add that a man who has thought and acted as I have done should be armed against fear of death.[40]

Except for a moment right at the beginning of the trial when he had asked rather agitatedly for a glass of water, he seemed to some 'unmoved and unterrified throughout'.[41] But the Marquis of Buckingham who was present at the trial commented the same day that he thought Tone was 'much agitated and I cannot help thinking that he means to destroy himself on Monday' (the day appointed for his execution).[42] Cooke, the under secretary, expressed the same fears to Cornwallis on the Saturday.

Tone's one request in court had been that instead of being hanged he should, out of respect for the uniform he wore, be shot 'by a file of grenadiers'. The request was transmitted to Cornwallis. All weekend Tone lay in prison listening to the gallows being erected outside his window and waiting for an answer. On the Sunday evening he was told that his request had been refused. The government's intention was to make as public an example of him as possible.

Next morning, when the gaoler came to rouse Tone at about four o'clock, he found him exhausted and weltering in his own blood with his throat cut. He had in fact missed the main artery but cut through his windpipe with a penknife he had kept concealed. 'I find then I am but a bad anatomist', he is reported as saying.[43] His head was kept in one position and a sentry placed over him to prevent him moving.[44]

While a legal wrangle proceeded as to whether or not Tone should have been tried by a court-martial at all since he was not one of His Majesty's soldiers and the normal processes of law were available, Cornwallis suspended the execution, though there were those, including the fellow student from Trinity who had greeted him on landing, who thought his neck should be sewn up immediately and he should be summarily hanged. After a week of agony his condition deteriorated and it is said that on hearing a surgeon remark that if he were to move or speak it would be fatal to him, he managed to utter: 'I can yet find word to thank you, sir. It is the most welcome news you could give me,' and died at once.[45]

Whether or not the story is mythical is unimportant, for it was as a mythical figure that Tone was to make his greatest contribution to history. For to this sympathetic young man, most remote of all the influential United

Irishmen from practical events in Ireland during the years of conspiracy and rebellion, but most articulate expounder of the theory that Ireland should be a sovereign independent country separate from England, there was to attach a legendary significance which long after his death did more for the cause in which he believed than he himself had ever been able to do during his lifetime.

After the great events of the decade to which Tone had been witness, political attitudes in Ireland could never be the same again. Up to this point in Irish history no Irishman, of whatever origin, when thinking of his country had considered it as being one that had to be made separate from the Crown that was shared with England. Now at least that idea had been planted. And with it had been planted that notion of a republic which, originally adopted as the desirable constitutional form in imitation of America and France, was long afterwards to become an Irish ark of the covenant in its own right.

From these years, at the end of the eighteenth century, dates much of the manner and style of a movement that was often to be mannered and stylized. A song of the period runs:

> See, Erin's sons, yon rising beam
> The eastern hills adorning,
> Now freedom's sun begins to gleam
> And break a glorious morning . . .

Such a golden sunrise, literally depicted against an emerald green background, was to become the standard of the republican movement in the course of the nineteenth century. 'Sunburstry', as it came to be called, or the habit of talking of freedom with this sort of flourish without actually getting down to more practical politics, became one of its most popular vices. An increasingly rhetorical question was to arise: how far were separatists prepared to try to make separatism practical politics? How far was it practical politics at all?

'Plant, plant the tree, fair freedom's tree' – the song's chorus continues –

> Midst danger, wounds and slaughter,
> Erin's green fields its soil shall be,
> Her tyrants' blood its water.

In this decade after the French Revolution blood – though not so much of the tyrants – had flowed in plenty. And by blood too, for all the fanciful sunburstry, freedom of a sort was to be won in the end.

PART THREE

1

The Making of the Union

It is easy to see turning-points in history where turning-points later turned out to have been; but to do so often misrepresents the way things looked at the time. The events of the year 1798 proved a major turning-point in the history of Irish nationalism. They left an inspiration, however vague and emotional, for the future; and more important they led directly to a Parliamentary Union with Great Britain, the long-term effects of which seemed to confirm Ireland as a province and not a country at all. But the last defeat in October 1798 of French attempts to assist rebellion in Ireland that year seemed to contemporaries only the end of one immediate cause for anxiety. Even this was revived within days when the news reached Dublin that yet another French squadron had actually anchored again in Killala Bay.

These were the same three ships that had brought Humbert in the first place. They had been back to France in the meantime and had now returned with some three thousand more men and supplies. When they heard of the defeats of Humbert and Admiral Bompard, they made good their escape without attempting a landing. But their reappearance emphasized what, for contemporaries, was the most important fact of all about the Irish situation at the time: the constant possibility, even probability, of the arrival on those discontented shores of a force from the great land power in Europe which was England's enemy. The very real likelihood of invasion from France remained a most vivid threat at least until 1805.

In Ireland itself by the end of 1798 the original United Irish movement had been most effectively broken. Seventy of its most intelligent leaders were in prison, and others and many subordinate organizers were dead. But because of its obscure ties with the vast bodies of the Defenders, an internal as well as external threat appeared to pervade the situation in Ireland for a long time. While it was possible, on the one hand, to accept that the guerrilla activities of Holt and Dwyer and their men in the fastnesses of the Wicklow mountains were simply the dying echoes of an old convulsion, there were at first enough ominous new signs to keep alive a general apprehension too. So soon after the breaking of the rebellion as September 1798, a traveller on the mail coach between Cork and Dublin was stopped and held for thirteen hours while he was tried by a rebel court-martial consisting of two colonels, one major and four captains, and finally given a pass, permitting him to proceed to Dublin 'free and unmolested by any of the Friends of Liberty'.[1] The Quaker lady of Ballintore, County Kildare, who had herself experienced many of the terrible events of the early summer, felt that the business was by no means over that autumn. She could hear the sound of the trees being felled at night for pike handles and the creaking of the carts which took them away.[2] The darkness was frequently lit up by the fires of houses burned by insurgents, and the funeral of a man who had been hanged moved through the village 'with a kind of indiscreet solemnity'. During that winter of 1798–9, she wrote afterwards, 'the country was far from being settled; it was like the working of the sea after the storm'.[3]

In February 1799 an English militia captain serving in Ireland wrote in his diary that 'although this immediate neighbourhood and the Kingdom at large appears to wear a face of Tranquillity, it more resembles the Pause of Expectation and the silence of Fear ...'.[4] Whole bodies of the lower orders of Catholics, he added, were sworn United Irishmen. On 24 February a strong party of mounted rebels were encountered by a detachment of yeomanry some twenty-five miles from Youghal in County Cork. The yeomanry pursued the rebels so hard that many jumped from their horses into the River Blackwater where they were supposed drowned.[5]

In other parts of Ireland the outlook was equally uncertain. The Member of Parliament for Mayo had already reported that Ireland was 'in a very precarious state that winter'[6] and in the middle of March 1799 none of the main roads into Dublin itself were passable except to large parties or military escorts.[7] In the North, though the short-lived alliance between Catholics and Dissenters continued to break up, Defenderism itself was again on the increase, particularly in Antrim, where many former United Irishmen were now absorbed into the Defenders. Nightly raids for arms were taking place there and a system of intimidation by flogging with the cat o' nine tails began in macabre imitation of established authority. A rising was confidently expected for 10 April 1799 and special messengers were said to have been sent to the French Directory to arrange assistance. Bonfires lit the hillsides at night both in Antrim and Derry, when orders were said to have been received from France to hold themselves in readiness.[8] Nor was the continuing threat of clandestine conspiracy confined to Ireland alone. Irishmen still composed a very large proportion of the seamen in the British fleet and late in 1798 and during 1799 numerous plots were uncovered among crews to seize British men-of-war in the name of the United Irishmen, run up the green flag and sail for French ports. Dozens of such prospective mutineers were hanged: others were flogged through the Fleet.

It is against this assumption of a continuously unresolved dangerous situation in Ireland for any foreseeable future that the political manoeuvrings which led to the Parliamentary Union between Great Britain and Ireland, and the abolition of a separate Irish Parliament after five hundred years, must be understood.

When the rebellion of 1798 took place, the concept of Irish nationality had twice been put forward, each time in much common nationalistic language but from different standpoints – that of the Protestant ascendancy, and that of the radical United Irishmen, also largely Protestants. Simultaneously with the United Irish movement, there had also sometimes emerged among the uncouth and ill-coordinated bodies of Defenders a vague awareness that the wants and grievances which were the source of their own political motivation could be thought of dramatically in terms of a green flag. Such dramatic coherence, however, containing perhaps the crude beginnings of a mass nationalism, had been abruptly and chasteningly shattered by the rebellion's failure.

The strongest and most effective expression of nationality to date – that of the Protestant ascendancy – had been analogous to the colonial nationalism of eighteenth-century America. Since in Ireland, however, a quarrel with the mother country had been avoided, Irish patriots of this type had been able to feel that they had the best of both worlds, always emphasizing, like Grattan, their pride in Ireland as an independent sovereign country simultaneously with their sense of connection with Britain in the wider British Empire. But the rebellion of 1798 had exposed the artificiality in such thoughts, painfully emphasizing that only in the most highflown theoretical sense could they claim to speak for Irishmen as a whole.

The United Irishmen had put forward a more democratic version of Irish patriotism, using the same nationalistic phrases by tying them to Republicanism and to a proposed separation from Britain and the Empire altogether. The easy defeat of the rebellion, notable for the failure of the Irish masses to respond coherently to the new Republican appeal, emphasized that this too was unrepresentative and ineffectual.

Neither form of nationalism looked particularly convincing immediately after the events of 1798, and though obviously this conclusion did not present itself to contemporaries with simple analytical clarity, their uncertainty is plainly expressed in the eighteen months of political groping that took place before the passing of the Parliamentary Union.

The British Government had a practical problem to solve. Unlike the Protestant ascendancy, they had been getting the worst of both worlds. They had total final responsibility for the situation in Ireland and yet only an indirectly geared and cumbersome machinery with which to deal with it. And the one thing the outbreak of 1798 had proved conclusively was that the situation in Ireland needed dealing with. As a former lord lieutenant wrote at the time with the sense of urgent desperation about Ireland that so many people were feeling: 'something new must be attempted'.[9]

Early in June 1798, even before the Wexford rebellion had reached its , climax, Pitt, the British Prime Minister, was working on a plan for a union of the two countries' parliaments. It was to be a few months before the British cabinet concentrated on the problem of getting the project accepted by Irish opinion. But thereafter it never once relented in its determination to carry the Union through.

The idea of a legislative union between the English and Irish parliaments was not a new one. Such a union had even existed for a few years in the time of Cromwell's Commonwealth, but the *status quo* of two separate Parliaments had been restored with Charles II. Early in the eighteenth century before a sense of Irish Protestant nationality had developed very widely, the Irish House of Commons had actually unsuccessfully petitioned Queen Anne to extend the blessings of the new Anglo-Scottish Union to Ireland. In 1751, a pamphlet advocating a union had prophesied with some accuracy that the Irish (meaning the Protestant Irish) though not yet a nation, would soon be too vain and insolent to accept a union at all. One of the many replies to this pamphlet, which immediately expressed horror and contempt at the idea of a union, tried to formulate the mystical ambivalence which lay beneath the Protestant Irishman's developing sense of nationality. Unlike America, which was a simple colony, said the pamphleteer, 'Ireland should be looked on rather as a sister whom England has taken under her protection on condition she complies with the economy of the family, yet with such distinction and deference to show that they were once upon an equality'.[10] By the end of the 1770s the emphasis had shifted: it was the equality of the present that was being stressed, and Protestant Irishmen were considering themselves Irishmen as proudly as the English considered themselves English. The idea of a union was hardly ever broached and then only to be mistrusted.

When, therefore, towards the end of 1798, the subject of a legislative union again began to be seriously put forward, there was a situation which in the light of later events seems a paradox: it was among the Protestant Irish gentry that the great body of opposition to a union was to be found. However, their opposition to it was not so solid or coherent as, in the light of former events, one might have expected. For rebellion had delivered a profound social shock to their whole way of thinking. And the notion of joint sisterhood in the British connection was already so well-established at the back of their minds that a shift of ground towards closer connection was still at least something conceivable.

Later nationalists often extolled eighteenth-century opposition to the Union as activated by patriotic principles analogous to their own, but the analogy is imperfect. Even Foster, the Speaker of the Irish House of Commons, who emerged as the most implacable and influential of all the Protestant Irish leaders against the Union, was not unequivocally opposed to the measure on principle. Pitt, discussing the projected Union with him, found him 'strongly against the measure of an Union (*particularly at the moment*), yet perfectly ready to discuss the point fairly'.[11] And Protestants who had previously presented a single political front for legislative independence now divided not on principle but on how they assessed the chances of their own élite society surviving within the British connection in these troublous times.

Clare, the Chancellor (formerly Fitzgibbon) who had been urging Union since 1793, proclaimed predictably: '. . . it is utterly impossible to preserve this country to the British Crown, if we are to depend upon the precarious bond of union which now subsists between Great Britain and Ireland.'[12] But many who had previously been among the foremost protagonists of legislative independence agreed with him and opted for a union. Sir George Hill on the other hand, the loyalist who had felt so vindictive about Wolfe Tone that he wanted him hanged with his neck stitched up, was strongly against it. The Earl of Charlemont, founder of the Volunteers of twenty years before, was against a union, as might be expected, but the terms in which he expressed his opposition are revealing. 'Next to the liberty of my country,' he wrote, 'its perpetual connection with its beloved sister has ever been the dearest wish of my heart, the gratification of which could only have been endangered by the plan now in agitation, the disuniting union, a measure which I reprobate as an Irishman, and, if possible, still more as a member of the empire and an adorer of the British constitution.'[13]

Separation from the British connection was the last thing men like Charlemont and the Speaker, Foster, wanted; they opposed the Union just because they thought it was likely to bring that about. As Foster said: 'If a resident Parliament and resident gentry cannot soften manners, amend habits or promote social intercourse, will no Parliament and fewer resident gentry do it?'[14] J. C. Beresford, a man who had helped put down the rebellion with great savagery and from whose family riding school in Dublin the shrieks of the tortured had been clearly audible, was equally against the Union, whereas his father was strongly for it. In other words, the vast majority of opponents of the measure were not at odds with Unionists about the need for a connection. Their argument was that this was not the way to strengthen it. The Irish Parliament had shown itself impeccably loyal and resolute during the rebellion, and the rebellion had been broken militarily by Irish troops and the Irish militia. The withdrawal of most of the influential inhabitants which would inevitably follow a union 'would leave room for political agitators, and men of talents without principle or property, to disturb and irritate the public mind'.[15]

However, even the anti-Unionists in their certainty about the disadvantages of a legislative union did not conceal an uneasy awareness of the need for a new approach in Ireland after the events of 1798. Ideas such as a reform of the tithes system, or some financial provision for the Catholic clergy, or an increase in the amount Ireland should pay Britain for her protection within the Empire were all put forward as a tentative basis of some comprehensive new deal universally acknowledged to be necessary.

Opinion about a union did not run clearly down any political or social dividing line. The most solid opinion seems to have been among the Orangemen, who were very generally described as being against it. This too may seem a paradox in the light of later events, but it was a logical attitude at the time, for the Orangemen simply represented the most extreme expression of the Protestant point of view, namely, that they held a dominant position in Irish society and the legislature as things were, and what they held they wanted to hold. Even in later times, after they had identified their interests with the Union they were always to make clear that, in the event of a clash between those interests and the Union, it was the Union they were prepared to sacrifice. But even the Orangemen were not now unanimous, for a Unionist supporter while accepting that they were chiefly against the measure thought they could be brought to be neutral though it was the utmost the friends of the Union could hope.[16] The Masters of the Orange Lodge did in the end opt for neutrality.

The lawyers and bankers of Dublin, whose particularist interests were threatened, were outspoken against a Union. 'We look with abhorrence,' declared the bankers, 'on any attempt to deprive the people of Ireland of their Parliament and thereby of their constitution ...' And they added that, '... impressed with every sentiment of loyalty to our King and affectionate attachment to the British connection', to propose a union was 'highly dangerous and impolitic'.[17] For the Dublin poor, the Union did not seem an urgent issue one way or the other, though as Castlereagh wrote they might 'easily be set in motion, should their cooperation become of importance to the leading opposers of the measure'.[18] Indeed, siding with the bankers, they were within a short time to be triumphantly drawing the Union's opponents in carriages from the Irish House of Commons and pelting Clare, its leading protagonist, with mud.

The mixture and confusion of opinions was observable not only in social and political groupings but geographically. Dublin, for instance, since it was going to lose its special status as an independent capital and the seat of the national legislature, was strongly against the Union. Cork, because it might hope by the Union to achieve something like parity with Dublin, was strongly for it. Elsewhere in Ireland opinion divided geographically in an arbitrary fashion, determined often by the individual opinions of whoever exercised great influence in any particular county. Sligo, Limerick, Waterford, Wexford, Derry, Antrim and Cork were all reported as being in varying degrees for; Carlow, Cavan, Fermanagh, Roscommon, Kildare, Louth and Wicklow against.[19] In the North, though the Orangemen were broadly against, the division of opinion was often determined by a straight conflict of view as to what the Union would or would not do to the linen trade. Thus some argued that within a union the linen trade would now all go to England, and since the linen trade in the North was flourishing this argument was said to be having some effect in promoting anti-Unionism. Others countered that the very security of their trade was bound up with the security of the British connection, and that only a union could ensure that. Linen merchants themselves were said to be too busy to take part in the argument very actively one way or the other, but on the whole they inclined to this latter view and favoured a union.

In short, the real argument about the Union was not over any major issue of national principle at all but over what its effects were going to be on certain interests. The largest single set of interests involved was that of the Catholics, who still had much to gain and many recent gains to lose.

All laws penalizing Catholics for the exercise of their religion or excluding them from ownership or other acquisition of land had long been abandoned. In 1793 they had been admitted to the vote on exactly the same terms as Protestants. However, no State or municipal offices were yet open to them (though they could be magistrates) and above all they were disqualified from entering Parliament by the need to make a formal abjuration of their beliefs in order to do so. The claim for rights of full equal citizenship with Protestants was obviously a matter of real concern only to the better-off Catholics, who incidentally had proved themselves zealously loyal to the Crown in the rebellion, with many fewer exceptions than among well-to-do Protestants. For the Catholic peasant masses Catholic Emancipation was, as it had always been, at best only a remote symbol of their own far more down-to-earth aspirations, and, as Thomas Emmet the United Irish leader had already remarked, they did not 'give a feather for it'.* Deprived, by the defeat of the rebellion, of more dramatic hopes of seeing their down-to-earth aspirations realized, symbols were all that was left to them. But Emancipation was such an oblique one that, without anyone consciously to make it a part of their lives, as Daniel O'Connell was eventually to do, the strange rituals of the secret societies seemed to provide more satisfying evocations of their hearts' desires.

Since the better-off Catholics all identified themselves as strongly as Protestants with the maintenance of the British connection, and yet had been admitted to a much smaller share of the pride in independent Irish nationality, they saw no objections to a union in itself. Their concern with the issue confined itself largely to whether or not it would make Emancipation more or less probable. But this was an extremely difficult question to

* Cf. above, p. 42 (Emmet, *Pieces of Irish History*, p. 221.)

decide. On the one hand, it might be said that if the Orangemen were mainly against the Union as likely to undermine their dominant position then Catholics should be for it. And on the whole this was the attitude which the majority of Catholics took up. It seemed to them that they were more likely to obtain from a united kingdom, in which they would be only a minority, those concessions at present withheld from them through fear of their majority in Ireland. On the other hand, this argument could be turned the other way round. It could and was argued by some Catholics that their numerical preponderance in Ireland gave them greater power to wring concessions either now or later out of an Irish Parliament alone. And certainly, if the future development of parliamentary institutions on democratic lines could have been foreseen, the argument for Catholic interests opposing a union would have been overwhelming. But, as things were, their best chance seemed to lie with the generosity of a united parliament in which they would escape from the narrow bigotry of the apprehensive Protestant minority which had so often thwarted them in an Irish one. The vote itself had, after all, only been given to Catholics because the British Government had put pressure on the Irish Parliament.

Pitt's earliest ideas for a union had indeed been drafted on the assumption that the project would include Catholic eligibility for Parliament and all offices of state.[20] He himself was in favour of this, but was not prepared to press it if it should make for difficulties. Difficulties in fact threatened on all sides from the king downwards. And when Clare went to London in October 1798 to add his weight to the argument against immediate Emancipation he was soon able to write back to Ireland that the Union was to go forward 'unencumbered' by it.[21] Cornwallis, the lord lieutenant, though he also personally thought that Emancipation should have been part of the deal, accepted the decision. In order to convey some hint of flexibility for the future the stipulation in the Union arrangements that Irish parliamentary representatives must take the Protestant oath of supremacy was qualified by the phrase 'unless it shall be otherwise provided for by Parliament'.

This rather vague and distant prospect of undefined hope suited the Catholic gentry and priesthood well enough. They were opposed to any further pressure for Catholic Emancipation at present on the very grounds that it would be 'injurious to the Catholic claims to have them discussed in the present temper of the Irish Parliament'.[22] And they officially decided to play things coolly. A meeting of influential Catholics just before Christmas 1798 to discuss the projected union decided it would be 'inexpedient to publish any resolution at present' and adjourned *sine die*.[23]

Responding to this careful attitude of the Catholics, both pro- and anti-Unionists set about wooing them. The prospects of Emancipation which the anti-Unionist Foster could offer were necessarily limited since the solid bulk of his support against the Union came from those who wanted to maintain the Protestant ascendancy. The government, on the other hand, though they could not offer immediate Emancipation, dropped vaguely encouraging hints about the future more and more frequently. As Castlereagh, the Chief Secretary, had put it quite candidly: 'I conceive the true policy is by a steady resistance of their [the Catholics'] claims, so long as the countries remain separate, to make them feel that they can only be carried with us, through an union.'[24] And Pitt's speech for the Union in the British House of Commons was full of general hints that concessions to the Catholics could be discussed more safely within the constitution of a united kingdom than within that of Ireland alone. Of the lower orders of Catholics he said: '... A united legislative body promises a more effectual remedy for their grievances than could be likely to result from any local arrangements.'[25]

Since, not only with the Catholics but with all groups, it was a matter of persuading people that the Union would benefit their interests, the government embarked on a series of similar persuasive tactics in other directions. The chief material cause for complaint about the re-arrangements required by the Union was of course the inevitable reduction in the number of Irish parliamentary seats and in the power and influence that went with them. The three hundred seats in the Irish Parliament were now to be reduced to one hundred in the Imperial Parliament.*

But before Cornwallis and Castlereagh could start effectively deploying every technique of persuasion and compensation to placate the interests which controlled these seats, the strength of the opposition to the Union in the Irish House of Commons revealed itself. A motion to reject any discussion of the Union as projected in the king's speech for the session of January 1799 was passed by 111 votes to 106. 'We are yet a nation,' wrote Charlemont to a friend. 'The abominable project is defeated; I can think or talk of nothing else.'[26] But within a week he was sounding more cautious: 'I now begin to perceive that our victory though glorious is not absolutely decisive.'[27]

It was not only 'not absolutely decisive'; eventual defeat was almost certain. The British Government had always ultimately held the Irish Parliament in its power through its control of the patronage system. The full range of patronage was now deployed by Cornwallis and his Chief Secretary, Castlereagh, to secure the objective on which the British Government had set its mind.

There were certain steps they could not take. For instance, when the Marquis of Downshire, an opponent of the Union, showed some signs of wavering if the Irish representatives in the new House of Commons were to be kept at their present figure of three hundred, it was clearly impracticable to meet him on the point. But where individuals might be influenced by rewards of title or office to support the Union every possible effort was made to make them do so. And since the chief arguments *against* a union were

* These became 105 after the Reform Act of 1832.

that it would work out against individual interests, to make it in individual interests to vote for the Union was not perhaps as despicable as it has sometimes been made to seem. Altogether, as a result of Cornwallis's and Castlereagh's ceaseless activity, sixteen important borough-owners were given English peerages, twenty-eight Irish peerages were created, and twenty Irish peerages were increased in rank. As a further general inducement to the Irish peers to seek their prestige within a union rather than outside it, twenty-eight of them were to be virtually nominated by the government as representative Irish peers in the British House of Lords.

This trade in inducements to vote was certainly a two-way one, and was conducted by the opposition just as vigorously as by the government, though clearly the same resources were not available to them. But direct money bribes were undoubtedly offered by the opposition; one man who had voted for the Union in the debate in 1799 voted against it in 1800 in return for a sum of £4,000, though even this man's venality had its limits, for an attempt by the government to win him back once again by a still larger bribe is said to have been unsuccessful.[28] Few direct bribes seem in fact to have been made by the government, though this accusation was often levelled afterwards. Financial compensation, on the other hand, was certainly offered to and taken by the owners of the close boroughs on the straightforward principle that such boroughs were private property like any other. It is illustrative of the inadequacy of the word 'corruption' for the whole procedure that one-third of those to whom such compensatory payments were made actually voted against the Union.[29] Lord Downshire, who received the largest single payment of this sort, maintained his opposition to the Union to the end.

The government's most effective single measure to secure the passage of the Union was the creation of vacant seats in the Irish Parliament, which were then filled with Union supporters before the crucial final debate. This was done partly by approaching men who, though they were not prepared openly to vote for the Union, were willing to accept rewards for vacating their seats – perhaps the most dishonest individual attitude to be found in all the various Union transactions. Exploitation of such moral dishonesty proved very effective. Altogether, including vacancies from deaths and other causes, one-fifth of the Irish House of Commons changed its representation in the eighteen months before the crucial debate took place in 1800 and many of the newcomers thus brought in for what proved to be the death throes of the Irish Parliament were Englishmen. Indeed, the very thoroughness with which Cornwallis and Castlereagh pursued their task itself converted many people in the end to the inevitability of the Union. Already by the end of June 1799 a correspondent was writing to Castlereagh that the impression that the Union would be passed was itself helping to do the trick. 'Little alternative is left to people but to reconcile their minds to its advantages, and which they seem to do with a very good will.'[30] And towards the end of September one of the under secretaries told him that even in Dublin the talk of the coffee houses was that the Union would be carried.[31]

Although Cornwallis and Castlereagh did their work extremely well – almost too well, for the king and the British Cabinet were slightly appalled when they realized the scale on which the Irish ministers had been offering rewards for support[32] – Cornwallis himself had felt distinctly squeamish at times. 'I despise and hate myself every hour for engaging in such dirty work,' he wrote, but he added that what kept him going was the thought that without a union the British Empire must be dissolved.[33] Castlereagh was less emotional. 'The Irish government,' he wrote, after the Union had been carried, 'is certainly now liable to the charge of having gone too far in complying with the demands of individuals; but had the Union miscarried, and the failure been traceable to a reluctance on the part of the Government to interest a sufficient number of supporters in its success, I am inclined to think we should have met with, and in fact deserved, less mercy.'[34] The final voting in the Irish House of Commons was conclusive: a majority of forty-six for the Union where only the year before there had been a majority of five against it. It was to come into force on 1 January 1801. And so, what one member of the British Cabinet described as 'the greatest and most desirable measure which ever was in contemplation' was brought into being. Something of this extravagant mysticism continued to surround the Union for the 120 years of its existence.

At once exaltation on the part of the British Government and the pro-Unionists achieved almost religious dimensions. According to Cornwallis, the Empire was now so completely united that the Union would remain 'in all future ages, the fairest monument of His Majesty's reign already distinguished by so many and such various blessings conferred upon every class and description of his subjects'.[35] What had been achieved, Unionist supporters felt, was the almost magical formula which Pitt had expressed in a speech in the House of Commons: 'the voluntary association of two great countries, which seek their common benefit in one Empire, in which each will retain its proportionate weight and importance, under the security of equal laws, reciprocal affection, and inseparable interests, and in which each will acquire a strength that will render it invincible'.[36]

Grattan, however, in his last speech in the Irish House of Commons opposing the Union, had struck a very different note.

The Constitution may, for a time, be lost – the character of the country cannot be so lost. The Ministers of the Crown may at length find that it is not so easy to put down for ever an ancient and respectable nation by abilities however great, by power and corruption, however irresistible. Liberty may repair her golden beams, and with redoubled heart re-animate the country. ... I do not give up the country. I see her in a swoon, but she is not dead; though in her tomb she lies helpless and motionless, still there is on her lips a spirit of life and on her cheek a glow of beauty . . .[37]

Both attitudes were misleadingly rhetorical. What golden beams of liberty, it might have been asked, had the wretched masses intoxicating themselves with the mumbo-jumbo of the Defenders ever known? The Constitution as it had existed for nineteen years was indeed going down but no 'ancient and respectable nation' had been truly identified with it – only the propertied classes, and many of these, even, without the right to function within it. The country in the sense that Grattan was talking about was indeed helpless and motionless but not in her tomb, or even in a swoon, for she had still to have life breathed into her.

The challenge to Pitt's rhetoric lay in the future. It was not by any means inconceivable that the Union might turn out to benefit Ireland in the way he foretold. But whether or not she would acquire the promised invisible strength would depend entirely on the reality given to phrases like 'common benefit' and 'equal laws', and how exactly an attempt was going to be made to meet those 'interests' which were now to be 'inseparable' from the rest of Britain's.

The fact that the Union was to fail the challenge of reality was not, as has sometimes been maintained, the result of treacherous English villainy. The Union was not intended as a trap for Ireland although it turned out afterwards to have been one. What was to make it fail was not villainy, or even neglect, but inability to understand until almost too late the fundamental problem of Irish society. This problem, so long evaded not only by the British Government but by Irish patriots themselves, was the historically conditioned land system which covered the greater part of the country. This system's injustice, its lack of acknowledgement of any rights for those who worked the land and lived by it – as distinct from those who owned it – was the result of the ancient religious conflict between Protestants and Catholics long conceded to be irrelevant where land was concerned. The injustice was magnified by another historically conditioned factor: the absence of any alternative form of livelihood but land. The land system had to be changed, even at the cost of interfering with the rights of property, if the population of the country was ever to come within sight of the decent satisfactions of normal everyday life. When eventually understanding did break through and relevant action was taken, it was still just not too late to save the Union in its widest form and certainly not too late in any case to save the British connection through a joint Crown. That both were eventually lost was due to another failure, not this time of understanding, but of imagination.

2

Robert Emmet's Fall and Rise

The actual passing of the Union turned out to be something of an anti-climax at the time. The issue had always given rise to more calculation than passion and such passion as had been generated was spent. From all over the country, including Dublin, came reports of perfect tranquillity.[1] Even those forces which by definition existed to disturb Irish tranquillity seem hardly to have been affected one way or the other. Agrarian disturbances came and went, as they had done for decades, in Lecky's phrase 'like the passing storms that sweep so rapidly over the inconstant Irish sky'.[2] Part of the pro-Union argument had in any case always been that it would in time work to eradicate such disaffection. As for the United Irishmen, they had been opposed not particularly to the Union but to the British connection which existed whether there were a union or not. They had been broken not by the Union but by their own incompetence and lack of effective organization three years before, and by the consequent military defeats both of the rebels and the French. But there was to be one last attempt to revive their cause. And total failure and puny in scale though it was, it was to echo through history with almost as much effect as the convulsion of 1798 itself.

While the Union arguments had been proceeding in the course of 1799 the government had received information that a new United Irish executive had been formed in Dublin and that one of its guiding spirits was the Protestant Robert Emmet, youngest son of a sometime physician to the Vice-Regal Lodge and younger brother of Thomas Addis Emmet, then a state prisoner in Fort George in Scotland. The year before, Robert had been a noticeably brilliant student at Trinity College where he had studied science, but he had been expelled for holding radical political views like those for which his brother had got himself into much more serious trouble. Robert had visited his brother and MacNeven, O'Connor and the rest in Kilmainham gaol before they were moved to Scotland. The prisoners had had considerable latitude and freedom of association in Kilmainham, and Robert had taken out instructions from them to such members of the United Irish executive as were still at large, and had himself become a member of the executive. Now, in 1799, on receipt of information about his activity from an informer, the government ordered his arrest. They found that he had already fled.

Robert Emmet's whereabouts for the next year or so are obscure though he undoubtedly had contacts with his brother and the others in Fort George, where conditions were even more lax and civilized than they had been in Kilmainham. Early in 1801 he went to France, where for about a year he seems to have been the Paris representative of such United Irish directory as was functioning in Ireland. But the apparent half-heartedness of the French towards the cause made it an unrewarding post. Certainly it seems that Bonaparte was more interested in making the British fear an invasion of Ireland than in actually carrying one out. Emmet optimistically studied military textbooks, including a history of the Seven Years War.[3] Among acquaintances he made was the American engineer and armaments specialist, Robert Fulton, who was then trying to sell the idea of a submarine to Bonaparte and who imparted to Emmet his fascination with rockets and explosives. But the chances of putting theory into practice receded further than ever when France concluded the Peace of Amiens with England in 1802.

The United Irish prisoners were now released from Fort George in delayed implementation of their compact with the British Government, and it was Robert Emmet's first wish to join his brother in exile in America. But the loneliness of his ageing parents in Ireland troubled him and he eventually decided with some reluctance to return there.[4] Presumably he felt free to do so because Habeas Corpus, which had been suspended when the government wanted to arrest him earlier, had now been restored, and there was probably little solid evidence against him which would have held up in front of a jury. The private letter in which he writes of the difficulty this decision caused him also makes clear that he was not then contemplating anything in the way of radical conspiracies, but rather reluctantly considering them a thing of the past.[5]

He returned to Ireland in October 1802, leading for a time a purely social life, dining out in merchants' houses in Dublin and emphasizing that he had come about private and not public affairs.[6] But there was in fact already a conspiracy on foot in Dublin, with which in its first stage he apparently had no connection. This was a curious affair timed to coincide with a three-part rising of radical republicans in the British Isles – in England, Scotland and Ireland simultaneously. The chief branch of the conspiracy was in England, where it was headed by an eccentric military figure of previous good standing named Colonel Despard. Despard had had a respectable public career up to a point but had developed a bitter sense of grievance against the British Government when they dismissed him from a post in the West Indies, and this sense of grievance transformed him into a violent republican. The London end of the plot, which was to begin by blowing George III to bits with a cannon aimed at him from the park, was foiled in plenty of time. Despard was arrested, tried with six other conspirators, found guilty and hanged in a row with them, in spite of a recommendation to mercy by the jury on account of past services to the nation and personal testimony to his character from Lord Nelson. Altogether, Despard in fact appears as a rather absurd and pathetic figure in history who only keeps his place there thanks to his tenuous connection with another conspiratorial failure to whom myth was kinder: Robert Emmet.

It seems unlikely that Emmet had any part in the Irish end of the conspiracy while Despard was alive, but it must have been soon after Despard's execution that he once again became entangled in United Irish activity in Dublin. In his Proclamation of July 1803, headed very like another more famous proclamation of over a century later, 'The Provisional Government to the People of Ireland', Emmet declared that such a government had been organizing for eight months and referred to the 'failure of a similar attempt in England', clearly meaning Despard's.[7] It must therefore have been around the end of 1802 that he entered into his plan for a new United Irish rising in Dublin. Certainly the police began to show an interest in him again about that time, because they paid a visit to his father's house where he was living at the end of December 1802, but he evaded them by means of an elaborate series of trap-doors, ropes, pulleys and concealed hiding-places which he had constructed there.[8]

Emmet does not appear to have been the prime mover in the new conspiracy at first, though it is not clear who was. Certainly, by the time his ill-assorted band took to the streets in the following July he, in his general's uniform of green and lace with gold epaulettes on each shoulder, was the chief person in authority – though authority is an inappropriate word in the circumstances.

In spite of past disappointments with France, the conspirators had been plainly encouraged by the renewal of the war in May 1803, and a messenger was sent to France, to Robert's brother Thomas, with the familiar sort of wildly optimistic assertions about the state of affairs in Ireland. There was 'a new and closer plan' . . . communication between North and South had been thoroughly established . . . respectable men had come forward . . . Kildare, Wicklow and Dublin were in a very forward state . . . one depot in Dublin alone held 2,500 pikes already fitted with handles . . . the government did not seem to have the slightest suspicion, etc.[9] Thomas Emmet was to procure arms and money and officers from Bonaparte, but in this he proved unsuccessful, being unable even to obtain personal access to Bonaparte, a problem aggravated by a split among the exiled revolutionaries in Paris.*

* Arthur O'Connor, who seems more to have enjoyed the First Consul's favour, and was made a French general, was the leader of the rival group to T. A. Emmet.

In any case, after past experience the Dublin men do not seem to have been relying too heavily on the French, stressing in their application for help that they were disgusted with France and would not take her assistance if they could do without it.[10] In Emmet's excited proclamation, it was positively stated that the conspiracy had been conducted 'without the hope of foreign assistance'.[11] Certainly, whether hoped for or not, French help was not forthcoming, for, in what was to become the tradition of Irish nationalist rebellions, the rising went off at half-cock.

The plan itself was reasonable and practical, its execution lamentable to the point of farce. Bad luck played its part but need not have played such a disastrous one if organization and leadership had been efficient. The chief objective was Dublin Castle, the seat for centuries of the Irish executive which had been retained intact after the Union, though responsible now directly to the British Parliament. The Pigeon House fort in the harbour and the Artillery Barracks at Islandbridge were to be captured first. Meticulous care had been given to the planning of this operation. Points in between the main objectives where loyalist forces might be expected to give trouble were detailed, and an elaborate defensive system worked out whereby certain streets were to be chained and padlocked and strategic nearby houses occupied. The bridges over the Liffey were to have boards covered with long nails fixed into the roadway to impede entry. A special feature of the rising was to be the ingenuity of weapons employed. In secret arms depots in Dublin men had for weeks been manufacturing not only the conventional pikes in use five years before but also an improved version which folded in half so that it could be carried concealed under a man's greatcoat, and, more revolutionary still, a great quantity of explosives including rockets, grenades and fixed wooden blocks full of explosive and shrapnel which could be set to go off in the street like mines. It was in fact the preoccupation with explosives that set off the disastrous sequence of events in which Emmet's attempt ended. On 16 July 1803 an accidental explosion took place in one of the depots in Patrick Street, Dublin, drawing the attention of the police to the house.

One of the most remarkable features of Emmet's ill-starred attempt was that, unlike the business of five years before, the secret of the conspiracy had been kept very close. This part at least of the message to his brother in France had been no boast. Although the government had some general uneasy feelings that something was afoot they had no suspicion of what it was, or who was involved in it. Even after the explosion in Patrick Street the police were unable to discover anything like the real nature or extent of what had been going on there. Many of the remaining arms had been removed before the police arrived; others were stored in specially prepared hiding-places which were not discovered. But Emmet reasonably concluded that it would only be a matter of time before the government were on to him and decided not to postpone the date of the rising already fixed for the following Saturday, 23 July 1803. Thomas Russell, Tone's old friend, the only one of the exiled prisoners from Fort George to come over from France to join him, was sent off to alert the North which, he assured Emmet, was all ready to rise.

It had been a conscious part of Emmet's strategy not to try to organize the country outside Dublin to any large extent. He thus hoped to avoid the pitfalls of conspiratorial bureaucracy which had helped undo the men of '98. His assumption was that large areas of the country were ready to rise in any case if given the proper signal, and that there could be no more proper signal than the taking of the Castle and victory in Dublin. This replaced the old previously awaited signal of a French landing.

In his Proclamation Emmet said he was counting on the support of nineteen counties. When he finally launched his abortive attempt that Saturday, the country so conspicuously failed to rise that it is easy to say his assumptions were ludicrous. But then, no signal was given. Not only did Emmet fail to take Dublin; he came nowhere near any success at all. And the cautious and individualistic nature of the discontent in the country was such that without any very clear indication of success it inevitably remained inert.

The trail of disasters after the accident of the Patrick Street explosion was almost continuous. There was a remarkable lack of any firm leadership or preparedness to deal with them. Apart from sending Russell off to the North, the only practical arrangements Emmet had made with forces other than his own were with the men of Kildare and those remnants of the '98 rebellion still holding out under Michael Dwyer in Wicklow. But these arrangements, and Emmet's entire system of communications, proved highly unreliable. Through a failure of the messenger sent to summon Dwyer's men from Wicklow, they never arrived at all. The men from Kildare did come into Dublin, principally on the evening before, but did not like what they found. Emmet had to spend hours arguing with them not only about whether the arms provided were sufficient but also, at this absurdly late stage, about whether or not the rising ought to wait for a French landing. These Kildare men spent much of the day itself waiting for the zero hour of 9 p.m. in the Dublin public houses, and many actually moved out of the city about 5 p.m. on receipt of a false report that Dublin was not going to rise after all. A message had been circulated by some treacherous or cowardly person, wrote Emmet later, that the rising was off till the following Wednesday.[12] The Wexford men who did assemble at the right place in Dublin waited in vain on the night for their prearranged signal – the firing of a rocket. It was never fired, because by then Emmet had been so overwhelmed by the magnitude of the other disasters that he had decided to call the whole adventure off.

'There was failure in all,' Emmet wrote afterwards, 'plan, preparation and men.'[13] Until as late as five o'clock on the day of the rising he was desperately trying to find money to buy more blunderbusses. The last two days, which should have been spent in perfection of plans, had to be devoted to making good the shortage of pikes after losses in the Patrick Street explosion. '... Even this, from the confusion occasioned by men crowding into the Depot, from the country, was almost impossible.' The man who was to make the fuses for the wooden explosive devices forgot about them. The man in charge of the depot 'mixed, by accident, the slow matches that were prepared with what were not, and all our labour went for nothing. The fuses for the grenades he had also laid by, where he forgot them, and could not find them in the crowd. The cramp irons could not be got in time from the smiths, to whom we could not communicate the necessity of dispatch; and the scaling ladders were not finished (but one).'

At Dublin Castle itself the government had had many indications to supplement their vague suspicions of the past few weeks. On the morning of 23 July itself a publican came in to report that he had heard some men discussing over breakfast a rising due for that evening, and an employer arrived to say that some of his men had asked to be paid off early that night so that they could take part in it.[14] A state of increased alert was maintained but no positive move made and the government was afterwards heavily criticized for not having taken the situation more seriously.

Meanwhile, the Proclamation of the Provisional Government was arriving wet from the presses* in the depot where Emmet in his general's green uniform and his feathered cocked hat was assembling his men. Three hours – from six to nine – had been allotted for the assembly of two thousand men. By nine o'clock eighty had arrived.[15] 'You are now called upon,' began the Proclamation, 'to show the world that you are competent to take your place among the nations; that you have a right to claim their recognisance of you as an independent country. ... We have now, without the loss of a man, with our means of communication untouched, brought our plans to the moment when they are ripe for execution. ... We therefore solemnly declare that our object is to establish a free and independent republic in Ireland ...'[16] The 'Provisional Government of the Republic' appended to the Proclamation a list of thirty decrees, abolishing tithes, making Church lands the property of the nation, and suspending all transfers of land and securities until the formation of a national government. A new sovereign assembly was to be elected on universal suffrage by secret ballot, to consist of three hundred representatives as in the old Parliament but now elected in proportion to the population of the thirty-two counties.[17]

Over such matters at least considerable care had been taken, and this evidence of it may at the last moment have given some confidence to the

* So described by the soldiers who arrived on the scene shortly afterwards.

group assembled round their small uniformed general in the confusion of the Thomas Street depot. If so, it could not have lasted long. News suddenly arrived that the horses pulling the coaches on which they had been counting to carry the assault force under cover to Dublin Castle had bolted on their way there, after an incident in which one of the escorting rebels had fired his pistol at a patrol. Soon after, a near panic ensued when word came that the military were approaching. The news was to prove false but there and then Emmet drew his sword and, accompanied by about a hundred men, sallied forth into the night in the name of the Irish Republic. The streets were filled with the usual Saturday night crowds, many of them drunk.

An indeterminate mob was soon rampaging through the streets with pikes and blunderbusses. It eventually found itself, quite fortuitously, surrounding the coach of Lord Kilwarden, the Lord Chief Justice, and a remarkably humane man, who with his son-in-law was now savagely piked to death. Emmet, striding on with a band of followers which soon dwindled to about twenty, was quite unaware of this grisly occurrence, and afterwards wholeheartedly deplored it. But the catastrophic nature of his failure was already plain to him, and, refusing to give the signal for the Wexford men to move to the now useless shedding of blood, he took himself off into hiding. As he himself conceded, what had happened did not even have the respectability of insurrection.[18] About thirty lives were lost in the course of the desultory rioting that completed the night.

Elsewhere in Ireland, almost nothing happened at all. The faithful Russell, as 'General of the Northern District', issued a proclamation that 'vast multitudes in all parts of the country were engaged',[19] but this was quickly recognized as untrue and treated accordingly. One claim Emmet could, and did, justifiably make for the whole disastrous undertaking. It had always been predicted that any new attempt at a rising would fail, but for quite different reasons. It was impossible, it was said, to hatch a conspiracy that was not known at the Castle. This at least Emmet had proved to be not so. When the government afterwards discovered the scale on which preparations had been made, unknown to them, they took considerably more fright than the actual events of the rising seemed to justify. There was an internal political row and the army commander was rather unfairly made the scapegoat.

But Emmet's real contribution to the cause in which he had so far cut such a forlorn and ludicrous figure was still to come. Under the name of Mr Ellis, his *nom-de-guerre* throughout the whole affair, he remained at large for nearly a month but, once caught, the result of his trial was a foregone conclusion. His speech from the dock must have had considerable effect in the darkening court room even at the time, for a number of his fellow students from Trinity days who were in court wearing the king's uniform went up and shook him by the hand afterwards, and the judge who sentenced him to be hanged, drawn and quartered, a notoriously callous man, is said to have been profoundly moved.[20] But the effect of the speech at the time was as nothing compared with the force it was to have as, with increasingly romantic persistence, it echoed through the history of the next hundred years into our own time. Since it was as a legend that this speech took wings it seems unimportant that the exact text is probably not wholly accurate. Certainly Emmet's words must have been close to the form in which they so popularly and effectively survived. He concluded:

I have but one request to ask at my departure from this world. It is the charity of its silence. Let no man write my epitaph; for as no man who knows my motives dare now vindicate them, let not prejudice or ignorance asperse them. Let them rest in obscurity and peace, my memory be left in oblivion and my tomb remain uninscribed, until other times and other men can do justice to my character. When my country takes her place among the nations of the earth, then and not till then, let my epitaph be written.

There is said to have been a curious delay at the scaffold. Emmet, who was allowed by the hangman to give the signal for his own drop by letting go of a handkerchief, continually replied, 'Not yet' to the hangman's repeated question: 'Are you ready, sir?' Finally, the hangman lost patience and tipped him into eternity in mid-sentence. The incident gave rise to some speculation as to whether or not Emmet was hoping for a last-minute rescue by some of Dwyer's men from Wicklow. But no rescue could have achieved the dramatic effect of the execution itself. After hanging for half an hour his unconscious form was cut down and, in accordance with the judicial custom of the day, his head was cut off with a butcher's knife. It was exhibited by the hangman who strode about the scaffold crying, 'This is the head of Robert Emmet, a traitor'. Dogs were seen licking up the blood. Handkerchiefs were dipped in the blood and jealously prized and preserved. Metaphorical handkerchiefs were dipped in it for over a century.

A few years later Emmet's old friend and fellow student at Trinity, the poet Tom Moore, wrote some lines which he included in his *Irish Melodies* without a title:

Oh! breathe not his name, let it sleep in the shade,
Where cold and unhonoured his relics are laid;
Sad, silent and dark be the tears that we shed,
As the night dew that falls on the grass o'er his head.

But the night dew that falls, though in silence it weeps,
Shall brighten with verdure the grave where he sleeps,
And the tear that we shed, though in secret it rolls,
Shall long keep his memory green in our souls.

Moore's poem, picking up Emmet's own last words from the dock, set the tone for the future of the legend.

The reason why exactly the Emmet débâcle should have become transformed into a myth of such powerful emotive force, and thus indirectly of political importance, is not immediately easy to see. His failure could hardly have been more ignominious and complete. It is true that the myth gained incidental colour from Emmet's romantic attachment to Sarah Curran, the daughter of the prominent barrister John Philpot Curran. Letters compromising her in his treason were found on Emmet at the time of his arrest. She was disowned by her father and there is a story of her waiting down a street in a closed carriage and waving a last farewell to him as he proceeded to the scaffold. But what still needs explaining is why it should be such a romantic ethereal figure so much closer to the sentimental balladist's heart than to practical politics who was to become Ireland's noblest hero. Why was it Robert Emmet's portrait above all others that was to go up along with the crucifix in countless small homes in Ireland for over a century and may even be seen there still?

The proximity of the crucifix may provide a clue. The success of the Emmet myth lay in the very need to ennoble failure. For tragic failure was to become part of Ireland's identity, something almost indistinguishable from 'the cause' itself.*

* Compare the speech made by Padraic Pearse, who was to be Commander of the Republican forces in the Easter Rising of 1916, at Wolfe Tone's grave the year before. 'No failure,' he said, 'judged as the world judges these things, was ever more complete, more pathetic than Emmet's. And yet he has left us a prouder memory than the men of Brian victorious at Clontarf or of Owen Roe victorious at Benburb. It is the memory of a sacrifice Christ-like in its perfection.'

3

The Failure of the Union

If the Union were to be a political success, it had to bring about some definite change in Irish life. Its justification lay in ushering in a new era. The one thing it could not afford to be in everyday terms was meaningless. Yet, for the vast majority of Irishmen clinging with unceasing precariousness to their small holdings of land, the Union made no practical difference at all; if anything, by making them more remote from government, it made things worse. The ground swell of social discontent remained as before, a vast unwieldy incoherent force, available to any political skill that might be bold enough to try to harness it.

There is an uncanny similarity about the way in which all eye-witnesses describe the conditions of the majority of the population of Ireland over a vast span of nearly two centuries. In the middle of these two centuries stands the Union of 1801, an almost irrelevant landmark. The commonest feature of all such descriptions is the comparison between Ireland and other countries to the detriment of Ireland, and this is stressed even more heavily after the Union.[1]

'I have seen several countries,' said a Resident Magistrate of Cork in 1824, 'and I never saw any peasantry so badly off.'[2] Richard Cobden, the Free Trader, told a friend that once after spending three months in Ireland he had gone direct to Egypt and that, taking the difference of climate into consideration, the condition of the fellaheen was infinitely better than that of the Irish cottier, or labouring class.[3]

'The wretchedness in some of the western parts of the County of Clare,' stated a Constabulary Inspector in 1824, 'is as great as human nature can almost be subjected to.'[4] And Sir Walter Scott visiting Ireland a year later noted in his diary: 'Their poverty has not been exaggerated: it is on the extreme verge of human misery.'[5] Nor were the years 1824–5 years of famine as 1817 and 1822 had been. Nor had anything like the worst yet been seen.

In 1844 a German traveller echoed many earlier comments with the words: 'To him who has seen Ireland no mode of life in any other part of Europe however wretched will seem pitiable.'[6] And a year later the Devon Commission, the last government inquiry to report on Ireland before the

Great Famine, confirmed this with a reference to 'the patient endurance which the labouring classes have generally exhibited under sufferings greater we believe than the people of any other country have to sustain'.[7] But by that time the greatest disaster of all in the Irish common people's long history of suffering was already befalling them. It was a disaster which everyone, including the government, had in one sense been able to see coming for decades, but which, since they felt quite powerless to do anything about it, they had preferred to treat as if it might never materialize.

A Frenchman, De Latocnaye, who toured Ireland fifty years before in 1796 had confirmed the continuation of the middleman system that had even then long been in existence.*

... A rich man, unwilling to be at any trouble, lets a large tract of country to one man, who does not intend to cultivate it himself, but to let it out to three or four others; those who have large shares farm them to about a score, who again let them to about a hundred comfortably situated peasants, who give them at an exorbitant price to about a thousand poor labourers, whom necessity obliges to take their scanty portion at a price far beyond its real value . . .[8]

Fifty years later this situation had become a nightmare. The early years of the nineteenth century saw a great surge of agricultural prosperity in Ireland, started partly by earlier government corn bounties to farmers in the days of the Irish Parliament, but accelerated by the high farm prices obtainable as a result of the Napoleonic War. Yet in Ireland, where land was virtually the only source of livelihood, and competition for land therefore unlimited, agricultural prosperity meant prosperity only for those who received rents. For the rest of the population, who would pay any price that gave them a minimum subsistence, prosperity meant only that subsistence was at least for a time not in doubt, and that more such subsistence was available for more such people.

More such people soon appeared by the normal processes of nature to take advantage of the fact. The census of 1841 gave a population of just over eight million, probably double what it had been at the beginning of the century.† Middlemen on the land, taking a natural commercial advantage of the multiplying masses' desire and indeed absolute need for land, themselves multiplied accordingly on the pattern described by Latocnaye. Holdings were increasingly subdivided and sub-let to others who increasingly subdivided and sub-let in turn. Soon tenants on any sizeable piece of land were increasing at a terrifying rate of progression, and it became common enough to find a chain of succession on any one piece of land going down four or five times from the initial landlord. In the early 1820s when the

* See above, p. 22.

† This census also revealed that Irish was still the common speech of the majority. The Irish population was at this time just about half that of Great Britain – then sixteen million.

simple lease of one of the Duke of Leinster's 500-acre farms fell in, he found that on some parts of it there were tenants at seven removes from himself.[9] And the Catholic barrister Daniel O'Connell said he knew of farms, where he remembered only two farmhouses, supporting, in 1825, nearly two hundred families.[10]

All this was possible because land was the only means by which a man could procure a living for his family. The vast majority of the population naturally found themselves at the end of these series of middlemen; almost half the total number of holdings being less than five acres, and, by 1841, only seven per cent of them more than thirty acres.[11]

As each middleman in each series had to take his profit, the rent paid by those at the end of the series was all that a man could possibly afford to pay and continue to survive. Indeed, the series only came to an end in any given piece of land when that point had been reached.

The competition for land had 'attained something like the competition for provisions in a besieged town or in a ship that is out at sea'.[12] Whatever the size of a holding (and few were more than fifteen acres) the tenant-farmers lived almost entirely on potatoes, selling their crops to pay the extortionate rent. Frequently they could not even afford salt for their potatoes, which themselves were of the coarsest quality.

The Irish [wrote a desperate tenant farmer to the lord lieutenant] are reduced to the necessity of entirely subsisting on the lumper potato – a kind that grows something better in the poor man's impoverished land than the potatoes of good quality. The lumper is not indeed human food at all. Mix them with any other kind of potatoes and lay them before a pig, and she will not eat one of them until all the good kind are devoured. . . . People like you cannot have the least idea of our misery. The great governors of nations ought to go in disguise through the country and enter the hovels of the peasantry to make themselves acquainted with the kind of food they live on and how they must labour for that food.[13]

Bread itself was hardly eaten by the average Irishman from one year's end to the other. Nor was this only true of the poorest. A farmer with a holding of above average size on the Marquis of Conyngham's estate in 1846 declared: 'Not a bit of bread have I eaten since I was born, nor a bit of butter. We sell all the corn and the butter to give to the landlord' [for rent] 'yet I have the largest farm in the district and am as well off as any man in the county.'[14]

During the first half of the nineteenth century a number of most thorough inquiries were made by Parliament into the state of Ireland, and all reveal clearly this wretched life lived by the majority of the inhabitants, paying rents, 'by which it was impossible for the tenant at any time to pay, reserving the means of decent subsistence', living huddled together without distinction of age or sex, usually in the company of their livestock, on the bare floor of cabins through which ran open sewage, possessing hardly any bedding except straw, and often only able to go to Mass on alternate Sundays because there were not enough clothes to go round.[15] The lowest class of all could not even afford to pay rent, but in return for a minimum plot on which to grow enough potatoes for survival gave their labour for nothing all the year round like serfs. Some families of this type occupied as little as a quarter of an acre (though not less than two to three acres was regarded as necessary for the proper support of a large family).* So far down the economic scale were many of them that they hardly ever handled money at all.

Moreover, with a drop in agricultural prices after the Napoleonic War and the general trend for grazing land to become more profitable than tillage, landlords, appalled by the number of poor people they found multiplying on their land, understandably enough began to try and consolidate their property. A parish priest described what happened when they did.

'About three weeks or a month ago,' he said in May 1824, he had seen 'a certain farm (about 500 acres) that had 40 families residing on it, thinned in this manner. These 40 farms consisted of 200 individuals. When the lease fell in ... 28 or 30 of these farms, consisting of 150 individuals, were dispossessed; they were allowed to take with them the old roofs of the cabins, that is the rotten timber and the rotten straw; and with these they contrived to erect stands upon the highway. The men could get no employment, the women and children had no resource but to go and beg; and really it was a most affecting scene to behold them upon the highway, not knowing where to go.'[16] Some, thus evicted, moved to the towns where they crowded into small apartments and perhaps four or five families would live huddled together in a garret without proper clothes or bedding or food, while the men scavenged for casual labour, which was seldom to be had.

In all these circumstances it needed no social or economic genius to foretell what would happen if the potato crop, which alone was keeping the vast majority of the population alive, were to fail. In any case, the potato crop had failed quite frequently before, and history had already recorded the terrible famines which then ensued. There had been famines with particularly appalling spectacles of misery and death in 1720, 1739, 1741, 1800, 1817 and 1822. The great famine of the years 1845–8 was only the worst because by that time the population had grown to such a size that the pressure on land was that much greater, and the whole precarious system that much more disastrously balanced. A little over twenty years before, a parliamentary inquiry had asked a witness: 'Looking ahead to 15 or 20 years or more, what must this increase in population without employment end in?' and he had replied, 'I do not know; I think it is terrible to reflect upon.'[17]

Terrible indeed it proved to be, killing probably about a million people altogether and reducing the population of Ireland by death or agonizing

* An Irish acre was slightly larger than a normal British acre, being in the relation of about $1\frac{3}{5}$: 1.

emigration by as much as a quarter in six years. Men found that the scenes long spoken of with awe as characterizing earlier famines were now taking place, on an even more horrifying scale, before their eyes. The dead were already lying unburied six or eight days in the streets of Skibbereen and it was possible to plead on behalf of a sheep-stealer that his wife was so hungry that she had been eating the thigh of her own daughter who had died from famine fever.[18] And since starving and dying people had not the strength to till the soil to pay the rent – only the potato was affected by blight: other crops were good in the famine years – eviction on an unprecedented scale now took place in horrifying circumstances. One eye-witness described the eviction of 143 families (700 persons) from an estate in Tipperary as 'the chasing away of 700 human beings like crows out of a cornfield'.[19] Often they were too weak to be chased or had to be evicted dead. In either case, their corpses were found soon afterwards littering the hedgerows.

The opportunity was also seized of clearing *all* unwanted people off land, even those who were managing to pay their rent regularly. In one such case, seventy-six families, or about three hundred persons, were evicted from the estate of a Mr and Mrs Gerard in County Galway in spite of having the rent ready, and they were even driven from the ditches to which they had·fled to try to fix up some sort of shelter with sticks and mud.[20] A bizarre individual instance of an eviction where no rent was owing was that of James Brady, cleared with his family from a holding near Kells in the rich farming county of Meath, though he had always paid his rent regularly. After spending nine days and nights with his wife and four little girls in a ditch, he dug the family a living grave in a churchyard on the plot of a man called Newman. Newman then served him with an eviction order but, before it could be enforced, himself died of famine fever and was buried in the grave beside the squatters, who thus continued to defy him into eternity.[21]

Sir Robert Peel, who had been Prime Minister when the potato crop first failed in 1845, said of one set of evictions at Kilrush in County Mayo involving the clearance of some fifteen thousand people like rubbish over a period of twelve months, that he did not think the records of any country, civil or barbarous, presented materials for such a picture.[22] And he went on to quote a government inspector's account of one significant but poignant incident involving a man employed breaking stones.

He [the inspector] saw that man suddenly seize on the remnant of a pair of shoes and run across a heath. He followed the direction the man took and saw a fire blazing. On making inquiry as to the cause of it, he was told that upon the man being driven from his home, he had occupied a still more wretched hovel of his own construction and that it was this last place in which he had sought shelter that had been set fire to in order to get rid of him.[23]

There are countless descriptions of what happened in those years on such a vast scale in the workhouses and fever hospitals, in the prisons to which people chose entry by the most direct means only to find the packed cells riddled with typhus, in the lonely derelict cabins where families of dying and dead were stretched out one above the other in layers, in the cramped emigrant ships in which as many as one-fifth of all the passengers sometimes had to be buried at sea, and in the fever-ridden camps on the other side of the Atlantic. But it was in millions of individual memories, often incoherent and inarticulate, handed down in America and Ireland from one suffering generation to the next, and from them to men and women who were young in the twentieth century, that the sense of fundamental outrage and resentment at this monstrous thing that had happened under civilized government to the humble people of Ireland lived on.[24]

It is easy, over a hundred years later and after the successful establishment of an Irish Republic, to look back and say, quite correctly, that the accusations of genocide made by some Irish writers at the time and since were unjust and absurd; that the government was the prisoner of the economic philosophy of the day, which taught that economic laws had a natural operation and that to interfere with them was to breed chaos and anarchy; that, far from looking on callously, the government looked on with an increasing sense of dismay at what it regarded as its helplessness before irresistible economic and social forces; that, eventually, by what seemed a superhuman effort at the time, it succeeded in abandoning at least some of the principles it held most sacred and brought itself to distribute government charity, expecting only in return that its recipients should continue to live. All this is true.

It is also true, as the appalling conditions from which the English working classes suffered at the same time make clear, that there was no specifically anti-Irish callousness in the government's outlook. The agricultural lower classes of Ireland were of no less theoretical concern to the government than the industrial working classes of England. The trouble was simply that in neither case was the concern great enough. Complex situations had developed within both patterns of lower-class living with which government had never contemplated having to deal. In Ireland the problems, besides being physically more remote, were also more complex, being bound up with a historical land system that went much further back than the industrial revolution; and the sufferings of the lower classes there were correspondingly greater. But the government were dealing 'with their own people' in both cases, however ironic the phrase may seem in the circumstances.

It is also necessary to say that the rigidity of the formula from which the government of the day had to escape in order to govern better is, at this distance of time, very difficult to appreciate. A Poor Law Commissioner of the famine time declared that he had heard the opinion stated both implicitly and explicitly that 'it was desirable to allow things to take their normal course; not to assist the people in their suffering but to permit disease and want to go to their natural termination'. And he added that 'many individuals even of superior minds, who seemed to have steeled their hearts to the suffering of the people of Ireland, justify it to themselves by thinking it would be going contrary to the provision of nature to render assistance to the destitute of that country'.[25] And this was at the height of the disaster when the government were in fact already distributing free soup. It was held then and continued to be held even for long afterwards that 'the economic laws which govern all human society are fixed by divine wisdom, and that any attempt to struggle with them by human legislation invariably results in making matters worse'.[26]

In the current of such a social philosophy clearly the government of the famine time showed some courage and enterprise in grappling with the disaster even to the inadequate extent it did. Yet it must finally be said of men who, when faced by the manifold unmistakable warnings they had received, had felt unable to grapple with the situation earlier or more effectively, that there was about them a lack of imagination and a fear of acting outside the civilized conventions of their time that amounted to a blot on civilization itself. Certainly it made nonsense of all the fine phrases about 'common benefit ... equal laws ... reciprocal affection ... inseparable interests and invincible strength' with which Pitt had ushered in the Union over forty years before.

There was also a flaw in their economic philosophy which amounted to something very like hypocrisy. For this society had no scruples about interfering by human legislation with 'natural' economic laws where the interests of property demanded it. It was only where the demand was in the interests of the poor that their principles were so sternly unyielding. As a future Prime Minister, Gladstone, was to comment, the law was amended over and over again in favour of the landlord but there was not to be, until 1870, a single act on the statute book in favour of the tenant.

If, then, it must be the calm judgement of history that the government which could allow such a thing to happen stands condemned, it is easy to imagine how bitter and outraged was the reaction at the time of those who survived and who understood only the pain they and their loved ones suffered. This deep resentment was to take on a profound historical importance.

For the famine and its after-effects played a role in Irish history long after the grass had grown over the mass graves and the unwanted roads and pointless earthworks which the starving had had to construct in return for the first attempts at relief. In the late forties and early fifties well over a million Irish of the poorer class, hating what passed for government in Ireland, became literally physically separate from that government when they emigrated to the other side of the Atlantic. Given the conditions under which their class had lived ever since the penal laws, there had obviously never been much enthusiasm for government as such but, in a primitive struggle like theirs, the real enemy had appeared not so much in the form of the government itself as in the more get-at-able form close at hand of a landlord or his agent, or, most frequently, of another member of the Irish peasant class refusing to combine in the common interest. Moreover, hostile as the government had been felt to be, it had been the only government there was; there had been no real conceivable alternative. Now, for a considerable section of the Irish people this was no longer so. They had separated from it. And since they and their descendants and followers to America long continued to be very Irish, for the first time in Irish history a very large body of Irish common opinion, often retaining close personal links with Ireland, could feel itself politically anti-British without the confusing factor of being somehow British too.

In Ireland itself the situation was less clear. The famine and its evictions had been only the worst in a long series of cruelties to which the humble people of Ireland had been exposed for centuries. Over and over again they had suffered and died, and society had been shocked, or had 'steeled their hearts', and the dead had been buried and society had continued as before, with more fine laments simply added to the stock of legend. In one sense the famine could be seen as the last straw, demanding at last some form of political atonement to the nameless millions who had suffered for centuries and, for the living, a better future. Yet to think, in Ireland itself, of creating a 'separate' Ireland demanded a much greater effort of the imagination than it did on the other side of the Atlantic. For the whole external fabric of society in Ireland was British, and, more confusing still, this British society in Ireland was Irish too.

One of the British Government's nineteenth-century Chief Secretaries for Ireland, the Earl of Mayo, a descendant of one of the most ancient Norman–Gaelic families, spoke no more than the truth when, in 1868, he declared that he had considerably less Anglo-Saxon blood in his veins than 'many of the gentlemen in green uniforms flourishing about New York' at that time.[27] And by then, too, religious divisions in Ireland, though more obvious than racial ones, were themselves becoming of less and less social or political significance. By the 1820s Catholics had once again accumulated considerable landed property in Ireland. By 1834 they owned about one-fifth of the land of Ireland outright – compared with one-fourteenth at the height of the penal laws – and a further half was held by Catholics on long lease, compared with almost none under the penal laws.[28] Thus, though the land system itself had not changed, Catholic landlords now exploited it together with Protestants. When, immediately after the famine, one-third of the land of Ireland changed hands as bankrupt estates were sold off, ninety per cent of the new landlords were Irishmen of one religion or the other, and particularly harsh in increasing rent and effecting clearances they proved to be. The important divisions in Irish society were no longer those of race or religion, but those of class.

In such circumstances the idea of Irish nationalism, never precise for the masses, took on a blurred image, and, inasmuch as it came to mean something positive at all, meant different things to different people.

4

Daniel O'Connell
and Catholic Emancipation

Some years before the famine a new form of Irish nationalism, rejecting republican separation altogether, had taken shape under the leadership of the lawyer Daniel O'Connell, one of the great pioneers of popular democracy. It had in fact, until swamped by the famine, acquired the power of the people behind it unlike anything put forward in the name of Irish nationalism before; being the first real effective organization of Irish mass opinion since the days of James II.

The new movement had different names at different times depending on O'Connell's immediate political objective, but its real objective, under whatever label, was the improvement of the lot of the Irish common people as a national aim in itself. Nationalism, or Irish-consciousness, with its heavy and romantic sense of the past and its love of the beautiful landscape in which this flourished, became primarily a powerful emotive auxiliary in the drive towards political goals which were to mean better times for all.

For the rest of the century and beyond, this was what Irish nationalism was to represent for the majority of the Irish population. Republican separatism, though it could often call on wide passive sympathy, became only a small minority movement, and remained so until almost the final moment of its surprise success in the next century. Only the swelling numbers of separate Irishmen in the great republic across the Atlantic, nursing the bitterest memories of government in Ireland, gave it a significance out of proportion to its Irish presence.

Daniel O'Connell was twenty-five at the time of the Union. He was by then a promising lawyer, born of a prosperous Catholic family from one of the remote promontories of County Kerry in south-west Ireland. As a Catholic, he had been rather untypical of his faith in strongly opposing the Union in 1800, declaring that if offered the alternatives of Union and the re-enactment of the penal laws in their full severity he would choose the latter. Certainly his own family history showed how some well-to-do Catholics could survive through long years of difficulty and darkness.

The O'Connells had been High Sheriffs of Kerry in the sixteenth century, but had suffered setbacks in the seventeenth when the head of the family was transplanted under Cromwell's anti-Catholic measures to Connaught. However, another O'Connell, by not joining in the rebellion of 1641, had managed to retain his own land. Throughout the eighteenth century the O'Connells had continued to cling to a nucleus of their ancient estates in Kerry and even before the repeal of the penal laws had been adding to them by the fairly common device of buying land in the name of a cooperative and friendly Protestant. One of O'Connell's uncles had emigrated to reach high rank in the French Army, another to become chamberlain to three Emperors of Austria. But another, after the abolition of the penal land laws, had added further to the family estates in Kerry and become an owner of grazing cattle on a considerable scale. He had also carried on a productive sideline in the smuggling trade with France for which the innumerable wild bays and inlets of Kerry made it so suitable. He virtually took over his nephew's upbringing.

O'Connell, like better-off Catholics throughout the eighteenth century, was educated in France where he stayed during the early part of the Revolution, leaving on the day of Louis XVI's execution. After studying law in London he was called to the Irish bar in May 1798, on the day Lord Edward Fitzgerald was arrested. Appalled by the bloodshed of the rebellion of that year, he was, by the time of Emmet's fiasco, a member of the loyalist Lawyers Artillery Corps.

But although O'Connell rejected the United Irishmen's ideas of separatist nationalism, he had a very strong emotive Irish-consciousness rooted in his own family history and he was successfully to take over much of the United Irishmen's rhetorical thunder and convert it to his own uses. A lot of his language was to be often almost indistinguishable from that of separatist nationalists. Thus, although he attached his own constitutional limitation to what he meant by 'liberate', he echoed Tone when he declared in 1810: 'The Protestant alone could not expect to liberate his country – the Roman Catholic alone could not do it – neither could the Presbyterian – but amalgamate the three into the Irishman, and the Union is defeated.'[1] Again, later in his career he said: 'In the struggle for nationality I recognize no distinction of creed or party. Every man who joins with me for Ireland is my sworn brother.'[2] And he could talk about 'the desire for National Independence' or 'the want of Nationhood'[3] with as much emotive power as anyone.

But for O'Connell the British connection and acceptance of the Crown were never questioned. Late in his life he insisted that he would abandon all his political aims overnight if he thought them in any way 'dangerous to the connection between the two countries, or dangerous to our allegiance to our sovereign'.[4] More than twenty years earlier, when George IV had visited Ireland in 1821 and the port of Dunleary was renamed Kingstown in his honour, O'Connell presented the king with a laurel crown on bended knee on his departure.[5] The address from the citizens of Dublin on that occasion referred to the king uniting 'six millions of a grateful people in a bond of brotherly love to one another, and of affectionate attachment to your Majesty's person and throne'.[6] O'Connell afterwards suggested the formation of a Royal Georgian club to dine six times a year, wearing cloth of Irish manufacture and rosettes of blue. 'Loyalty,' he declared, 'is not the peculiar prerogative of one sect or another, but it is the legitimate and appropriate characteristic of all His Majesty's subjects of every class, every rank, every denomination.'[7]

In other words, the sort of Irish nationality and Irish independence in which O'Connell believed was an extension to all the people of Ireland of that very sort of independence within the Empire which Protestant Irishmen had so proudly insisted on for themselves in the eighteenth century. What he meant by liberating the Irish people was liberating them all to this equality of rightful national pride within the connection. Ultimately this would bring about their liberation from the whole tyranny of their everyday conditions. The reason why he stuck so firmly to the British connection was not from any profound mystical convictions about it such as Grattan had had. O'Connell had simply learnt from recent history that any attempt to break the connection not only got the Irish people nowhere, but actually increased their dreadful suffering a thousandfold. On the other hand, anything on the right side of treason might theoretically be obtained. Thus the only insuperable obstacle to his aims became treason itself.

It was in the 1820s that the first stage of O'Connell's political career opened with his great campaign for Catholic Emancipation. This issue had simmered on for some twenty years after the Union, as a middle- and upper-class affair of polite petitions to Parliament. It was of direct interest only to those Catholics who might aspire to the relatively few high offices and functions, including membership of Parliament, from which they were still debarred. The peasantry concentrated on their own immediate interests through the network of the secret societies. Even as a symbol Emancipation had lost much of its force, for the major concession to Catholics had been made in the 1790s, when they received the vote on the same terms as the Protestants.

Yet it was precisely by managing to organize the masses so effectively in a campaign for the little that remained that O'Connell succeeded in raising a new issue of national political principle altogether. The real issue now, and for the first time in modern Irish politics, was this: were the masses, well-organized, but acting constitutionally, to be allowed to have their way against the government? It was this new subtle threat that accounted for the bitterness with which the government now fought Emancipation thirty years after Pitt had been prepared to concede it.

Although O'Connell had long been in favour of more vigorous action on Emancipation, it was only in 1823 that he began to give his full energies to the cause. Many sophisticated Catholics that year felt that the prospect of Emancipation had never been so dim. One wrote afterwards: 'I do not exaggerate when I say that the Catholic question was nearly forgotten.'[8] But that year O'Connell founded the Catholic Association for the purpose of adopting 'all such legal and constitutional measures as may be most useful to obtain Catholic Emancipation'.[9] The outstanding feature of the new organization was the broad democratic basis O'Connell gave it by introducing an associate membership, for which the subscription was only a shilling a year. The 'penny a month' became known as the Catholic Rent and soon vast sums, sometimes of £1,000 a week and more, were pouring in to the organization from all over Ireland, providing it with a regular campaign fund. The only immediate political objective for which the Association could campaign was the return to Parliament of Protestants who favoured Emancipation, but something like an embryonic political party apparatus on a democratic model had come into being.

The old oligarchic political system had survived the Union unreformed. But it did contain one odd democratic feature ready to hand for anyone with the will and determination to use it. When Catholics were enfranchised in 1793, the qualification had been the forty-shilling freehold. Almost any bit of property, sometimes even a bit of furniture, could be and often was spuriously dignified with the title of a forty-shilling freehold, for, with no secret ballot and the tradition still holding good that a tenant voted for his landlord, it was in a landlord's interest to have as many forty-shilling freeholders as possible. Anyone who voted against that interest could expect immediate eviction. But during the second decade of the nineteenth century evidence began to appear that Catholic forty-shilling freeholders could, if given support and encouragement by their priests, be brought to defy their landlords at the polls. The numerous forty-shilling freeholders were thus potentially a considerable democratic force. Some years even before the appearance of the Catholic Association the forty-shilling freeholders of Leitrim, Wexford and Sligo, mobilized by their priests, had successfully defied their landlords and obtained the election of liberals favourable to Catholic Emancipation. And just before the foundation of the Association the landed proprietors in County Dublin itself had also seen themselves outvoted.

O'Connell seems to have been slow to realize the powerful instrument made available to him by this new trend. A picture had long ago impressed itself on his mind of freeholders being driven by their landlords to the polls, like so many cattle to market. In spite of recent evidence he thought they were more a political liability as automatic landlord votes than an asset, and was even prepared to see their disfranchisement. Thus the initiative to overthrow the entrenched Tory landlord interests in a new election pending in Waterford in 1826 did not actually come from him.

Waterford was the property of the Beresford family, the most powerful in Ireland for influence and patronage. Only ten days before the actual election, for which preparations had been going on for months, O'Connell and the Catholic Association finally decided to throw themselves into the fight against the Beresfords' nominee. But they did so with a masterly organization which immediately struck fear into the government. The frightening thing was not the expected disorder, but the reverse. The police major in charge in Waterford reported to Dublin Castle that, quite unlike normal Irish elections, there was very little drunkenness and no rioting.[10] The Catholic Association itself patrolled the town to keep order. Green handkerchiefs, sashes, cockades and ribbons were being worn everywhere and green flags flew in all parts of the city.

The Emancipation candidate at Waterford was elected. It was a staggering blow to the landed proprietors, one of whom emphasized what to him was the really ominous feature, namely that all those very Catholics who had most loyally helped him put down rebellion in 1798 had now voted contrary to his wishes. The prospect of an organized mass political opinion which could no longer be dealt with as treason was thoroughly alarming. An equally sensational result took place soon afterwards at Louth, where a man whose family had controlled the county for half a century was defeated by an Emancipation candidate.

One of the ways in which Association funds were used was to give help to tenants evicted in reprisal for voting against their landlord's wishes. Publicity given by the Association to such acts of vindictiveness also discouraged the use of this ultimate landlord's sanction against the rebellious Catholic freeholder. Further elections followed, in which the Association continued to be successful.

The government, alarmed by this new democratic phenomenon, had already passed one act which made the Catholic Association illegal. But O'Connell always boasted that with his lawyer's skill he could drive a coach and six through any act of Parliament. He soon founded a New Catholic Association, 'merely for the purposes of public and private charity ... promoting public peace and tranquillity as well as private harmony among all classes of His Majesty's subjects throughout Ireland'.[11] Peel, the Home Secretary, and Wellington, the Prime Minister, strongly pressed the law officers of the Crown to prosecute the new organization. They were advised that, although the Association had technically broken the Convention Act of 1793 which had been specifically designed to prevent Catholics organizing extra-parliamentary power, it would be 'hazardous' in the present climate of Ireland to risk a prosecution by bringing the case before a jury. The climax of the Association's campaign came when O'Connell himself decided to stand for County Clare in 1828.

There was nothing illegal about a Catholic actually standing at an election, though none had done so for nearly 150 years. It was only after election that the test of his suitability to sit in Parliament was made. On presenting himself at the House of Commons he had not only to take the oaths of allegiance and supremacy. but also to testify that 'the invocation or adoration of the Virgin Mary or any other saint and the sacrifice of the Mass, as they are now used in the Church of Rome, are superstitious and idolatrous'.[12] If, in full knowledge of this, an electorate voted for a Catholic it was clearly as arrogant a defiance of the political establishment as could constitutionally be made. The Clare election presented the government with the most serious challenge it had had to face since the passing of the Act of Union.

There was a threat, too, behind the challenge, which, though largely unspoken, was a real consideration to the government and an essential, if risky, aspect of the tactics of O'Connell and the Catholic Association. The bloody horrors of 1798, though now some thirty years old, were very much a part of living memory. Any organization of the Irish masses in their incredible poverty and misery and their fierce resentment of their conditions could not help conjuring up the old spectre of violent and terrible insurrection. Though all leadership for political insurrection had disappeared, the masses' instinct for violence as a last resort had continued to manifest itself in the activities of the agrarian secret societies, particularly in the period between 1815 and 1824, which had seen two serious potato famines. In the circumstances, the government and the established order made no nice distinction between agrarian and political activity, between the masses collected in night bands of Rockites and Ribbonmen and the masses collected in their constitutional organization under O'Connell. One Orangeman, the Earl of Clancarty, thought that in 1824 Ireland was in a more dangerous state than on the eve of the rebellion of 1798, and in letters to the government there was exaggerated talk similar to that of the 1790s, of nightly meetings and arming with pikes and firearms.[13]

O'Connell's own horror of bloodshed was founded in recent Irish history. He had made technical legality and a constitutional attitude the cornerstone of his political faith. But he was not beyond implying that but for him and the Catholic Association violence would gain the upper hand. And in thus drawing attention to the threat he was averting, he uttered a sort of threat himself. The vivid and emotive metaphorical language of his speeches heightened the effect. His technique was to use those very dark forces of violence, which he was holding back, as a force obscurely at the back of him. This was to become even more blatantly his tactic in his later campaign for Repeal of the Union.

There was a good deal of substance in O'Connell's and the Catholic Association's claim that by the broad democratic nature of their own appeal they kept the violence of the agrarian secret societies harnessed and under control. O'Connell boasted that they and they alone prevented 'civil war', at the same time warning Wellington: 'Why, even in London if Pat took it into his head, he would go near to beat the guards; but for efficient strength at home it is but folly not to appreciate us justly.'[14] Sheil, another prominent member of the Association, sailed even closer to the wind by drawing attention in public to the 'vast body of fierce, fearless and desperate peasantry, who would be easily allured into a junction with an invader'.[15]

Certainly agrarian violence diminished after 1824 and the government reluctantly had to admit that this was due to the Association and its ability to assert discipline. 'We are in that happy state in Ireland,' wrote Peel to Wellington, bitterly, 'that it depends upon the prudence and discretion of the leader of the Roman Catholic Association whether we shall have a rebellion there or not in the next few months.'[16] And O'Connell continuously reminded the British Government of their predicament, playing sometimes too on their fear of French and even American[17] intervention. In his address to the people of England early in 1825, he stressed that 'Those who are labouring under oppression ... will be exposed to the strong temptation of receiving (if they can obtain it) assistance from any part of the world', and he talked of 'the possibility of seeing foreign fleets or bands the deliverers of Ireland'.[18] Moreover, by 1828, the year of O'Connell's own candidacy in the Clare election, the government were beginning to have serious doubts about the reliability in any emergency of the Irish troops.

Thus in the Clare election of 1828 the Irish bogey loomed almost as large as if rebellion had broken out, with the additional disadvantage that it could not be dealt with as if it had.

O'Connell stood in Clare as 'Man of the People'. The discipline of the crowds was again uncanny for an Irish election. Drunkenness was actually made a subject for mob punishment, offenders being thrown into the river, where they were kept for two hours and subjected to repeated duckings.[19] The commander of the troops described how the people marched in regular columns under officers who gave orders like 'keep in step' and 'right shoulders forward' which were immediately obeyed.[20] Peel himself wrote of the 'fearful exhibition of sobered and desperate enthusiasm'.[21]

O'Connell won the election by an overwhelming majority.

'Such a scene we have had!' wrote Peel. 'Such a tremendous prospect it opens to us! ... no man can contemplate without alarm what is to follow in this wretched country.'

With reports coming in that columns of men wearing green sashes and carrying green flags were parading in the West of Ireland,[22] Wellington and Peel, who even before the election had been facing up to the need to accept the inevitable, were in no doubt about one thing that had to follow. 'No one can answer for the consequences of delay,' wrote Wellington to the king in November.

A Catholic Emancipation Bill was introduced early in 1829 and received a pained and angry royal assent on 13 April of that year. It was immediately followed by an act which did something to reduce O'Connell's political power in Ireland for the immediate future by raising the franchise qualification from a forty-shilling to a ten-pound freehold. But, dazzled by his victory, O'Connell does not seem to have thought this important.

His victory meant much more than that Catholics could now sit in Parliament and become judges. The real victory consisted in the fact that for the first time ever the down-trodden Catholic masses had taken on the government and won. They had won by organization and discipline, by courage and leadership, by keeping just on the right side of the law and a long way on the right side of loyalty. There was a lesson to be learnt from this victory in contrast with the disastrous defeat into which the far cruder methods of the Defenders and the United Irishmen had led them. And in the first flush of this first victory, it either escaped them or seemed unimportant that the victory brought no real change to their everyday lives. In any case, the new strength by which they had won Emancipation could presumably be brought to bear on other issues too.

O'Connell, whose election had taken place before the passing of the Emancipation Act, now tried to take his seat in the Commons. But by a piece of government spite the act had not been made retrospective. Though O'Connell knew what the outcome of an attempt to take his seat must be in the circumstances, he made the most of the occasion for political ends. He went down to the House and, putting on his spectacles, laboriously read through to himself the wording with which he must have been perfectly familiar, of the oath of royal ecclesiastical supremacy together with the passage about the superstitious and idolatrous nature of the adoration of the Virgin and of the Mass.

'I see,' he declared aloud, 'in this oath, an assertion as a matter of opinion which I know to be false. I see in it another assertion as a matter of fact which I believe to be untrue. I therefore refuse to take this oath.'[23]

O'Connell had to travel all the way back to Clare to re-submit himself to the electorate. But again he made the most of the occasion, travelling much of the road in triumph and entering Ennis, the county town, escorted by a procession of forty thousand people with bands and banners.[24] This time he was elected unopposed, and under the Emancipation Act could now take his seat. The government's spite had deprived him of a personal ambition to be the first Catholic to enter Parliament, for the Duke of Norfolk and other peers had already been able to take their seats in the House of Lords.

A great triumph was behind O'Connell. He immediately set out in pursuit of a greater one. His next campaign would be Repeal of the Union itself.

5

The Repeal Debate

It was O'Connell's unforgettable campaign for Repeal of the Union, which consolidated for Ireland a strong mass national feeling that was political but not separatist. The important part of the campaign took place in the early 1840s; but it was to be preceded by a false start ten years earlier.

The outlook had seemed promising. O'Connell founded a popular organization similar to that which had just won Emancipation, and the government was soon suitably alarmed by its proportions. But the very different nature of the difficulties which confronted O'Connell on this new issue equally soon became plain.

In the Parliament that met after the great Reform Act of 1832 O'Connell found himself able to muster something very like a parliamentary party of his own in the House of Commons from among those Irish members who supported Repeal. There were thirty-nine Repealers out of a total Irish representation of 105 (the remainder being Tories and Liberal-Whigs). But the earlier issue of Catholic Emancipation had been supported by many more than thirty-nine members of the Union Parliament, for its supporters were not confined to Irish members. The mass agitation in Ireland and the election results had acted on a live political situation inside the Union Parliament. But Repeal was a dead issue in the Union Parliament. There were virtually no supporters for it other than the thirty-nine Irish Repeal members.

When in 1834 O'Connell first moved the Repeal of the Union in the House of Commons, the futility of his position on the new issue was revealed at once. The great debate that followed was notable not for its actual outcome, which was a foregone conclusion, but for a first parade of arguments for and against the Union which were to become more or less standard for the rest of the century.

O'Connell stated clearly the exact constitutional position he was aiming at. Ireland, he said, should be regarded 'not as a subordinate province, but as a limb of the empire – as another and distinct country, subject to the same King, but having a Legislature totally independent of the Legislature of Great Britain'.[1] He put this forward as a simple call to restore Ireland to the station she occupied 'when I was born'.

But it was of course naif to pretend, as he thus did, that what he sought was no different from the old Protestant Ascendancy's idea of national sovereignty, something traditional and normal and in no way revolutionary. Political circumstances had changed out of all recognition since 1782. Catholic Emancipation and the Reform Act had altered the whole balance of political power in Ireland. Irish national sovereignty under the Crown now meant not an oligarchic but an increasingly democratic 'nation'. However sweepingly O'Connell asserted that it was the Union which was 'the great source of Ireland's wrongs' he would have been doing no great service to Ireland in simply returning her to the conditions prevailing just before it. After all, there had been wrongs enough then to bring about the desperate catastrophe of 1798. His claim for independent Irish legislative power made little sense unless he intended to use it.

Irish national sovereignty within the Empire would now mean something like a social revolution in Ireland, however constitutionally it might be proposed. In the circumstances his conservative claim made little appeal to conservatives, particularly in the British House of Commons. Put forward as an old national claim, it was in reality something new. Given, however, a prior concern for the fate of the Irish masses rather than that of the landlords, it was a new claim which made good political sense.

There was sense too in O'Connell's final political argument. 'Repeal', he said, 'cannot endanger the connection – continuing the Union may . . .'[2] This was to remain the central point of debate for the rest of the century. The arguments would apply whether the issue at stake was Repeal (a wholly independent Irish legislature under the Crown) or, as later, Home Rule (an Irish legislature under the Crown with limited domestic powers only). Opponents of Irish legislative freedom of either kind always argued that it would lead to still further Irish national demands and eventually total separation. Conversely, Repealers and Home Rulers always argued that the only danger of separation arose from a refusal to grant Irish demands within the connection. This, they said, would play into the hands of the small minority of separatists.

In this first Repeal Debate in the Commons of April 1834, the chief government spokesman was the Secretary for War and the Colonies, Spring Rice, a Protestant Irishman. He argued as an Irishman whose national pride was satisfactorily fulfilled by the theory of the Union. His argument was ingenious to the point of absurdity.

'Why,' he declaimed, 'who contends that England has or ever had a right of domination over Ireland, either derived from conquest or concession? England exercised such a right, it is true, and strongly contended in its defence, but the claim was founded on usurpation alone. . . . Who governs Ireland? Who legislates for Ireland? Why the Parliament of the United Kingdom, not the Parliament of England . . .'[3] The 'usurpation' had been rectified in 1782 and 1783, and the Union had merely been a fresh development of the rights which Ireland had then won for herself. He actually cited the Union as a fruit of the Renunciation Act of 1783 by which the English Parliament abandoned all claim to legislate for Ireland. English members, he maintained, were as much charged with the maintenance of Irish interests and the protection of Irish rights, 'as if you had Irish constituents at your backs.[4] ... I deny that Ireland is a province of Great Britain. ... We are all parts of the United Empire, and I [Spring Rice, the Irishman] as much belong to England and have as much right to all the privileges of an Englishman as the proudest Howard who walks the earth; and in like manner the Howard belongs to Ireland as fully as if born there. We are all subjects of one King – we live under the protection of one and the same law – we belong to one United Empire ...'[5]

The argument in theory was impeccable, but it depended in practice wholly on the manner in which the Union Parliament did in fact protect Irish rights. Unfortunately, the privileges of the Howards and Spring Rices were hardly relevant to the Irish peasant of the day.

Spring Rice made an attempt to meet the obvious charge that England had in fact done nothing for Ireland. His soundest point lay in what he called 'the industry set in motion in the North'.[6] But the very truth of this claim weakened the rest of his argument. For the North of Ireland, with the industry it already had, had been able to enter England's industrial revolution and was the one part of Ireland in which something like a real union of interests had come about. Since 1801 the town of Belfast had been utterly transformed. Its· population rose from around 20,000 in 1803 to little short of 100,000 by 1851.[7] With the Reform Act of 1832, the core of the Protestant North's original revolutionary grievance had been removed and from now on it associated its interests as closely with the Union as in earlier days it had associated them with the cause of revolution.

But no such change had been wrought in the daily lives of people in the South. When Spring Rice came to refer, in the same tone, to the 'agricultural improvement developed in the South',[8] such a ludicrous gloss on the true facts could only be explained by the government's ignorance. Indeed, it was this ignorance which was the real indictment of the Union. Spring Rice proudly drew attention to the remarkable fact that between 1801 and 1833 there had been sixty government Committees of Inquiry into Ireland, and 114 Reports of Commissioners, making 174 altogether bearing on Irish interests. Then, anticipating the objection that these in themselves did not necessarily constitute the fulfilment of Ireland's wants, he cited as an instance of practical results: free trade between the two islands in butter and corn. That he could do so showed total misunderstanding of the message which these reports conveyed. For what they made clear was that the average Irish peasant lived so far below the poverty line that he could not afford to eat butter or bread however cheap. He produced it to pay the rent with. To lower the price actually struck him a blow because it meant he had to work harder and produce more to pay the rent. As the English radical, Hume, said in answer to Spring Rice's claims of agricultural improvement: 'It was but of little consequence what a country produced, if the inhabitants of that country partook not of that produce.'[9]

As further high points in the Union's achievements for Ireland, and equally irrelevant to the central problem of Irish agricultural poverty, Spring Rice proudly cited administrative acts such as one for the Assimilation of the Currency and another – marginally more relevant – for the Encouragement of Fisheries by the Construction of Piers and Harbours. The Union had also doubled the number of schools, made possible the charitable provision of dispensaries for the sick and 'built noble asylums for the lunatic poor'.[10] That a Union government could talk with such complacency at a time of such universal distress as continued to prevail in Ireland in the 1830's was final total refutation of the Union's claim to concern itself with Irish interests.

On the purely political front Spring Rice's argument in this debate of 1834 was sounder. Voicing what was to become the traditional fear that Repeal would lead to a total separation, he cited O'Connell's use of ambivalent menace at its crudest: 'The United States of America', the Liberator had said, ' – the western boundary of Ireland – threw off the British yoke, and gained freedom by the sword; they were three million and we are eight million.'[11] And it was on this constitutional point of the danger of separation that pro-Union arguments increasingly concentrated. To simplify the whole Irish question into a political issue conveniently glossed over the real problems of government in Ireland. 'I feel and know,' declared Peel sweepingly, 'that the Repeal [of the Union] must lead to the dismemberment of this great empire; must make Great Britain a fourth-rate power of Europe, and Ireland a savage wilderness.'[12]

But if one eye in the Unionist attitude remained exaggeratedly wide open to constitutional dangers, the other remained obstinately closed to those on the economic front.

'Of what grievance did the people of Ireland complain?' asked a member of the House of Lords. 'They [their Lordships] knew not. Of the book of Ireland's wrongs little now remained, except one or two chapters which would speedily by the wisdom and justice of Parliament be erased out of its pages.' Everything was the fault of agitators who preferred trouble-making to honest industry.[13] And this was some years before that great famine which all who had any knowledge of Irish conditions were already dreading.

The 1834 motion for Repeal was lost in the House of Commons by 529–38, and O'Connell had to recognize that to attempt a Repeal of the Union by conventional parliamentary methods was not in the realm of practical politics. Later, he said that he would never have introduced the issue in this manner at this time, had he not been pressed to do so by hot-headed colleagues.* His immediate reaction to failure was not to try and obtain Repeal by unconventional methods, as he later did, but to use conventional parliamentary methods to try and obtain benefits for Ireland in other ways. In the following year, 1835, O'Connell, dropping his demand for Repeal, gave the support of his members in the House of Commons to the Whig government in return for a policy of concessions to Ireland. The alliance was sealed in the so-called Lichfield House compact between O'Connell's party and the Whigs. It introduced a short period when Ireland was certainly administered more sympathetically – that is to say, with less immediate recourse to 'Coercion' Acts suspending the constitutional rights of the individual – than at any other time since the Union. Thanks for this were largely due to a remarkable Under-Secretary in Dublin Castle, Thomas Drummond, who enunciated the, for Ireland, revolutionary principle that 'property has its duties as well as its rights'. But nothing was done to strike at the roots of Irish agricultural poverty, for to do this would mean striking, in a way that seemed inconceivable, at the whole system of land-ownership.

Some well-intentioned governmental measures were passed. The tithe problem, which had reached its climax during the 1830s in a savage war between the secret societies and the authorities, was nominally solved by an Act of 1838. The tithe was in future to be paid by the landlord, but he was entitled to add a corresponding charge to the existing rent. All this really did was to simplify the sense of economic oppression felt by the tenant farmer. It was easier now for his hatred to concentrate wholly against rents.

A Whig Irish Poor Law and a Municipal Reform Act for Ireland proved equally rather tame compromises. O'Connell acquiesced in them despite his stated objections, for the sake of preserving the political alliance and as being at least better than nothing. But increasing criticism from Ireland that he was sacrificing what should be Ireland's real goals in order to maintain the alliance at all costs was inevitable. O'Connell often went far out of his way to be moderate, in order not to embarrass his political allies. He used, for instance, the full weight of his political machine to oppose the Protestant Irish liberal member for County Down, Sharman Crawford, an Ulster landlord who though not himself a Repealer had actually proposed the abolition of tithes altogether, and who at this time was concentrating much more single-mindedly on the real issue of tenant rights than O'Connell. On matters outside Ireland, O'Connell's attitude to the government even bordered on the sycophantic, and he appalled even many English radicals by his conservative attitude to both Canada's struggle for freedom within the Empire and the movement for a ten-hour day in factories.[14]

* Chiefly Feargus O'Connor, the Chartist leader of the forties and son of Roger O'Connor; see above, p. 78. See O'Connell's later speeches on Repeal at Monster Meetings, *The Nation*, 1843.

In Ireland his final political objective was still theoretically Repeal, but he had stated more than once that if he could get justice for Ireland by other means he would be prepared to drop it. 'A real Union or no Union' was his motto at this stage.[15] His trouble was that he was getting neither. When in 1838 a new Association was formed in Dublin to Repeal the Union, all reference to Repeal itself was omitted in order not to embarrass O'Connell's Whig allies, and it was called the Precursor Society. In 1840, with the probable end of the Whig Administration already in sight, an avowed 'Repeal Association' was formed, but it made no difference to O'Connell's continued support of the government and the new Association's first two principles hastened to make clear its constitutional aspect. These were:

1. 'Most dutiful and ever inviolate loyalty to our most gracious and ever beloved Sovereign Queen Victoria and her heirs and successors for ever.'

2. 'The total disclaimer of, and the total absence from all physical force, violence or breach of the law.'[16]

These two principles represented no retreat on O'Connell's part, for they had always been at the foundation of all his political ideas. However, the reality of any repeal movement at all was inevitably in question with O'Connell so devoted to alliance with a government which would always oppose Repeal as relentlessly as the Conservative opposition. The power of his party had in any case been seriously weakened during the course of the alliance, for ten of its thirty-nine members had accepted places, titles or offices under the government.

From this awkward dilemma of trying to alter the course of the ship of state without rocking the boat O'Connell was finally released by the results of the General Election of 1841.

The Whigs, who had been almost continuously in office for ten years, were swept away and Peel and the Conservatives returned to power. O'Connell himself, as the Whigs' ally, understandably suffered a personal setback in the elections; only eighteen repealers were now returned instead of the previous thirty-nine. But impotent as he was to be in Parliament the net result of the election was not to restrain his political power but to release it. For with the Whigs out of office, O'Connell could now clamour for Repeal without embarrassment. By the nature of the situation it had to be a clamour outside Parliament altogether.

6

O'Connell and Davis

To win Catholic Emancipation more than ten years earlier, O'Connell had mobilized mass opinion to a point where it became a national movement. But the movement had lost its momentum since Emancipation had been won, and since O'Connell had become linked with the Whigs' own inability radically to change Irish society. The local secret societies had resumed their hold, contributing effectively to the bloody battles fought against tithe-collectors and police in the early 1830s. From November 1841, however, when the Whigs lost office, O'Connell set about rebuilding a national political movement similar to that which had won Emancipation.

The Repeal Association founded in 1840 while the Whigs were still in power, with an old Protestant Volunteer of the '82 period as a symbolic chairman, had made little headway. But in the following year, renamed the Loyal National Repeal Association, it was effectively re-organized on the model of the old Catholic Association. Its principal democratic feature, as with the Catholic Association earlier, was the penny a month subscription which bought Associate Membership and now became known as the Repeal Rent.

The Association was firmly under the control of O'Connell, who addressed its meetings week after week, hammering home his basic argument that only a native Irish Parliament under the Crown could bring about those measures which were necessary to change the conditions of everyday life in Ireland. Though always inclined to use 'Repeal' as an emotive inspiration, and careful not to commit himself in much detail to the practical measures required to change society, he did definitely commit himself to the general principle of fixity of tenure for the tenant, making it clear that he was prepared to interfere with the basic structure of the landlord–tenant relationship.

This was enough to make his high-sounding claims for Repeal ('... fraught with the richest benefits to our common country ... in an eminent degree calculated to advance the interests of all classes ...' etc.)[1] seem plausible. It meant that a native Parliament would be different from the British one, which regarded the landlord–tenant relationship as virtually sacrosanct. At a time when the British Home Secretary was solemnly able to write that the most difficult problem of practical government in Ireland was that of financing the Maynooth priests' college and of Roman Catholic education in general,[2] and when even the future Irish rebel Smith O'Brien thought it impossible to intervene directly between landlord and tenant,[3] the Repeal movement's continuous insistence on the need to do so made Repeal seem a practical alternative as well as a rousing slogan. Repeal itself thus began to assume something of the nature of a mystical goal for the ordinary Irishman. When several hundred labourers on the Shannon works defied their overseers to attend a Repeal meeting in 1842, one of them remarked: 'If we lost our work for it, do you think we would have skulked away from the day's meeting? Oh no, we love the Repeal too well for that!'[4]

But the problem of how the Repeal of the Union was actually to be brought about in the face of the British Parliament's uncompromising refusal to consider it was another question. O'Connell was fond of brushing this fundamental problem aside, sometimes by saying that it was only necessary for the Queen to sign the requisite writs for the Irish Parliament's summons,[5] and at other times drawing attention to earlier causes such as Reform, which had received slender support in Parliament almost up to the moment of their acceptance.[6] But the weakness of the Repeal movement was that there was no prospect whatever of support from anyone in the British Parliament save the small handful of Irish Repealers. In the prevailing parliamentary situation, with one English party holding a large majority over the other, the Repeal movement had no means of putting pressure on the government, except by the threat of armed rebellion which O'Connell made clear he would not countenance. All he could do was to bluff, leaving the government to wonder whether or not he was as opposed to armed rebellion as he maintained, or, alternatively, whether he would always be able to control the vast numbers whose support he commanded. This tactic of openly playing on the government's fear had worked with Emancipation. Moreover, the size of the demand for Repeal which he was about to call forth was to prove even more imposing than anything Emancipation had produced.

In his great Repeal campaign, which reached its first climax in the autumn of 1843, O'Connell was immeasurably assisted by new allies, who though very different in age, background and temperament from himself were eventually to have an equally profound influence on nationalism in Ireland. This was a group of middle-class young men, half of them Protestants, who later came to be known as Young Ireland, but who for the present simply acted as a strong pressure group inside the Repeal Association. The nucleus of this group, consisting of Thomas Davis, John Blake Dillon and Charles Gavan Duffy, had come together in 1842 to found on their own initiative a new newspaper, *The Nation*. The first copy of *The Nation* appeared on 8 October 1842, and, though selling at sixpence, it had within a very short time a higher circulation than any other newspaper in Ireland. Its editor, Gavan Duffy, calculated that because of its wide distribution through reading rooms and from hand to hand it was read by a quarter of a million Irishmen.[7]

Duffy, a Catholic from Ulster and the only one of the three with much journalistic experience, was the official editor and manager of the paper. But the greater part of the editorial writing was done at first by Thomas Davis, a Protestant, who was to prove one of the key formative figures in the development of Irish nationalism.

Just as O'Connell had been the first man to mobilize Irish opinion effectively on a national scale, so Davis was the first man to construct for such national opinion a coherent theory of nationality. Irishness was something which the Catholic O'Connell did not need to think about intellectually for it was such a recognizable part of him and his long family tradition. But for Davis, the son of an English army surgeon and an Irish mother whose maiden name was Atkins (though with both Gaelic and English settlers' blood in her veins), Irishness was something which he found he consciously needed to work out and acquire for his own self-respect. He became, as it were, the grammarian of Irish nationality.

Trained as a barrister, though he never practised regularly, Davis, who had been born in County Cork in 1814, was considered by a man who knew him in 1838 as 'more like a young Englishman than a young Irishman'.[8] He had at first looked to England and made some attempt to concern himself with English radical politics, but had become disillusioned and after about a year turned back to his native land.[9] It was the very sense of provincialism thrust upon him in the country of his birth that he felt undignified and that he set out to overcome by elevating into a sense of nationality.*

A sense of Irish nationality was still very much something that seemed to need justification.

'Surely,' Davis wrote in December 1840, 'the desire of nationality is not ungenerous, nor is it strange in the Irish (looking to their history); nor, considering the population of Ireland, and the situation of their home, is the expectation of it very wild.'[10]

But it was still something to be hoped for and formed as nationality in Europe was being formed among the Czechs, or the Italians. Davis had spent some time in Europe after studying at Trinity College, Dublin, and his concept of what Irish nationality should be like was something all-embracing and creative in the new romantic European tradition, a conscious spiritual launching of the self into patriotism. Though Mazzini, the Italian nationalist and leader of Young Italy, was to maintain that Irish nationalism could not in fact be equated with Italian or any other conventional nationalism because the Irish were not sufficiently distinctive from the English,[11] the whole of Davis's short life's work was devoted to assertion of the opposite.

* Cf. Davis: 'Verily, we repeat, we are provincials.' (February 1841, quoted Duffy, *Thomas Davis*, p. 49.)

When in 1840, as outgoing President of the Historical Society, Dublin, he addressed a gathering of his young contemporaries from Trinity, he used the occasion to exhort them to seek out a national identity for themselves in Ireland. Speaking to 'what are called the upper classes of Ireland', he told them, as if opening their eyes to what was around them:

'Gentlemen, you have a country. . . . Reason points out our native land as the field for our exertions. . . . The country of our birth, our education of our recollections, ancestral, personal, national; the country of our loves, our friendships, our hopes, our country. . . . You are Irishmen, she relies on your devotion.' [12] And he reminded his audience, the majority of whom were young Protestants, of the great days of 1782.

It was exactly among Protestants that the most difficult part of Davis's creative nationalist task lay. Protestants were to be brought into an all-embracing definition of Irish nationality that included both themselves and the Catholic peasantry. Yet the only Protestant national tradition that had existed, and to which he was appealing, had been one which emphasized their ascendancy over Catholics. Davis's appeal for a united front was similar to that which Wolfe Tone had made fifty years earlier. But Tone had been able to stress the need for it in utilitarian political terms. Protestants had then been seeking something the British Government refused to give them, namely Reform. But now Davis could only make a vaguer and more general utilitarian appeal to Protestants about the future prosperity of the country as a whole and had to rely vainly on the appeal of his doctrine as a spiritual end in itself.

In the prospectus which he wrote for *The Nation*, he put forward a prospectus for nationality itself. Nationality, he said, was the paper's first object,

... a Nationality which will not only raise our people from their poverty, by securing to them the blessings of a DOMESTIC LEGISLATURE, but inflame and purify them with a lofty and heroic love of country – a Nationality of the spirit as well as the letter ... which may embrace Protestant, Catholic and Dissenter – Milesian and Cromwellian – the Irishman of a hundred generations and the stranger who is within our gates ... [13]

Over and over again Davis spelt out this same doctrine.

'We must sink,' he wrote, 'the distinctions of blood as well as sect. The Milesian, the Dane, the Norman, the Welshman, the Scotsman and the Saxon, naturalized here, must combine regardless of their blood – the Strong-bownian must sit with the Ulster Scot and him whose ancestor came from Tyre or Spain must confide in and work with the Cromwellian and the Williamite ...' If a union of all Irish-born men ever be accomplished Ireland will have the greatest and most varied materials for an illustrious nationality and for a tolerant and flexible character in literature, manners, religion and life of any nation on earth.[14]

In order to give this nationality substance Davis industriously reinforced his argument with a wealth of historical and cultural research into Ireland's past. Articles on Irish antiquities, Irish music, Irish art, Irish ballad poetry, Irish scenery, Irish ethnology and the Irish language poured from his pen in great profusion, appearing week after week in the columns of *The Nation* and always related to the cult of nationality. A few Irish Protestant patriots of the eighteenth century had shown an interest in Irish antiquities and the Irish language as part of their national consciousness, as had also some of the radicals of the 1790s. But such studies had been the prerogative of scholars and amateur specialists even though spoken Irish was still the vernacular for almost half the population. Davis was the first man to try to make such matters of popular concern, to try to link the past with the present as a continuing relevant force.

> That a country is without national poetry [he wrote] proves its hopeless dull-ness or its utter provincialism. National poetry is the very flowering of the soul – the greatest evidence of its wealth, the greatest excellence of its beauty . . .[15]

Soon romantic stanzas of trite but often stirring quality, written largely by Davis himself who had hardly written a line of verse before, were resound-ing through the columns of *The Nation*, and being repeated all over Ireland.

> When boyhood's fire was in my blood,
> I read of ancient freemen
> For Greece and Rome who bravely stood
> Three Hundred men and Three men.
> And then I prayed I yet might see
> Our fetters rent in twain
> And Ireland, long a province, be
> A NATION ONCE AGAIN.

The original attitude of Young Ireland to force as a solution to political problems was the same as O'Connell's and was made clear in a typical poem in the very first number of *The Nation*. Entitled 'We Want No Swords' it began

> We want no swords, no savage swords,
> Our fetters vile to shatter . . .

and ended:

> With conquering mind alone we fight –
> 'Tis all we need for freedom!

But from the start, also like O'Connell, *The Nation* had the best of both worlds by use of ambivalent metaphor. Inspiration for the political present

was continually being drawn from ancient war-like deeds, and its Poets'
Corner at least was not shy of the clash of steel.

> For often, in O'Connor's van
> To triumph dash'd each Connaught clan –
> Sing oh! how fleet the Normans ran
> Through Corlieu's Pass and Ardrahan!

> And later times saw deeds as brave
> And glory guards Clanricarde's grave –
> Sing on! they died their land to save
> At Aughrim's slopes and Shannon's wave.

> And if, when all a vigil keep
> The West's asleep, the West's asleep –
> Sing oh! poor Erin well may weep;
> That men so sprung are still asleep.

> But – Hark! – some voice like thunder spake:
> 'The West's awake, the West's awake' –
> Sing oh! hurra; let England quake,
> We'll watch till death for Erin's sake.

Of the Irish language Davis wrote: 'A people without a language is only
half a nation'; [16] and he vigorously urged a revival until 'the brighter days
shall surely come, and the green flag shall wave on the towers, and the
sweet old language be heard once more in college, mart and senate'.[17]

Often an admonitory note was to enter these national exhortations.

'We have Irish artists, but no Irish art,' he complained. 'This ought not
to continue; it is injurious to the artists and disgraceful to the country.'[18] And
with the constructive diligence which characterizes all Davis's writing he
proceeded to suggest a number of suitable subjects that truly national
painters might get down to right away: Brian Boru, for instance, reconnoit-
ring the Danes before Clontarf; James II entering Dublin; Wolfe Tone with
Carnot; the Battle of Oulart Hill and 'The Lifting of the Flags of a National
Fleet and Army'.[19]

In an article on Foreign Travel, Davis recommended that those who
travelled abroad should 'carry a purpose for Ireland in their hearts'.[20] Celtic
words mixed in classical French or the patois of Brittany or Gascony should
be noted and compared with Irish; Irish saints should be tracked down
wherever possible, and monuments and museums in France, Spain, Italy and
Scandinavia studied with reference to the antiquities of Ireland to make a
summer both pleasant and profitable. Useful tips might also be collected
abroad to help serve Ireland's defective agriculture and her untapped
mineral resources and waterpower, while encouragement might be derived
for that cultivation of the fine arts and design that was so sadly neglected in
Ireland. 'Our Irish cities,' wrote Davis, 'must be stately with sculptures,

pictures and buildings, and our fields glorious with peaceful abundance.' This was not, he maintained, just a Utopian dream. '. . . To seek it is the solemn, unavoidable duty of every Irishman.'[21]

It was in this emphasis on the spiritual dimension of what was otherwise basically the same as O'Connell's view of nationality that the special contribution of Davis and the rest of *The Nation* writers lay. Yet *The Nation* also from the start closely concerned itself with practical politics and like O'Connell and the Repeal Association, of which Davis, Duffy and Dillon were all committee members, concentrated specifically on the land question. Fixity of tenure was a basic objective, and an early issue of *The Nation* had a neat epigram about rents.

> 'Well, Pat, my boy,' said I, 'I've heard some chat
> With the ground landlord of this wilderness.'
> 'The *grinding* one your Honour means,' grinned Pat.
> 'It is the tenants that are ground, I guess.'[22]

An article headed 'Rents the Question of the Day' quoted with approval the Ulster Liberal Protestant landlord, Sharman Crawford, who, while agreeing that a landlord had a right to do what he willed with his own, denied that land was a landlord's own except subject to the principle that those who tilled it should get a fair and honest living out of it. Like O'Connell, Davis and his friends publicly proclaimed that there was only one major political remedy which would enable all Ireland's thousand grievances to be put right, and that was Repeal of the Union and an Irish legislature. And just as they spiritualized O'Connell's concept of nationality, so they turned Repeal into something like a moral principle in words which were to have an echo in the twentieth century.

> The work that should today be wrought
>   Defer not till tomorrow;
> The help that should within be sought
>   Scorn from without to borrow.
> Old maxims these – yet stout and true –
>   They speak in trumpet tone,
> To do at once what is to do
>   And trust OURSELVES ALONE.*

Not only did *The Nation* bequeath a slogan to later nationalists, but also specific tactics. A correspondent in *The Nation* of 19 November 1842 proposed that the sixty Irish Liberal Members of Parliament should not go to Westminster at all, but should join with two hundred and forty other 'Irish gentlemen' to form a Parliament of their own. (Three hundred had previously been the number of representatives in the Irish Parliament.) The

---

* *The Nation*, 3 December 1842. 'Ourselves alone' is an accepted translation of the Irish words Sinn Fein.

idea was to be elaborated in the next year in O'Connell's plan for a Council of Three Hundred. He proposed circumventing the Convention Act of 1793, which made any extra-parliamentary convention of representatives in Ireland illegal, by turning the delegates nominally into mere bearers of special Repeal Rent contributions of £100 from their localities. Similarly, 'arbitration courts', or an indigenous Irish system of court-administered justice to supersede the work of the official Crown Courts, were put into operation for a time in 1843.

In none of this was there any suggestion of a constitutional break with the Crown itself. The Repeal Association and O'Connell himself continued to go out of their way to assert their essential loyalty to the queen.

'The political principles', wrote a prominent member of the Repeal Association in *The Nation*, 'that have struck their roots deepest in the Irish peasant's heart are, devoted allegiance to the Queen, and undying hatred of the execrable legislative union.'[23]

This was probably a fair enough statement of the truth. Certainly, O'Connell often thought it worth his while to play on a crowd's emotional feelings about the monarchy.

'I want you,' he said, at a public meeting at Trim in March 1843, 'I want you not to violate your allegiance to the lovely and beautiful being that fills the throne – our gracious Queen, long life to her [great cheers]. I want you to preserve your allegiance unbroken to her as I do mine; but I want you, at the same time, to remember that you have another allegiance equally dear and higher in its quality, though not so binding in law, but equally binding in an Irish heart, and that is the allegiance you owe to your country [cheers]. I call on you to be loyal men – loyal to the Queen and loyal to your country.'[24]

On another occasion, after bringing in mention of the queen, he cried: 'May heaven bless her! – three cheers for her [tremendous cheering]. ... She was the Queen of their affections, as she had invariably been the Queen of their unswerving loyalty and allegiance.'[25]

He argued that it was the queen's enemies who came between her and her devoted and loyal subjects in Ireland, and declared that when the Irish people had conquered these enemies the first use they would make of their victory would be 'to place the sceptre in the hands of her who has ever showed us favour, and whose conduct has ever been full of sympathy and emotion for our sufferings'.[26]

Triumphal arches at O'Connell's meetings were inscribed 'The Queen, O'Connell and Repeal', and fulsome toasts to the queen were drunk at Repeal banquets.

There was little of this fulsomeness towards the monarchy in Davis's writing. He even at times seems to have used words associated with Tone intentionally to blur Young Ireland's precise constitutional image.

'Once,' he wrote in *The Nation* in December 1842, 'once the Irish People declare the disconnection of themselves, their feelings and interests from the men, feelings and interests of England, they are in the march for freedom. Ireland must bid all whom it concerns to know that her interests are separate and her rights peculiar.'[27]

Yet it was made positively clear elsewhere in *The Nation* that although the Irish Parliament was to be independent and separate, there would be a unity of the two kingdoms under a joint Crown. A parallel was drawn between the future relationship of the two countries and the relationship then existing between Norway and Sweden, in which the Norwegians had complete control of their affairs, with their own flag and navy, but shared a common crown and foreign policy with Sweden.[28] Davis was quite prepared to accept that England should have the chief say in affairs that concerned the Empire as a whole.

'It is right', he wrote, 'that England should have the preponderance in matters of Imperial interest; it is wrong that she should have it where those interests are not at all involved.'[29] On imperial matters he was content that decisions should be taken by a joint vote of both Parliaments and that the majority of the combined vote should prevail.

These words were written in *The Nation* in the course of an objective examination of a new proposal being made in some quarters for something less than total Repeal of the Union. This was the idea known as Federalism being urged by that same Liberal Ulster landlord, Sharman Crawford, who had already shown enlightened views on the land question. Federalists stood for an independent domestic legislature for Ireland, to be concerned with Irish interests only, while all wider responsibilities were to be assumed by the Imperial Parliament, in which Ireland should have a reduced representation. This in essence was that solution to the Irish problem which was to be put forward in the late nineteenth and early twentieth centuries as Home Rule.

Davis himself, though he saw the wider claim of total repeal as the only one consistent with the elevating doctrine of nationality, was by no means hostile to Federalists and thought that they should be supported as advocating a step in the right direction.[30] Realistically he admitted, in a private letter to a friend late in 1842, that Federalism was in fact all that Ireland stood a chance of getting out of the present political situation.

'Things have come to that pass,' he wrote, 'that we must be disgraced and defeated, or we must separate by force, or we must have a Federal Government.'[31]

In another letter to the same friend he made a hopeful appraisal of the Repeal movement's resources. He concluded: 'I think we can beat Peel (the British Prime Minister). If we can quietly get a Federal Government, I for one shall agree to it and support it. If not, then anything but what we are.'[32]

7

'Monster Meetings'

O'Connell had declared that 1843 was going to be 'Repeal year'. Though his young colleagues thought this a rash declaration, they threw their entire energy into his new campaign, acting for him as a sort of general staff and infusing the movement with their own particular flavour of historic national consciousness. 'To the work then, ye millions of Irish people,' *The Nation* exhorted. 'To the work! Catholic – Dissenter – Protestant band together under the green standard of your common country! Bear aloft that proud, stainless banner; and with the blessing of the great and just God, it will soon wave over your heads in the temple of the Irish constitution!'[1]

By March 1843 a new card for Members of the Repeal Association had been issued. It was green, and had four key battles of Irish history in the four corners and a flag in the middle, displaying the symbolic rays of a sun bursting over the horizon, together with a shamrock with 'Catholic', 'Dissenter' and 'Protestant' in each leaf and *'Quis separabit?'* up the stalk.

The chief feature of the campaign was the series of vast public demonstrations addressed in the open air all over Ireland by O'Connell, often at places of historic emotive appeal selected by Davis. *The* (London) *Times* in its indignation came to dub these demonstrations Monster Meetings, and the appellation stuck. In spite of the size of the crowds the meetings were conducted with a disciplined order which frightened the government much as the self-imposed discipline at elections had done in the Emancipation era.

The alliance between O'Connell and his young supporters worked harmoniously and effectively in this year. O'Connell himself preached nationality as proudly as *The Nation* itself, if in a less sophisticated style.

'Irish patriotism is alive,' he proclaimed at a public dinner. '... It is not buried, it only sleeps and I am the cock that shall crow for its morning.'[2] Though already a man in his middle sixties he crowed through the spring, summer and early autumn of 1843 to such effect that Peel and the Duke of Wellington felt the Empire shaken to its foundations.

In his speeches O'Connell continually repeated his abhorrence of violence and his belief in constitutional action, but, like the writers of *The Nation*, he often employed an ambivalent language which enabled him to raise the maximum amount of public emotional enthusiasm at all levels.

'I came here to recruit,' were the words with which he began his monster meeting at Trim, and as the cheers died away he continued: 'I want you to enlist with me; and reversing the old method of enlisting, where they give the recruit a shilling, I want you to enlist by giving the shilling to me ... [a reference to the penny a month of Repeal Rent].'

Later in the same speech he referred to himself as 'one who would give the last drop of his life's blood, and smile to see it flow to do any good for Ireland'.

The words were followed by loud cheers and cries of 'Long life to you', and O'Connell went on: 'I would wish to have life to make Ireland free, to get that without which she can never be prosperous or happy, to get Ireland for the Irish and the Irish for Ireland.'[3]

The following week *The Nation* published a poem which, though not by Davis himself, expressed in verse Davis's strong feeling that the actions of the United Irishmen and others, who had been under a polite historical cloud for nearly half a century, were nothing for Ireland to be ashamed of.

> Who fears to speak of '98?
>   Who blushes at the name?
> When cowards mock the patriots' fate
>   Who hangs his head for shame?
> He's all a knave or half a slave
>   Who slights his country thus:
> But a true man, like you, man,
>   Will fill your glass with us ...
>
> Then here's their memory – may it be
>   For us a guiding light
> To cheer our strife for liberty,
>   And teach us to unite!
> Through good and ill be Ireland's still
>   Though sad as theirs, your fate,
> And true men, be you, men,
>   Like those of '98.*

O'Connell's own disapproval of the methods of '98 had not changed, but he was not beyond infusing his own national appeal with martial ardour. At an open-air meeting at Roscrea in County Limerick he asked, to the cheers of the crowd, whether there was any man among them who would not, if necessary, die for Ireland, and himself immediately supplied the answer:

'There was not a man amongst them that would not brunt the battle's blaze, and glory in achieving victory for Ireland.'[4]

* The author was John Kells Ingram, who died, a forgotten scholastic recluse, in Dublin in 1907.

He continued in a vein that was always to play as powerful a part in Irish nationalist sentiment as any intellectual theory of nationality or inspiration from history – an appeal to the deep emotions aroused by the physical beauty of the land in which Irishmen lived. Small blame to them, he said, if they wanted to die for Ireland:

... there is not a lovelier land on the face of the earth – a more fruitful or fertile land the sun never shone upon [hear, hear, hear, and cheers]. I will repeat that the sun never shone upon a lovelier, or greener, or brighter land [hear, hear, hear, and great cheering]. Oh, it is a land to fill one with patriotism – its picturesque beauties please and delight the eye – its majestic mountains rise to the heavens – its limpid waters irrigate the plains, and its harbours are open to the commerce of the entire world, asserting for Ireland the great prerogative of being the first nation on the earth; and the period is coming, when standing forth in their native dignity, the people will be prosperous and free [cheers].[5]

The year 1843, not 1798, was the real emotional storehouse on which future Irish nationalism would always draw for its reserves.[5]

In the course of this year, in a long series of such monster meetings, O'Connell touched on every patriotic note in the vast range of rhetoric he commanded. Some contemporaries, drawn to Ireland to hear him because of his world-wide reputation as a national orator, were disappointed and found only crude demagoguery. But all testified to the magic spell he was able to cast over the crowds themselves. Bulwer Lytton, the English novelist and poet, wrote of him:

Once to my sight the giant thus was given:
Walled by wide air and roofed by boundless heaven,
Beneath his feet the human ocean lay,
And wave on wave flowed into space away.
Methought no clarion could have sent its sound
Even to the centre of the hosts around;
But, as I thought, there rose the sonorous swell,
As from some Church tower swings the silvery bell.
Aloft and clear, from airy tide to tide
It glided, easy as a bird may glide;
To the last verge of that vast audience sent,
It played with each wild passion as it went;
Now stirred the uproar, now the murmur stilled,
And sobs or laughter answered as it willed.

And a peasant said of O'Connell's voice: 'You'd hear it a mile off as if it was coming through honey.'[6]

At a great open-air meeting at Cork in May 1843 half a million people were estimated to be present, many of them having travelled great distances from other parts of Ireland to hear him. The streets of the city were packed, as a long procession of trade groups with banners (printers, rope-makers, chandlers, etc.) made its way past O'Connell's carriage. Every house-top, every lamp-post even, was occupied, and the procession took three hours and five minutes to file past. After the meeting nine hundred Repealers sat down to dinner, including many priests, one of whom said grace in Irish.[7]

The active support of the Catholic priesthood and many of the bishops demonstrated the true national impetus of the movement. The Catholic gentry and middle classes, together with a few Protestants, also appeared regularly on Repeal platforms emphasizing that what was by nature a mass movement was also deeply respectable. By midsummer 1843 Repeal Rent had topped the then enormous sum of £2,000 in a single week.

The British Government played the situation on the whole skilfully. One short-sighted action had been the dismissal from office of twenty-four Catholic gentry for attending Repeal meetings. This offended the sort of non-political Irish pride that was by no means necessarily committed to the agitation for Repeal. A number of other gentry resigned their commissions of the peace in sympathy with the dismissed magistrates, among them the Liberal Member of Parliament for Limerick, William Smith O'Brien, an old Harrovian who liked to trace his descent from Brian Boru, and another Protestant, Henry Grattan, the son of the great orator patriot. An attempt was also made by the government to introduce a new Arms Bill, facilitating the search for privately held arms, but it was held up by an early example of Irish 'obstruction' in the House of Commons. Otherwise the government did not try to check O'Connell by coercive measures. Reasonably, Peel had accepted the advice of his officials in the Irish administration and was letting O'Connell have his head, in the belief that he must in the end either commit himself to plain illegality or beat an ignominious retreat.

But the more conservative element in Peel's Conservative ministry were unhappy, and becoming increasingly convinced that Ireland was on the brink of civil war. 'Ireland,' wrote the Duke of Wellington, 'is in truth no longer in a social state.'[8]

Even the moderate Peel himself and his Home Secretary, Graham, soon became anxious. Graham expected the situation to 'lead to bloodshed and convulse the empire'.[9] Peel had already declared that in the long run there were no steps he would not take to maintain the Union and that even civil war would be preferable to 'the dismemberment of the Empire'.

At a meeting at Longford, O'Connell promised the crowd that they would be getting back their Parliament in College Green whatever Peel might say. He went on:

'They tell us there will be civil war if we attempt to get the Repeal – bah!'

The crowd cheered loudly and laughed.

'We will put them in the wrong, and if a civil war should break out it must be of their making ... and I tell you what, it they attack us then' – here

O'Connell slapped his breast and the crowd went wild with enthusiasm – 'who will then be the coward?' (More cheers.) 'We will put them in the wrong, and if they attack us, then in your name I set them at defiance.' (Great applause.)[10]

He repeated the defiance more solemnly at a dinner in Mallow later in the month, declaring again that though he and his supporters would never resort to force so long as they were left 'a rag of the constitution' to stand on, it was a mistake to think that the enemy would not attack them, and if that were to happen, then it was his dead body England would have to trample on, not the living man.[11]

O'Connell was pushing his old strategic bluff further and further towards the point where it would either have to succeed or be called in question.

At Ennis, capital of County Clare, the scene of his great victory of fifteen years before, he recalled that an ancestor of his who had led a battalion for James II at the battle of Aughrim was killed and buried nearby and he quoted the lines:

> We tread the land that bore us,
> Our green flag flutters o'er us,
> The friends we tried are by our side
> And the foes we hate before us ...

'Yes,' he concluded, 'the green flag of Clare is flying again.'[12]

At Murroe he caused a sensation by suddenly crying: 'I want you to get arms', but added typically: 'Now, mind me, do you know the arms I want you to get? – the Repeal Society's cards! Everyone who has that is well armed ...'[13]

Military images appeared increasingly in his speeches, while the crowds themselves, marshalled by Repeal 'wardens', preserved a well-ordered discipline. At Donnybrook, Dublin, before a crowd estimated at between 150,000 and 200,000, he said:

'It has never happened to me to behold such an assemblage as I have congregated here today. No; it is impossible to have more power. I have power enough – the only question is how to use it. I have more strength and more physical force than gained the battle of Waterloo – I have more physical force than ever monarch commanded or general led – I have abundance of physical force ...'[14]

The Nation criticized some of the 'Cockney and Italian' tunes played at this meeting as insufficiently national. It also complained that too many people had been marching out of step and that there had not been that minute subdivision into twelves and sixties, or tens and hundreds, 'which is essential to the permanent ordering and handling of arrayed men'.[15]

At Wexford O'Connell addressed crowds which, he declared, the Emperor of Russia himself did not have the power to put down. The Nation wrote:

'Never was organization more complete than it is in this noble county ...'[16] And when the county sent in a remittance of over £600 to the Loyal National Repeal Association, O'Connell commented that Wexford had done its duty, but then 'it was an old truth for Wexford to do its duty'.[17]

O'Connell and his young supporters now commanded by far the most comprehensive national movement in Irish history. They had woven together the traditions of the Wild Geese, of the Protestant Patriots of '82, of the Defenders and United Irishmen themselves, into one ideal. All the many different and often conflicting causes that had been fought for in Ireland in the past were now recognized as 'Ireland', a mystical cause which must continue to be fought for in the future.

But for all the unmistakable national character of the movement, O'Connell continually insisted that this was not a movement to separate England from Ireland:

'We encourage loyalty,' he said. 'We preach attachment to the Crown and submission to the laws ...' The only rebels in sight, he continued, were those who instigated the public against the queen, and maligned the loyal people of Ireland who were actually striving to uphold the security of the throne by basing it on the rights, the liberty and the prosperity of the entire nation.[18]

For the Repeal meeting at Tuam, where crowds estimated at 300,000 collected, with 400 gentry and over 100 clergy on the platform, the green flag on the Market House was overshadowed by a Union Jack flying from the top of the cathedral 'to mark the true character of the Repeal movement'.[19] It was the first object, viewable from an immense distance, seen by the multitudes coming from far and wide to hear O'Connell.

Yet, in spite of all the protestations of loyalty by Repealers, and all the undoubtedly sincere arguments of Federalists that their main concern was the preservation of the connection, it was not unreasonable for Unionists to take the view that *any* form of concession meant the thin end of the wedge of separation. To the Unionist the very blurring of the distinctive lines between Repealer and Federalist was itself ominous, for the Repealers themselves often blurred the lines between Repeal and separatism. And while renouncing ultimate separation O'Connell and his supporters continued to play on fears of it adroitly. A Wexford priest, criticizing the enemies of Repeal for continually harping on the danger of separation, commented that it was not wise thus 'to be throwing temptation' in the people's way. The sort of emotions which O'Connell and the Young Irelanders of *The Nation* were stirring delved deep into a past in which ancient hostilities and resentments lurked dangerously. In the same week as both O'Connell and *The Nation* expressed approval of Federalism, John Blake Dillon, who had founded the paper with Davis and Duffy, made a speech at Castlebar. The country, he said, had been visited with many sorrows, but even the sorrows it had endured were now playing their part in the work of regeneration. '... Even now from the graves which the tyrants have opened like wounds upon her bleeding breast, there comes a voice instructing, encouraging, purifying the people for the trial through which they have to pass. It searched the depths of the nation's memory.'[20] Powerful confused emotions were being played upon. No one could reasonably be certain how this would end.

'War harps of Erin!' sang *The Nation*'s Poets' Corner,

> I strike thee again.
> To echo the challenge of mountaineer men,
> While they climb the tall summits, and gazing afar,
> Shout aloud for the foemen and pant for the war.[21]

The largest of all O'Connell's monster meetings took place at Tara, the seat of the old Irish High Kings. A correspondent of *The Nation* claimed 'without the slightest fear of exaggeration' that there were three-quarters of a million people present.[22] O'Connell himself, never worried by fear of exaggeration, put it at a million and a half.[23] A contemporary ballad-maker gives as good an idea of its vast size as any.

> On the 15th day of August in the year of '43,
> This glorious day I well may say, recorded it shall be,
> On the Royal Hill of Tara, Irish thousands did prevail,
> In Union's bands to join their hands with Dan, for the Repeal.
>
> Such a good sight was never seen nor will till times no more,
> His lasting fame will long remain around Hibernian shore,
> No pen or talent can describe the glories of that day,
> As there was seen on Tara's Green a matchless grand display.
>
> There was Wexford, Wicklow and Kildare, sweet Dublin and Ardee,
> Westmeath, King's County and Dundalk most glorious for to see
> Cork, Limerick, Tuam, and Waterford, Strabane and sweet Kinsale,
> On the Royal Hill of Tara stood to sign for the Repeal.
>
> I topt the hill with heart and will – and cast my eyes around,
> With alarming consternation I viewed from the rising ground,
> The approaching legions of the Earth advancing from afar –
> With floating Flags and beating Drums like thundering claps of War.
>
> It baffles my description to portray the sight I seen,
> From Tara to Dunseeny and the lofty hill of Screen
> Ballinter, Trim and Bectivet with Kells, Navan and Altboy
> Came as one man for to see Dan their hearts' delight and joy.
>
> To see the flags of Drogheda with each harmonious band,
> Which with sacred pious music round the Croppies' graves did stand,
> Where is the heart that could not feel or eye refuse a tear,
> To see those noble heroes, for their country sleeping there.*[24]

---

* The last three lines refer to the graves of rebels slaughtered at Tara in 1798. See above, p. 106.

O'Connell began his speech with a pardonable romanticization of history. 'We are at Tara of the Kings,' he cried, '. . . emphatically the spot from which emanated then the social power – the legal authority – the right to dominion over the furthest extremes of this island . . .'

He went on: 'The strength and majority of the national movement was never exhibited so imposingly as at this great meeting. The numbers exceed any that ever before congregated in Ireland in peace or war. . . . It is a sight, not grand alone, but appalling – not exciting merely pride but *fear*. Such an army – for you have the steadiness and order of trained men – no free state would willingly see in its bosom, if it were not composed of its choicest citizens. . . . The great review of the Volunteers was the precursor of Ireland's independence – the Repealers at Tara outnumber as three to one the Citizen Army of '82. Step by step we are approaching the great goal itself; but it is at length with the strides of a giant.'[25]

The real question was whether the giant had a giant's strength. The closer O'Connell got to his goal the nearer came the moment when the question of how exactly he hoped to get Repeal if the government continued to stand firm would have to be answered. This critical moment was in fact just seven weeks away.

At the end of August O'Connell published his nine-point plan for a restoration of Irish parliamentary activity in Ireland. It included the ballot, household suffrage and a restoration of the Irish House of Lords. Of the rest of the nine points three were concerned with constitutional questions and in themselves could not have been objected to by the most die-hard Unionist. The first laid down that 'the Irish people recognize, acknowledge, maintain and will continually preserve and uphold for the throne of Ireland

HER MAJESTY QUEEN VICTORIA
WHOM GOD PROTECT',

and that they would give true allegiance to her heirs and successors for ever. Another stipulated that the Monarch and Regent *de facto* in England was the Monarch or Regent *de jure* in Ireland. The last ran: 'the connection between Great Britain and Ireland, by means of the power, authority and prerogatives of the Crown, to be perpetual and incapable of change or any severance or separation'.[26]

The picture of a new form of Irish nationalism commanding the enthusiastic support of the vast majority of the country was now complete. It had been evolved by the joint talents of an Irishman of the old Catholic and Gaelic strain, O'Connell, and an Irishman of the Protestant colonists' strain, Davis. It had its emotional roots in the glories and sorrows of the people of Ireland of both strains in the past, and derived its political dynamic from the misery and degradation of the majority of the population in the present. Both as part of its heritage from the past and as the acknowledged necessary condition for its existence in the present, it recognized an unalterable tie with the sister island on the other side of the Irish Sea. But it asked to be granted, in the now more democratic political circumstances of the mid-nineteenth century, the same sovereign right to manage Ireland's own affairs as Ireland had been granted constitutionally in the late eighteenth. As a slogan displayed at a great meeting at Lismore at the end of September 1843 had it: 'The rose of England shall never fade as long as it is entwined with the shamrock of Ireland; the only way to entwine it is by justice to Ireland.'[27]

The monster meetings continued as successfully as ever, even when as at Loughrea on 10 September they were deluged in torrential rain.[28] They became more and more brazen in their display of discipline.

At Clifden on 16 September green flags flew outside every home though sometimes there was a green, white and blue [sic] tricolour. Some six hundred men came to the meeting on horseback. They were drawn up in troops of what *The Nation* called 'peasant cavalry', five deep, with Repeal cards in their hats bound with green ribbons, and they answered with implicit obedience to the commands of farmers. O'Connell singled out these 'mountaineer cavalry' for special praise, admiring the precision with which they manoeuvred and declaring that no field-marshal was ever more punctually and willingly obeyed by his troops.[29] And he indulged himself in a particularly provocative version of his usual ambivalent language: 'He had demonstrated, to England,' he said, 'that more men of an adult age – why should he hesitate to say it? – that more men of fighting age [cheers] than had ever made a declaration for any other country in the world, had met together in Ireland to denounce the legislative Union [loud cheers] and yet they made no attack, nor allowed any threat of attack against their enemies . . .'[30]

A fortnight later, yet another monster meeting took place at Mullaghmast. At it for the first time, men with the words, 'O'CONNELL POLICE' printed on tickets in their hats and armed with staves marshalled the crowd.[31] Truly, as O'Connell himself had said, he had dared the government to their teeth.

The issue of *The Nation* of that week, beginning 30 September, contained a leading article headed 'The Coming Struggle', which declared: 'The clouds are thickening – Heaven only knows with what they are charged.' Its front page carried an advertisement for yet another monster meeting to be held at Clontarf, scene of Brian Boru's victory over the Danes, on 5 October. The notice was headed 'Repeal Cavalry' and continued:

'Muster and March of the Repeal Volunteers!!! [sic] . . . each troop to consist of 25 Horsemen, to be led by an officer in front, followed by 6 ranks 4 abreast, half distance, each bearing a wand and cockade . . .' It ended '. . . God Save The Queen. March for Repeal! March for Clontarf!'[32]

The government waited until the day before and then prohibited the meeting. The bluff was called. The question was now whether O'Connell and the Repealers would go ahead all the same and defy the troops sent to Clontarf to prevent them assembling?

Fully supported by his young allies on *The Nation* O'Connell called off the meeting.

Going in to dinner that night in England after hearing of the ban, the Duke of Wellington remarked contentedly to a neighbour: '*Pour la canaille, faut la mitraille.*'

8

Biding Time After Clontarf

Many years later, Gavan Duffy maintained that he and his Young Ireland friends on *The Nation* had been dismayed by O'Connell's capitulation after Clontarf, regarding it as a craven act, and his power as thereby 'recklessly squandered', his policy 'practically relinquished'.[1] However, an examination of the contemporary files of *The Nation* shows that Duffy and his Young Ireland colleagues in fact gave O'Connell immediate and unhesitating support on the decision.*

'The man who dares adopt any policy not sanctioned by O'Connell will deserve the deepest execration . . .' proclaimed *The Nation* in a leading article the week after Clontarf. 'Trust in O'Connell and fear not.'[2] A few weeks later Davis expressed the prescribed attitude for the Repeal movement in verse:

> Bide your time – one false step taken
> Perils all ye yet have done.
> Undismayed, erect, unshaken,
> Watch and wait and all is won.
>
> 'Tis not by one rash endeavour
> Men or states to greatness climb –
> Would you win your rights for ever
> Calm and thought bids bide your time.[3]

O'Connell now bided his time. The bluff of the monster meetings had been called. But, with the bluff called, what was future policy to be? How, practically, was the goal of Repeal, for which they were biding their time, in the fullness of time to be attained?

The one unmistakable asset remaining after the monster meetings was the fact that the Irish masses and the Catholic clergy (whose influence was always so closely linked with mass opinion) were overwhelmingly behind O'Connell. The government ban on Clontarf had brought further proof of

---

* Randall Clarke, *Irish Historical Studies*, vol. iii, p. 21 (1940), was the first historian to draw public attention to the inaccuracy of Duffy in this respect. But even he seems unaware of the full extent to which Gavan Duffy in his two books *Young Ireland* and *Four Years of Irish History* distorted the history of the post-Clontarf period. See below, pp. 219 and 225.

this, for, at less than twenty-four hours' notice, O'Connell and the Repeal Association had been able to prevent the assembly of perhaps half a million people, many of whom were already on their way to the meeting from many different parts of Ireland. Additional proof that the setback itself did not diminish O'Connell's authority with the Irish people was immediately forthcoming in the shape of the Repeal Rent, which rose sharply in the third week of October to the then record sum of £2,287.[4] However, evidence of popular support was of only limited advantage in a political situation which, before the great extensions of the franchise later in the century, was only in a limited sense democratic. The Irish upper and middle classes, a considerable proportion of whom were Protestants, were still widely opposed to Repeal just because of its character as a powerful popular movement, although the support of the Catholic Church made the movement seem more respectable to Catholic than to Protestant gentry.

As for support for Repeal in the British Parliament, where in the end Repeal had to be won, there was as little sign of it as when the issue had been debated there ten years before. The analogy with Catholic Emancipation which O'Connell was fond of drawing was still far from realistic. All in all, despite the past success of the monster meetings, the future for Repeal now looked bleak. And Peel's Tory government displayed its confidence when, within a week of Clontarf, it instigated a prosecution against O'Connell, Duffy and five others for 'conspiracy'.

Now, however rashly O'Connell and others had indulged in the ambivalent use of martial language during the year's campaign, there had never been anything conspiratorial about the Repeal movement. O'Connell had expressed *ad nauseam* his hatred and contempt for secret societies – partly a matter of genuine principle and partly because the agrarian secret societies were an unfathomable menace to his own influence over the Irish people. The Association's meetings had always been careful to assert their character as legal attempts by citizens of the Crown humbly and constitutionally to petition for a change in the law. So that it was possible at least that, by a prosecution, Peel was carrying his new confidence too far, and might arouse English Liberal sympathy for O'Connell.

While waiting to be brought to trial O'Connell embarked on the long laborious campaign that inevitably lay ahead if he were to win over to Repeal enough of the Irish gentry and, still more important, enough English support to give him a realistic force to manoeuvre with in the House of Commons. The arguments put forward in these years, and the arguments used to refute them, like those in the Repeal debate of the decade before dominated the question of constitutional Irish nationalism for the next seventy-five years.

In November 1843 O'Connell publicly examined the two evils which he said must be avoided if Repeal were to be obtained. The first was the separation of Ireland from the rest of Great Britain, which would be a great calamity'.[5] The other was the danger of what he called 'a Catholic ascendancy'.[6]

As far as separation was concerned, O'Connell insisted once again that not only was there not the least danger of separation in Repeal, but that Repeal would actually consolidate the connection between the two islands by removing all cause of further strife. To which Unionists could reply that they only had O'Connell's word for this, and that even he at times was careful to point out that he could not bind posterity beyond his lifetime.

As to the danger of a Catholic ascendancy, O'Connell made an interesting point that was relevant enough for his own day, but which would be less valid for the future. Catholic ascendancy, he maintained, could never come about because, although in an Irish House of Commons Catholics might well outnumber Protestants, yet in an Irish House of Lords Catholics would always be in a minority and there was therefore a cast-iron constitutional safeguard against the passing of any anti-Protestant measures.*[7]

Some encouraging signs were to be found that the Protestant gentry of Ireland were at this time not automatically wed to the inevitable continuation of the Union. It was, after all, a Protestant, the progressive landlord Sharman Crawford, who had already put forward Federalism – the proposal for an Irish legislature for domestic affairs only – as an important compromise between orthodox Unionism and total Repeal. It was a compromise of which Davis himself had already noted the tactical attractions.† Ten days after Clontarf, the Repeal Association declared Federalists eligible for membership; though Sharman Crawford himself did not in fact join. O'Connell made it clear that he himself, in accepting Federalism, was accepting no compromise, but that, in so far as an arrangement such as a Federalist might suggest would literally require the repeal of the Act of Union, he would consider such a man a Repealer.[8] 'We will not require him,' he continued, 'to go to the full length with us in every particular – we will go to that length ourselves and never give it up; but we will take the assistance of every man that is for a domestic legislature of any kind in Ireland.'[9]

The Nation, while also stressing its own more uncompromising aim, equally saw no reason to fear that a Federal Union could impede the march of nationality.[10] What it rightly did fear was what it called 'the deadly bane of Ireland – DIVISION ...'[11] and it welcomed Federalists with the words: 'They strike for nationality; they honour Ireland; they demand self-government; they ask part of what we ask – nothing against it.'[12]

But even Federalism was very much a minority creed among Protestants,

* In the Home Rule Bills later in the century, special Irish Upper Houses were envisaged which would not have had the same total veto on legislation which the House of Lords had in O'Connell's time.

† See above, p. 201.

and O'Connell's main problem, that of bringing Protestants into the fold of any sort of Irish nationalism, remained as formidable as ever. The government had, however, helped him acquire one Protestant recruit of considerable standing.

The ban on Clontarf and the prosecution of O'Connell had been too much for a forty-year-old Protestant landlord, named William Smith O'Brien, a man of some distinction and moral standing who had already resigned his commission of the peace in sympathy with those magistrates dismissed for attending Repeal meetings.*[13] O'Brien had been a member of Parliament for many years, first representing Ennis, in County Clare, and then County Limerick. Educated in England, like all the Protestant Irish upper classes of his day, he had the speech and mannerisms of an English gentleman and was often regarded by the Irish as stiff and stilted in a typically English fashion. One of his new Repeal associates remarked of him soon after he had joined the Repeal Association that the amalgam was unskilfully made: there was too much of the Smith and not enough of the O'Brien.[14] But these very characteristics were what made him such a sensationally imposing addition to the Repealers' ranks. For Smith O'Brien was a living embodiment of that nationalist theory first put forward by Tone and reiterated and substantiated by O'Connell and Davis that the Protestants of Ireland could and should make common cause with Catholics as Irishmen first and foremost in their allegiance. Moreover, he was a particularly suitable example of the theory, for although his family had been long of the ascendancy in style, and his new political views were to lead to painful difficulties with his mother, Lady O'Brien, yet he also traced his descent from Brian Boru, while a more recent ancestor had been one of the Wild Geese, had fought for the French at the battle of Ramillies and fathered a future Marshal of France.[15]

Again, although Smith O'Brien had been in favour of Catholic Emancipation in the twenties and had consistently taken up an attitude sympathetic to the Irish common people in the House of Commons, he had actually first been elected as a Tory. As a Whig-Liberal from 1835 onwards he had continued to oppose Repeal. As late as the summer of 1843, when moving in the House of Commons that the House should 'examine the causes of discontent in Ireland with a view to the redress of grievances and the establishment of a just and impartial government', he had used as one of his arguments for doing so the desirability 'of consolidating the legislative Union.[16] His decision now to join the Association was a powerful advertisement for the Repealers' argument that for all true Irishmen of whatsoever creed or class the Union was no longer supportable. Before the end of 1843, Smith O'Brien was taking part in the discussions on Federalism in the columns of The Nation, and agreeing that even a mere Federal constitution

* See above, p. 205.

would be better than 'the present miscalled Union which carries eternal weakness into the heart of the Empire, and which to Ireland is fraught with ruin and danger'.[17]

In the general desire to welcome all men of goodwill, particularly Protestant gentry, to the cause of the Repealers' Irish nationalism, there was certainly a tendency to skate rather optimistically over the sort of problems that Federalism would give rise to. For instance, with a domestic Irish Parliament concerned only with internal Irish affairs, and an Imperial Parliament which contained only a minority of Irish members, decisions on such questions as foreign treaties and the issue of peace or war would inevitably be those of the British and not of the Irish Government. Yet this hardly fitted the concept of Irish nationality which Davis and the other writers of *The Nation* and even O'Connell had been preaching. Certainly, they all emphasized that they would accept Federalism only as an experiment rather than as a final solution, but the half-way solution had to seem fairly stable if the British Parliament were ever to be brought to consider it seriously.

In a letter to *The Nation* at the end of the year Smith O'Brien faced up to the real problem with typical straightforwardness though not with altogether convincing arguments. He admitted that under Federalism there might theoretically be head-on conflicts over foreign treaties and peace or war, but the very danger of this would, he thought, be likely to prevent England from acting rashly on such matters. There would, O'Brien continued, be a two-way check on either England or Ireland allowing such conflicts to develop to a point where total separation threatened. When the Union was repealed England would have everything to lose and Ireland, if wisely governed, nothing to gain by separation. And in stating this he elaborated on an aspect of Irish life which was always to be a complicating, it not downright confusing, factor in the majority of Irishmen's national thinking.

'Nearly a million of our countrymen,' he continued, 'have fixed their homes in England and Scotland. Every family in the kingdom is linked by domestic connection with England – every British colony teems with the children of our soil.'[18] In these circumstances he held it very unlikely that Ireland would 'wantonly, without cause – nay, contrary to her own interest – desire to overthrow that majestic fabric of Imperial greatness on which she has lavished her energies to rear, and which she has profusely cemented with her blood. Deep indeed must be the wounds inflicted upon our national pride, and upon our national interests, before we can consent to deplore the associations which belong to identity of language, similarity of institutions, connection of kindred, and community of glory.'

The Nation, in spite of its own reservations about Federalism, applauded this letter from its new star recruit and welcomed Federalists with equal enthusiasm. Since *The Nation* group were to have their first major public difference of opinion with O'Connell almost a year later on the very subject of Federalism, this earlier agreement is of some interest.

At the beginning of the new year, 1844, the problem of what tactics to adopt were still the Repeal cause's principal concern. *The Nation* itself had nothing practical to suggest beyond general consolidation of the movement. It reiterated the two main principles of the cause: 'Ourselves Alone' and non-violence. 'Ireland must attempt nothing which can fail,' it wrote. 'Our fathers failed because they yielded to passion. ... Hoard your passions as though they were coined gold. ... Your policy is clear – organization, union, order.'[19] 'Bide your time', in fact, as Davis had put it earlier. A week later, *The Nation* had the grace to quote, from *Blackwood's Magazine*, a parody on Davis's poem.

'Bide your time,' wrote *Blackwood's*,

> ... bide your time,
> Patience is the true sublime;
> Heroes, bottle up your tears –
> Wait for ten, or ten-score years;
> Shrink from blows, but rage in rhyme –
> Bide your time, bide your time.

'But,' commented *The Nation*, 'neither scolding, or jibbing bayonets or proclamations shall push us a hair's breadth from the track on which prudence beckons us. We will bide our time and to some purpose.'[20]

In February 1844 something happened which increased the element of caution in O'Connell's natural pragmatism. The State trial of himself and the six other repealers which had dragged on throughout the winter came to an end and he and his co-defendants were found guilty of conspiracy. The actual sentence was postponed until the following law term, which meant a respite of three months or so on bail, but the verdict made the most profound impression on O'Connell.

His whole policy to date had been based on the necessity of keeping within the law. Its premise, rooted in his memory of '98, had been that illegal activity brought disaster. His determination and ability to make legality itself work for the Irish cause had so far been his most redoubtable asset. Now suddenly as a convicted conspirator he found himself virtually bracketed with the United Irishmen after all. An even greater sensitivity to the dangers of illegality was to characterize his political speech and behaviour for the rest of his life.

He at first considered dissolving the Repeal Association altogether and establishing some new organization quite uncompromised by the verdict. But dissuaded from such a drastic step by *The Nation* group, he turned his thoughts to the practical possibilities of the political situation in England.

There, a movement for a quite different sort of repeal – that of the Corn Laws – was under way and though this was not in itself of primary concern to Ireland, it opened up the possibilities of greater manoeuvrability for O'Connell on the English political scene, because the ruling Tory party was split on the issue. Conversely, the Whigs, united and energized by it, were already looking towards the end of the Tories' natural term of parliamentary office.

The bluff of the monster meetings had failed principally because the degree of English support for Repeal of the Union had been nothing like what it had been for Emancipation. But in the new political situation O'Connell had something to offer. His own parliamentary support became infinitely more valuable to British politicians. To trade one form of support for the other now became the underlying tactical principle of all his political action.

O'Connell had to wait between law terms for the pronouncement of sentence against him and his fellow 'conspirators' and used the interval to proceed to England to try to condition at least the English middle classes in favour of the Repeal cause. He went, in *The Nation*'s words, 'with the approval of the warmest Repealers'[21] and the Repeal Association soon afterwards passed with acclamation a resolution conveying their gratitude towards the Liberals and the sympathetic section of the British people whom O'Connell was meeting.[22]

But behind the scenes in Ireland there were already signs of that disquiet and even distaste with which the Young Irelanders were increasingly to view O'Connell's whole style of political activity. As yet it was more a question of differences of attitude rather than of policy. O'Connell, after years of political in-fighting, was the professional politician, with the professional's intuitive ability to adjust between the idealistic and the pragmatic approach to political problems. Davis, Duffy, Dillon, and the other young men whom they were begining to collect round them were unburdened by experience in politics. They were filled with the iconoclasm of the intelligent young for whom politics is a field for idealistic integrity, a practical extension of the written word, rather than a different element altogether. Even in the great monster meetings the year before there had been *sotto voce* disapproval for some of O'Connell's cheaper flights of demagogic oratory and now too, even before O'Connell's departure for England, Davis had already expressed some irreverent doubts about his firmness on Repeal to Smith O'Brien, who at this stage still stood aside both from the Liberator and Young Ireland in the Repeal movement. 'If O'Connell were firmer,' Davis wrote to O'Brien, 'I would say he ought not to go to England; but fancy his speeches at ten meetings here with the State trial terror on him! I fear we must keep him out of that danger by an English trip till Parliament meets, and then all will be well.'[23]

The Nation too had hinted at some doubts, when in the week of O'Connell's departure for England it published a leading article headed 'No Compromise'. The article's apparently innocuous intention was to disabuse any members of the Whig opposition of any idea they might have that all O'Connell was seeking in England was a political alliance on the of of the old Lichfield House Compact of the 1830s. If the Whigs were thinking this, then, said *The Nation*, speaking as ·if on O'Connell's behalf, they were making a mistake.[24] But what *The Nation* really meant was that if O'Connell himself were thinking this then he was making a mistake.

A still clearer public glimpse of such doubts appeared two days later in a meeting of the Repeal Association. A brief exchange of words took place between O'Connell's son John – his favourite of four, and always the acknowledged deputy of his father in his absence – and one Young Irelander, M. J. Barry, on what exactly the Lichfield House Compact had amounted to. John O'Connell showed himself very anxious to expunge any possible inference that might be drawn from Barry's words to the effect that O'Connell had compromised the full Repeal goal at that time and therefore might be supposed to be about to do so in the future.[25] The matter was at once cleared up to everyone's apparent satisfaction, but this fear that O'Connell might settle permanently for something less than Repeal, and a reciprocal resentment of this suspicion on his part, was to become a more and more painful feature of the O'Connell–Young Ireland relationship and finally seriously to damage the whole Repeal movement.

Modern historians, while rejecting some earlier detail of Gavan Duffy's account of this period,* have acquiesced in his general contention that soon after Clontarf O'Connell lost interest in Repeal and was overcome by physical debility. The very writer who first exposed Duffy's lapse in claiming to have opposed the Clontarf decision, himself declared that from the time of the trial verdict onwards O'Connell 'seems to have lost all faith in the Repeal movement'.[26] Thereafter, he continues, O'Connell had no real hope of achieving Repeal and only continued the agitation because the Young Irelanders and O'Brien forced him to do so. In fact, any close study of O'Connell's activity in the years 1844 to 1846 makes it impossible to accept that he could have carried an interest in Repeal to such impressive lengths or with such energy and enthusiasm, as he did, if he had been as disingenuous or as senile as Duffy implies.

The imaginative technique of the monster meetings had proved by itself inadequate. While not, in fact, as will be seen, abandoning the moral power which massed displays of Irish popular opinion lent his other efforts, he now combined this with more conventional pragmatic manoeuvres in the political field. Before, however, such manoeuvres could be effective, the entire Irish scene was overshadowed by the appalling catastrophe of the famine.

* See above, p. 212.

Pragmatic politics suddenly meant simply trying to preserve life itself for the starving common people of Ireland. And only when overwhelmed by the relative failure to do even this in which all politicians were to be involved did O'Connell succumb quite rapidly to debility and advancing age.

9

O'Connell's Imprisonment and After

In the very week of March 1844 in which the exchange of words took place in the Repeal Association between the Young Irelander, Barry, and John O'Connell about his father's intentions in England, Thomas Davis himself wrote John O'Connell a private letter expressing his own anxiety. He suggested that the success which the Liberator was soon enjoying in England was 'embarrassing' and even contradictory to the Repeal policy. There was an almost panicky note in Davis's letter.

'I do not, and cannot suppose,' he wrote, 'that your father ever dreamt of abandoning Repeal to escape a prison, yet that is implied in all the Whig [newspaper] articles.'[1]

Yet when the record of this short campaign of O'Connell's in England is examined, it seems that Davis was paying an almost obsessional attention to what the Whig newspapers were saying, rather than to what O'Connell himself was saying. And in view of the fact that no alternative to O'Connell's practical attempt to win English support had been suggested by anyone else, Davis's implied suspicions seem unworthy of him.

In O'Connell's public references to Repeal on this visit he usually made clearer than was strictly necessary his intention to seek, in the long run, nothing short of full Repeal. But his chief concern was to make Repeal acceptable to English ears. Thus, at Birmingham, where on 9 March 1844 he spoke on the same platform as the Federalist Sharman Crawford, he admitted openly that if the Union had been a fair bargain between Britain and Ireland it ought to be preserved, but denied that it was a fair bargain. (The emphasis was different from that of the thirties when he had talked openly about 'testing' the Union.) At the same time he denied that Repeal of the Union meant separation, maintaining that he would be against it if it did and insisting that one of his chief reasons for being in favour of 'a just and equitable Repeal' was that it alone could prevent eventual separation. (His tactful use of the adjectives 'just' and 'equitable' in Sharman Crawford's presence made it unnecessary to go into any precise distinctions between Federalism and full Repeal.) His way of putting things was not that of the

Young Irelanders, but then their more aggressively expressed nationalism would not have won many voices for Repeal of the Union within the British political system. In fact, O'Connell's argument was to become the basic argument of the vast majority of nationalist Irishmen for the rest of the nineteenth century and the first sixteen years of the twentieth.

The day after this Birmingham meeting another large meeting took place in Manchester – this time without O'Connell – to direct the government's attention to 'the public grievances under which the people of Ireland labour'.[2] The Mayor presided. Professors, bankers and clergy were among the sponsors. There was enthusiastic applause at the mention of O'Connell's name. Certainly, it was primarily a Whig rally. But it was also a valuable part of that necessary process of softening up English opinion if Repeal were ever to be won by constitutional means. And no Young Irelander was then in favour of it being won by any other.

In the following week a great dinner was given to O'Connell in the theatre at Covent Garden, where the auditorium was entirely boarded over and made level with the stage.[3] A number of Whig notables were present, including the Earl of Shrewsbury who proposed the toast of 'The People', and particularly 'The Irish People', though in a rather confused and dated way he seemed to mean by this the Irish country gentlemen. However, he announced the opening of a new era in history, and the toast of 'O'Connell' was received with immense cheering, the whole audience rising *en masse* and cheering and waving handkerchiefs for several minutes on end.

But though playing for British support, O'Connell was aware of the anxiety of the young men who were his political élite in Ireland, and was careful to consider them too. At Coventry on the following Monday he took up the remark of an earlier speaker who had said, in an over-accommodating manner, that what O'Connell was looking for was not in fact really Repeal of the Union at all, but simply justice for Ireland.

'Now,' said O'Connell of this speaker, 'he was mistaken in his views of my objects for although it is true that I am looking for justice to the Irish people, yet I see no prospect of justice. I believe there is none in any other means than by a restoration of her domestic legislature to Ireland. . . . If,' he went on in familiar vein, 'by looking for Repeal of the Union I sought a separation of the two countries, I would be wrong in seeking it – but a Repeal of the Union would not produce separation – it would unite the two countries more closely.'[4] He refused to leave his audience with any comforting sense of ambiguity about his final purpose: 'You can never convince me that any other than an Irish Parliament will give justice to Ireland, and I will go to the grave with that feeling.' But he compensated by concluding in his woolliest vein with a call for 'a strong pull and a long pull for England and Ireland – for Ireland and for England; a strong pull and a long pull, and a pull altogether'. He sat down amid loud and renewed cheering.

Before leaving England for Ireland at the end of March 1844 O'Connell told a great indoor meeting at Liverpool, for which tickets had been changing hands at treble their official price, that if justice were not done to Ireland and the Union repealed there would be 'a bloody revolution and separation between the two countries'.[5] After a night at the Adelphi Hotel he sailed for Ireland, where Smith O'Brien was quick to approve his visit and wholly refute any suggestion that it had been nothing but a Whig manoeuvre.[6]

The date was approaching on which O'Connell and his six co-defendants were due for sentence on the conspiracy charge. Temporary loss of O'Connell's leadership would inevitably be a serious tactical blow for the Repeal Association. He made clear how he wished its affairs to be conducted in his absence. At a dinner at Cork on 8 April 1844, at which a letter of support from MacHale, the Archbishop of Tuam, was read, O'Connell laid down the principle that 'the Repeal must continue', adding: 'If you want to confer on me comfort when in my dungeon, you will rally for Old Ireland and Repeal.'[7]

On 30 May 1844 he was sentenced with the others to a year's imprisonment. *The Nation* protested between black borders: 'He, the King of your hearts, cannot step this land which he has so served, beyond the walls of his gaol.'[8] Smith O'Brien, at the first meeting of the Repeal Association after the sentence, swore to vehement applause that he would not allow a drop of intoxicating liquor to pass his lips until O'Connell was released.[9]

O'Connell's dungeon in fact turned out to be a luxurious one. The Dublin prison in which he was confined was under the control of the Dublin Corporation and the Governor graciously vacated his own house for O'Connell's use. He was allowed as many visitors as he liked. Food was sent in from outside and very large dinner parties of twenty-four people or more were frequent, sometimes held in a special dining tent in the garden from which a tricolour flag was flown until over this at least the Governor put his foot down.*[10] Smith O'Brien, who now assumed something of the position of O'Connell's deputy in the Association, was able to consult with him continually, while Davis, who ran *The Nation* while Gavan Duffy served his sentence, was equally able to consult with him as much as he liked. Nevertheless, a great wave of sympathy and protest at the sentences was felt all over Ireland, and the additional enthusiasm for the Repeal cause in which it resulted was immediately signalled in a sudden prodigious rise in the Repeal Rent. The weekly sum had been drifting sluggishly around the £500 mark until O'Connell's imprisonment, but it rose sharply to over £2,500 in the week in which he was sentenced and climbed still higher to over £3,000 a week for several weeks afterwards.[11] These amounts, which in the money values of the mid-nineteenth century were considerable, were subscribed

* There is no indication as to the nature of the tricolour. It was probably the French red, white and blue, a symbol of progressive defiance. The orange, white and green as an Irish variant of this first appeared in 1848. See below, p. 265.

almost entirely in small sums by people in all walks of life – carmen, coach-lace weavers, solicitors, stockbrokers, priests, peasants, etc. Almost all of it came from Ireland itself. Of the tally of £3,389 14s 8d recorded in *The Nation* of 22 June 1844, only £34 came from America. More progress, wrote Davis in *The Nation* of 15 June, heading his leader 'Third Week of the Captivity', had been made in the previous fortnight than in any other quarter of the agitation.[12]

Davis now gave his mind to the question of how this favourable situation was to be turned to more practical advantage. He stressed particularly the need for internal unity and, on the principle that any sort of domestic legis-lature would at least give nationality 'a temple', he added that a Federalist was 'a Repealer of the Union as decidedly as if he never called himself a Federalist'.[13] He made it clear that *The Nation* itself thought that a claim in the government of the Empire and consent to contribute taxes and soldiers towards its upkeep 'seems to us unwise' but that this was 'not such a difference as should make us divide'.[14]

Signs of a broad, if vague, sort of Irish unity were indeed coming from some unexpected quarters. In July 1844 an Irish National Society was formed in London to bring peers and gentlemen together for the promotion of social and intellectual intercourse among Irishmen, irrespective of political differ-ences. The Earl of Clanrickarde and Lord Castlereagh were listed among its members, together with one of O'Connell's sons, Maurice. This was the first of a number of such attempts made in these years to bring Irishmen of all parties together in London on the basis of nothing but their Irishness. Such groupings never led to anything very positive or constructive, but in retrospect they can be seen as a residual flickering of that sense of Protestant gentry nationalism which had partly inspired the more broadly based Irish nationalism now at work. At the time, to the young men of *The Nation*, they seemed more like the flickering of a reviving than a dying fire, a first faint sign of their vision being fulfilled.

Late in August 1844 a development in foreign affairs suggested a much more promising analogy with the years of the Volunteers. France became engaged in a series of actions against the Sultan of Morocco to which the British Government reacted with traditional sensitivity. *The Nation* declared that if war were to come between England and France then Repeal must be made to follow. There was no specific proposal as to how exactly this might be done beyond increased nationalist efforts to acquire knowledge and improve organization. But the inference was obvious. At the end of the month the paper spelt things out. The Prince de Joinville had bombarded the island and town of Mogador, while on land Marshal Bugeaud had defeated twenty-four thousand Moorish cavalry. 'We heave a sigh for Morocco,' wrote Davis in *The Nation*. 'We rejoice for Ireland. There is hope for us in every volley ...' He drew the parallel with 1779. 'The opportunity

of 1779 may come again – our garrisons empty – an invader on the horizon.'
He addressed himself to Peel, telling him how rapidly he should endeavour
to conciliate the people by releasing their leaders and yielding Ireland to the
Irish; for 'nationality consecrates a coast'. How too he 'should accept their
volunteer battalions, and strengthen their Patriotism by arsenals and
discipline'.[15]

Yet even in this prospective concrete situation *The Nation* offered no
practical scheme to nationalists. There was no call for the formation of
volunteers, merely one to strengthen the Association by forming Repeal
Reading Rooms and increasing contributions to the Repeal Rent. The
furthest Davis went was to exhort Repealers to 'carefully study every book
and map that may qualify them for the defence of their soil'.[16]

The war did not materialize, but within a fortnight something happened
which gave almost as much hope to the Repeal movement. Against all
expectation, the judgement on O'Connell and his fellow prisoners was
reversed in the House of Lords. They were released the same day, but
chose to return to the prison for the night so that a triumphal procession of
some 200,000 citizens could make the most of the event on the following day.
Similar rejoicing took place all over Ireland. In Cork there was 'the very
ecstasy of joyous delirium'.[17] The bands turned out. Bonfires were lit. Houses
were decked with laurel. Torchbearers and blazing tar barrels turned night
into day and beacons flared from hill to hill across the countryside.[18]

But when the first natural excitement was over, the same question which
had faced Repealers before O'Connell's imprisonment still remained: what
was the next step to be?

Duffy's retrospective account of events, coloured by Young Ireland's subsequent quarrel with O'Connell, tries to establish that a physical and mental
deterioration of O'Connell set in after his release from imprisonment.[19] But
there is no evidence of this at the time. There is no contemporary comment
on a physical deterioration in O'Connell until November 1846. Then it is his
friend, W. J. O'Neill Daunt, who notes specifically that while 'his physical
energies are plainly decaying' he displays 'unimpaired intellectual power'.[20]
Even in the following year, only a few months before O'Connell's death,
Daunt records that, though complaining of the feebleness of age, O'Connell
declared himself otherwise 'very well'.[21] And Daunt was no sycophant, like
Tom Steele, O'Connell's so-called 'Head Pacificator' and others of his supporters in the Association. Certainly Duffy's implication of O'Connell's
rapid decline into enfeeblement and senility after his release cannot be sustained, though his need to find some explanation that was not too painful
for events which even forty years later were painful to look back upon is
understandable.

In his first speech to the Association a few days after his release, O'Connell
faced up to the problem of what the next step was to be without claiming to

be able to supply the answer. Though he maintained that the Clontarf meeting had been legally summoned and illegally prohibited, he was on the whole against risking another challenge of that sort. Pre-eminent in his mind was the need to preserve what had always given his movement its strength: namely, the fact that, unlike the United Irishmen's demand for nationality, it was not treasonably expressed.

The trial and the original legal decision against him had plainly given him a fright, and something like an obsession with this fright can be seen in his first suggestion – soon dropped – to prosecute those British authorities who had brought about his imprisonment; the Attorney General, the Judges and the British Ministers themselves. His other positive proposal was to proceed with the plan for the summons of a Council of Three Hundred (the same number of members as had sat in the old Irish Parliament). Since this plan had been actively under review when the prosecution was instigated he approached the subject now with extreme caution, and emphasized that it was full of legal difficulty. The fifty-year-old Convention Act, expressly designed to prevent any such extra-parliamentary body from meeting, was still on the Statute Book and O'Connell's old confidence in his ability to drive a coach and six through any Act of Parliament had been rudely shaken. However, he was in favour of summoning the Council 'as a Preservative Society' which, while initiating nothing, should act as the supreme sanctioning and consultative body for the Association itself.[22]

Duffy, in his later history, suggests that Young Ireland's reaction to this speech of O'Connell's was one of disappointment bordering on dismay. But the issue of *The Nation* which reported it does not bear him out. The leading article appearing under its regular heading, 'Remember the 30th May',* in summarizing the Association's prospects said: 'the Preservative Society must be made a reality, though we concur with O'Connell that it must be done slowly and carefully'.[23] It also agreed with O'Connell in deprecating a Clontarf meeting. Further, it advised a renewal of those arbitration courts which in the previous years had heard something like four thousand cases in an indigenous Irish process altogether outside the machinery of British law, and had obtained acceptance for their verdicts in all but a minute percentage of cases.[24]

O'Connell himself was in favour of these courts, though again he was anxious to keep their activities separate from the Association lest their possible illegality should endanger it.[25] Nor was there anything in the rest of *The Nation*'s article with which O'Connell would not have agreed. Better organization was needed. The Reading Rooms should be extended. The men of the North should be educated, and England must be taught that it was in her interest to have Ireland a friendly neighbour helping her in danger, rather than a discontented province. In general the paper struck a most

* The date of O'Connell's imprisonment.

realistic note: '... while legally we are in the same position as on the day they [O'Connell and the other defendants] were impeached, politically we are far stronger. We have rallied good and generous men in our adversity. .... We are far stronger than we were a year ago. ... We have got where we are by organization, conciliation and peace. Our peace cannot be improved – the People cannot do better than adhere to their present obedience to the law.' [26]

In a speech at a banquet in his honour a few days later O'Connell echoed *The Nation*'s general tone. Their first duty, he said, was 'to combine together the Irish of every sect and persuasion – to unite and combine Irishmen of every gradation of opinion who agree with us in thinking one thing necessary – the Repeal of the Union'.[27]

Many hopeful portents for such a combination were in the air. The Federal idea was becoming increasingly popular among men who had been previously opposed to the Repeal movement, and Sharman Crawford had actually sent a letter to this very banquet in O'Connell's honour, apologizing for his absence. O'Connell took up an inference in this letter that Repealers ruled out Federalism, which he said was quite incorrect. It was true that most members of the Association preferred 'simple Repeal, but there is not one of us that would not be content to Repeal the Act of Union and substitute a Federal Parliament, not one. I don't think Federalism to be the best, but I was never one of those who had such an overweening opinion of the infallibility of my own judgement as not readily to yield to argument, and cooperate with anyone that thinks better. I am ready to join with Federalists to repeal the Act of Union.' [28] He even went so far as to propose that he should hand over leadership of a combined movement to a new Protestant recruit for Federalism, a former Orangeman who was now High Sheriff of County Fermanagh, named Grey Porter.

Though such extravagant and uncharacteristic humility can be discounted as oratorical display, O'Connell was again undoubtedly sounding the one note which seemed likely to promise real advance for the Repeal movement, namely conciliation of those forces which were in any case moving towards it. Some time before this banquet a high Tory of distinction on the Dublin Corporation, a Dr Maunsell, had written to him with a proposal which while not going so far as Federalism was significant enough of a general shift in opinion. This proposal was that while the Act of Union itself should not be altered, the Imperial Parliament should meet in Dublin every three years. In this case O'Connell could only reply politely that much though the prospect of working together for Ireland with such men as Dr Maunsell delighted him in principle, he could not support this particular measure as it was clearly intended as a substitute for Repeal. Nevertheless, as Davis himself pointed out, the proposal did represent at least a 'loosening of ideas, an abandonment of the old superstition that all was right'.[29]

That the general conciliatory line of tactics was a promising one seems confirmed by the British Government's own reaction to these straws in the wind. Graham, the Home Secretary, wrote to Peel, the Prime Minister, voicing his suspicion that 'the Federal arrangement will be the middle term on which for the moment opposite parties will agree: and some scheme of national representation will be devised, to which the Whigs will agree'.[30] And the fact that the proposal for occasional Imperial Parliaments in Dublin should come from such a high Tory as Dr Maunsell alarmed him still further.[31] Even Lord John Russell, the leader of the Whigs, seemed frightened by the way things were going and wrote to the Duke of Leinster asserting his determination to maintain the Union and reject any Federal solution.[32]

All this makes the breach that was about to take place between O'Connell and Young Ireland on the subject of Federalism difficult to understand. For *The Nation*, under both Davis's and Duffy's editorship, at first appeared wholly to endorse O'Connell's tactic. 'Mr O'Connell,' it wrote, two days after his banquet speech, 'is prepared to welcome Federalism. ... We too will hail the concession of Irish supremacy in Ireland and will give this plan a fair trial.'[33] And a week later, in another leading article headed 'Conservative Repealers', it drew attention to the fact that the Protestants felt sold out by the government and were therefore ready to listen to new suggestions that might be in their interests.[34] 'Federalism is making such way,' *The Nation* continued, 'both among Tories and Whigs, here and in England, as to lead us to hope that that great object will be gained without a shot being fired.'[35]

The new spirit among Conservatives derived partly from the developing political split between Peelites and anti-Peelites within the party. And it was not just wishful thinking to suppose that this internal split might be turned to advantage by advocates of the Repeal cause. An anti-Repeal English journal, the *London Examiner*, commented on the advance of the Repeal cause as moderate and sensible men came to see that in their own interests some new parliamentary organization was necessary 'to adjust appropriate legal capacity and attention to the peculiar needs of different parts of the country'. 'Affairs,' continued the *London Examiner*, 'have become too complex for the careless scrambling legislation in a mob of six hundred members ... a very considerable portion of the thinking classes ... are of opinion that the duties of the legislature have outgrown its means of performing them.'[36]

At the weekly meeting of Belfast repealers in those days it was no unusual thing now for Protestants 'and Orangemen to be proposed as members or associates. And the ultra-Tory *Belfast Newsletter*, in commenting that there were now many distinguished Conservatives openly supporting Federalism, wrote of 'most extraordinary times' and that the crisis of Ireland's fate was approaching.[37] No wonder *The Nation* felt optimistic. 'Let the people go on as they had begun,' it wrote, '– growing more thoughtful, more temperate, more educated, more resolute – let them complete their parish organization, carry out their registries, and above all establish those Reading Rooms which will inform and strengthen them into liberty; and 'ere Many Years Work, the Green Flag will be saluted by Europe, and Ireland will be a Nation.' None of this fits in with the 'silent discontent and dismay' which Duffy nearly forty years later remembered to have greeted O'Connell's utterances on his release.

After the necessary three weeks or so of speech-making and celebration O'Connell retired to his home, Darrynane Abbey in County Kerry, for a short holiday. This was reasonable enough for a man of seventy who had just emerged from three months' confinement, even of a comfortable sort. He found his farm in excellent shape with the richest crop of hay of any-one in the district, and he was soon out on the hills delightedly hunting hares with his pack of beagles. Acknowledging his debt to 'my merciful God for my health and strength' he concluded a letter to one of his closest friends, 'I am becoming very impatient to hear authentically from "the Federalists".'[38] Ten days later, he wrote a letter to the Repeal Association almost ten thousand words long containing his thoughts on future policy.

In this letter O'Connell started from two premises. First, it would be 'criminal' not to exploit their great legal victory 'to achieve the great object of our desires – the restoration of an Irish Parliament'.[39] Secondly, the con-ciliation of a sizeable body of Protestants was necessary in order to do so. Having demonstrated from ancient and recent history that Protestants had nothing to fear from a Catholic ascendancy, he proceeded to examine that movement which, for the first time since the Union, seemed to show Protes-tants again moving towards the idea of an Irish Parliament, namely Federal-ism. He recommended some alliance with it, and in terms of political tactics in the prevailing situation it was a realistic enough recommendation to make. Although O'Connell already knew enough of *The Nation* group to realize that political realism was not their strong point, it was not unreasonable to expect their support in this policy in view of their frequent editorial blessings on Federalism in *The Nation* in the past, and in particular in view of the fact that Davis himself was even at that moment in Belfast conducting negotia-tions with prominent Federalists.[40]

In fact the only practical difficulty O'Connell appeared to see was that the Federalists were not yet themselves precisely agreed on how their scheme was to work. But while admitting this reservation and making clear that no such precise scheme could be expected to come from him he went so far as to declare: 'For my own part, I will own, I do at present feel a preference for the Federative plan, as tending more to the utility of Ireland, and to the maintenance of the connection with England than the mode of simple Repeal.'[41]

The qualification 'at present' seems to denote plainly the waiting game on which he was embarking. Davis himself had specifically approved such a game, writing of O'Connell the day after he had left for Darrynane: 'He is wisely playing a slow game to let the Federalists ... show themselves.'[42]

In the end O'Connell's attempt at a new tactical move came to nothing for the Federalists remained unable to agree publicly on a precise formula. Indeed, his rather transparent eagerness to embrace them may have scared some of them off altogether. But their failure to respond gave him a way of escape from an even greater embarrassment. For O'Connell's statement on Federalism rather surprisingly led to the first major public disagreement between *The Nation* and himself, a portent of disastrous things to come.

Duffy alone of those prominent in *The Nation* group had been in Dublin when O'Connell's letter to the Association was inserted in the minutes.[43] Without consulting any of the other Young Irelanders he published in the leader column of *The Nation* an open letter to O'Connell, signed by himself, repudiating the idea of any compromise on pure and total Repeal of the Act of Union.

It is possible to read between the lines of Duffy's later writings that Davis himself did not approve of Duffy's action.[44] It would have been odd if he had approved, since he was then negotiating with Federalists in Belfast. And at the time Davis even described O'Connell's letter as 'very able of its kind', though he thought his gesture of embrace towards the Federalists was too precipitate.[45] Federalism could never be a final settlement, but it deserved a fair trial and toleration; in any case, whether they went through Federation or not, he believed there would be no limit to Irish nationality in twenty years.[46] However, once Duffy in *The Nation* had made his purist stand for principle regardless of political expediency, Davis could only back him up. A fortnight later in *The Nation* he himself was stressing that Ireland's aspiration was 'for UNBOUNDED NATIONALITY'.

O'Connell seems to have been genuinely surprised, and not without reason, at the sudden indignation of his young supporters. He quickly seized on the Federalists' failure to agree a detailed scheme as justification for reappearing as 'a simple Repealer' again, literally snapping his fingers in public at Federalism, as something that had let him down.[47] But though *The Nation* soon radiated a conciliatory tone, reassuring its readers that all was going well with Ireland and that cordiality and resolution were perfectly restored,[48] the situation was in two senses unalterably different after the incident. In the first place, the relationship between O'Connell, the experienced politician, and those literary idealists who were the intellectual élite of his movement, had taken an open turn for the worse. Secondly, a possible new tactic by which the Repeal movement might break through the post-Clontarf political deadlock had disintegrated. Though public enthusiasm for Repeal remained as great as ever, it was now again as difficult as ever to use that enthusiasm to effect.

In this frustrating situation the differences of temperament and outlook between O'Connell and Young Ireland grew more and more inescapable, and were increasingly reflected within the transactions of the Repeal Association. Contempt for many of the sycophants and provincial time-servers by whom the Liberator was surrounded, including his favourite son John; embarrassment about the lack of sound accountancy with which the Repeal Rent and other funds were administered; a dislike, though many Young Irelanders were themselves Catholics, of a routine sectarian flag-waving which even O'Connell was inclined to fall back on in the absence of other emotive material; but above all youth's natural leanings towards uncompromising political puritanism in a power vacuum which O'Connell alone was seriously committed to fill – all these things made Young Ireland more and more impatient with the undoubted fact that O'Connell was the only conceivable leader who commanded the affections and loyalty of the Irish people.

Reciprocally, O'Connell, shouldering all political responsibility in a power situation which by the nature of the Union Parliament was heavily loaded against him, and in any case inevitably feeling something of an older man's natural resentment for the cocksureness and intransigence of youth, found his particular style of pragmatic manoeuvre increasingly cramped by Young Ireland's independent spirit, and longed to be able to contain it within the confines of what today would be called party discipline. The mutually irritant effect of the two parties on each other was only exacerbated by mutual recognition of the fact that each needed the other badly. Without O'Connell's power of leadership over the Irish people, Young Ireland knew that they were only a minority middle-class group who commanded virtually no following at all. Without the practical drive and energetic intelligence of Young Ireland, and particularly its effective propagandizing influence through the columns of *The Nation* newspaper, O'Connell knew that the movement was in danger of acquiring a hack Catholic sectarian image against which the Protestants of Ireland and even some of the Catholic gentry would remain steadfastly united. When the break finally came the worst fears of each party were to be realized, to the sole benefit of the Union they had combined to repeal. Whether or not the internal stresses in any case made the final break inevitable is uncertain. What they could not stand was the additional dislocation of the political situation by the appalling consequences of the potato disease which settled on Ireland in the autumn of 1845.

10

More 'Monster Meetings'

In spite of increasing internal strains, the Repeal movement for the greater part of 1845, though not breaking new ground as in the sensational days of '43, was certainly not retreating. And for the first ten months of 1845 O'Connell continued to commit himself energetically and unequivocally to Repeal and the restoration of an Irish Parliament.[1]

The central problem remained: how to bring majority Irish opinion to make an impact on government. Hope of building and bargaining for English support for Repeal within the House of Commons had become, after Clontarf, the only solution that seemed realistic to O'Connell. But this inevitably seemed a very long-term affair, although O'Connell continued to draw analogies with both Emancipation and Reform to show that the House of Commons could change its mind very suddenly.

On the whole, feeling was consolidating among Repealers that they would have to wait for some sort of situation analogous to that of 1778–82. They must be ready for some external threat to Britain to arise which would enable them to show their strength while nominally organizing to help meet it.

In December 1844 *The Nation*, in supporting a public demand that had been made for Irish Volunteers, had written: '... it is our right by God's ordinance and the old constitution of both realms to link our citizens into an army, and therewith to smite all who invade our land or our liberties'.[2] The next week *The Nation* drew a parallel between Ireland, within the British connection, and Hungary, that 'loyal province of Austria', which not only had her national Parliament but her own army, voted by that Parliament and dressed in national Hungarian uniform.[3]

In January 1845 an '82 club was formed in Ireland with O'Connell as its president and the veteran Protestant Volunteer of 1782, Cornelius McLoughlin, as one of its vice-presidents. In emulation of the splendours of the old Volunteers the uniform, designed by Davis, was a green coat with a velvet collar, white lining and gilt buttons (inscribed 1782, in a wreath of shamrocks), green trousers with patent leather boots, white kid gloves and a black satin cravat.[4] In response to some criticism that this all seemed rather too military, Smith O'Brien, who hoped that the club might prove a sort of alternative to the Council of Three Hundred until the legal difficulties surrounding that body could be overcome, declared: 'I am not sorry that the government should feel that the dress we wear wants nothing but the sword attached to it to constitute us officers of the Irish people.'[5] It was as an officer class, too, that Davis seemed to envisage its membership, for he had accepted that the uniform should cost a minimum of twelve guineas.[6] When a banquet for 'the Repeal martyrs' was held at Kilkenny at the end of March, attended by the Mayor and Corporation in their municipal robes preceded by outriders dressed in orange and green, '82 club members appeared in their uniform for the first time in public, and *The Nation* held out high hopes of it for 'the people'.[7] While admitting that the uniform was 'yet to be decorated by achievements and honour', it continued: 'Inconsiderate men may ask what it will accomplish – let them for that take the words of the very practical men who have assumed it – time will show its uses.'[8]

Within a month *The Nation* was hailing what it called 'Our First Triumph':[9] Peel's decision to increase very substantially the annual grant made by the British Government to the Roman Catholic priests' training college at Maynooth.

In comparison with the sort of triumphs for Irish national pride on which *The Nation* had set its sights, this may today hardly seem anything of great significance. But within the context of the time it was an imaginative and courageous step, and one which very considerably increased Peel's own difficulties within the Conservative Party. Its remarkable welcome in Ireland was a measure of the Repeal movement's frustration on the main count of Repeal itself. *The Nation* exulted in one particular remark of Peel's in the House of Commons to the effect that, when trouble came to a head with the United States that month over the annexation of Texas and Oregon, he had been able to recollect 'with satisfaction and consolation, that the day before I had sent a message of peace to Ireland' – namely, the proposal for the increase in the Maynooth grant. Thus, claimed *The Nation*, Ireland's foreign policy had been recognized and the Repeal Association had shown itself 'a permanent nation within the Union'.[10] But the Repeal Association had come into business for more substantial proofs of nationhood than the Maynooth grant.

In fact, the Maynooth grant was part of a series of conciliatory measures with which Peel hoped to weaken the Irish nationalist demand. Concessions intended to placate Catholic feelings in Ireland were made in other fields too, principally that of education, where Peel proposed to found and endow three regional university colleges for Ireland which, unlike Trinity, Dublin, should be equally open to Catholics and Protestants alike and wholly undenominational in character.

The effect of these conciliatory measures on some Irish ultra-Conservatives was paradoxical in the extreme. For, in their blind fury at any concessions to Catholics at all, they became ready to assert Irish independence themselves. And it is one of the strange ironies in which Irish history abounds that it was a right-wing Protestant newspaper which first proposed for Ireland in 1845 the underlying conception of that flag which is today the emblem of the Irish Republic. Arguing that the Protestants of the North might very well be able to get better terms out of the Repealers than the government themselves proposed, the *Dublin Evening Mail* on 2 August 1845 wrote that 'the Repeal banner might then be orange and green, flying from the Giant's Causeway to the Cove of Cork and proudly look down from the walls of Derry upon a newborn nation'. Nevertheless, the total effect of these measures was, in general, as Peel had intended, to consolidate rather than disrupt the Union. In the words of a modern Irish historian, 'they certainly made it easier for a Catholic to be a conservative and an anglophile and so facilitated the growth of a quiet but influential body, the Catholic Unionists'.[11] And to do that was to strike at the very heart of Repeal.

One of Peel's measures – the proposal to create three undenominational regional university colleges – was the immediate cause of the next public clash between O'Connell and the Young Irelanders, a further portent of disastrous quarrels to come. For some time temperamental differences between the two groups in the Association had been polarizing round the issue of Catholic sectarianism. Disputes usually took the form of indignant denials by each side of the attitude of which the other was accusing it. O'Connell continually, and plainly sincerely, reiterated his determination to have no Catholic ascendancy in an independent Ireland. 'I would rather die upon the scaffold,' he declared in April 1845, 'and I say it with all the solemnity of truth – than consent to a Catholic ascendancy in Ireland.'[12] And he was always quick to resent any Protestant criticism of what appeared to Young Ireland as Catholic sectarian tendencies. Yet it would have been unreasonable to expect O'Connell and his intimates, who derived the great bulk of their support from a people whose chief identifying feature was their Catholic religion, not to make that identity an occasional rallying cry.

Davis, on the other hand, a Protestant himself, whose nationalism was based wholly on the belief that religion was irrelevant where an Irishman's nationality was concerned, deplored any attempt to accentuate Catholic views as part of the movement. Once, in 1844, he had even written to Smith O'Brien threatening to withdraw altogether from politics because he thought exclusively Catholic interests were being pushed to excess.[13] And as he went out of his way to issue private and public warnings against Catholic bigotry in the movement, the chief O'Connellite newspaper, *The Pilot* (over which, however, O'Connell always insisted rather disingenuously that he had no control) responded in kind. It accused Young Ireland and *The Nation* of being not only anti-Catholic but even godless and irreligious.

In Peel's university colleges Davis and the other Young Irelanders welcomed at least a step in the right direction of extending educational facilities to Catholic Irishmen. But the Catholic hierarchy was uneasy about the idea of an education that was not specifically a Catholic education and decided to reject the proposal unless provisions were made to protect the faith and morals of Catholics. Quite apart from a natural pleasure at re-emphasizing his identity with the Catholic Church – a far more indispensable ally to him than Young Ireland for all their value as an élite – O'Connell seems to have decided from the first to make an issue of the matter as a means of keeping Young Ireland in their place. To these colleges, in which Davis and the rest saw so much hope for the Ireland of the future, O'Connell applied the epithet 'godless'.[14] When on 26 May the question was publicly debated in the Repeal Association he went out of his way to provoke the Young Irelanders, and a remarkable incident took place.

The Young Irelander, M. J. Barry, a Protestant, applauded the likely educational effects of the proposal and declared himself 'utterly indifferent' to the fact that their character was undenominational. The next speaker, a young Catholic named Conway, assailed this statement with indignation, drawing somewhat florid attention to the traditional Christianity of Ireland and exclaiming ' "Utterly indifferent!" What a sentiment for a Catholic!' The Young Irelanders, he maintained, understood nothing of the Irish character or Irish heart.

At this O'Connell took off his cap, waved it repeatedly over his head, and cheered vociferously in approval.

Davis then rose to speak in reply, as he put it, to 'my old college friend, my Catholic friend, my very Catholic friend, Mr Conway'.[15]

O'Connell interrupted him:

'It is no crime to be a Catholic, I hope?'

'No,' said Davis, 'Surely no, for —'

'The sneer with which you used the word would lead to the inference.'

Davis quickly did his best to disavow the inference, declaring that some of his best friends were Catholics and making it clear that he thought that the proposals of the Catholic bishops (which included the appointment of Catholic chaplains to the colleges) would actually improve the bill. But O'Connell was determined to humiliate him. He emphasized that Young Ireland and *The Nation* had approved of the bill from the start, before the Catholic amendments were proposed, and launched into a broad attack on what he called 'the section of politicians styling themselves the Young Ireland party'.

'There is no such party as that styled "Young Ireland",' he continued. 'There may be a few individuals who take that denomination on themselves. I am for Old Ireland. 'Tis time that this delusion should be put an end to. Young Ireland may play what pranks they please. I do not envy them the name they rejoice in, I shall stand by Old Ireland. And I have some slight notion that Old Ireland will stand by me.'

There was general consternation. Then O'Connell rose to withdraw the nickname Young Ireland since he had been told by those sitting near him that they did not call themselves this. Davis also got to his feet and in avowal of the affection in which he held O'Connell burst suddenly into tears of emotion.[16]

O'Connell was equally overcome and the two men shook hands. 'The result,' declared *The Nation* in its next issue, 'was a better understanding and closer amity than ever', and it emphasized that differences were bound to occur from time to time in a confederacy such as theirs, but hoped that in future they would be confined to a committee and not aired in public.[17]

But *The Pilot* was less conciliatory, revealing the intense feeling that lay behind the incident and which any further political pressures were bound to exacerbate. The Young Irelanders, it wrote, were 'a party of young men, actuated by a morbid self-esteem, who have latterly been assuming an un-earned and fancied importance among us ... but their temerity has been checked, and their presumption chastised in a manner that will be, if they bear it in mind, of essential service to them'.[18]

Smith O'Brien, who had for some time now been getting confidential letters from the Young Irelanders expressing their exasperation with O'Connell, was not yet, in any way, their leader. His central position at this time is best ex-plained by an appeasing joke he made after the emotional scene over the 'Queen's Colleges'. He, he said, personally belonged to 'Middle-Aged Ireland'.[19]

After the row, the movement outwardly again proceeded on what seemed its continuing even course. Large open-air meetings reminiscent of 1843 were again held. One at Dundalk, in the North, on 1 May 1845, was described by *The Nation* as 'characterized by all the zeal and enthusiasm which the people manifested during the progress of the monster meetings of 1843. In truth it was a monster meeting in the full sense of the word.'[20] The paper added that it was even of a 'much more important character than any that occurred that year [1843]' because addresses were sent to it from some of the most remote and Orange districts of the North. After a procession through evergreens and triumphal arches which included 'every variety of vehicle from the dashing barouche to the humble car', O'Connell told the men of the North that he had come there to meet them half-way. Let the Protestants of the North, he proclaimed, join them, and the Union would not last a month. He hoped there were some of them listening to him.

A voice called out from the crowd:

'There are thousands of us.'

Above the chairman's seat at the ensuing banquet, which was rather a crush because the stewards had sold seven hundred tickets for six hundred places, hung a shield optimistically inscribed:

> If again the sword we draw,
> True men that none may sever,
> For Ireland's right and Ireland's law
> We'll cross the Boyne together.
>   Each for the altar of his love
>   But all for Ireland's glory.

But this claim to be uniting Protestant and Catholic, North and South, at last, was to prove, as so often in Irish history, dream rather than reality.

'Repeal – No Compromise – Repeal' was another slogan on the walls of this banqueting hall at Dundalk, and O'Connell at the beginning of his speech drew attention to it, saying, 'I repeat again: Repeal, no compromise, and nothing but Repeal.' There was loud and long continued cheering and O'Connell then added: 'All that I say, all that could be written is comprehended in that short sentence.' He returned to the theme again later when he insisted: 'We are disciples of a political faith which we will never for one moment abandon.'[21]

Week after week now O'Connell repeated this same refrain – a fortnight later at Navan, where 200,000 people had come to hear him, some 50,000 of them assembling first on the Hill of Tara; and in the Association itself when Smith O'Brien, asking rhetorically whether they would ever abandon Repeal, however many other concessions might be made to Ireland, was answered by O'Connell with great emphasis:

'Never.'[22]

At a great meeting in Dublin on the anniversary of his release from prison on 30 May, O'Connell declared:

'They are now offering us a price for not agitating. They say that if we don't agitate they will give us something good. ... Let them make the experiment. I give them the fullest opportunity to do so; and when they are done with experiments, I will have one answer to the entire lot – THE REPEAL OF THE UNION.'[23] And a pledge was taken by all participants to continue the campaign for Repeal until final victory.

A few days later, in describing to the Association the pleasure he had felt at this anniversary meeting, he let loose the full flood of his oratory to convey his emotional commitment to the cause.

'I never,' he said, 'felt such ineffable delight as I felt on Friday last. I never before so completely perceived that the Repeal of the Union is inevitable – that its progress is irresistible. ... Yes, from north to south – from east to west the voice for Repeal is spread abroad – it is borne on the wild winds of heaven – it careers throughout our sea-girt land – it is heard

238

in the resounding of the waves, and all nature seems to cry out with me Repeal! Repeal!'[24]

Although O'Connell in a difficult political situation could be as full of tricks as any good politician, he was fundamentally an honest man. It is inconceivable that he can have so constantly repeated the refrain of No Compromise all over Ireland throughout the greater part of 1845 if he had not then meant what he was saying. The political situation was then neither more nor less difficult than it had been since Clontarf, and according to *The Nation* the Repeal movement had made more progress in self-organization since O'Connell's release from prison than in the whole of the monster meetings year of 1843.[25]

The situation was made even more promising by the prospect of a change of ministry in England. When O'Connell said in one of these speeches that no candidate for Parliament should get endorsement from him or the votes of Repealers unless he became a member of the Repeal Association, and actually named his friend Sheil, Liberal member for Dungarvan, as a man whose personal friendship with O'Connell would not win him exception from the rule, there seems no reason to doubt that he then meant what he said.

Although over seventy, he continued the series of vast open-air meetings with which he had begun the summer. At Cork on 10 June he addressed a crowd estimated at half a million. Tar barrels, sugar hogsheads and other improvised torches blazed through the night.[26] On 12 June he addressed five open-air meetings in the county in one day.[27]

'I am told I will not carry Repeal,' he declared on Sidney Hill outside Cork. 'Did I not carry Emancipation against the most cunning minister England ever had, Sir Robert Peel, and against the greatest General she ever had, the Duke of Wellington [loud cheers] ... Repealers, then, stand together in union, in firmness, in continuation, in undoubted allegiance to our gracious Sovereign – God bless her – in firm attachment to the value of the connection with Great Britain, but with a more inviolable determination to have our parliament in College Green [loud cheers]. ... Who without feeling the glow of patriotism within him, could stand on the spot I now occupy and view that superb scene before him – that beautiful landscape now before my eye – the placid waters of the Lee rolling among the green fields and cultivated demesnes, and the distant mountains rising in fertility, grandeur and beauty? Ireland! Land of my fathers – Ireland! birthplace of my children – Ireland! that shall hold my grave – Ireland! that I love with the fondest aspirations, your men are too brave, your women are too beautiful and good – you are too elevated among the nations of the earth, too moral, too religious to be slaves. I promise you that you shall be free!

His words were, as usual, followed by loud and continuous cheering.[28]

Although the Young Irelanders had a certain sophisticated disdain for O'Connell's demagogy, they seem often to have been carried away on his moods of general optimism that summer. A leader in *The Nation* in July headed 'Growth of an Irish Nation' began: '... In our days Ireland undergoes a marvellous change.'[29]

In the middle of this month there was another monster meeting, this time at Wexford, where some quarter of a million people listened to O'Connell in a field. One of the flags in the procession was green with orange binding and inscribed with the slogan 'Tenant Right and No Mistake'.[30] On 27 July O'Connell was in the West, where his reception 'exceeded anything of the kind ever before attempted in the province of Connaught'.[31] He had been given an enthusiastic reception along the entire line of the route from Dublin to Galway, and was greeted on the platform with the strains of 'See the Conquering Hero Comes'. He promised the crowd of a quarter of a million Repeal for 1846.

Retiring to his Kerry home at Darrynane for a well-earned summer holiday, O'Connell wrote to the Repeal Association telling them how impressed he had been by the demonstrations in Wexford and Galway, and, on the analogy of Emancipation and the Clare election, declared that sixty members of the Repeal Association returned to the House of Commons would 'demonstrate irresistibly to the present government the still greater necessity of repealing the Union'.[32] The voting registry must be carefully attended to, and proper candidates for Parliament elected.

The Nation backed up this call by O'Connell for Repealers to get their names on the registry. Smith O'Brien wrote to the paper agreeing that the most important thing that could possibly be done for the cause was to get a large majority of Irish members returned as Repealers to Westminster. Then on 16 September 1845, the movement was dealt an unexpected blow.

On the 9th Duffy had received a note from Davis, who was at home, to say that he had had an attack of some sort of cholera and perhaps had slight scarlatina.[33] There was no cause for alarm, but he could not be relied on to write for the paper for a while. Two days later Duffy received another note to say that Davis hoped to be able to do some light business in four days. In reply Duffy passed on a bantering message from a friend to the effect that Davis now had the opportunity of rivalling Mirabeau by dying, but begging him not to 'be tempted by the inviting opportunity'. Four days later Davis was dead. He was not quite thirty-one.

It is impossible to say whether or not future history would have been different if he had lived, though his death was the sort of event which automatically raises such a question. Certainly, in him, the movement lost the most imaginative and generous mind among the Young Irelanders at a time when imagination and generosity of mind were to be badly needed. Yet it seems unlikely that the presence of Davis could have altered the subsequent course of political events. For a disaster far greater than that of Davis's death and with far more inexorable consequences for the Repeal movement was about to break over Ireland.

O'Connell, still on holiday at Darrynane, wrote in a moving letter to a friend that his mind was so bewildered and his heart so afflicted by the news of Davis's death that he didn't know what to say.[34] He paid an honourable tribute to his qualities, declaring that his death was an irreparable loss and that there was no one who could be so useful to Ireland in the present stage of her struggles.

As yet no indication had reached him of the desperate phase of Ireland's troubles that lay immediately ahead. A few days earlier he had actually written from Darrynane in another letter: 'The poor man's harvest in particular is this year excellent ...' His only complaint was that in the hot weather the scent would not lie for his beagles, even though he had been getting up at six in the morning while the dew was still on the ground.[35] He concluded with the cry: 'Register! Register! Register!', for in a consolidation of the Repeal vote at the polls he still had high hopes of winning the Irish independence for which he stood.

The Nation was in equally optimistic mood, despite its natural sense of shock at the news of Davis's death. The leading article which preceded the obituary of Davis was entitled 'Our Future Prospects' and declared: 'The autumn is waning sunnily and cheerfully. It is a busy and hopeful time ...'[36]

Some days later, O'Connell went to address a new monster meeting in Tipperary. According to *The Nation* 'the Liberator was never in more robust health or better spirits'.[37] His progress from Limerick to Cashel was a triumph and he was met outside the town itself by the Young Irelander, Michael Doheny, with whom he was to stay. A Repeal Band dressed in green uniforms with gold lace also awaited him together with thousands of people carrying green boughs whose acclamations were taken up as he entered the city by well-dressed ladies crowding the windows of the houses. An address from the Cashel Juvenile Reading Class proclaimed:

'Welcome, welcome, not to Cashel, not to Tipperary, for these we own not and cannot give, but welcome, ten thousand times welcome to our green hearts.'[38]

The procession, accompanied by bands and groups representing various trades, proceeded to Thurles. In the countryside the ditches were full of cheering people and the fields were darkened by the crowds crossing them to catch a glimpse of their Liberator.[39] A meeting of some 100,000 people, it was estimated, assembled half-way at the fair green in Holycross and the procession was two miles long as it finally passed through a triumphal arch into Thurles where the streets were packed to suffocation. At another vast open-air meeting held just outside the town O'Connell summed up in a few sentences what this massed display of public opinion stood for:

'Let England give us liberty and I will stand by her to the death.... Ireland for the Irish is my motto. ... Repeal! Repeal! ...' He had carried Emancipation, he said, against Peel and Wellington, but this had been partly in the interests of the gentry . . . 'what I am now working for, what I ask for now, will be for the benefit of the working man'.[40]

At a banquet in honour of O'Connell, attended by about a thousand people that evening, Michael Doheny asked in his speech: 'Who that saw or will read of the multitude today and hears of physical force that will not smile? There is no power from Hindustan to the Pole that could crush that great multitude.'[41]

The Repeal Rent for the week was, at £600, nearly three times the figure it had been running at for some time. But a letter, tucked away in the issue of *The Nation* that announced this heartening fact, drew attention to an event soon to loom larger in Irish minds that all enthusiasm for Repeal: 'the lamentable and nearly universal rot in the potato'.[42]

Oblivious of the significance of such news, the series of monster meetings continued. In the first week of October they were extended to Kerry, O'Connell's own home county which so far, oddly, had shown little enthusiasm for the idea of nationality. Now, as *The Nation* put it, it was 'as if touched with an enchanter's wand'.[43] But here, too, reality broke in awkwardly for a moment. O'Connell rhapsodizing about Kerry and Repeal in the open air, was interrupted unusually by a voice in Irish crying: 'Our houses are tumbled about us every day.'[44]

Still, the significance of what was happening was not apparent. *The Nation* could see 'victory wooing the people of Ireland and not from afar', and O'Connell wheeling his triumphant progress up the West of Ireland through County Sligo to County Mayo spoke of 'the near and approaching prospect of success'.[45] At a banquet for five hundred attended by MacHale, the Archbishop of Tuam, O'Connell's mind was wholly concentrated on the issue of Repeal. He put the constitutional part of his case in a nutshell, when he said:

'I tremble for the connection unless we place it on such a footing that it will be the interest of both countries to maintain it, and never violate it . . . on a footing that is limited to the wants and wishes, to the virtues of the Irish people. If we don't succeed in placing the connection on such a footing I defy any rational man to assert that ten years after my death the countries will be connected at all.'[46] He had, he thought, sufficient influence to promise that nothing would happen in his lifetime, but he could not promise beyond that.[47]

John MacHale, the Archbishop of Tuam, also made a strong speech asking for legislative independence for the Irish people 'to secure Her Majesty's throne in peace, prosperity and freedom of religion'. And though the exact details of the future connection had not been worked out any more clearly than in the year before, its indispensability was still wholly taken for granted by all Irish Nationalists in 1845. That autumn Smith O'Brien, drawing attention to the number of friends he had in England, again said he had no wish to see the great British Empire of which Irishmen formed so glorious a part broken up.[48]

Meanwhile, 'the State of the Crops,' wrote the *Farmer's Journal*, 'is still the subject of much anxiety. . . . Regarding the potato failures we still continue to receive the most melancholy accounts.'[49]

The last of the 1845 monster meetings took place on 23 October at Rathkeale in County Limerick. A hundred thousand people were said to be present, and the procession, which started from Smith O'Brien's house at Cahermoyle, where O'Connell had been staying, stretched for three miles.[50] Prominent banners in the procession, inscribed 'Repeal and No Surrender' and 'No Compromise', reflected the impending political change in England, where it was becoming clear that Peel's ministry, increasingly at odds with a section of its own Conservative Party, could not last much longer. Repealers were about to be wooed for political support by Whigs under Lord John Russell.

But the potato disease was at last attracting attention. Dublin Corporation appointed a special committee of inquiry, and a priest from Kells reported of his parish his 'inexpressibly painful conviction that one family in twenty would not have a potato left on Christmas Day'.[51] The situation was soon to be much worse than that, though conservative newspapers were at first quick to insist that it was not nearly so bad as 'alarmists' made out and that there was a great deal of exaggeration. *The Nation* summed things up more accurately:

'It may now be stated,' it declared on 25 October 1845, 'that fully one half of the crop on which millions of our countrymen are half-starved every year is, this season, totally destroyed or in progress to destruction.'[52]

The inexorable approach of these two events – what Smith O'Brien called 'the awful calamity . . . impending'[53] and the fall of Peel's Tory ministry – now dominated O'Connell's mind.

In normal times a political situation in which the Whigs needed Irish support would have been ripe for exploitation in the Repeal interest by a man of O'Connell's skill and experience. But now his room for wider political manoeuvre was almost totally restricted by the famine, which made Ireland desperate for any sort of help at all.

He himself had been one of the first publicly to appreciate the enormity of the crisis and his mind was soon largely concentrated on the business of getting the, then still Tory, Government to carry out any government's most elementary duty, and prevent its citizens from dying of starvation. In the circumstances Repeal inevitably became a second priority.

For the famine, it was already clear, was going to be the most terrible of all the terrible disasters in Irish history.

11

Repeal, Famine and Young Ireland

In December 1845, when it was thought (prematurely as things turned out) that Lord John Russell and the Whigs were about to take over from Peel, O'Connell had explained to the Repeal Association something of the political dilemma which faced him, and his proposed attitude towards it. After announcing as a dramatic gesture that he was doubling his subscription to the Association, he came to the business of the day:

'Hurra for the Repeal,' he began orthodoxly, being received with orthodox cheers. 'No compromise – no surrender – no postponement ... let parties shift and scenes vary – let their view of politics be changed by others – we are firm and immovable [cheers], the high heart of Ireland beats for Ireland ... come weal, come woe, we will struggle for the Repeal.'[1]

He then quoted a letter he had received from Smith O'Brien, in which O'Brien pledged him his support and declared that if the incoming Whig ministry were to succeed in winning the Irish people from Repeal in the course of a mere struggle for party ascendancy, 'indescribable would be the scorn with which the people of Ireland would be named'.[2] After reading this O'Connell repeated three times the slogan 'Repeal and No Compromise!'.

He then went on to explain the nature of his present difficulty: 'While we seek Repeal without compromise and without postponement, it is our business, our sacred duty to look into the present awful state of the Irish people, and to see what is to be done for their relief ... while I desire Ireland's liberty, I desire also the preservation of her people.'[3]

He asked the prospective ministry to give them food and to come forward with finance for public undertakings, such as the immediate construction of railways in Ireland. He had, he said, hopes of such things from Lord John Russell, though not from the Duke of Wellington.

'And when,' he went on, 'I promise conditional support to Lord John Russell, it may be asked if I purpose to compromise Repeal?'

There were loud cries of 'No! No!' and O'Connell responded:

'I thank you for that "No", but I had the very same in my own mouth.

[Cheers and laughter.] There shall be no compromise. But I tell Lord John Russell I will act fairly by him.'

He then named two things he wanted for the Irish peasant, which, in the light of the immediate situation, were even more relevant than cash for the purchase of food to be earned through public works. First, he wanted the law of property amended so that it would become illegal to evict a tenant without giving him compensation for the improvements he had wrought on the land. And in the course of making this proposal he enunciated a theory of property which, to landlords at least, then seemed revolutionary. The land, he said, was by right the property of the landlord; but the labour which went into the land was equally by right the property of the tenant, 'and his claim to that right came from a higher source than the landlord's title to his estate. If the landlord wanted his land given up, he must pay the tenant in cash the full and fair value of the tenant's expenditure.'[5]

This doctrine was to remain a fundamental part of Irish nationalist thinking on the land question for the rest of the century, though O'Connell himself is seldom given credit for subscribing to it.

O'Connell also wanted the law amended to prevent any evictions taking place at all except where the tenant held by twenty-one year lease.

Thus, as the first evictions of hungry people unable to pay rent began on a serious scale, O'Connell rightly named as the most necessary immediate terms for Ireland two of those 'three Fs', – Free Sale and Fixity of Tenure – which were not finally to be conceded by a British Government until another land crisis nearly thirty years later.* In pressing at the same time also for a supply of cash to be earned by public works, O'Connell was putting forward an altogether coherent plan for dealing with the famine. Everyone knew that Ireland was short only of the potato and otherwise full of food in the form of oats, wheat, butter, eggs, sheep and pigs, all of which continued to be exported to England on a considerable scale throughout the famine.[5] And all these measures were what O'Connell hoped for immediately from the new ministry in return for his parliamentary support.

'I will get all I can for Ireland,' he declared, 'and when I can I will take the rest.'[6]

Finally, so that there should be absolutely no doubt about where he stood on the constitutional issue, he restated his basic position:

'I believe you understand me distinctly. I am totally against any compromise and postponement, or any surrender of the Repeal Cause. Repeal is the great object of my existence – it is the first and last thought of my heart – it is the entire text of my life and if there are marginal notes upon it they

---

* The third 'F' was to be 'Fair Rent', a truly revolutionary principle, implying the government's right to tell a landlord what rent he could charge for his own property, and conceded by Gladstone's Land Act of 1881.

are mere appendages to the great cause of Repeal. Repeal is all we desire and with the blessing of Providence we shall obtain that Repeal.'[7]

There were loud cheers as he sat down.

The Nation's own position was, at this stage, not so far apart from O'Connell's. A leading article in the paper on 20 December 1845 stated that a Whig ministry, resting its right wing on the anti-Corn Law League and its left on the Repealers in Ireland, making Repeal itself an open question and giving the lord lieutenancy and chief secretaryship to Irishmen, and office to Repealers as Repealers, would unquestionably command *The Nation*'s allegiance.

'We would be bound to sustain them by every sacrifice and every labour that a people can offer to their country,' *The Nation* added.

But new divisions were about to appear between O'Connell and the Young Irelanders of *The Nation* at this critical time. Since the death of Davis, Duffy had brought on to *The Nation* a handsome and iconoclastic young Protestant solicitor from County Down called John Mitchel. His father, a Unitarian minister, had been 'out in '98'. Mitchel himself was now imparting a fresh, strident and aggressive note to the paper, and in November 1845 had suddenly caused O'Connell considerable alarm.

A government newspaper had just published an article urging that the agitation for Repeal should itself be made high treason. The paper congratulated itself on the fact that the new system of railways then being built in Ireland would make it easy to put down such treason by bringing troops from Dublin to any point in Ireland within six hours. The article itself must have been unpleasant enough for O'Connell, containing as it did insulting references to him and other 'convicted conspirators'.[8] But Mitchel's reply in *The Nation* upset him still further.

'As the Dutch dealt with the French by laying land under water,' wrote Mitchel, 'ruining their fertile plains of waving corn – so Ireland's railways, though most valuable to her, were better dispensed with for a time than allowed to become a means of transport for invading armies. Every railway within five miles of Dublin could in one night be totally cut off from the interior of the country. To lift a rail, fill a perch or two of any cutting or tunnel, to break down a piece of embankment seems obvious and easy enough.'[9] He added that it should hardly be necessary to point out the uses to which railway material such as good hammered iron and wooden sleepers might be put. As if this evocation of the now traditional Irish rhetorical symbol of the pike were not enough to dismay O'Connell, Mitchel recommended that Repeal Wardens should be familiarized with the best ways of 'dealing with railways in case of any enemy daring to make a hostile use of them'.[10]

O'Connell at once went round to *The Nation* office to protest against linking the Repeal Association with such militant policy in this way. He demanded that Duffy should in the next issue of the paper make clear that neither *The Nation* nor its editor had any official connection with the Association[11] – which was true, for the separation of identity had been made for tactical purposes after *The Nation* had been cited in the general indictment of the year before. In the next issue Duffy obligingly pointed out the lack of connection between *The Nation* and the Repeal Association. But O'Connell observed in the Association that, though he bore no ill feeling towards the paper, 'he had admired its talents more in the time of the illustrious dead' – meaning, of course, Davis.[12]

Smith O'Brien's political position within the Repeal movement still remained somewhere between Young Ireland and O'Connell. He agreed within the Association that subjects like Mitchel's railways article should not be pressed into discussion, since they might 'endanger the safety of the Association'.[13] Temperamentally, however, he was closer to Young Ireland, if for no other reason than that he, like them, was less a practical politician than a man for whom politics meant primarily the pursuit of high principles often in somewhat rhetorical attitudes. He had already been emphasizing strongly his own mistrust of any prospective deal with a Whig government. In January 1846 he declared that 'complete neutrality' between the contending British political parties should be observed; and concluded this speech with the words '. . . we shall prove ourselves steadfast to the cause for which we are ready if necessary to lay down our lives'.[14]

'I trust,' he said in the Repeal Association the following month, '. . . that the time is not far distant when men of all parties in this country will see that it is in vain to place any trust save in ourselves – ourselves alone is the motto I would wish the Irish people to assume . . .'[15]

But such ambitious thoughts were becoming increasingly irrelevant to the immediate condition of the Irish people. From almost every county in Ireland more and more alarming reports were coming in as the earthed-up potatoes were uncovered and found to be masses of loathsome rottenness. Agrarian outrages in the old Whiteboy tradition, which had long been diminishing in proportion with the success of the Repeal movement, became commoner again as Repeal itself now seemed of less immediate urgency. As the two million-odd of the rural population who lived even in normal times on the verge of starvation,* now faced the reality of total famine, they began to take such desperate action against landlords and their agents as their strength still allowed. The peasantry's enthusiasm for Repeal and *The Nation*'s ennobling principles of nationality had been rooted in the hope that conditions on the land would thereby be changed for the better. O'Connell had always acknowledged this with his prominent insistence on tenant right. Now, as the people began to struggle with the basic problem of physical survival, thoughts of nationality became middle-class luxuries. The Repeal Rent which had been running at a fairly steady level of between

---

* The figure of 2,300,000 was given by the Poor Law Commissioners of 1835.[16]

£300 to £400 a week for eighteen months began a slow and fairly steady decline from which, under the full impact of the famine, it never recovered.

Young Ireland meanwhile tended to consolidate its position of detachment, meeting as a group from time to time in the gold and green uniforms of the '82 club, often with Smith O'Brien in the chair while O'Connell, the titular president, was away in London. Gavan Duffy, John Mitchel, M. J. Barry and Michael Doheny were joined by other bright young men, mainly Catholics, often dandified in their dress and speech [17] and drawn with the others from the middle classes but making up for their lack of contact with the Irish people by the zeal with which they held the principles of nationality in trust for them. Prominent among the newcomers were Thomas Meagher (pronounced Maher), son of a Mayor of Waterford, and Richard O'Gorman, son of another prosperous merchant. Speaking with an English accent derived from his education at Stonyhurst in England,[18] Meagher made a strong 'No Compromise' speech in the Association in February 1846;[19] and Richard O'Gorman in the same month made oblique references to 'others choosing the sword' but himself at present preferring 'the might of mind' as they were not yet driven to 'the last resource'.[20] But the signs of a vast social catastrophe were now unmistakable. The Duke of Cambridge as late as January 1846 subscribed to the view that talk of famine was greatly exaggerated, adding 'they all knew Irishmen could live upon anything, and there was plenty of grass in the fields, even though the potato crop should fail'.[21] But the following month O'Connell was telling the House of Commons that hope had now quite vanished.[22] He also emphasized strikingly the very special character of this freak famine, which was in one sense no famine at all. More wheat, barley and wheat meal flour, he pointed out, had in fact been imported into Great Britain from Ireland in 1845 than in any other of the three previous years, and between 10 October 1845 and 5 January 1846 over 30,000 oxen, bulls and cows, over 30,000 sheep and lambs, and over 100,000 pigs had sailed from Ireland to English ports.[23]

Impotence before the overwhelming catastrophe sharpened people's sense of political frustration. Attitudes became more desperate; quarrels developed more quickly. *The Nation* began nagging at the Repeal Association more openly for not publishing its accounts. *The Pilot*, the specifically O'Connellite paper, replied that *The Nation* was trying to subvert Christianity. John Mitchel expressed a growing restlessness within the Association in words which indicated still further the direction in which his thoughts were heading. He had, he said, been a member of the Association for three years and would continue to remain so until the policy it had been originated to try had been fully tried, and until he saw 'whether the peaceful and moral organization could effect the good it was intended to effect for Ireland'.[24]

In April 1846 Smith O'Brien wrote from London to the Repeal Association, declaring that the proceedings of Parliament convinced him daily more and more that the affairs of Ireland could only be dealt with properly in an Irish legislature.[25] And a leading article in *The Nation* that week, commenting on the situation in Poland, declared meaningfully: 'Better a little blood-letting to show that there is blood, than a patient dragging of chains and pining beneath them slowly for generations leading to the belief that all spirit is fled.'[26]

A display of militancy on the part of Smith O'Brien provoked a further scene of public dissension between O'Connell and Young Ireland, and as a result of it O'Brien began to gravitate from his central position in Repeal politics towards Young Ireland.

As long ago as 1844 Davis had proposed that one tactic for the Repealers might be for their Members of Parliament to refuse to sit at Westminster but meet instead as a body in Ireland. The proportion of Ireland's total number of representatives who were Repealers was small, and a more suitable method of convening a specifically Irish representative body seemed to lie in the idea of a Council of Three Hundred. There was also a constitutional difficulty in the proposal for non-attendance. Repeal Members of Parliament had already attended the House of Commons and taken the oath.* There was some legal doubt as to whether non-attending Repealers summoned, for instance, to attend Committees of the House of Commons might not be committing an offence in refusing to respond to the Speaker's writ. However, O'Connell himself had decided in the middle of 1845, before the famine, that such action would be perfectly legal and certainly there was no greater stickler for legality in the Association than he. It had therefore been agreed as policy that when a summons for any committees on which they were serving should arrive for either John O'Connell or Smith O'Brien, they should reject the summons and announce their intention of attending to the needs of their constituents in Ireland instead. In June 1845 such summonses duly arrived and were duly rejected by both John O'Connell and O'Brien. But the session ended before the House of Commons had decided what appropriate action to take.

By the next session of Parliament the situation had been transformed by the famine. In April 1846, when O'Brien decided on his own account to renew the gesture of defiance and refuse to serve on the railways committee to which he was summoned, O'Connell was already in London, accompanied by his son John, devoting himself to measures of famine relief and engaged in fighting, together with the Whigs, the Coercion Bill introduced by Peel's government to deal with the recent rapid increase in agrarian violence.† John

---

* The Sinn Feiners of the twentieth century elected to Westminster never went there at all.

† Between 1 January and 16 May 1846 there had been eighty cases of murder in Ireland, in only seven of which convictions had been obtained (*The Nation*, 20 June 1846). It was to deal with such a state of affairs that the government proposed a suspension of the normal rights and processes of law in the new Coercion Bill.

O'Connell was actually already attending the railways committee. It is testimony as much to poor coordination of Repeal tactics as to O'Brien's undoubtedly high sense of principle and integrity that he nevertheless decided to defy the Speaker alone by refusing to attend the committee. He was rewarded with a month's imprisonment in a cellar beneath the clock tower of Westminster, the first Member of Parliament to be imprisoned by the House of Commons for two hundred years. His sense of betrayal and disillusion was naturally increased when he heard that O'Connell had taken steps to see that the Association should not too strongly associate itself with his gesture for fear of compromising its legality. O'Brien even drafted from his prison a bitter letter of resignation to his constituents in Limerick.

Both in *The Nation* and in the meetings of the Association itself, the Young Irelanders supported O'Brien valiantly. *The Nation*'s leading articles still appeared under the two-year-old banner heading 'REMEMBER THE 30TH MAY' (the date of O'Connell's own imprisonment), but one such article on 16 May appeared under the further heading: 'The Man in Jail for Ireland', and meant O'Brien. It described him as 'an Irishman intensely Irish' and not one of the 'pretended Irishmen – luke-warm, milk-and-water ... small-beer lovers of their country', to whom it applied the derogatory term 'West Britons'.[27] The Young Irelanders not only spoke up for O'Brien in the Association, where Michael Doheny described him as a man who 'dared to stand forth as the Defender of Ireland's rights',[28] but also summoned the '82 club, in which they outnumbered O'Connellites by two to one, and passed a resolution in O'Brien's support. A deputation of the '82 club, including Mitchel, O'Gorman, Doheny, Meagher and a new recruit T. B. McManus, then went to Westminster where, in their gold and green uniforms, they conveyed the club's respect and admiration to O'Brien in his cellar in the House of Commons, and persuaded him not to send the letter of resignation to his constituents after all.

On Smith O'Brien's discharge from imprisonment at the end of May, O'Connell immediately wrote him a handsome tribute in the form of a letter to the Association. It was impossible, he said, to estimate too highly O'Brien's services in the sacred cause of Irish nationality, adding: 'I am convinced that if necessary he would sacrifice his life to preserve union and harmony amongst the supporters of the cause ...'[29] Reciprocally, the Young Irelanders, M. J. Barry and Michael Doheny, then strongly expressed their gratitude to O'Connell, but with a gentle and firm reminder that they could not be expected to betray themselves or the memory of Thomas Davis. Michael Doheny concluded:

'Let me sincerely hope from this day forth we will be agreed in all things ... and that steps will be taken, under the guidance of the Liberator of Ireland [cheers] – to do honour to the martyr of the House of Commons and receive him upon the shores of this kingdom as the descendant of one of her Kings ought to be received.'[30]

When O'Brien 'the martyr' himself appeared at a great demonstration in his honour in Limerick, he too made a point of emphasizing ties with O'Connell, in spite of what had passed. At the same time he, too, affirmed nationalistic principles which in his case seemed to have hardened perceptibly in the course of his imprisonment. Arriving in a triumphal chariot in a field outside Limerick, through which the Shannon flowed, to address tens of thousands of people assembled from all over the West of Ireland, he declaimed that he could not contemplate 'that noble river without remembering that the flag of our country – the green flag, bearing the harp of our native land – cannot be hoisted lest it be pulled down with ignominy and disgrace'.[31]

'The mighty multitude,' which, according to The Nation, had marched to the field 'with waving flags and martial music through the country of the Wild Geese, proclaiming their hatred of British misrule', let out a great roar. 'For a hundred and fifty years,' wrote The Nation, 'the grey Shannon has not heard such a chorus of triumph.'

And though the evening banquet for two thousand guests was a decorous affair, with portraits of the queen and Prince Albert above the chair and attended largely by the middle classes, O'Brien was greeted there too with ten minutes of such thunderous applause that it 'actually pained the ear'.[32] After suitable expressions of gratitude, he declared that the occasion marked the most important day of his life and the opening of an era in the history of Ireland.

'I have appealed,' he said, rightly emphasizing the significant aspect of his imprisonment, 'from the British House of Commons to the Irish Nation.'[33]

In his speech that evening O'Brien hailed O'Connell as 'the undoubted leader of the Irish people' and said that although there were 'stories of a disposition to overthrow his leadership ... as long as O'Connell lives he shall have the guidance of the Irish nation'. But he also made a point of stressing the danger of trying to barter advantages for the country in return for a compromise on Repeal.[34]

Neither side in fact wanted a breach with the other, yet as the return to power of a Whig ministry became more and more certain, so a breach became inevitable. It was O'Connell's unalterable intention to work with the Whigs. Indeed, he replied to O'Brien's compliment from Limerick with the slightly testy remark that while Smith O'Brien had been very properly receiving a tribute of gratitude from his constituents, he himself had been in London busy trying to defeat the Tory Coercion Bill and could have done with his support.[35] But Thomas Meagher, who had hailed O'Connell's successful obstruction of the Coercion Bill in alliance with the Whig opposition generously enough, spoke for Young Ireland when he made clear in the Association that he regarded any sort of alliance with a Whig *ministry* as fatal.[36] Young Ireland was as determined to insist that alliance with the Whigs meant betrayal of Repeal as O'Connell was adamant that it meant no more than a temporary but necessary shifting of political priorities.

In June 1846 wordy public disputes between the two halves of the movement became frequent in the Association's meetings. These often took place in O'Connell's absence, and certainly his henchmen, Tom Steele and others, were by no means as sophisticated and flexible in debate as he himself could be, but the eventual parting of the ways began to look more and more inevitable. Speaking of a Whig alliance – and incidentally reminding his audience that Lord John Russell had actually voted for the first reading of the Coercion Bill – Meagher told the Association:

'It is not for this that . . . you looked back to the Church of Dungannon, and embraced the principles, though you could not unsheath the sword of the patriot soldiers of '82; that you gathered in thousands upon the Hill of Tara, and hailed your leader upon the Rath of Mullaghmast. . . . There you swore that Ireland should be called a free nation.'[37]

The implication was clear: a Whig alliance meant that Ireland would never be a free nation. In O'Connell's absence Steele replied indignantly. He took particular exception to a reference by Meagher to Davis as 'our prophet and our guide', and himself insisted that the people of Ireland had never had as prophet and guide any other than O'Connell, 'the crownless, sceptreless monarch of the hearts of the people – the lay pontiff of his religion, Catholicity.'[38]

The following week O'Connell wrote to the Association of 'the bitterest regret and deepest sorrow' with which he had witnessed 'the efforts which are made by some of our juvenile members to create dissension and circulate distractions amongst the Repealers'. He emphasized yet again that he had 'nailed the colours of Repeal to the mast and would not be taking them down until there was an Irish Parliament again on College Green'.[39] He reminded the Association of the pledges he had already taken to this effect and recommended that they be framed and glazed and hung on the walls of Conciliation Hall. 'This,' he added, 'may take away some claptraps from juvenile orators.'[40]

At the meeting at which this letter was read one of O'Connell's supporters again reiterated the substance of the Liberator's case, namely that it was quite possible to be a good Repealer and yet take what advantages you could get from the Whigs. But the Young Irelanders were angered by O'Connell's letter. M. J. Barry now raised the possibility that they might soon no longer be able to remain with the Association.[41] Meagher denied that they had suspicions of the integrity of their leader – a disingenuous statement, to say the least, for if they did not suspect O'Connell's integrity, it was difficult to see what the fuss was about. At the same time Meagher was intransigent. 'As we have united,' he continued of the Young Irelanders, 'thus shall we continue to act. You may exclude us from this Hall, but you will not separate us from the country.'[42]

It is unlikely that O'Connell actually wanted to exclude the Young Irelanders from the Repeal Association, though, being an emotional and sometimes impatient man, he must have known many moments when he longed to be rid of them. But when the Whig ministry finally did come into office in July 1846 it was imperative for him to have control of this brilliant but erratic element in his own party. The issue on which he decided to assert discipline was one he had chosen carefully. On 13 July 1846 two acrimonious debates took place in the Association. The first concerned the selection by O'Connell of his friend Sheil as parliamentary candidate for Dungavan in spite of the fact that Sheil had still not come out for Repeal and in spite of the fact that O'Connell had, before the famine, said that Sheil would not be selected unless he did. On this point O'Connell now successfully carried the Association with him. The second debate concerned the hypothetical issue of physical force and took the form of a discussion of a special committee's report. This contained declarations to the effect that the Association should call the country's attention to its policy of 'seeking amelioration of political institutions by peaceable and legal means *alone*, disclaiming all attempts to improve and augment constitutional liberty by means of force, violence and bloodshed'.[43]

Now this report really only stressed what had long been known to be the Association's attitude. The implication, that under no circumstances whatever was force justifiable, was not very strong; and the resolution elsewhere explicitly allowed the use of self-defence against unjust aggression. Indeed, Mitchel, who was the first of the Young Irelanders to discuss the report, began mildly enough. Though he and Meagher had been on the committee and had there voted against the resolutions, he accepted that they had been sanctioned by a majority of the committee and declared that it would not therefore be right to contest them in the hall, nor, he added, was there any necessity or disposition to do so. However, he could not resist just adding that he personally did not accept the abstract principle stated, namely that force was never justified. He did not, for instance, abhor the Volunteers of '82, nor his ancestor who had fought in '98.

O'Connell immediately jumped up and with some justification accused Mitchel of pretending to be with him when he was really against him. If, he said, Mitchel was not opposing the resolutions as he claimed, then he should not go on as he was doing, for the resolutions under discussion were not concerned with past events.

And at this point O'Connell too began to overstep the mark. The resentment and mistrust of many months were soon animating the debate. Sanctimoniously he announced that 'the greatest political advantages are not worth one drop of blood'.

It is often said that in this matter of 'physical force' O'Connell went out of his way unnecessarily to force an issue out of a purely abstract principle. Inasmuch as he was looking for an issue on which to assert his control over Young Ireland this is true. But it is equally true that the Young Irelanders, who themselves were all agreed at this stage that peaceful means alone should achieve Repeal, also went out of their way to make the question of abstract principle an outright challenge to O'Connell. Since they renounced physical force for the foreseeable future there was an intellectual dishonesty in pretending that the question was of such immediate importance.

The debate was adjourned for nearly a fortnight and *The Nation*, appearing in the interval, argued the case more sincerely. The present, it maintained, was a bad moment for the introduction of the 'peace resolutions'. To say that they would never use force now was 'to deliver themselves bound hand and foot to the Whigs'. It would make nonsense of what after all was O'Connell's dictum that England's weakness was Ireland's opportunity.[44]

The adjourned debate on the 'peace resolutions' took place on 27 and 28 July. This time O'Connell himself was not present. He sent a letter to the Association declaring that his spirit was 'sad, my heart heavy at the miserable dissensions', but he made his attitude uncompromisingly clear: 'The advocacy of the physical force doctrine renders it impossible for those who stand on the constitution to cooperate with those who will not adhere.'[45] But this of course was unfair. To say that Young Ireland were actually advocating the physical force doctrine was a travesty of their attitude. And now it was that Smith O'Brien finally decided to abandon his self-appointed role of 'umpire' between O'Connell and Young Ireland and commit himself wholly to the Young Ireland side. He stated bluntly that he was afraid the real object of the resolutions was to drive *The Nation* group from the Association altogether. If such an attempt to exclude them were to be made he himself would feel it impossible to cooperate with the Association until they had been restored to it.

The bitterness of the renewed debate was heightened by the fact that O'Connell's elder son John, much despised by the Young Irelanders, officially dominated the proceedings. An insolent 'little frog', Dillon, co-founder of *The Nation*, had once called him, '. . . There is no man or country safe from his venom.'[46] And another Young Irelander, MacNevin, had described him as 'the most mischievous public man in Ireland'.[47] Certainly much of his interest at this stage was to ensure his own final inheritance of the role of Irish leader and therefore to have Young Ireland crushed or at least conveniently out of the way in time.

As when the resolutions had first been debated, the nominal argument centred on the purely metaphysical point of whether or not at any time past, present or future in any situation, physical force was a justifiable means for anybody to use. Everyone continued to agree that moral force was the only viable instrument for the Repeal movement.

And during the last day's debate the line of division between the two parties on the ostensible issue became fainter and fainter. The discussion was about whether offensive rebellion was hypothetically as acceptable as defensive rebellion – for the O'Connellites were always prepared to concede the principle of the latter. But John Mitchel expressed the true point at issue when he declared: 'The real complaint against us is that we cannot endure any tampering with these Whigs.'

For a time the debate reached a creditable level as both sides argued the actual point of difference cogently. John O'Connell made the reasonable point that it was better for Repealers than enemies of the national cause to have places under a Whig Government because they could be 'eminently useful in situations in which details are carried on'.

'Do you think,' replied Mitchel putting the case against this in a nutshell, 'do you think that the men who have been begging one day at the gate of an English minister will come down here the next day to help you get rid of English ministers altogether? If some of the legal gentlemen now in this box accept commissionerships and assistant barristerships from Lord John Russell, will they be so eloquent afterwards in this Hall, denouncing English tyranny and English rapacity?'

But in the light of what was happening in the Irish countryside all hypothetical propositions were increasingly irrelevant. For the ravages of the potato blight had appeared for the second year in succession and this time the entire potato crop of Ireland seemed likely to be consumed. Unity at all costs in the face of the impending disaster was the only reasonable policy.

However, Meagher raised the argument back to a highly-charged emotional level, on which there could be no hope of settlement. Contending rightly that there was no need for the peace resolutions, he continued to argue dramatically against them as if there were a need to oppose them.

'Then, my Lord Mayor,' he said, addressing the chair in the speech's most famous passage, 'I do not disclaim the use of arms as immoral nor do I believe it is the truth to say that the God of Heaven withholds His sanction from the use of arms. . . . Be it for the defence, or be it for the assertion of a nation's liberty, I look upon the sword as a sacred weapon. And if, my lord, it has sometimes reddened the shroud of the oppressor, like the anointed rod of the high priest, it has, at other times, blossomed into flowers to deck the freeman's brow. . . . Abhor the sword and stigmatize the sword? No, my lord, for at its blow a giant nation sprang up from the waters of the Atlantic, and by its redeeming magic the fettered colony became a free republic . . .' He cited also the winning of Belgium's freedom from the Dutch Republic 'by effusion of generous blood'.

This was too much for John O'Connell and his supporters. They immediately declared that Meagher and themselves could no longer belong to the same Association. There were shouts and scenes of confusion as Smith O'Brien protested at Meagher being 'put down'. John O'Connell rose and replied that the question was not whether a young man should be put down in the Association but whether the young man should put down the Association. He played his trump card, saying they could try to turn Daniel O'Connell himself out of the Association if they wanted to. It was simply a question between him and them. O'Connell had founded the Association on the basis of these resolutions. Would they stand by them? If not, let them adopt other resolutions and another leader.

Emotional tension had now reached such a pitch that while the hall rang with enthusiastic cheering and loud cries of 'O'Connell! O'Connell!', Smith O'Brien abruptly got up and left, followed by Meagher, Mitchel, Duffy and other Young Irelanders. An eye-witness saw most of the ladies then leave the gallery while many people rushed to the doors to follow O'Brien and his companions. An impromptu enthusiastic reception took place for them in the street outside, but inside the hall the cries still resounded for 'O'Connell! O'Connell!'

It was an impulsive gesture rather than a calculated decision. It is unlikely that any of the seceders intended their secession to be permanent. Each side recognized that the split was harmful to them. The damage proved irrevocable.

12

The Irish Confederation

The rest of the history of the Repeal movement and Young Ireland is a dismal one.

By the end of August 1846, the month after the split between O'Connell and Young Ireland, the failure of the potato crop was total in almost every part of Ireland.[1] Each half of the Repeal movement heaped invective on the other. O'Connell mocked 'the paltry Young Ireland party' who 'while vapouring about physical force and vindication by the sword ... would be afraid to look at a poker'.[2] But he himself became increasingly helpless before the appalling fact of starvation spreading over the entire island. O'Brien and the Young Irelanders, aware of the fatal effect the split had had on Ireland's 'self-reliant' political strength, oscillated between attempts at reconciliation with O'Connell and uninspired efforts to regroup. For all the talk of physical force Smith O'Brien laboriously redefined his own constitutional position as non-separatist. He could advocate no newer policy than a Davis-like refurbishing of the literary and historical springs of Irish nationality.

Meanwhile, the common people of Ireland were being carried far out of reach of Repeal politics altogether. They were staggering into the towns and dying as they begged for food, or collapsing on the mountainsides either on their way back from work or before they could bring back to their starving families whatever they had managed to beg from the towns. 'No language,' wrote a curate in Mayo that winter, 'can describe the awful condition of the people – they are to be found in thousands, young and old, male and female, crawling in the streets, and on the highways, screaming for a morsel of food.'[3] A priest wrote to the *Cork Examiner:* 'No description that I could give would for a moment adequately tell the misery, the wretchedness and the suffering of my poor people – they are in the most frightful state of destitution that can possibly be imagined.'[4] Such people were living – when they lived – almost entirely on seaweed. From every port in Ireland cargoes of oats, barley, bacon, eggs, butter and other foodstuffs continued to sail out to England.

To all this the Young Irelanders replied with rhetoric, which, though often moving, was politically useless. 'I feel by the teachings of history,' Doheny prophesied hopefully in December 1846, 'that there is such a thing as an avenging angel – that he may sleep long and watch a wicked power until it is doomed – that he often springs all around from the maddened brain of a suffering people.'[5] It was mere wishful thinking.

In January 1847 O'Brien and the Young Irelanders founded a new organization known as the Irish Confederation, and O'Brien himself, dubbed by the Young Irelander D'Arcy Magee, 'as kingly a king as the most eminent among the number of his ancestors',[6] addressed it in April 1847 in tones of the deepest despondency. He pointed out in horror that what was happening in Ireland was being done in an Empire that called itself the most civilized, most powerful and most Christian in the world. Yet he himself had no new thought to break the spell in which all seemed gripped. When, eleven months after its foundation, the Irish Confederation issued its first major exposition of its principles, there was only the inevitable proclamation of the right of self-government, the disavowal of separation and physical force, the need to get the same sort of support from the upper classes for the principle of nationality as in 1782, and a reiteration of Davis's principle of self-reliance, with a special emphasis on home manufacture.[7] None of this was different from the policy of the old Repeal Association. None of it was relevant to the Irish peasant in his agony. Moreover, even if the large assumption were correct that Repeal itself would prove a political and social panacea, there was still no hint of how Repeal, so elusive hitherto, was to be achieved. What was to be *done* became the more and more insistent question in people's minds.

The only answer O'Connell thought relevant was relief from England. But he was soon forced to accept that there was no prospect of this, or at least not 'on that enormously large scale which is absolutely necessary to prevent hundreds of thousands of the Irish people from perishing of famine and pestilence'.[8] He was now seventy-one, and at last feeling the feebleness of age upon him. Ordered by his doctors to the south of Europe in March in the hope of restoring his strength for the coming autumn, he decided to make a pilgrimage to Rome. The horrors of the famine and his own relative impotence to obtain really effective relief from the Whig government had taken a terrible toll of him. Before leaving, he went down to the House of Commons at the start of the new session. Disraeli described his appearance:

... of great debility and the tones of his voice very still ... it was a strange and touching spectacle to those who remembered the form of colossal energy and the clear and thrilling tones that had once startled, disturbed and controlled senates ... to the House generally it was a performance of dumb show, a feeble old man muttering from a table; but respect for the great parliamentary personage kept all as orderly as if the fortunes of a party hung on his rhetoric.

The words O'Connell could be heard muttering were both a tragic admission of the failure of his campaign for Repeal of the Union, and at the same time total justification of the principle on which it had been based.

'Ireland is in your hands,' he told the House of Commons. 'If you do not save her, she cannot save herself. I solemnly call on you to recollect that I predict with the sincerest conviction that one-fourth of her population will perish unless you come to her relief.'

He had always been inclined to hyperbole. In fact, only about one-eighth of the population died. But before the decade was over more than another eighth had emigrated to the United States, and as a direct result of the famine the population of Ireland was almost halved in twenty years.

O'Connell himself did not live to know the worst. He died at Lyons on 15 May 1847. An autopsy revealed a brain severely damaged, its membranes inflamed and thickened with blood. His heart, in accordance with his wishes, was taken to Rome. The rest of him, the first man ever to give one voice to the mass of the Irish people, was buried in Ireland.

His death clarified nothing, actually adding to the sense of impotence and ineffectualness on the political scene. For although *The Nation* appeared edged with black borders for three successive issues, Young Ireland was said to have killed him by its opposition, and when Smith O'Brien asked with typical gentlemanly tact if he and his supporters might attend the funeral it was made plain to him that they would not be welcome. Bitterness between O'Connell's supporters and the Young Irelanders continued particularly at mob level for many months. When later in the year the Irish Confederation tried to hold a meeting in Belfast, it was not the Orangemen but the O'Connellites who broke it up.

An attempt to break out of the total impasse was made when a so-called Irish Council was formed of people from all sections of the Irish political spectrum, to represent at least that unanimity in horror which all Irishmen felt in face of the famine, whatever their class or political belief. It was to be above party, and followed the abortive attempt a few months earlier to get all Irish Members of Parliament to agree to act together at Westminster, an attempt which had predictably disintegrated the moment the members had been put to the first severe test of party loyalties. But though the Irish Council – composed of some Conservatives, some Federalists, John O'Connellites and the Young Irelanders of the new Irish Confederation – effectively expressed its unanimous sense of horror, and sponsored some worthy committees of investigation into social conditions, it was hardly surprising that it failed to achieve a break-through where those not handicapped by party differences could find none. Such non-party groupings were little more than gestures of self-respect in a situation of general impotence.

The Irish Confederation's own single practical step lay in the field of organization: the founding of so-called Confederate clubs in different parts of the country to fill the need for more knowledge and understanding of the principles of Repeal and self-reliance. But though a mere twenty persons were required to form the nucleus of a Confederate club, only twenty-three such clubs had been formed by November 1847, four of which were in Dublin and some of the rest in Great Britain.[9] As the different parts of the country entered on yet another winter of famine the majority of the population were wholly absorbed by the more practical need to keep alive. At Skibbereen in County Cork a workhouse designed by no very generous standards for 800 persons was holding over 1,300, and hordes of others besieged the doors waiting for those inside to die and yield them a place.[10] The *Cork Examiner* described similar scenes from Bantry and Killarney while the *Galway Vindicator* reported from further up the west coast that nothing could exceed the frightful conditions of the poor of that district.[11] Two eleven-year old boys in Enniskillen had been sentenced to seven years' transportation each for stealing a pint of Indian meal porridge from a workhouse.[12] The queen's speech for the winter session of 1847 promised only a bill for the better prevention of crime and outrage.

The situation had deteriorated to the point where only original or revolutionary thinking was relevant. All the 'national' talk was now grotesquely out of touch with reality. Most of the Young Irelanders were in varying degrees trapped in the ineffectualness of their own familiar rhetoric. But one serious attempt was made to carry nationalist thinking forward into new areas. In keeping with events, it introduced a harsh, unconciliatory note which in time led to a further split in the movement.

This new thinking was provided by the hitherto unknown eldest son of a prosperous Protestant farmer of Queen's County, named Lalor. The father had himself helped organize the peasant resistance to tithes in the thirties, and had been an O'Connellite Member of Parliament. His son, Fintan Lalor, suffered from a disease of the spine and was almost a hunchback. He was an ardent reader of *The Nation* and his physical handicap had given him time in which to brood over the political and social impasse in which Ireland seemed trapped. When the Irish Confederation was founded in January 1847, he immediately wrote to Gavan Duffy with some fundamental suggestions which Duffy, impressed, passed on to the other leading Young Irelanders.

Even today, to come across some of Lalor's words suddenly in the middle of a history of the Young Ireland movement is to experience a breath of fresh air. His argument was that the Confederation, with its old slogan of Repeal, was based only on a collection of vague impulses and emotional generalities. 'Men,' he wrote, 'keep theorizing and dreaming too long – and building up, or restoring an airy and ideal nationality, which time is wearing down, and wasting away faster than they can work it up; and when they awake from their dreams they will find, I fear, that one other people has gone out of the world, as nations and races have gone ere now.'[13]

Repeal, he said, as an objective in itself must now be abandoned as 'an impracticable absurdity'. It had been shown by the events of past years to be unattainable by constitutional means. Military means were out of the question not so much because of the inevitable superiority of government strength but chiefly because, with the events of the famine, Repeal had become a remote and meaningless abstraction to the Irish peasant. The only thing the peasant could be roused about was the land.

In any case, to try and establish two independent sovereign legislatures within one framework was 'an arrangement repugnant alike to common sense and experience'. The analogy of 1782 was invalid; it was, after all, this very arrangement which Tone and Lord Edward Fitzgerald had found it necessary to try and dissolve. Therefore, total national independence must be the objective. And this the peasant was to help achieve.

Lalor had nothing in principle against the idea of the peasant arming himself, but to bring the government to its knees more immediately and with less general suffering he proposed another way, which he defined as 'moral insurrection'. And the area of this moral insurrection would be something the peasant really did care about, namely the land, specifically the landlord–tenant relationship. Rents were to be refused until the land-lords agreed to a quite new land system to be negotiated directly between the Irish people and their landlords, based on the principle that the people who worked the land held by right a co-equal ownership of that land with the landlord. All future rents and conditions of tenure would start from that premise. Any landlord who did not recognize this inalienable right of the Irish people to their land would receive no rent and forfeit his property. From such an assumption by the Irish people of sovereign authority with regard to land titles and land tenures would flow automatically all other law-making rights.

They were already half-way there, Lalor maintained, for the famine and its consequences had begun their work for them by demolishing the old land system for ever. In this he was to be proved unduly optimistic. Social systems are tougher and more resilient than the human beings who compose them. Though the famine was to remove one quarter of the population from the land altogether and change twenty per cent of the landlords, the system itself survived for over another thirty years.

There was much that was imprecise and much that was fanciful in Lalor's radical thinking. As practical policy it was itself unreal in pre-supposing that the peasantry were prepared to stand up to the landlords. In fact, whether or not they could or could not pay their rents the peasantry were allowing themselves to be driven, famished and submissive, off the land into the ditches and hedgerows in tens of thousands. As Gavan Duffy objected, Lalor's 'angry peasants, chafing like chained tigers, were creatures of the imagination – not the living people through whom we had to act'.[14]

Yet by linking, even in theory, the violent power and passion which the Irish peasant in more normal times had manifested for his land to loftier thoughts of Irish nationalism, Lalor at least made an attempt to bring Irish nationalism down to earth. O'Connell in the early days of Repeal had had an instinctive feeling for the same principle, emphasizing as he constantly did tenant right, together with the need for Repeal. But Fintan Lalor formulated it more positively as a radical political theory. Other men in other times were to try and turn it into practice.

In his own day Lalor failed to convert the Confederation to his ideas, but he did at least force them to acknowledge that they themselves were lacking in practical policies and must adopt a more positive attitude. He also made one important individual convert, John Mitchel, who, inspired by Lalor, was soon to adopt the spirit at least of his argument and add a page to that record of history which was itself always to influence Irish history. Even Duffy had been convinced that while rejecting Lalor's scheme it was necessary to substitute another as specific.[15] And *The Nation* itself, for which Mitchel was still writing, continually voiced the need. '... It is indeed full time that we cease to whine and begin to act.... Good heavens, to think that we should go down without a struggle.'[16]

When at the beginning of 1848 Duffy wrote in *The Nation* that the coming year would witness great changes, he himself echoed: 'But how?', adding immediately: 'Our readers will not long be ignorant now.'[17]

Duffy had a plan of a sort. But it was hardly revolutionary, depending as it did for its effectiveness on that old assumption of national unity of all classes which never materialized. His proposal was that from all the present legal institutional functions of the Irish people in corporations, grand juries, boards of guardians, and as town commissioners, and Members of Parliament, there should be constituted a new National Authority in Ireland. Representing this at Westminster, Irish members would make Englishmen listen to the justice of Irish national claims by 'making Irish interests cross and impede and rule the British senate'.[18] They would '... stop the entire business of Parliament till the constitution of Ireland was restored'.[19] If the Members of Parliament failed to achieve this then they would withdraw from Westminster and together with representatives from the other institutions and other elected delegates form a Council of Three Hundred and 'demand the reassembly of the Irish Parliament'.

It is significant that the proposal did not even go so far as to make such a Council of Three Hundred in itself a Constituent Assembly, but only empowered it to make a final 'demand'. Altogether, the plan expressed what was increasingly to become the Confederation's attitude: namely that of wanting a revolution without having to bring one about.

By the end of 1847 John Mitchel, stimulated by the radical nature of Lalor's thought but dissatisfied with Duffy's plan and maddened with frustration, at last came to the conclusion that constitutional methods should be abandoned altogether.

He left *The Nation* and soon afterwards seceded from the Confederation itself. From among the prominent Young Irelanders he took with him only the young journalist Devin Reilly, but the general mood of the rank and file was by now so desperate that two-fifths of those present at the debate which led to his secession voted for him. He immediately founded a new weekly, brazenly named *The United Irishman*, from which he preached in a sort of violent vacuum the general principle of revolution. In his very first issue he openly defied the viceroy, giving him what he called 'a true account of ... the rules, signs and passwords of our new United Irish Society Lodge A 1'.[20]

Mitchel had in fact no organization whatsoever. He had only the sympathy of fanatical members in the new Confederate clubs in the towns, and virtually no support at all in the countryside. He simply assumed that the frenzied indignation he himself felt and expressed would somehow reproduce itself widely enough to generate revolution spontaneously. He hardly seemed to care what such a revolution's outcome might be.

'I hold it is a more hideous national calamity,' he wrote, 'for ten men to be cast out to die of hunger, like dogs in ditches, than for ten thousand to be hewn to pieces, fighting like men and Christians in defence of their rights.'[21]

It was not long before he was publishing articles on how to form hollow squares of pikemen against cavalry, and extolling the pike itself as 'the queen of weapons ... the weapon of the brave'.[22]

Smith O'Brien and the rest of the prominent Young Irelanders had deprecated Mitchel's extremism as soon as it had become apparent within the Confederation. O'Brien had called it 'utterly fatal to the liberties of the country'.[23] Even Meagher ('of the sword') wrote to O'Brien in January 1848 that for all his own increasing sense of desperation he was convinced that 'the only policy which we can successfully conduct is the constitutional policy advised by Duffy'.[24] O'Gorman took the same line, writing of Mitchel and Devin Reilly as 'Infant Ireland', and dissociating himself altogether from 'opinions so dangerous'.[25] Doheny, who, though a barrister, had himself been bred on the soil and had actually helped Fintan Lalor form a Tenant Right Association in the previous year, maintained that with the priests against them they had no chance with the peasantry. Moreover, he continued: 'If the peasants do take to arms they'll be faced by England's disciplined soldiery and end as corpses on their native fields, or, if they did manage to have a local success, on the gibbet.... But even if that were not so, where are your peasantry? – sicklied, hungry, wasted, exiled or in their graves. If you want to arm – I tell you your best chance – go to Skibbereen, re-animate the corpses that are huddled there and bid them arm ...'[26]

O'Brien finally made it clear that he would rather retire from the Confederation altogether than allow himself to be 'compromised by the reckless violence of men who care very little what is their destiny.... If I understand their policy,' he continued, 'I feel persuaded that it can lead to nothing but to confusion, anarchy and bloodshed, and must inevitably, for one generation at least, defeat all efforts for the attainment of our liberties.'[27] He moved finally in the Confederation that 'to hold out to the Irish population the hope that in the present broken and divided condition they can liberate their country by an appeal to arms ... would be in our opinion fatal misdirection of the public mind'.[28]

Within six months Smith O'Brien and the rest had all taken the field and every word they had said about the disastrousness of such an enterprise was proved correct.

The Young Ireland group were respectable, comfortably-situated, middle-class nationalists; the sort of men who even at the height of the famine could and did winter abroad for their health's sake.* They were men of unquestionable personal courage and integrity, as was soon to be shown. But for all their theoretical talk of physical force in the time of O'Connell, they were congenitally unfitted by temperament and tradition to abandon the safety of constitutionalism, particularly when the alternative was a desperate rebellion for which no preparation had been made and for which there was little positive inclination on the part of a starving and exhausted populace. O'Connell's cruel gibe that they were men afraid to look at a poker had a certain simple truth in it. It was a desperate determination to escape at all costs from their natural ambience in such desperate circumstances that had made Mitchel consciously adopt his wild course, and it is impossible not to admit the logic in his illogical gesture. The others were to allow themselves to be forced into such an attitude against their will.

It is, however, possible to sympathize both with the main body of the Confederation and with Mitchel. Each can be seen to be doing the wrong thing where no right thing was discernible. Cautious and sensible as was the main group, audacious as was Mitchel, both were utterly ineffectual. Mitchel was anxious to provoke a climax as quickly as possible. The others, in what now seemed a parody of Davis's motto, continued to 'bide their time'. What they were really waiting for was a miracle.

In February 1848 the miracle seemed to have arrived.

The Young Irelanders had been looking for inspiration to a number of developing nationalist movements on the continent of Europe. Speaking in 1847 of the movement then gaining force in Italy, Meagher had ended a Confederation meeting at Cork with the words: '... the beautiful, the brilliant and the gifted Italy is in arms! ... Glory! glory! to the citizens of Rome, patricians and Plebeians, who think that liberty is worth a drop of blood!'[29] and he had been received with tremendous cheering.

* Dillon, who suffered from tuberculosis, spent the winter of 1846–7 in Madeira; Richard O'Gorman spent it in London.

Now, in February 1848, with all Italy itself alight with nationalist fervour, there came on the 26th the astonishing news that an almost bloodless popular revolution had taken place in Paris. Louis Philippe had fled with barely a shot being fired. The thought of such a thing – a revolution achieved with no more than rhetorical blood, and with a poet and orator (Lamartine) himself one of the leading figures – went to the heads of the Irish Confederation. A revolution without the embarrassing task of making one had been shown to be possible. Many people now appeared to think that it only had to be hailed and glorified for a similarly painless reversal of the *status quo* to take place in Dublin.

The assumption was made that somehow the entire situation in Ireland had already changed overnight. At the next meeting of the Confederation Gavàn Duffy, making one of his rare appearances on a public platform, declared:

'If we are no slaves and braggarts, unworthy of liberty, Ireland will be free before the coming summer fades into winter.... All over the world – from the frozen swamps of Canada to the rich corn-fields of Sicily – in Italy, in Denmark, in Prussia and in glorious France, men are up for their rights.'[30]

But they were not up for their rights in Ireland. Nothing in Ireland had in fact been changed by these events. The one small straw which many hurried to seize was the remote possibility of war between the new French Republic and England. The common-sense arguments by which members of the Confederation and Smith O'Brien himself had felt restrained hitherto and with which they had censured Mitchel only a few weeks before were now thrown to the winds. 'The day of our deliverance is at hand,' wrote Duffy in *The Nation* in positively Mitchel-like tones.[31] 'Ireland's opportunity has come at last.'[32]

As he himself was to admit much later: 'The men who a few weeks before had fearlessly resisted anarchy, now as fearlessly embraced revolution.'[33] They were to pay dearly for their euphoria.

O'Gorman, who had thought Mitchel's opinions so mischievous, foolish and dangerous in January, now declared that all honest men were bound to arm.[34] O'Brien himself thought that the moment of Ireland's liberation was at hand, though typically he counselled patience, still hoping to bring the gentry on to the right side of the barricades.[35]

All the previous arguments still held good. The British Government was as strong, the populace as weakened by starvation and disease, the gentry as disinclined to repeal the Union as ever. But at the first meeting of the Council of the Confederation after the February revolution it was officially decided that if one last effort to get a national Parliament by negotiation should fail then there should be a revolution within the year.[36]

The nature of the goal had not changed. The Confederates still wanted another and better '82. The only change consisted in the miraculous renewal of their hopes that they could achieve it, winning it bloodlessly by the same combination of moral and physical pressure with which the Protestants had won their victory in '82. 'If the English government give us our freedom we will fight for England,' declared a prominent Kilkenny Confederate only in March. 'If that freedom be withheld, I cannot answer for my country or myself.'[37] Mitchel, who was now somehow regarded as largely vindicated by the events in Paris, was brought back into the Confederation's discussions, though his paper, *The United Irishman*, was hardly counselling patience in the manner of O'Brien. Addressing Clarendon, the Viceroy, as 'Her Majesty's Executioner-General and General Butcher of Ireland', it declared openly that its object in publishing, as he did, treasonable articles about street-fighting and barricades was 'to sweep this island clear of British butchers and plant the green flag on Dublin Castle'.[38]

The excitement of the Dublin Confederates was echoed in other Irish cities. A new Irish flag made its appearance. French red, white and blue tricolours had been widely hoisted in honour of the new young French republic from the start, but in the first week of March there appeared in the celebrations at Enniscorthy in County Wexford a tricoloured flag of orange, green and white, hopefully 'expressive of the union of the parties'.[39] And at a dinner given in April by the Dublin Trades Committee to O'Brien, Meagher and other members of a deputation that had carried Ireland's congratulations to the new French republic, Meagher presented his hosts with a silken orange, white and green flag surmounted by an Irish pike which he had brought back from Paris. He explained that the centre signified a lasting truce between the 'Orange' and the 'Green'. Mitchel, speaking at the dinner, declaimed:

'Brighter days are coming to us; this noble weapon glittering above us, this majestic banner, are of good omen to us. Ah! the gleaming pike-head rises through our darkness like a morning star; this magnificent Irish tricolour, with its orange, white and green, dawns upon us more glorious than ever Sunburst flashed over the field of Brunanburgh, or blazed thro' the battle haze of Clontarf. My friends, I hope to see the flag one day waving, as our national banner, over a forest of Irish pikes.' *

But if the mood of victory and optimism had been miraculously restored, the old question soon began to re-impose itself: what exactly, apart from

* The delegation's reception in Paris had been enthusiastic, but the British Government, through their Ambassador, had put pressure on Lamartine to state that the new republic did not wish to interfere in the internal affairs of the British Empire. This caused dismay to some extremists in Ireland who were hopefully thinking of an analogy with '98, but to O'Brien, thinking in terms of '82 and hoping for success without resort to war, it was only marginally disappointing. The general intoxication of the optimistic Paris scene, with everyone under arms and trees of liberty in every square, more than made up for it. (See O'Brien's *Personal Memorandum*, quoted Gwynn, *Young Ireland and 1848*, pp. 167-8.)

defying the government in the press, was to be done? Though the potato crop, or such as people had managed to plant, had not been so severely damaged by the blight in this winter of 1847–8, the ravages of starvation and disease after two years of famine were if anything worse than ever. People were dying daily in all parts of Ireland. Early in March 1848 the Mayo Constitution wrote: 'The streets of every town in the country are over-run by stalking skeletons.'[40] An inquest on a man found lying dead face downwards on the roadside near Westport revealed that his mouth was full of masticated turf and grass.[41] A Galway woman ate part of the legs and feet of her own daughter.[42] In Galway gaol, intended for 110 persons, there were 903 prisoners and 34 children, while 44 other people had died there in the previous week. In the prison hospital it was common to find three persons to a bed, one or more of them often dead.[43]

In the general revolutionary excitement, *The Nation* sounded a sobering warning note that Ireland's last chance had come.

'... If this be another roar of blank cartridge, if once again the passionate sobbing and straining of the people for liberty end in some shameful disappointments, hundreds of thousands of our truest hearts will fly from the land for ever, and the black hopeless darkness of slavery will settle down on it for a hundred years. For all the living race of Irishmen this is indeed the last chance.'[44]

Duffy issued a call for a 'National Guard' in imitation of the French revolutionaries. The Confederate clubs would provide a nucleus.

Even Smith O'Brien began to sound a new note of realism and urgency. He described how night after night he had sat in the House of Commons listening to the government and becoming more and more convinced that they were utterly indifferent to what was taking place in Ireland – '... never at any time did that Parliament seem to me to treat with more disdain than at present the claims of the Irish people'.[45] He thought it was time they bid the British Parliament 'good morning' and went home to take care of the Irish people. Yet none of the other Irish members would have followed him.

On 15 March 1848, speaking before a meeting of the Confederation three thousand strong, Smith O'Brien came out in his most theoretically rebellious mood to date. 'I trust,' he said, 'I speak in all true humility when I say that, if by surrendering my life, either upon the scaffold or the field, I could thereby secure the redemption of this land from the bondage under which it now suffers that life would be cheerfully given in my country's cause.'[46] He had, he said, the utmost possible horror of bloodshed, but an Irish parliament, an Irish army, an Irish national guard were what the vast majority of Ireland now wanted. Whether the final form of government were to be a republic or not, was at this stage unimportant. He personally believed that 'at present at least' the Irish people would be content to remain subject to the sovereignty of the British Crown.

O'Brien clearly envisaged the national guard as the principal lever to be used against the government, performing a similar function on behalf of the whole of Ireland to that which the Volunteers had performed on behalf of the Protestant ascendancy in 1782. To be composed of about 300,000 men, it would both be ready to protect social order and to act in defence of the country. It should enrol publicly and 'not by your night walkings, and by your ribbon societies, which have been the curse of the country'.[47] He recommended 'fraternizing' with the army and with the police, reminding his audience that the latter were Irishmen like themselves, 'as fine a body of men as ever held a musket; and if their energies were properly directed they would become the safeguard of this country . . .'.[48]

The Confederates indeed now resolved to draw up a roll of enlistment for a national guard and to summon a Council of Three Hundred. But almost nothing was actually done. The pulse of revolution was still quickening mainly in words. Mitchel drew attention to the fact.

'Speeches,' he said, 'or resolutions here never will avail or do one bit of good unless we all have arms and are ready to turn out.'[49]

But these were words too.

Increasingly aware of the need for some practical move, O'Brien decided to undertake a tour of inspection to discover the real state of the Confederate movement in other parts of the country. But the omens, even for a united front among Repealers, at once seemed poor. When he addressed his first meeting in his own home town of Limerick it was broken up by old O'Connellite supporters, angered by the presence at the meeting of Mitchel. Smith O'Brien, potential leader of an Irish revolution, was assaulted by other Irishmen with sticks and stones and received a black eye and bruised jaw and ribs for his pains. Though it was hurriedly pointed out to him that no offence had been intended to him personally, he was so disgusted that he threatened to retire altogether from public life.

It was the British Government which, understandably alarmed in such a year of revolutions by the talk in Ireland and unaware of how much effectiveness might or might not lie behind it, gave the revolutionary movement some apparent coherence by its counter-actions. In the circumstances these were not really excessive. A few counties had already been 'proclaimed' under the Crime and Outrage Act of the previous year, but in the others it was still quite legal to possess and even manufacture weapons including pikes, though little of this was going on.[50] Then in March the government instituted prosecutions against Smith O'Brien, Meagher and Mitchel for sedition in recent speeches and articles, though the three were allowed out on bail.*

'The war between the people and their English rulers has begun,' declared Duffy in *The Nation*, hopefully.[51] But it was not until the end of April that

---

* It was while out on bail that O'Brien and Meagher had been able to carry Dublin's congratulations to the new republic in France.

the viceroy issued a specific proclamation declaring any national guard and the summoning of the Council of Three Hundred illegal.

O'Brien, Meagher and Mitchel all came up for trial in May. The indictment itself did the mild O'Brien something of a service by describing him as 'a wicked, turbulent and seditious person'.[52] He was suitably escorted to the trial by a number of the Dublin Confederate clubs, one of which was called the Sheares Club after the unfortunate brothers of 1798.[53] In both his case and that of Meagher the juries failed to agree, in spite of intensive packing by the government with likely Unionist supporters. O'Brien and Meagher were released in triumph.

Mitchel himself was tried under a recent act creating the new offence of treason–felony, which allowed much severer penalties for sedition than hitherto, but did not demand the full rigours of treason. An article in *The United Irishman* – written in fact by Mitchel's young lieutenant Devin Reilly – had only recently advocated the throwing of vitriol into the eyes of soldiers in street fighting,[54] and this and the far more radical and violent republican tone Mitchel had long adopted made his conviction seem more certain. When some of the rank and file Confederates demanded that if Mitchel were convicted there should be an armed attempt to defy the government, rescue him and raise the country, the Confederate leaders took a desperate look round at their organization and resources.

They found there were only just over seventy Confederate clubs in Ireland altogether, almost half of which were in Dublin, containing between two and five hundred members each.[55] There was virtually no organization by the Confederates in country districts at all. The Dublin clubs themselves, probably the best organized, were, for all their enthusiasm, found by Meagher and O'Gorman after a rapid inspection to be unfit for any sort of action with a reasonable expectancy of success.[56] Against them the government had ten thousand police and troops in the city and forty thousand in the rest of Ireland. Though many in the Dublin clubs wanted to make a rescue bid all the same, they were restrained by Meagher and O'Gorman after O'Brien himself had advised very strongly against it.[57]

On 26 May 1848 Mitchel was found guilty and sentence was postponed till the following day.

One eye-witness described Dublin at midnight that night as wearing the aspect of a city on the eve of insurrection. Men walked the streets distractedly, as if they had forgotten all sense of time and weariness. Carriages drove constantly to and from the several military and police stations while large bodies of police patrolled the streets.[58] But the night passed off quietly, and the next day Mitchel came up for sentence. Many of his old friends were in court. The sentence was that he should be transported beyond the seas for a period of fourteen years.

'I do not regret anything I have done,' he cried from the dock, 'and I believe that the course which I have opened is only commenced. The Roman who saw his hand burning to ashes before the tyrant promised that three hundred should follow out his enterprises. Can I not promise for one' (and here he pointed at Meagher in the courtroom) – 'for two?' (at Reilly) – 'for three?' (at O'Gorman) – 'aye, for hundreds?'[59]

There was a rush of outstretched hands towards the dock and the judges withdrew in disorder while Mitchel was forcibly taken below. One man he could not promise for so confidently was Smith O'Brien, who had circumspectly withdrawn to Wicklow during the trial, still suffering from the battering he had received a month before at Limerick.[60]

Mitchel was taken aboard a warship in Dublin Harbour that afternoon, stumbling over the chain which fastened his hand to his right leg as he reached the deck.[61] Special instructions were given by the government that he should be treated without vindictiveness.[62] He was soon allowed to change his convict dress for his own clothes and the Governor of Spike Island outside Cork, where he was held for a few days, even bought him some shirts.[63] On his way to Bermuda, where he was to spend a year of close confinement, he took his meals at the Captain's table. Even in Bermuda, where he was lodged in one of the prison hulks offshore, he had a quite spacious room to himself with books. He was kept apart from the other convicts, could go ashore for exercise and did not have to work.

It is still sometimes said that Mitchel lived through 'appalling privations and physical sufferings'[64] during this period, but this is not strictly so. He was treated as a 'gentlemanly' prisoner with, relatively, considerable privileges, and the fact was more than once made the subject of angry comment in the House of Commons. Apart from the damp climate of Bermuda, which was bad for his asthma, the worst he had to endure was the shrieking of the ordinary convicts being flogged with the cat o' nine tails on the decks above.[65] But though he found this unpleasant, it did not trouble his sensibilities unduly for he was a stern man who did not disapprove of flogging as such and even thought it too good for most common criminals.[66] After a year he was sent to Tasmania where, immediately given his parole, and receiving a ticket of leave, he spent some years sheep-farming and kangaroo-hunting.[67] Then one day, having made his plans, he suddenly announced that he was giving up his parole and escaped to America.

But, for Ireland, Mitchel had become a martyr – a martyr second in that century only to Emmet. And, as with Emmet, the total ineffectualness of the defiance seemed no reflection on the individual, only an inspiring evocation of the hopelessness of the Irish people's plight.

13

Smith O'Brien's 'Rising', 1848

What is often described as the rising of 1848 in Ireland was not in any practical sense a rising at all, nor until the very last minute was it ever intended to be one. There was no previously drawn up military plan of campaign, no secret organization, and such conspiracy as there was had previously been overtaken by events and made irrelevant. Though a confrontation of sorts between the Young Irelanders and the government had been planned in theory for the autumn of 1848, the confused series of events which actually took place in July and August was no more than a desperate last-minute attempt by would-be Irish leaders to avoid arrest and thus force the government into a negotiating position. It failed hopelessly, for the same reason as the more positive effort vaguely proposed for the autumn would have failed. The gap between words and deeds, but above all between leaders and people, was too great. In such a situation the initiative remained throughout with the government.

Immediately after Mitchel's transportation one of the few priests who had come out not only in favour of the Irish Confederation but also of the extreme viewpoint expressed by Mitchel had arrived in Dublin to see Duffy. He was a Father Kenyon of Templederry in County Tipperary. Even before Mitchel's sentence he had expressed some impatience with mere histrionic gestures and talk. Addressing a crowd at Kilkenny in April 1848 he had said:

'You have often met before in crowds like this; you have been hitherto accustomed to shout and cheer and take off your hats, until shouting and cheering and taking off your hats has come to be worth a pinch of snuff. ... I ask you again, are you ready to die for Ireland?' And the crowd had replied: 'Yes, yes, all ready to die this minute', whereupon he had expressed himself content.[1]

Now he put it to Duffy that some positive preparations should be made for armed action if necessary. Duffy, all too aware how little had been done, agreed.[2]

But activity was largely restricted to sending agents to France and America to enlist general support, one of whom dramatically carried his commission to America smeared with gunpowder in a loaded pistol so that it could be blown to pieces in the event of arrest.*[3]

O'Brien himself, only kept vaguely informed of the moves, remained brooding at home. He was still unable to 'stoop or stretch without pain' after his Limerick injuries, but he was also as late as June on his own admission still 'not one of those who wish to plunge recklessly' and this must have played its part in delaying his recovery.[4] However, he kept quite closely in touch by letter with developments, and one of the most important of these was a reunion at last between the Confederation and the old O'Connellite Repeal Association.

For the Confederation the benefit of this reunion was more psychological than organizational, for under the combined influence of the famine and John O'Connell's leadership the old Repeal organization had become moribund and inactive. The Repeal Rent, which had once run into thousands of pounds per week, had for a long time barely reached double figures. But the reunion did bring theoretically to the Confederation the potential sympathy of those masses for whom the name O'Connell was still the only one which held any political magic at all. The reunion also seemed to promise some tentative approval from the bulk of the Roman Catholic clergy, who had so far largely held aloof from the Confederation and were the key to all popular support in Ireland. Out of the reunion a new political body was formed to replace the Irish Confederation. It was named the Irish League.

O'Brien, still at home, wrote on 1 June a letter to *The Nation* approving the Irish League's formation, in some of his most committed language to date.

'Our controversy,' he wrote, 'will soon narrow itself into the single question how often uttered with impatience – When will the Irish Nation strike?',[5] though typically he also quoted the Young Ireland poet who had written:

... Your worst transgressions
Were to strike, and strike in vain.

And it is clear that by 'striking' he still meant more the striking of a defiant attitude, backed by an armed organization, rather than literally taking the field.

The effectiveness of the new united front was soon reduced by two events. The first was a decision taken by John O'Connell to retire from public life. In making his decision known he also let it be known that the new note of militancy in O'Brien's letter had contributed to it. The second event was another revolution in Paris at the end of June. This, unlike that in February, was

---

* This was the conspiracy made irrelevant by subsequent events. The money raised in America for arms arrived in Ireland too late for anything but a defence fund for those members of the Confederation who were by then under arrest. (See Duffy, op. cit., pp. 693–5.)

extremely bloody, and openly socialistic and anti-clerical. It alarmed many wavering middle-class supporters of the Irish League and put a sharp brake on the clergy's approbation of radical methods.

Nevertheless, the spirit of optimism among the faithful of the Confederate clubs was running high. Meagher and O'Gorman in particular were busy travelling about the country working up enthusiasm. The press, in the shape not only of *The Nation* but of a new paper, the *Irish Felon*, which had replaced Mitchel's suppressed *United Irishman* and was edited by a close personal friend of his, John Martin, with help from Fintan Lalor, was striking a more and more openly revolutionary note.

Letters were appearing in *The Nation* on how to look after steel weapons, whether pikes, sword blades or daggers, and how to cast bullets.[6] Duffy was promising that one of the first duties of the Irish League would be to plant the country with clubs from end to end.[7] O'Brien himself, in his more militant mood, actually wrote that he was bound to tell the people of Ireland that injustices and wrongs were 'rapidly bringing us to that period when armed resistance to the oppressors of our country will become a sacred obligation, enforced by the highest sanctions of public duty.'[8] Meagher, fully extravagant again, declaimed: 'Generation transmits to generation the holy passion. From the blood which drenched the scaffolds of 1798 the felons of this year have sprung.'[9]

Duffy had been subtly encouraging the more militant side of O'Brien's nature and trying to goad him at least into committing himself to leadership. 'There is no half-way house for you,' he wrote to him probably on 17 June. 'You will be head of the movement, loyally obeyed, and the revolution will be conducted with order and clemency; or the mere anarchists will prevail with the people and our revolution will be bloody chaos. . . . If I were Smith O'Brien I would shape out in my own mind . . . a definite course for the revolution and labour incessantly to develop it that way.'

He blamed O'Brien for allowing the projects for a National Guard and the calling of a Council of Three Hundred to lapse, but thought it was now too late to try and revive them. The Confederate clubs were now the one real hope. 'Forgive me for urging this so anxiously upon you, but I verily believe the hopes of the country depend upon the manner in which the next two months are used.'[10]

And at the beginning of July O'Brien came out from his home at last and went on a tour of the country. In spite of the 'abject looks' rather than 'glad faces' he met among the peasantry,[11] he began, under the combined influence of the beauty of the Irish countryside and the enthusiasm he found in the Confederate clubs, to drift more and more positively towards a guarded revolutionary fervour. In Cork he held a sort of review by moonlight in a city park of some seven to ten thousand members of the clubs, many of whom marched past him in military order.[12] The next day he wrote to his wife that 'we shall be able to make the whole of this force available for good purposes . . .'.[13]

But how exactly these good purposes were to be worked out was still left vague. There was no practical plan of rebellion such as Lord Edward Fitzgerald and even Robert Emmet had developed. It was clear that both O'Brien and Duffy too were still thinking primarily in terms of a display of armed organized clubs which, when the time came in the autumn, would stand as a challenge to the government behind the demand for Repeal and succeed in getting it to back down, much as the Volunteers had achieved their objectives in '82.

However, some awkward voices were beginning to be raised.

Another new radical paper had appeared, the *Irish Tribune*, edited by two students, Dalton Williams and Kevin O'Doherty. 'Why?' asked a letter in this on 1 July, echoing Duffy's private letter of a fortnight earlier, 'Why is not the Council of Three Hundred, which alone is required to save the country, proceeded with? ... We call upon Smith O'Brien – we call upon T. F. Meagher to rouse from his apathy.' The harvest, the letter continued, would be ready in two months and it must be prevented from leaving Dublin and other ports by the clubs. '... No faltering, no hesitating, no suspense. Ever keep before your minds the GREAT CAUSE.... Think of those great victims whose names, still unappeased, cry out for vengeance – FITZGERALD, and EMMET and TONE. Think of MITCHEL.... Think, think and BE COURAGEOUS.'[14]

A letter in the *Irish Felon*, also at the beginning of July, came even closer to the point when it stated that though the clubs were numerous they were not well-armed. There was too much braggartry, the writer complained. He discerned only the desire for freedom – not the energy to win it. Each club that was aware of its own deficiencies imagined that the others were better equipped. 'Cork looks to Dublin and Dublin looks to Cork.' Defeatism was spreading with 'each new postponement of the revolutionary drama which seems necessary to our cautious managers.... The words you speak are meaningless, for you have spoken them so frequently already; and the attitudes you adopt are lifeless and unimpressive, because custom has exhausted passion.... Our alternative now is ... the hillside or the court. I for one would rather die with the green flag for my shroud than pine into the grave with the insignia of felony on my limbs ...'[15]

Duffy himself had expressed similar reservations about the clubs only a short time before. Certainly the number of members in Dublin had doubled in three weeks after Mitchel's sentence, but there were still large blanks on the map of Ireland where there were no clubs at all.[16] This knowledge, however, did not prevent the issue of *The Nation* which revealed this from carrying an article entitled 'Night Thoughts on The Bayonet'.[17]

Then, while O'Brien was still down in Cork intending to continue his leisurely tour of inspection through Youghal and Dungarvan and up to

Dublin, the government struck. It arrested Gavan Duffy for sedition. He was joined in prison the same night by John Martin, Mitchel's friend and editor of the *Irish Felon*, for whom a warrant had been out for some time. Next day the two young students who had started the *Irish Tribune* were there too, having only been allowed to bring out three issues of their paper. Early the following week Doheny and Meagher, whose oratory had been becoming increasingly violent, were also arrested, as was D'Arcy Magee, Duffy's assistant editor on *The Nation*.

Doheny, Meagher and Magee were all allowed bail. Duffy and the others were not, though, as had been the case with O'Connell, the prison regime under the control of Dublin Corporation was lax. Both Duffy and Martin were able to keep in contact with their papers and, being allowed any visitors they liked, could continue to confer on general 'revolutionary' policy.

This remained as imprecise as ever, except for the principle that nothing rash or premature should be attempted. As Duffy himself was being taken to prison in a police van on the night of his arrest, a vast crowd had collected round it in the streets of Dublin, forcing it to walking pace in spite of a large police escort. Shouts of 'Take him out! Take him out!' had arisen, and the president of one of the Confederate clubs climbed up on the steps of the van and asked Duffy if he wanted to be rescued.

'Certainly not,' replied Duffy, and then at the request of the police officer appealed to the crowd to let him be taken to prison.[18]

Similar scenes had occurred the next week when Doheny was arrested in Cashel and Meagher in Waterford. Meagher had had to appeal to the clubs from the top of the vehicle on which he was being taken to gaol to remove a barricade blocking the bridge and to abandon their determination to occupy the town.

They agreed reluctantly, saying: 'We fear you will be sorry for it, sir.'[19]

But clearly not all initiative could be left to the government. Smith O'Brien cut short his tour and returned to Dublin by sea on 14 July to discuss what should be done. On the 15th a meeting of the council of the Confederation took place together with representatives of the clubs. It was a private meeting, but there was nothing secret or illegal about it, though the government had taken the precaution of infiltrating an informer.*

O'Brien, after going through the strength of the organization of the Dublin clubs with their representatives, gave an encouraging report on his experiences in Cork. But, as he truly said, they were not yet well-enough informed of the state of the clubs' organization in Ireland as a whole. When discussion arose as to the desirability of a rescue attempt on behalf of the new prisoners should they be convicted, he said that he personally would rather ascend the gallows himself than let anyone lose his life by a premature step on his

---

* James Stephenson Dobbyn. The bulk of his information as revealed in evidence in court was admitted afterwards by Meagher to have been accurate.

account. But the consensus of the meeting seems to have been that a rescue should be attempted in the event of the prisoners' conviction. Since the next law term in which convictions might be expected was not until October no thought of an immediate insurrection seems to have been contemplated by anyone.

A quite different situation had, however, arisen when the council met again four days later, with O'Brien again in the chair. For the government had again taken the initiative. On 18 July the lord lieutenant issued a proclamation declaring the holding of arms in Dublin and a number of other counties as illegal. At the Irish League council's meeting a resolution was immediately put forward that the clubs should no longer wait for the harvest in the autumn but should start an insurrection at once. This was proposed by the young man from Cork, Joseph Brenan, who had written the fiery letter to the *Irish Felon* earlier in the month.*

An amendment to Brenan's motion was moved by John Blake Dillon, to the effect that the clubs should merely conceal their arms and offer only passive resistance to the proclamation, refusing to open any door or lock voluntarily.[20] This was eventually carried by a small majority.[21] Brenan, arguing that the clubs were at the peak of their morale now, declared in exasperation that they were always waiting – till American or French aid came, 'till rifles are forged in heaven and angels draw the trigger'.[22]

During these days since his return to Dublin, O'Brien had been touring Confederate clubs in towns in the capital's vicinity. At Drogheda, Navan and Trim he had received great welcomes and told his audiences that the day might not be far distant when they would be called on 'to afford sterner indications of patriotism than mere cheers'.[23] But at a meeting of the League itself on the evening of 19 July (the day of the council's decision to offer passive resistance to the arms proclamation) he insisted that the organization would continue constitutional efforts 'until we find all constitutional efforts exhausted'.[24]

On 21 July a further meeting of the council took place which O'Brien purposely did not attend. The object of this was to elect a small inner executive to manage the clubs, a directory whose deliberations would be less unwieldy than those of the thirty-strong council, and both swifter to take any necessary emergency action and more secret. O'Brien refused even to let his name go up for election, objecting to the whole idea on the grounds that such a directory would be a source of jealousy and weakness.†[25] Those elected were Duffy, Meagher, Dillon, D'Arcy Magee and Devin Reilly; three were to form a quorum. Pressed by the rest of the meeting to give a

* See above, p. 273.
 † Both Duffy and Gwynn, following him, say that the directory never met; but since, on the evidence of the informer Dobbyn, three were to form a quorum, they are not strictly correct (see below, p. 277).

pledge that a rising would take place before 8 August Meagher refused, though he said he would do everything he could to expedite one even before that date. But the general feeling seems to have been that nothing would occur to precipitate a rising for three or four weeks, and the feeling was shared by O'Brien.

On the next day, 22 July, Smith O'Brien went down by invitation to stay near Enniscorthy in Wexford with an old friend, John Maher, Deputy Lieutenant for that county and formerly its Member of Parliament. There was a plan for them to go the following day to visit some mudlands then in process of reclamation in Wexford Harbour, a subject in which O'Brien, with his admirable civic sense, had expressed considerable interest.[26]

The same day, after O'Brien had left, the news reached Dublin that the government was rushing a suspension of the Habeas Corpus Act through the House of Commons.

O'Brien never visited the mudlands. Soon after six o'clock on the morning of 23 July he was woken to be told that Meagher and Dillon, whom he thought were in Dublin, were in the house and wanted to speak to him urgently. They were shown to his bedside where they told him that Habeas Corpus was being suspended and that a warrant was said to be out for his arrest. After consulting with them for over an hour he asked his host to come to his room and, while dressing, told him the news.[27]

'My dear Maher,' said O'Brien, 'I did not come to your house to disturb its peace; get us some breakfast, and send us on our way. I do not wish that any arrest should take place in your house. Send for a car, that we may go towards Kilkenny, where we have some friends with whom I wish to consult in this crisis.'[28]

With these unambitious words began the 'rising' of 1848.

O'Brien had rejected both the idea of submitting to arrest and that of flight. As he wrote soon afterwards:

'So much had been said by the Party with which I was associated and by myself, about the necessary preparation for conflict, that we should have been exposed to ridicule and reproach if we had fled at the moment when all the contingencies which we had contemplated as justifying the use of force were realized ...'[29] But he continued, '... In order to leave as little as possible to conjecture I resolved before I summoned the country to arms, still further to test the disposition of the people.'[30]

In other words, having come South without any idea of an immediate insurrection in mind, and having been forced by circumstances to recognize that the moment for some sort of decisive action had at last arrived, he decided to prolong that moment as long as possible.

The town of Kilkenny, with its historical associations from 1642, and its dominating position over much of southern Ireland, had for some time been commanding the Confederates' attention. Only three days earlier, when positive action was still far from O'Brien's mind, he had been publicly looking forward to holding the next meeting of the Irish League there.[31] A prominent citizen of Kilkenny, Dr Cane, was an enthusiastic supporter of the League and there had been a newspaper report to the effect that the Confederate clubs there were organized to a strength of seventeen thousand men.[32] In the adjacent county of Tipperary, at Templederry, lived Father Kenyon, the fiery priest who had tried to jolt Duffy into some sort of action two months earlier. On the other side lay Waterford, where in the county town Meagher had his own personal Confederate stronghold. In deep support to the southwest lay the city of Cork, where O'Brien himself had witnessed the militant dash of the Confederate club members.

To Meagher, already thinking more single-mindedly of insurrection than O'Brien, certain tactical military considerations reinforced the advantages of Kilkenny as a base. The railway from Dublin still stopped fourteen miles short of the town, and the undulating landscape and twisting roads flanked by high walls and hedges made it suitable territory in which to confront regular troops with spirited irregulars. An additional coincidental factor thought to be of advantage was that the Annual Show of the Royal Agricultural Society was being held in Kilkenny that week in the presence of the Duke of Leinster, the Marquis of Ormond, the Earl of Clancarty and other gentry who might prove useful as hostages while the cattle themselves could also be put to good purpose.[33]

Such thoughts had run through the minds of Meagher and Dillon the day before, when they had taken a number of hurried decisions with D'Arcy Magee, the only other member of the inner directory available in Dublin. (In tune with the general feeling that nothing unexpected was likely to happen for a few weeks, O'Gorman had left Dublin to continue the organization of the clubs in Limerick, and Doheny was in Cashel on a similar errand.) Now, given the recent resolution of the clubs to offer only passive resistance to the arms ban and the known effectiveness of the government's Dublin garrison, it seemed mad to take responsibility for blood-letting in the streets of the capital and call out the clubs.[34] The three looked naturally to the areas of the South which were less heavily garrisoned, and in which in any case the most respected figure of the movement was known to be staying. Agreeing that D'Arcy Magee should go off to Glasgow where he had connections and, with the help of the very large Irish population of the city, try to organize a supply of arms by sea for the moment of insurrection, Meagher and Dillon then themselves travelled all night down to O'Brien in Wexford.

Soon after ten o'clock the next morning, Sunday the 23rd, after collecting O'Brien, all three were on their way by coach to Kilkenny.

They stopped at a number of points en route to try to rally feeling. At

Enniscorthy, since it was Sunday, Meagher and Dillon went to Mass. Afterwards they were joined by O'Brien, and all three were soon surrounded by a large crowd who assured them that, though not prepared or organized for an insurrection, they would protect them if any attempt were made by the police to arrest them. O'Brien expressed some disappointment that a town of the size of Enniscorthy did not have more than one Confederate club. He did not call them out to insurrection, but told them that they had to prepare for an emergency. The townspeople were asked to pledge themselves to take the field should the people of a neighbouring county rise, and a ringing shout came back that they would 'and with God's blessing too'.[35] But in this they were over-stepping the mark. In the peasantry's eyes, at any rate, it was the priests who were the final arbiters of God's blessing.

It was raining heavily that Sunday and, stopping occasionally by the roadside for shelter, O'Brien, Meagher and Dillon were left in no doubt by the famished and dispirited peasantry they met that they had no enthusiasm for any rising. A longer stop at the small town of Graigue-na-mana was also discouraging, for the priest there would not commit himself to approval of an insurrection, remarking merely that 'the whole affair was a very difficult subject to decide upon'.[36] Spirits recovered a little, however, when it was remembered that Thomas Cloney, the old rebel of '98,* now a venerated citizen, lived in the town, and O'Brien, Meagher and Dillon went to see him.[37] Cloney, long popularly known as 'General' Cloney, threw his arms round O'Brien and wept with emotion. Speaking to a crowd of between three and four hundred from Cloney's house, Meagher told them the news of the suspension of Habeas Corpus and urged them to form a club, but also told them to beware of 'the claws of the law' and to commit no breach of it.[38] It may well have seemed unclear to the crowds whether they were actually being called to insurrection or not. The position roughly was that O'Brien and the others were saying they would take up arms if the people supported them while the people were saying they would support them if they took up arms.

The three arrived in Kilkenny at about eight o'clock that Sunday evening and went straight to the house of Dr Cane. There they received their first serious shock. There were not 17,000 members of the clubs in the town as reported, but 1,700. It had been a misprint in the newspapers. Only about one in four of the members had arms.[39]

Abandoning the idea of an immediate insurrection in the town, O'Brien, Meagher and Dillon proceeded next day on a tour of the surrounding countryside. They hoped to mobilize support for those ardent spirits in Kilkenny who, in spite of all, had encouraged Meagher and Dillon to think that within a week the green flag would be flying from Ormond Castle.

The travels of O'Brien, Meagher and Dillon now continued in the same

* See above, p. 112.

pattern as the day before, only with the difference that the longer such travels continued the more desultory and inconclusive they seemed. At Callan a party of the 8th Irish Hussars was in the town when they arrived, but they left O'Brien unmolested as he again asked a crowd, this time about nine hundred strong, if they would let him be arrested and the crowd replied emphatically: no. One Englishman among the Hussars, alarmed by the prevailing mood, prepared to leave the Market House where the troops were quartered. But Meagher reassured the men that there was no need to leave the building and that they and their arms were quite safe.[40]

'We know that, Sir,' replied a corporal of the Hussars. 'We know well you wouldn't take an unfair advantage of the poor soldiers; at any rate, you wouldn't do it to the Irish Hussars.'[41]

Again the gist of the message to the people was two-fold. They should help O'Brien resist arrest if arrest were attempted. They should also organize and be ready, for the time was at hand. It was still not made clear what the time was at hand for, other than being ready.

That evening on the road between Callan and Carrick-on-Suir, O'Brien, Meagher and Dillon stopped at a halt to change horses and chatted with the country people. They learned that though many were disposed to rise against the government even if they only had bill-hooks and pitchforks rather than guns, the priests were overwhelmingly against it. However, some of the more enthusiastic people they spoke to said that if only one priest could be found in favour of action that would do 'for the people were tired of keeping so quiet and dying from day to day'.[42]

Just short of Carrick itself they pulled up at some cross-roads to talk to some men digging in a field. On hearing that a young Catholic land-owner named John O'Mahony, who had done much to organize the local clubs, lived in the neighbourhood they asked to see him. Twenty minutes later O'Mahony himself came galloping up on a black horse to vouch personally for the local enthusiasm.[43]

In Carrick town itself therefore O'Brien, on being brought into the presence of the club leaders, asked for six hundred men with guns and ammunition to guard him and his companions while they raised the countryside. Since Tipperary was a proclaimed county, this was to propose an open act of war. But though O'Brien was beginning to commit himself his request met with dismay. One man asked pointedly why it was that the leaders should have come to Carrick of all places to start the rising. Was it because they had been rejected everywhere else?[44]

The most influential priest in the neighbourhood, a Father Byrne, who had in his day made inflammatory enough speeches, would have nothing to do with the project, saying that O'Brien 'must be mad', and that he should at least wait until the harvest had been brought in in a fortnight's time.[45]

That other well-known Tipperary priest, Father Kenyon at Templederry, was also backing out of any positive action on the grounds that an attempt now would be suicidal.

O'Mahony, ashamed for Tipperary, pledged himself to go out and raise the neighbourhood. He actually succeeded in collecting four hundred men from his own club with about eighty guns and a large number of pikes. But there was apparently no immediate work for them to do. For by next morning O'Brien had moved off in the direction of Cashel, hoping to get some encouragement from Michael Doheny, whose home town it was. Before leaving Carrick he addressed a crowd of some five thousand in the streets, telling them positively this time that he was calling them to the field. Meagher also spoke and was quite carried away by his own oratory, for after first appearing to contradict his leader and telling the crowd that they must all deliberate a little longer he also cried:

'What care I for all their force? They may threaten us with death; they may tear from us our lives; more they cannot do for they have already deprived us of all else besides. Death is the worst they can inflict. Death is the utmost bounds of their threats. They are again renewing the bloody deeds of '98 ...'[46]

It was half a century since '98, but memories of the appalling government brutalities that had followed its failure were still vivid. Any reminder of them was a doubtful rhetorical gambit, for apprehension of failure was growing daily.

The whole of the rest of the week was spent in similar dilatory and cumulatively demoralizing fashion. Day followed day without any very positive action being taken by anyone. O'Brien and his companions simply moved from place to place within a relatively small area of Tipperary, often visiting the same town or village more than once. Those who at first had had a certain amount of heart for a fight became understandably cautious, while those who were already pessimistic became even more determined not to involve themselves in the consequences of disaster. The priests did all they could to discourage premature audacity, coming out increasingly into the open to argue against O'Brien.[47]

Meagher went off to his own city of Waterford, hoping to raise the clubs there and return with a thousand men. He returned alone, having been unable to get the leaders to move against the advice of their own radical priest, Father Tracy. Meagher seems, however, to have accepted their reply a little too readily, for later in the week another young Confederate, Michael Cavanagh, found the boatmen of Waterford disappointed and feeling let down by Meagher who had sent them no word when 'thousands' of them were still waiting for a summons to the fight. They felt, they told Cavanagh, 'something was wrong somewhere'.[48]

Almost nothing was right.

O'Mahony, by force of his own local appeal and vigorous personality, continued to rally the countryside effectively for a time. He reckoned afterwards, probably with some exaggeration, that he had some twelve to fifteen thousand men ready to march by the night of Tuesday, 25 July, and Michael Doheny, who had by then joined him, substantiates at least the enthusiasm with which pikes were being forged in the area round the Slievenamon hills.[49] But O'Mahony, waiting for a signal from his leaders that never came, was unable himself to give his followers any very clear indication of the purpose for which they were being summoned.

A number of other enthusiastic middle-class young Irishmen had by now made their way south to swell the group round O'Brien. Among them were P. J. Smyth, son of a prosperous Dublin merchant, and a successful young shipping agent, named T. B. McManus, who had crossed over from Liverpool specially for the purpose. Also in this group was a twenty-five-year-old employee of the Limerick and Waterford Railway Company who, though he had never been a member of the Irish Confederation, had come to join O'Brien from Kilkenny. His name was James Stephens.

It was in the company of Stephens, armed with a double-barrelled gun, that on the morning of Wednesday, 26 July, O'Brien made his first overt move against the forces of the Crown. Wearing the gold and green cap of the '82 club, and with a number of pistols tucked into his coat, O'Brien, with Stephens and one other companion, marched into the police station at Mullinahone, in County Tipperary. It was garrisoned by a head constable and five others.[50]

An enthusiastic crowd had gathered in the village the night before, but in the morning, under the influence of their priests, they had begun to have second thoughts. The presence of the police was given as an excuse for their new-found timidity. O'Brien decided to tackle the problem head on. He had been maintaining throughout the last three days that the police were as good Irishmen as any, and when the time came would know how to act. He proceeded to the police station to prove his point, and asked the police to surrender.

The head constable said afterwards in court that he replied: 'I would be unworthy of the name of Irishman if I gave up my arms.'[51] And though O'Brien, who is probably more reliable, stated that the constable had by no means been so firm as he later pretended, the fact that this was at least thought to be the right answer to give is significant. O'Brien, like other Irish nationalists before and after, was up against the awkward fact that Irish nationalism was not the clear-cut cause he made it out to be.

Another eye-witness maintained, many years later, that while O'Brien and Stephens were inside the police station, a big policeman put his head out of an upper window and exclaimed to the crowd: 'Yerrah! sure the time isn't come yet to surrender our arms. D'ye wait till the right time comes!'[52]

Whatever the truth of this, while O'Brien gave them further time in which to deliberate, they worked out their own compromise and made off with their arms to a stronger police post.

This new appearance of resolution on O'Brien's part had first taken shape the night before, when he had sent P. J. Smyth off to Dublin with orders to 'start an insurrection there'.[53] Nevertheless, a man who saw O'Brien that same night later described him as having been 'like a man in a dream'.[54] And it was a fact that the secretary of the Dublin clubs, James Halpin, was actually already in the South looking for O'Brien in order to get instructions for his clubmen. These had been left 'disheartened and bewildered',[55] without any indications of what was going on or how to communicate with their leaders. Some isolated manoeuvres were carried out in a few parts of Ireland on the initiative of a few individuals who hoped for news from the South to give coherence to their movements. Richard O'Gorman, for instance, began to raise the peasantry in Limerick, and D'Arcy Magee, after he had had to fly from Glasgow to escape arrest, had landed in Sligo and organized some qualified support from the agrarian secret societies there.[56] But by then total fiasco had overtaken O'Brien's perambulations in Tipperary.

Without any proper organization, or even effective communications, with the priests against him, and beset by failures such as that of Meagher's in Waterford and his own before the police station in Mullinahone, O'Brien must by mid-week already have begun to grasp that his chances were forlorn in the extreme. Nevertheless, the same eye-witness who described him as having been like a man in a dream at Mullinahone, also saw him not many hours after looking dreamy still, but happy and smoking a cigar as he left on a jaunty car.[57] He stubbornly refused to requisition private property for supplies, as his companions urged him to, maintaining incongruously that the last thing he wanted to start was a *jacquerie*.[58]

A certain amount of shambling drill seems to have taken place in Mullinahone itself and other villages where he appeared. But always the parties of peasants, armed mainly with agricultural implements and a few muskets, melted away after entreaties from their priests not to risk their lives without hope of success, or on realizing that supplies of free food were not unlimited. (O'Brien paid for more than 160 loaves of bread on one occasion out of his own pocket, but another day solemnly issued an order that each man among the starving peasantry should appear with at least four days' rations.)[59]

However, on Friday, 28 July, at the small town of Killenaule, O'Brien had the nearest thing to a victory that came his way during the whole week. A party of dragoons was seen approaching the town and, it being assumed that they had come to arrest O'Brien, barricades were thrown up in their path. When the captain of dragoons, a Captain Longmore, halted before the first barricade a rifle was presented at him by James Stephens, and he was asked by Dillon if he had a warrant for O'Brien's arrest. On giving an assurance that he had not and that he had no intention of trying to arrest O'Brien, the barricades were lifted and he and his men were allowed through and out of the town.[60] It was a transaction from which on reflection neither party considered it had emerged with credit. O'Brien, after all, was a proclaimed outlaw, and it would have seemed Captain Longmore's duty to proceed against him whether he had a warrant or not. To this extent it was a victory for O'Brien. On the other hand, if O'Brien had really been wanting to start an insurrection and put heart into those thousands in the area who were understandably wavering, this had been an opportunity for forcing a body of government troops to surrender which had not been taken.

But it was still perhaps not wholly O'Brien's policy to commit himself to a fighting insurrection. Future policy was indeed the subject of a conference held that night in the small town of Ballingarry, the centre of a colliery district from which O'Brien hoped for support from the miners. Earlier that evening Meagher had told the miners that they were to be ready in three weeks' when the wisp would be lit over the hills'.[61] Another, unnamed, companion had stated more directly that they would 'hunt every English bugger to his own side, and let him live there'.[62]

The conference at Ballingarry was the nearest thing to a council of war the Confederates ever held. Doheny and O'Mahony, as well as Meagher, had managed to join O'Brien for it, along with Stephens, Dillon, McManus and the others already there. The conference lasted only an hour and a quarter. Everyone declared himself dissatisfied with the course which events had taken during the week. In the circumstances most people were in favour of going into hiding and waiting for the harvest. But O'Brien, whose strong personal sense of honour prevented him from becoming a fugitive at this stage, determined to try and continue to raise sufficient force to be effective. It was decided that Dillon, Meagher and Doheny should once more go off to rally the neighbouring districts while he stood firm where he was.[63]

Prospects had been doubtful enough before. Now nothing seemed in their favour. After so much delay already the only hope of rallying the countryside lay in the news of an outstanding success. As Father Kenyon, the former militant priest of Templederry in Tipperary, told Dillon and Meagher when they arrived: it was not becoming in a priest to start a hopeless struggle; they were perfectly at liberty as far as he was concerned to raise a green flag on a pole anywhere in his district and see just how many men would rally round it.[64]

And soon there came to Templederry and elsewhere news not of a success but of a particularly lamentable failure.

On Saturday, 29 July, the government forces slowly began to move towards O'Brien, penned up in his Tipperary box. He had spent the night writing a letter to the mining company, saying that if they withheld wages from the miners who joined him, then the colliery would be confiscated as national property in the event of the Irish Revolution succeeding.[65] It was the one truly revolutionary step he took in the whole week. Next morning McManus reviewed the local forces. Two days before, few people in Ballingarry had even heard of O'Brien, let alone had any clear idea of his cause.[66] Now McManus counted twenty men armed with guns and pistols, and eighteen with crude pikes.[67] The decision was taken to try and join up with another more powerful force optimistically thought to be in the neighbourhood and attack the nearest police barracks.

Before they could move, a member of one of the Dublin clubs, named John Kavanagh, who had come South to join O'Brien, galloped up to say that on his way he had spotted a large body of police approaching Ballingarry.[68] He had come via Kilkenny, where incidentally the rumour was that the town of Callan was in rebel hands and O'Brien himself at the head of twenty thousand men. All the approaches to Kilkenny were now guarded by the military, but he thought the government were in a panic and urged O'Brien, who seemed elated by this news, to strike rapidly. At that moment another messenger came up to say that an even larger body of police was now approaching from Thurles. O'Brien and McManus decided to defend Ballingarry.

A barricade, manned by O'Brien himself, was thrown up. Stephens and some of those armed with guns occupied the houses immediately overlooking it. McManus and another party lay flat on their faces in a hollow about 250 yards ahead of the barricade, waiting to catch the police in the rear as they approached it.[69]

The police whom Kavanagh had spotted had now arrived within a mile or so of Ballingarry. But seeing the barricade and the large crowds assembled – the majority of whom can only have been sightseers – the police veered prudently away and made for cover in a solid one-storey stone house with a slate roof about a mile northwards at Farrinrory.[70] This house belonged to a widow, a Mrs McCormack. She was out at the time, but her five children, all under ten, were inside when Sub-Inspector Trant and forty-six men entered, and chorusing 'The British Grenadiers' started breaking up the furniture to put the house in a state of defence.[71]

Without waiting for orders the mob rushed towards the house, sweeping Smith O'Brien before them. McManus decided the best policy would be to try and smoke the police out by setting fire to some straw in the stables at the back, and was in the process of doing this when he was stopped by O'Brien who said that the widow herself had now arrived and was appealing to him to save her house and her children from destruction.[72]

She, O'Brien, McManus and a few others then went through a gate into the small cabbage garden that surrounded the house, and O'Brien boldly went up to one of the windows. Climbing up onto the sill he asked to speak to Sub-Inspector Trant, the police commander. Trant had taken up his post at an upstairs window and there was a delay while someone went to fetch him. Meanwhile, O'Brien talked to the policemen at his window telling them that he was an Irishman and a soldier too, and asking them to give up their arms. To this they replied: 'We would forfeit our lives rather than give up our arms.'[73]

Whereupon O'Brien said he would allow them five minutes in which to make up their minds, and got down from the window sill.

The next thing that happened was that, as O'Brien turned away, someone – clearly not O'Brien – shouted:

'Slash away, boys, and slaughter the whole of them!' or words to that effect.[74]

Some stones were thrown. Possibly a shot was fired from the crowd.

The police were in an unpleasant situation and very nervous. They fired a volley. They continued to fire intermittently for the next hour or so, expending some 230 rounds in all.[75] Two of the would-be besiegers were killed and a number wounded. None of the police were wounded.[76] There was a general retreat of the besiegers, including eventually even O'Brien, who had at first refused to leave the scene declaring formally that an O'Brien never turned his back on an enemy.[77]

The local priest, a Father Fitzgerald, now came on the scene. O'Brien enlisted his help in making one more attempt to persuade the police to lay down their arms. But the priest received only a harangue from the agitated Sub-Inspector, who conjured up visions of '98 and threatened martial law, the burning of houses and summary executions for this resistance to lawful authority. On his return to O'Brien Father Fitzgerald advised him to give up all notion of attacking the house and O'Brien seemed disposed to take the advice.[78]

Another policeman had arrived during the fighting with a message for Sub-Inspector Trant about reinforcements on the way but had been made prisoner by the mob and had his horse taken from him before being released. Some time later this policeman ran into O'Brien wandering about on this horse of his in a state of some distraction. O'Brien, thinking that the man had come to arrest him, produced a pistol and prepared to sell his life dearly. The policeman hurriedly reassured him, and when the misunderstanding had been cleared up they had something of a heart-to-heart conversation.

The policeman told O'Brien he had no hope of success with the clergy against him, and asked him how, in any case, he hoped to be able to take on regular troops. O'Brien's reply was that he had been working for his country for twenty years and his country could redeem itself if it liked. The policeman said the only way it could be redeemed was with blood. O'Brien said he wanted no blood and gave him his horse back.[79]

Two hours later another force of police arrived, and after a brief engagement with the mob, which James Stephens attempted to rally, they relieved the widow McCormack's house and its loyal defenders.* Further bodies of police followed. O'Brien, McManus and Stephens went off into hiding. They had little alternative since McManus's attempt to raise a force from the citizens of Ballingarry to avenge their fallen comrades produced only three volunteers.[80] The 'rising' was over.

As an eye-witness of Ballingarry declared a few days later: the idea that it had been a rebellion was ridiculous.[81] O'Brien himself called it an 'escapade' and added, echoing Emmet, 'it does not deserve the name of insurrection'.[82]

Large bodies of troops and police soon poured into the area round Ballingarry. There was no repetition of the horrors of '98. Many arrests were made and according to the local parish priest 'whole families were left mourning and desolate, for many died in captivity and exile, others perished from long concealment in bogs and mountains'.[83] But there were no executions.

None of the leaders were betrayed in hiding. O'Brien himself remained at large for over a week and was eventually captured on the platform at Thurles railway station, trying to make his way back to his home near Limerick.[84] He was wearing a black hat, a blue coat and light plaid trousers at the time, and had just bought himself a second-class ticket and forgotten to collect his sixpence change. An English railway guard named Hulme made the initial arrest and received the £500 reward.[85]

Others arrested while more conventionally on the run included McManus, taken on board a ship bound for America in Cork harbour, and Meagher, caught on the open road near Cashel after nights spent in ditches, haylofts and peasant cabins. James Stephens's death from a bullet at Ballingarry was reported in the *Kilkenny Moderator*. The paper, while regretting the loss of this 'most inoffensive young man, possessed of a great deal of talent', and lamenting 'his untimely and melancholy fate', nevertheless trusted it might prove a 'wholesome warning to the hot young blood of Kilkenny'.[86] However, the *Moderator's* rival, the *Kilkenny Journal*, scooped it a couple of months later when it was able to announce that Stephens had written to a friend in Tipperary from Paris, where he had found sanctuary and where refugees were, he revealed, being received in the highest circles.[87] Stephens had made his escape to France via Bristol and London, after spending adventurous weeks in hiding together with Doheny who also got to France. O'Mahony, thanks to the local loyalties he commanded, kept some-

---

* More than thirty years later Stephens gave a rather fanciful account of this engagement in the *Irishman* newspaper, in which he claimed that several constables were killed. None of the Crown forces were killed that day at Ballingarry. Stephens's exaggerations have unfortunately been repeated in Desmond Ryan, *The Fenian Chief* (Dublin, 1967). There is little doubt, however, that Stephens acted bravely.

thing of a force in being in Tipperary for a few weeks. In September he unsuccessfully attacked a police barracks at Glenbar with the loss of two men, and another at Portlaw in County Waterford with the loss of one. He then escaped to join Stephens and Doheny in Paris.[88]

O'Brien's trial for high treason was by then over. He was found guilty and sentenced to be drawn on a hurdle to the place of execution, there hanged by the neck until dead and then decapitated and cut into four quarters to be disposed of as Her Majesty thought fit – the routine formula of the day*.[89] The same sentence awaited Meagher, McManus and others involved in the misfortunes of that last chaotic week in July. From the dock, McManus, who had been earning the large sum of £2,000 a year as a shipping agent in Liverpool only a few months before, stressed that he had been activated not by animosity towards Englishmen, among whom he had spent some of the happiest and most prosperous days of his career. 'It is not', he added, 'for loving England less but for loving Ireland more that I stand now before you.'[90] Meagher had declaimed with dignity: '... the history of Ireland explains my crime and justifies it ... judged by that history, the treason of which I have been convicted loses all guilt – is sanctified as a duty – will be ennobled as a sacrifice'.[91]

The jury in O'Brien's case had brought in a strong recommendation to mercy, and it was not thought that the death sentence would be carried out. However, O'Brien typically refused to apply for a pardon, which was the only legal means of granting him a reprieve, and a special act of Parliament had to be passed in the following year enabling the government to transport him for life instead. He was sent to Tasmania with Meagher, McManus and John Martin, who had meanwhile been convicted for sedition in his paper, the *Irish Felon*. In Tasmania they were joined by Mitchel, who after his year in Bermuda had spent a further eleven months on the high seas journeying via South America and the Cape.

In Tasmania O'Brien, again typically, alone refused to give his parole at first. He was confined to a solitary existence in and around a cottage on a small island off the coast of Tasmania, and made an abortive attempt to escape which was betrayed. Later, as his health deteriorated, he gave in and became a ticket-of-leave man like the others, with the run of a district about thirty-five miles long by ten miles wide.

McManus, Meagher and Mitchel all eventually escaped from Tasmania to America, having planned their escapes while on parole with the aid of the Young Irelander, P. J. Smyth, who had come specially from America for that purpose.[92] O'Brien was finally pardoned with Martin in 1854, and allowed to return to Ireland and the bosom of his embarrassed family in

---

* Earlier in the queen's reign the time-honoured passage about disembowelling the traitors while still alive and burning their entrails in front of them had been relinquished.

1856.[93] Though it is sometimes said that he 'took no further part in public life',[94] this is not strictly so. A curiously dignified figure, even to those political enemies who regarded his antics of 1848 as ridiculous, he continued to appear on the fringes of public life, writing letters to newspapers and identifying himself with aspirations for constitutional nationality until his death in 1864. 'Erratic' was the respectful term of opprobium Unionists reserved for him. In 1859 he visited America, where he met Mitchel, Meagher and O'Gorman again. The *New York Express* wrote: 'There is a hesitancy and diffidence about him which perhaps does not attract favourably at first, but ... there is something in him which rivets the hearer in spite of himself.'[95]

Mitchel, Meagher and O'Gorman were all to make new lives for themselves in the stimulating and demanding conditions of the still evolving nation on the other side of the Atlantic. The need to earn a living there, to establish a social identity in a strange society, to find both the material and psychological security necessary for day-to-day existence always set up a personal conflict between the demands of America and Ireland in the minds of even the most spirited and determined emigrant advocates of the Irish 'cause'. The very imprecision of this cause and its slightly theoretical nature in contrast with the hard facts of life in the States was part of this conflict. The conflict was resolved in many different ways, but usually so as to dilute the amount of energy directly applied to Ireland.

Some, like O'Gorman, chose the easy way out, abandoning all further serious thoughts of Irish nationalism. He died in 1895, a distinguished New York judge. D'Arcy Magee, though he retained an interest in Ireland, equally firmly renounced the rebelliousness of his youth, became postmaster-general of Canada, and was assassinated by an extreme Irish separatist in 1867.

Meagher continued to breathe fire and lived quite successfully off it in the form of lectures or journalism. When he did finally take the field it was not in Ireland at all but in the country of his adoption. In the early years of the American Civil War he fought in the three-thousand-strong Irish brigade of the Union Army at the great battles of Bull Run, Antietam, Fredericksburg and Chancellorsville, taking command with the rank of general after its commanding officer had been taken prisoner. Both the brigade and its general showed outstanding bravery and dash. At Fredericksburg, of the twelve hundred men Meagher led into action only 280 were fit for action the next morning.[96] An exasperated Confederate general burst out during the battle: 'There are those damned green flags again',[97] and a Confederate soldier wrote home to his wife: 'Why, my darling, we forgot they were fighting us, and cheer after cheer at their fearlessness went up all along our lines.'[98] But out of the battle line Meagher's military career seems to have been less distinguished. He left the army under something of a cloud, with accusations of drunkenness and incompetence and even talk of a court-martial hanging over him.[99] He died in 1866 when acting-governor of the district of Montana, which had not yet become a State. Drunk or ill, or possibly both, he fell overboard from a steamboat moored on the Missouri where he was spending the night and disappeared in the rapid current. His wife searched the river's banks for two months for his body without success.[100]

Of all the *émigrés* of this time Mitchel perhaps maintained the best balance in his attitude to Irish affairs. He lived by journalism, running a newspaper himself first in New York and then in the South where he lived during the Civil War. He became a stern advocate of the Confederate cause, and, as one might have expected from his remarks about his fellow convicts on the Bermuda hulks, indulged in no sentimental libertarianism towards the Negro slaves. He was prepared to involve himself in Irish affairs whenever prospects seemed to him realistic, which was less often than more bombastic Irish patriots preferred to assume. Mitchel actually ended his life in Ireland in 1875 in the very house in which he was born, having just been elected Member of Parliament for Tipperary, though unseated as a convicted felon.

Curiously, T. B. McManus was to prove the most effective Young Irelander in the long run, but as a corpse. Having settled in California, where he showed little further interest in the cause of Irish nationality, he died there in 1861. The return of his body to Ireland and its subsequent funeral in the streets of Dublin was made the occasion for a mass patriotic demonstration which inaugurated in Ireland the first hopeful phase of a new movement altogether.

14

The Corpse on the
Dissecting Table

'For the first time these many years,' declared the leading article in the *Kilkenny Journal* for Saturday, 19 August 1848, 'this country is without any popular political association. There is no rallying point. ... A more prostrate condition no country was ever in ...'[1] It was true. The Irish Confederation and the subsequent Irish League had been proved by the events of July to be rallying-points of straw. Now even they were gone. There was not a single club left in Dublin.[2]

It was no use trying to find a convenient scapegoat in O'Brien. It was, as the *Kilkenny Moderator* put it, the 'absurd bravado and unmeaning rhodomontade' of the whole movement that had been exposed.[3] Those club leaders who did try and blame O'Brien's leadership conveniently forgot that 'by their grandiloquent ovations, by bragging of what they would do and what they could do, unfortunate O'Brien was led out absolutely under false pretences'.[4]

The ineffectualness of simply talking about nationality in the face of the realities of Irish life was most cruelly revealed. In the political silence that now prevailed, the sounds the Irish people heard were not the dying trumpets of a defeated cause, but the clanking of crowbars demolishing cabins, the cries of evicted women and children, and the moans of the starving, all of which had persisted for the past three years.[5] With the potato crop again blighted, the prospects for the autumn and winter of 1848 were as grim as they had ever been.[6] The ragged, barefoot crowds lucky enough to find outdoor relief still laboured ten hours a day on empty stomachs for food tickets, throwing themselves on the ground when the overseer's own dinner hour arrived, and staggering to their feet again like sea-sick men when he returned.[7] 'Travel where you would,' wrote a contemporary later, 'deserted and ruined cabins met the eye on every side. You frequently met large parties of emigrants proceeding to the ports.'[8]

Clearly the ideal of nationality had to be brought closer to the lives of the ordinary Irish people if it was to mean anything. A new sort of policy altogether was required.

For a year or so a few of the very young men who had been peripherally involved in the events of July 1848 tried to show that they could do better in the existing situation than their leaders. One was a former member of a Dublin Confederate club, a railway clerk named Philip Gray, one of whose uncles had been hanged in '98.[9] Gray had on his own initiative tried to rouse the peasantry in Meath while O'Brien was making his way round Tipperary at the end of July. Having totally failed, he had joined up with O'Mahony in the South in August and taken part the next month in the attack on Portlaw barracks. In November, with another Dublin ex-Confederate, an eighteen-year-old Protestant student of Trinity College, named John O'Leary, he planned to attack Clonmel gaol and rescue Smith O'Brien.

The rescue was arranged for the night of 8 November, but an informer gave away one of the assembly points, a piece of ground known as 'the Wilderness', and O'Leary and sixteen other young men under his command were arrested there and a few pikes and a large pistol found.[10] The matter was not treated very seriously by the authorities, presumably because of the youth of the apparent leader. Gray, the real leader, was not caught. O'Leary was released from gaol a few weeks later.

It is not quite so easy to dismiss Gray, and O'Leary's next moves as childish pranks. For although they too ended in fiasco they involved the formation of oath-bound secret societies to establish an Irish republic, and there were to be links at least in personnel between these and a later society of the same sort which finally altered the course of Irish history. The formation in 1848 by Gray and O'Leary of these secret societies in the South, and that of another by Joseph Brenan and Fintan Lalor in Dublin, showed at least a recognition, however amateurish, of the need to organize better in future. Their own particular deficiency in professional skill was revealed in the following year.

First, a bold plan of Brenan's to capture Queen Victoria on her visit to Dublin in the summer of 1849 came to nothing, though 150 men actually assembled one night for the purpose.[11] Then, when the different secret societies amalgamated under Fintan Lalor in September, they immediately embarked on a plan for a rising which was not only badly coordinated but also largely known beforehand to the authorities. On the night of 16 September 1849, an unsuccessful attack was made on the police barracks at Cappoquin by a force under Brenan, and the movement disintegrated. Lalor, and the son of a professor at Trinity named Thomas Luby, were imprisoned for a short time. Lalor, whose health had always been bad, died not long afterwards. O'Leary and Gray escaped arrest. Brenan fled to America. This abortive movement to assert Irish nationalism in a more openly aggressive manner than anything the Irish Confederation or Irish League had wished to undertake seemed only to confirm that all such purely nationalistic activities were doomed as unrealistic.

Of the realities of everyday Irish life two were paramount: the desperate hardship of trying to get a livelihood out of the land and the presence of the Catholic Church. The Church was, as it were, the only permanent form of national organization, or indeed true representation, the peasantry had. In Ireland, wrote a Catholic editor of this time, the priests occupied towards the people the role of a gentry or local aristocracy. They were the *only* educated class who truly sympathized with the people, and thus the only class to whom the poor Catholic farmer could turn for advice and guidance on matters temporal as well as spiritual.[12]

The Church was more important than any political association. It was more all-embracing than the agrarian secret societies, not only because it was open, but because it was both localized and universal at the same time. The only time the peasantry had shown themselves capable of being organized politically at all had been when political forces and the Church cooperated closely, in the days of O'Connell. At elections the extent of the priests' spiritual intimidation was often grossly exaggerated, but they exercised considerable influence.[13] Their general influence as day-to-day leaders was something no serious nationalist could leave out of account.

For the Irish farmer and labourer, national consciousness, such as it was, was an emotion rather than a doctrine, a powerful but vague adjunct to that identity of which the chief features were the passionate need to improve his material lot and his Catholicism. Irish nationality was not an end to be pursued for its own sake, as it had been for Davis. Any doctrinaire nationalist had to come to terms with this fact. It was not enough to appeal to national sentiment in order to assert it. If idealists wanted the Irish people to take the idea of Irish nationality seriously, they themselves must take the land situation seriously and must work if possible with the approval, or at worst the benevolent neutrality, of the Catholic Church.

This presented the doctrinaire exponent of nationalism with a dilemma. To work obliquely towards nationality was the only way of making it a reality; yet, by thus appealing primarily to other interests and other loyalties, the goal of nationality itself became secondary. It forfeited that overriding loyalty which should by definition be the essential characteristic of nationalism.

Thus for the rest of the nineteenth century and beyond – perhaps still even today – there remains a certain lack of distinctness about Irish nationality. Many questions have always lain, only half-asked, just below the surface of political life. What, for instance, really was nationality, in Irish terms, if it did not spontaneously and instinctively assert itself as a separate force? Was it something real enough to be pursued for its own sake at all? Or was it only a means to an end; a tactical slogan with which to achieve a better life for the majority of the people of Ireland? And if this could be achieved without pursuit of separate nationality, was there really a need for any positive nationality? Given the long historical tradition of political and racial entanglement with the rest of Britain, was there not something absurd about the idea of 'pure' nationality? Could there perhaps be such a thing as a half-way status between a nation and a province? If not, in view of the past, could Irish pride be satisfied with the status of a province? Events alone were to resolve these uncertainties, often with an arbitrary disregard for national considerations.

With the total humiliation in 1848 and 1849 of all grandiloquent attempts to assert Irish nationality, Irish political life proceeded to concern itself for a time with more down-to-earth affairs. Even a former ardent nationalist like Duffy saw no alternative but to rest his ardour and concentrate, in the appalling wake of the famine, on efforts to alter the land system and extend Ulster custom of tenant right by law to the whole of Ireland. At the same time, Catholic considerations inevitably figured prominently.

The Irish Catholic Church's attitude to the idea of Irish nationality was ambivalent. On the one hand, sympathizing with the people for whose material as well as spiritual welfare it was acutely concerned, it naturally favoured any emphasis on the people's identity which would help further an improvement in their appalling conditions. Similarly, there were specifically Catholic objectives which could be pursued and gained by an effective political rallying of the people. Emancipation itself had been one obvious example of this, and there were other outstanding Catholic issues in which the hierarchy had a political interest, not least of which were the disestablishment of the Protestant Church and the principle of separate denominational education for Catholics.

As far as the pursuit of nationality as an end in itself was concerned, the Church had inevitable reservations, which were not just confined to its spiritual need to assess the justifiability of violence. The Catholic Church itself was, after all, the supreme loyalty with which the hierarchy wanted the people to identify themselves. Any attempt to promote the spiritual idea of nationality must in some sense prove competitive with this. On the whole, therefore, the Church's attitude to nationality in the nineteenth and twentieth centuries proved pragmatic, being generally determined by tactical considerations. Inasmuch as Catholic interests seemed likely to be enhanced by nationality, it was in favour of it. Inasmuch as they seemed likely to be endangered by nationality, it tried to restrain it. In the last resort, where restraint eventually proved impossible, it was prepared to follow, for fear ultimately of losing the power to lead. All of which meant that individual members of the hierarchy, sometimes in conflict, were the forces that determined the Church's attitude to nationality at any given time.

The Irish Catholic Church in the fifties, sixties and seventies of the nineteenth century was dominated by two giant ecclesiastical personalities of very different outlook and temperament: John MacHale, Archbishop of Tuam, who had been a prominent supporter of O'Connell, and Paul Cullen, who became Archbishop of Dublin in 1852. Though Cullen is usually thought of – and rightly by comparison with the progressive MacHale – as having been an extreme conservative, his appointment was from the point of view of nationalists an improvement on his predecessor Archbishop Murray who had been an out-and-out supporter of the government.[14] But Cullen's approach to political developments was based on the cautious assumption that they should be judged by the experience of a dangerous past rather than in the light of an optimistic future. Whereas MacHale saw self-government as the eventual key to all other Irish political and social problems, Cullen feared that an Irish government would be controlled by the Protestant ascendancy. When something like an independent Irish party began to operate in the British House of Commons during the early 1850s, with its immediate objective a Tenants' Rights Bill, Cullen soon cooled towards it because, he said, 'if all Catholics were to unite in adopting such principles I am persuaded that the English government in self-defence would have to expel them from Parliament and begin to renew the penal laws'.[15]

The appearance in the 1850s of an independent Irish party in the Commons is of interest chiefly as an indication of more effective things to come. It eventually failed to obtain its objectives and had disintegrated by the end of the decade. But it was for a time quite an impressive political force, a working combination of the strongest feelings that dominated Irish opinion, namely those concerning the Catholic religion and the land.

Over a hundred thousand persons had been officially evicted from their holdings in 1849 and local tenants' organizations had sprung up in that year as simple measures of self-defence. By 1850 there were twenty such organizations in ten different counties in Ireland. Simultaneously, Ulster tenants, who though protected by the custom of tenant right had suffered hardship trying to meet their rents in famine conditions and were anxious about future security, agitated for legalization of the Ulster custom. A Tenants' League of North and South was formed, and this public recognition of common interest even on a purely material plane seemed particularly hopeful to a nationalist like Gavan Duffy.

Duffy had survived five attempts to convict him of treason felony in 1848 and 1849 when five successive juries failed to agree. He had returned to the editorship of *The Nation*, and in 1852 he entered Parliament as one of forty-eight Irish members of a so-called Irish Tenants' League. The members of this League took a significant public pledge. This was, to be 'perfectly independent of, and in opposition to, all governments who do not make it a part of their policy and a cabinet question to give to the tenants of Ireland a measure embodying the principles of Mr Sharman Crawford's tenant right bill'.[16]

In fact, the nationally unifying drive of the new political association was never very great, for relative agricultural prosperity began to return to Ireland with a series of good harvests beginning in 1851, and the Ulster share in the agitation became insignificant. To some extent the good harvests also lessened the impetus of the tenant right movement in the South. But here religious issues came to its aid.

Even before the election of 1852 Irish members in the House of Commons had been combining in the defence of Catholic interests, particularly against a bill to prevent Catholic bishops assuming territorial titles. In this way Irish Members in Parliament had already achieved some temporary solidarity, parading under the name of 'the Irish Brigade' or, as their opponents called them, 'the Pope's Brass Band'. They had assumed a position of obvious importance in the prevailing delicate balance of British political parties. One prominent member of the 'Brigade' (the Mayo Catholic land-owner G. H. Moore, father of the novelist George Moore) even proposed that they should employ methods of obstruction in the House, but was over-ruled by his colleagues. And it was the alliance of this parliamentary 'Irish Brigade' and the Tenant Right League which gave the forty-eight members elected in 1852 their appearance of independent strength. They took a public pledge to remain independent of any English party that did not commit them to Tenant Right.

But this notion of independence received a temporary shock soon after the new Parliament had assembled. For though the party's first action had been to help turn out Lord Derby's Tory government, yet when a new government under Lord Aberdeen was formed, also depending on the Irish vote for its majority, it was suddenly revealed that two members of the 'independent' Irish party, in spite of their pledge, had taken posts as ministers. These were John Sadleir, a junior Lord of the Treasury, and William Keogh, the new Solicitor General. No assurance of any kind had been given by Aberdeen that he would introduce a Tenant Right Bill. In the light of their public pledge, the behaviour of Sadleir and Keogh was cynical and undermining to the party. Both were men of over-riding personal ambitions.

The character of Sadleir in particular was soon afterwards shown to have been unsavoury by any standards. A gigantic financial swindle was uncovered in 1856, involving securities personally forged by himself, the collapse of the Tipperary Joint Stock Bank, the ruin of thousands of humble Irish farmers and his own suicide on Hampstead Heath. Something of the ill-repute thus attaching to him and Keogh, who though he was to become a judge, also in the end committed suicide, was often later extended by extreme nationalists to the whole principle of trying to work through the House of Commons at all. But at the time, the colleagues of Sadleir and Keogh, once they had recovered from their shock, hailed their departure as having a cleansing effect on the Irish party in the Commons. Ireland was stronger as a result, declared *The Nation*.[17] Frederick Lucas, editor of the *Catholic Tablet*, who had done much to bring the independent party alliance about, also thought that the prospects were good, or even better than they had been before the defection.[18] The term 'independent opposition' was in fact only used about the party after Keogh and Sadleir had left it in April 1853.[19]

A more serious threat to the party's effectiveness was the increasingly reserved attitude of Archbishop Cullen to the principle of 'independent opposition'. Cullen had originally shown some goodwill towards the Tenant Right League and had obviously been gratified by the mobilization in Parliament of pro-Catholic sentiment. But his fear of the possible consequences to Catholicism of too effectively thwarting the British Government was reinforced by the irrational obsession with which he viewed the activities of Gavan Duffy and any sort of national principle that stemmed from the Young Ireland tradition. Cullen had been at the Vatican during the Roman revolution of 1848, and the traumatic shock he had experienced there at the hands of Young Italy became indistinguishably associated in his mind with Young Ireland. Duffy, Cullen declared, was 'a wicked man ... the Irish Mazzini'.[20] Cardinal Newman related how Cullen always compared Young Ireland to Young Italy; and 'with the most intense expression of words and countenance assured me they never came right, never – he knew them from his experience in Rome'.[21]

It was partly due to the discouraging attitude of the Church that in 1855 Duffy decided to abandon hope for the Tenant Right movement and independent opposition altogether, and emigrate to Australia. Those, he said, who ought to have guided and blessed the people's cause had deserted it.[22] There was, he wrote in *The Nation*, no more hope for Ireland 'than for a corpse on the dissecting table'.

It so happened that this independent opposition did in the end achieve nothing. But its failure was not as foregone a conclusion at the time of Duffy's withdrawal as Duffy's own later history made out. His rival editor, Frederick Lucas of the *Tablet*, declared that Duffy's real reason for leaving Ireland was want of financial means, 'but he wants to go off in poetry rather than prose'.[23] The truth was that a number of different factors had made political life difficult for the 'independent party' – Sadleir, and Keogh's defection, the cold shoulder of Archbishop Cullen, Duffy's withdrawal itself, and above all perhaps the good harvests of the fifties which took the desperation out of the Tenant Right movement. But if the core of the party had been stronger, if there had been better organization and discipline, or if there had even been one figure of outstanding political ability to lead it, these setbacks might not have led to its disintegration.

By 1857, of the original forty-eight members who had emerged as 'independents' from the election of 1852 there were only fourteen left, the rest having drifted off into conventional party commitments. The party introduced a land bill every year until 1858, but without converting the government of the day to anything like the necessary radical reappraisal of the system of land-ownership. The greatest failure had been a tactical one: the party's incapacity to exploit the sort of political situation in the House of Commons most favourable to it. In February 1859, for instance, the Liberal Government fell and the Conservatives came into office with a minority vote. The Irish might have been expected to wring from them some major concession in return for their invaluable support. But all that was extracted from the government was a series of peripheral concessions to Catholics, such as the award to Catholic chaplains in the British Army of permanent rank and status along with Church of England chaplains. This concession, though long overdue considering that about one-third of the British Army were Irish Catholics, was of little relevance to the condition of the Irish tenant farmer and labourer. Admittedly, a government landlord and tenant bill was said to be in the course of preparation, but as yet only the intention had been stated. And when later in the year this bill actually appeared and became law it made virtually no difference to the existing situation on the land at all, inspired as it was still by the assumption that at all costs the rights of property must remain paramount. By then, however, the Irish party had already split on other issues and disintegrated.

The failure of this attempt to work through the Union Parliament even for limited Irish national interests was afterwards often taken to prove the hopelessness of trying to achieve Irish national goals through Parliament at all. But the collapse of the independent party of the fifties proved no such point. It proved only the inadequacy of one particular set of men in one set of circumstances. There was no intrinsic reason why in different circumstances, with the agrarian temperature rising and with more gifted men and better tactics, the principle of parliamentary action should not one day be highly successful. And with additional assistance from the widening franchise it was one day to be so, changing the face of Ireland and effectively deploying a widely based national movement for the first time in Irish history.

A potential nucleus of nominally independent Irish members remained, though long unorganized, in being in the House of Commons. The traditional aim of Repeal or some lesser restoration of Irish autonomy remained continually before the Irish people. In 1864 a National League was founded to recover Irish legislative independence, by constitutional means. It is now almost entirely forgotten because another contemporary movement, Fenianism, has retrospectively eclipsed it in Irish history. But it is remarkable that in the eyes of two contemporaries it was the constitutional movement and not Fenianism that then seemed the important national movement of the day. 'The Irish political movements since 1860,' wrote W. J. O'Neill Daunt, the old friend of O'Connell, in 1867, 'have been chiefly an attempt by John Martin [former editor of the *Irish Felon*, now a constitutionalist] and The O'Donoghue [a young ex-soldier MP for Tralee] to establish a National League for the recovery of our national cause of 1782.'[24] And the journalist A. M. Sullivan, himself to be a Member of Parliament, could write in 1878 the now seemingly incredible words: 'The men who led, or most largely influenced, Irish National politics from 1860–65 were William Smith O'Brien, John Martin and The O'Donoghue.'*[25] On the other hand it was the failure of such efforts to make progress that gave moral encouragement to other men, trying to promote a more effective way for nationalists to go about their business. These were the men soon popularly to be known as Fenians.

* Smith O'Brien, usually regarded as having withdrawn from public life after his release from exile, in fact afterwards engaged quite frequently in public controversy on national issues as a strict constitutionalist.

References

PART ONE

1 Treaty Night

1 *Daily Express*, 7 December 1921. Other weather details from *The Times* and other contemporary newspapers.
2 6 April 1893. Hansard, H.C. Debates, 4th series, vol. 10, col. 1597.

2 Contradictions of Irish Nationality

1 William O'Brien and Desmond Ryan (eds.), *John Devoy's Post Bag, 1871–1928*, 2 vols., Dublin, 1948, 1953, vol. ii, p. 522. Letter to Dr Patrick McCartan, 7 February 1918.
2 C. F. N. Macready, *Annals of an Active Life*, London, 1924, p. 573.

3 Strongbow (1170) to the Ulster Plantation (1609)

1 Cited in A. G. Richey, *A Short History of the Irish People*, Dublin 1869, p. 367; from State Papers, Ireland, vol. ii, p. 562.
2 Richey, op. cit., p. 489.
3 W. E. H. Lecky, *History of Ireland in the Eighteenth Century*, 5 vols., London, 1892, vol. 1, p. 5.
4 Richey, op. cit., p. 481.
5 Cited Lecky, op. cit., vol. i, p. 6.
6 ibid., p. 9.
7 Minutes of evidence taken before a *Select Committee appointed to inquire into the Disturbances in Ireland in the last session of Parliament, May 1824*, p. 338. Evidence of the Reverend Michael Collins, parish priest of Skibbereen.
8 *United Irishman*, 30 August 1902.

4 *Great Rebellion (1641) to Penal Laws (1703)*

1 Edward MacLysaght, *Irish Life in the Seventeenth Century after Cromwell,* Dublin, 1939, p. 30.
2 Aidan Clarke, *The Old English in Ireland,* London, 1966, pp. 179–80.
3 Quoted by Isaac Butt, Hansard, H.C. Debates, 3rd series, vol. 228, col. 771, 29 March 1876.
4 Lecky, *History of Ireland in the Eighteenth Century,* vol. ii, p. 182. See also the phrase of a modern Irish poet, Seamus Heaney, in describing the figure of an Orange drummer on 12 July: 'He is raised up by what he buckles under.' (*Listener,* 29 September 1966.)
5 Diarmuid Murtagh, 'The Battle of Aughrim', in G. A. Hayes-MacCoy (ed.), *The Irish at War,* Thomas Davis Lectures, Cork, 1964, p. 61.
6 J. G. Simms, 'Land owned by Catholics in Ireland in 1688', in *Irish Historical Studies,* vol. vii, no. 27, March 1951, p. 189.

5 *Majority Living (1703–1880)*

1 Jonathan Swift, *A Short View of the State of Ireland,* Dublin 1727–8, p. 13. Cited in James Carty (ed.), *Ireland from the Flight of the Earls to Grattan's Parliament,* Dublin, 1951, p. 108.
2 Swift, op. cit., p. 12. Cited in Carty, op. cit., p. 108.
3 Swift, *Proposal for the Universal Use of Irish Manufacture,* cited Lecky, *History of Ireland in the Eighteenth Century,* vol. i, p. 181.
4 Cited in Lecky, op. cit., vol. i, p. 184.
5 *The Querist* (Question 132). Cited in Carty, op. cit., p. 109.
6 J. Bush, *Hibernia Curiosa, giving a general view of the Manners, Customs, Dispositions and co. of the inhabitants of Ireland,* London, 1764, pp. 31–2.
7 Lecky, op. cit., vol. ii, p. 39n.
8 Francis Plowden, *An Historical Review of the State of Ireland from Henry II to the Union,* 2 vols., London, 1803, vol. ii, p. 157.
9 De Latocnaye, *Promenade d'un Français dans l'Irlande,* 1797, pp. 88, 147, 167.
10 *Devon Commission Report Digest,* vol. i, p. 343.
11 Lecky, op. cit., vol. i, p. 363.
12 G. C. Lewis, *On Local Disturbances in Ireland,* London, 1836, p. 107.
13 Hansard, H.C. Debates, 3rd series, vol. 257, col. 1754.
14 Lecky, op. cit., vol. ii, p. 23.
15 *Select Committee 1824,* Minutes of Evidence, p. 25.
16 Lewis, op. cit., p. 14.
17 Cited in R. R. Madden, *The United Irishmen, their lives and times,* 7 vols., London, 1842–6, vol. i, p. 26.

18 Bush, op. cit., p. 136.
19 Lecky, op. cit., vol. ii, p. 165.
20 Lewis, op. cit., p. 162.
21 *Select Committee 1824*, pp. 129, 135–6, 249.

6 Minority Politics, Eighteenth Century

1 Lecky, *History of Ireland in the Eighteenth Century*, vol. ii, p. 54.
2 Speech and address on motion for Declaration of Independence, 1782. Lecky, op. cit., vol. ii, pp. 300–1.
3 Lecky, op. cit., vol. ii, p. 217.
4 Lecky, op. cit., vol. ii, p. 284.
5 ibid., p. 313.
6 Cited in Plowden, *An Historical Review* . . ., vol. ii, pp. 296–7.
7 Lecky, op. cit., vol. iii, p. 7.

PART TWO

1 Ireland and the French Revolution

1 For a summary of Grattan's arguments see Lecky, *History of Ireland in the Eighteenth Century*, vol. iii, p. 135.
2 Charles Bowden, *A Tour of Ireland*, London, 1791, p. 158.
3 ibid.
4 See the speech of Fitzgibbon, Attorney-General, in the Irish House of Commons, 31 January 1787. Cited in Plowden, op. cit., vol. ii, p. 156.
5 Letter dated Dublin, 4 August 1763. B.M. Add MSS 32, 950, f. 123.
6 Francis Plowden, *A Short History of the British Empire*, 1792–3, London, 1794, p. 240.
7 Brother Laurence Dern, *Ahimon Rezon, or Help to a Brother*, Belfast, 1782, p. 3.
8 Plowden, op. cit., p. 276.
9 ibid.
10 Thomas MacNevin, *Leading State Trials, 1794–1803*, London, 1844; trial of James Weldon, pp. 297–347.

2 Wolfe Tone and Samuel Neilson

1 Lecky, *History of Ireland in the Eighteenth Century*, vol. iv, p. 235.

2 R. R. Madden, *The United Irishmen, their lives and times*, 1st series, vol. ii, p. 221.

3 Madden, op. cit., p. 276.

4 William Theobald Wolfe Tone (ed.), *Life of Theobald Wolfe Tone*, 2 vols., Washington, 1826, vol. i, p. 26.

5 Tone, op. cit., pp. 27–8.

6 ibid., pp. 36–7.

7 ibid., p. 43.

8 ibid., p. 36.

9 R. B. McDowell, *Irish Public Opinion, 1750–1800*, London, 1944, pp. 93–4.

10 Tone, op. cit., p. 140.

11 *Report from the Committee of Secrecy to the House of Commons*, London, 1797, p. 5.

12 Tone, op. cit., p. 140.

13 *Report from the Secret Committee of the House of Commons*, Dublin, 1798. Appendix IV. The authorship of the paper as quoted is anonymous. Evidence in D. A. Chart (ed.), *The Drennan Letters*, Belfast, 1931, p. 54, suggests it was probably the work of William Drennan, a radical doctor of medicine who was to be prominent in the early aspirations of the United Irishmen.

14 Tone, op. cit., p. 52.

15 ibid., p. 142.

16 ibid., p. 147.

17 ibid., p. 149.

18 ibid., p. 150.

19 ibid., p. 143.

20 *Report of the Committee of Secrecy to the House of Commons*, London, 1797, Appendix II, p. 46.

21 *Report from the Secret Committee of the House of Commons*, Dublin, 1798, Appendix V, p. 110.

22 ibid.

3 *United Irishmen and Defenders*

1 Tone (ed.), *Life of Theobald Wolfe Tone*, vol. 1, p. 55.

2 ibid., p. 158.

3 ibid., p. 163.

4 ibid., p. 164.

5 ibid., p. 168.

6 ibid., pp. 115–16.

7 ibid., p. 175.

8 ibid., p. 208.

9 W. J. MacNeven and T. A. Emmet, *Pieces of Irish History*, New York, 1807, p. 35.
10 Tone, op. cit., p. 202.
11 ibid., p. 203.
12 ibid., p. 247.
13 *The Times*, 14 November 1792.
14 Tone, op. cit., p. 179.
15 *The Times*, 1 October 1792.
16 ibid., 8 January 1793.
17 ibid., 9 January 1793.
18 ibid., 30 January 1793.
19 ibid., 20 February 1793.
20 ibid., 22 February 1793.
21 See an account of the trial of two Defenders, Lawrence O'Connor and Michael Griffin, in Walker's *Hibernian Magazine* for November 1795, p. 433. This source is given by Lecky, *History of Ireland in the Eighteenth Century*, vol. iii, p. 391. The first part of the trial is reported in the magazine's previous issue for October 1795.
22 Lecky, op. cit., vol. iii, p. 387.
23 *The Times*, 8 June 1793.
24 *Report of the Secret Committee of the House of Lords*, Dublin, 1793.
25 Plowden, *An Historical Review of the State of Ireland*, vol. ii, pp. 389–91.
26 Tone, op. cit., p. 97.
27 MacNeven and Emmet, op. cit., p. 47.
28 *Report from the Secret Committee of the House of Commons*, Dublin, 1798, p. 99.
29 ibid., p. 101.
30 See R. B. McDowell, 'Proceedings of the Dublin Society of United Irishmen', in *Analectica Hibernica*, no. 17, Dublin, 1949, pp. 3ff.
31 MacNeven and Emmet, op. cit., p. 67.

4 French Contacts

1 Lecky, *History of Ireland in the Eighteenth Century*, vol. iii, p. 103.
2 ibid., vol. iii, p. 104.
3 Thomas Moore, *The Life and Death of Lord Edward Fitzgerald*, 2 vols., London, 1831, p. 170.
4 Quoted in Frank MacDermot, *Wolfe Tone*, London, 1939, pp. 141–2.
5 Lecky, op. cit., p. 234, n. 1.
6 *Report from the Secret Committee of the House of Commons*, Dublin, 1798, p. 226, Appendix XXII. This incident is also described in Tone (ed.), *Life of Theobald Wolfe Tone*, vol. i, p. 117.
7 Tone, op. cit., p. 116.

8 Cited in MacNeven and Emmet, *Pieces of History*, p. 72.
9 Tone, op. cit., p. 114.
10 ibid. For Tone's own vindication of his later action in the light of his agreement, see ibid., pp. 125–6.
11 For this and subsequent details, see MacNevin, *Leading State Trials, 1794–1803*, pp. 274 ff.
12 MacNeven and Emmet, op. cit., p. 108.

5 Defenders and Orangemen

1 *The Times*, 22 March 1794.
2 ibid., 21 March 1794
3 ibid., 28 May 1794.
4 Lecky, *History of Ireland in the Eighteenth Century*, vol. iii, p. 218.
5 ibid., p. 387.
6 ibid., p. 385.
7 MacNevin, *Leading State Trials*, p. 387.
8 ibid., p. 313.
9 Walker's *Hibernian Magazine*, October 1795, pp. 351 ff.
10 MacNevin, op. cit., p. 319.
11 ibid., p. 303.
12 ibid., pp. 472–3.
13 ibid., p. 319.
14 ibid., p. 350.
15 ibid., p. 392.
16 ibid.
17 ibid., p. 467.
18 ibid., p. 380.
19 ibid., p. 466.
20 ibid., p. 423.
21 Plowden, *An Historical Review of the State of Ireland*, vol. ii, p. 548. The threat was quoted by Grattan in the Irish House of Commons.
22 Lecky, op. cit., vol. iii, pp. 430–31.
23 *Walkers Hibernian Magazine*, November 1795, p. 430.
24 ibid., p. 433.
25 Cited in Moore, *Fitzgerald*, vol. i, p. 274.
26 *Report of Committee of Secrecy* (printed 6 June 1799), House of Commons Report, vol. xliv.
27 Lecky, op. cit., p. 447.
28 J. T. Gilbert, *Documents Relating to Ireland, 1795–1804*, London, 1893, p. 153.
29 Gilbert, op. cit., p. 150.

6 *Bantry Bay*

1 Tone (ed.), *Life of Theobald Wolfe Tone*, vol. ii, p. 94.
2 Gilbert, *Documents*, p. 170.
3 Tone, op. cit., vol. i, p. 130.
4 Lecky, *History of Ireland in the Eighteenth Century*, vol. iii, p. 498.
5 Tone, op. cit., vol. i, p. 133.
6 ibid., vol. ii, p. 107.
7 ibid., p. 50.
8 ibid., p. 97.
9 For emigrés generally, see Lecky, op. cit., vol. iii, pp. 523–6.
10 Tone, op. cit., vol. ii, p. 92.
11 ibid., p. 152.
12 For a full account of Arthur O'Connor's life see Frank MacDermot, 'Arthur O'Connor' in *I.H.S.*, XV, no. 57 (March 1966), pp. 48–69. The family were not as Gaelic in origin as they sounded, being descended from rich London merchants called Connor who had settled in Cork several generations before.
13 See depositions by soldiers and letters between General Coote and Pelham in the summer of 1797. B.M. Add. MSS. 33104, 318–27.
14 Lecky, op. cit., vol. iii, p. 504.
15 ibid., vol. iii, p. 522.
16 ibid., p. 206.
17 ibid., p. 229.
18 MacDermot, *I.H.S.*, vol. xv, no. 57, March 1966, pp. 54–5.
19 MacNeven and Emmet, *Pieces of Irish History*, p. 187.
20 ibid.
21 *Report from the Secret Committee of the House of Commons*, Dublin, 1798, Appendix VI, p. 114.
22 B.M. Add. MSS. 33104/331.
23 Tone, op. cit., vol. ii, p. 240.
24 ibid., p. 241.
25 ibid., p. 252.
26 Cited in T. Crofton Croker, *Popular Songs Illustrative of the French Invasion of Ireland*, London, 1845. The account of the expedition that here follows is taken principally from Tone, and Lecky, op. cit.; but see also works by Guillon, Gribayedoff, Hayes and Stuart Jones, listed in the Bibliography.
27 Tone, op. cit., vol. ii, p. 260.
28 E. H. Stuart Jones, *An Invasion that Failed*, Oxford, 1950, p. 175.
29 Lecky, op. cit., vol. iii, p. 541.
30 ibid.

31 ibid., pp. 542–3.
32 MacNeven and Emmet, op. cit., p. 189.

7 *United Irishmen in Trouble*

1 Lecky, *History of Ireland in the Eighteenth Century*, vol. iv, p. 29.
2 ibid., p. 31.
3 ibid., p. 33.
4 ibid., p. 34.
5 Samuel MacSkimmin, *Annals of Ulster*, London, 1906, p. 47.
6 Lecky, op. cit., vol. iv, p. 32.
7 Cited in Charles Dickson, *Revolt in the North*, Dublin, 1960, p. 106.
8 ibid., pp. 112–13.
9 Lecky, op. cit., p. 45.
10 Sir J. F. Maurice (ed.), *The Diary of Sir John Moore*, London, 1904, vol. i, p. 284.
11 Lecky, op. cit., vol. iv, p. 208.
12 Maurice (ed.), *Diary of Sir John Moore*, vol. i, p. 287.
13 *Secret Committee*, Dublin, 1798, Appendix IX, p. 120.
14 ibid., Appendix VIII, p. 118.
15 Dickson, op. cit., p. 240. Information of James MacGuckin.
16 B.M. Add. MSS. 38759.
17 Lecky, op. cit., vol. iii, p. 430.
18 Cited in McDowell, *Irish Public Opinion 1750–1800*, p. 239.
19 Private letter dated Dublin 30 June 1797, B.M. Add. MSS. 38759.
20 De Latocnaye, *Promenade d'un Français dans l'Irlande*, p. 286.
21 Lecky, op. cit., vol. iv, p. 90.
22 ibid., p. 96.
23 ibid., p. 77.

8 *New French Preparations*

1 Tone (ed.), *Tone*, vol. ii, p. 414.
2 ibid., p. 416.
3 ibid., p. 420.
4 ibid., pp. 422, 424.
5 ibid., pp. 455–6.
6 ibid., p. 458.
7 *Report from the Secret Committee of the House of Commons*, Dublin, 1798, Appendix XIV, p. 147.
8 Plowden, *An Historical Review of the State of Ireland*, vol. ii, p. 566. The Reverend J. B. Gordon, *History of the Rebellion in Ireland 1798*, London, 1803, pp. 31–3.

9 *Report of the Secret Committee of the House of Commons*, Dublin, 1798, Appendix XVI, p. 168.

10 Lecky, *History of Ireland in the Eighteenth Century*, vol. iv, p. 252.

11 Tone, op. cit., vol. ii, p. 473.

12 ibid., pp. 471–2.

13 Moore, *Fitzgerald*, vol. ii, p. 84.

9 *Repression 1798*

1 James Caulfield (ed.), *The MSS and Correspondence of James, First Earl of Charlemont*, 2 vols., London, 1891–4, vol. ii, p. 301.

2 ibid., p. 304.

3 ibid., p. 306.

4 Coote to Pelham, 9 July 1797. B.M. Add. MSS. 33104. At a court-martial in Belfast in May, a sentence of 1,500 lashes had been pronounced on Private Thomas Redmond of the Galway Militia. *Report of Secret Committee of House of Commons*, Dublin, 1798, p. 291.

5 R. M. Young, *Ulster in '98*, p. 17.

6 Maurice (ed.), *Diary of Sir John Moore*, vol. i, p. 271.

7 James Alexander, *Some Account of the ... Rebellion in Kildare ... Wexford*, Dublin, 1800, p. 28.

8 ibid., p. 28.

9 Roger McHugh (ed.), *Carlow in '98*, Memoirs of William Farrell, Dublin, 1949; p. 75.

10 Maurice (ed.), *Diary of Sir John Moore*, vol. i, p. 294.

11 Mary Leadbeater, *The Leadbeater Papers*, 2 vols., London, 1862, vol. i, p. 227.

12 Thomas Cloney, *A Personal Narrative of those Transactions ... in Wexford ... 1798*, Dublin, 1832, p. 14.

13 B.M. Add. MSS. 41192.

14 Gordon, *History of the Rebellion in Ireland*, p. 62.

15 *Report of the Trial of Henry and John Sheares*, Dublin, 1798, p. 179.

16 ibid., p. 75.

17 ibid., p. 91.

18 McHugh (ed.), op. cit., p. 82.

19 ibid., pp. 82–3.

20 Gordon, op. cit., p. 86.

21 McHugh (ed.), op. cit., p. 90.

22 Gordon, op. cit., p. 92.

23 The following details of her experience are extracted from *The Leadbeater Papers*, pp. 227ff.

24 *McHugh* (ed.), op. cit., p. 95.

25 Charles Ross (ed.), *Correspondence of Charles, First Marquis of Cornwallis*, 3 vols., London, 1859, vol. iii, p. 357.

26 ibid., vol. iii, p. 359.

27 Gordon, op. cit., p. 100.

28 Lecky, op. cit., vol. iv, pp. 336–7. Lecky himself gives the loyalist losses for this action as only nine killed. However, *A History of the Rebellion in Ireland in the year 1798*, a competent factual compilation printed by W. Borrowdale in 1806, gives the figure of twenty-seven dead.

29 Cited in Charles Dickson, *The Wexford Rising in 1798*, Tralee, 1955, p. 16.

30 B.M. Add. MSS. 33104 and *Report of Secret Committee of House of Commons*, Dublin, 1798, Appendix XXIX.

31 Gilbert (ed.), *Documents 1794–1803*, p. 124.

32 ibid., p. 131.

33 Tone (ed.), *Tone*, vol. ii, p. 484.

34 ibid., p. 491.

35 Moore, *Fitzgerald*, vol. ii, pp. 112–18.

10 Rebellion in Wexford

1 B.M. Add. MSS. 32335.

2 B.M. Add. MSS. 41192.

3 B.M. Add. MSS. 37308.

4 ibid.

5 Dickson, *Wexford Rising*, pp. 21–2.

6 Edward Hay, *History of the Insurrection of 1798*, Dublin, 1842, p. 46.

7 Cloney, *Personal Narrative*, p. 98.

8 Wheeler and Broadley, *The War in Wexford*, London, 1910, p. 48.

9 Gordon, *History of the Rebellion*, pp. 104–5.

10 ibid., p. 106.

11 Account of an eye-witness named Peter Foley recorded by Luke Cullen and cited in Dickson, op. cit., pp. 51–6.

12 ibid., p. 53.

13 Cited in Dickson, op. cit., p. 55.

14 Wheeler and Broadley, op. cit., pp. 85–6.

15 Patrick F. Kavanagh, *A Popular History of the Insurrection of 1798*, London, 1898, p. 299. (An eye-witness account of the author's paternal grandfather.)

16 B.M. Add. MSS. 38102.

17 Gordon, op. cit., Appendix III, p. 373. Evidence at the trial of Andrew Farrall.

18 ibid., p. 168.

19 ibid.

20 *History of the Rebellion in Ireland in the Year 1798* (printed by W. Borrowdale, 1806), p. 78.

21 B.M. Add. MSS. 41192 (Letter of Lady Sunderlin dated 3 July 1798).

22 Charles Jackson, *A Narrative of the Sufferings and Escape of Charles Jackson*, 1799, p. 23.

23 *History of the Rebellion* (Borrowdale, 1806), p. 78.

24 Gordon, op. cit., p. 266.

25 Cloney, op. cit., p. 47.

26 Kavanagh, op. cit., pp. 341–2.

27 Charles Jackson, op. cit., p. 21.

28 The carefully calculated conclusion of Dickson, *Wexford Rising*, p. 34.

29 Cloney, op. cit., p. 20.

30 *History of the Rebellion* (Borrowdale, 1806), p. 102. For fuller extracts from Mrs Brownrigg's diary see Wheeler and Broadley, op. cit.

31 Dinah Goff, *Divine Protection through Extraordinary Dangers ... during the Irish Rebellion of 1798*, London, 1857, p. 9.

32 Goff, *Divine Protection*, pp. 13–14.

33 Cited in Dickson, op. cit., pp. 115–16.

34 Cloney, op. cit., p. 39.

35 Gordon, op. cit., p. 272.

36 Cited in Dickson, op. cit., p. 255.

37 ibid., p. 242.

38 Luke Cullen, MSS. cited in Dickson, op. cit., p. 260.

39 Gordon, op. cit., pp. 363–4.

40 Thomas Hancock, *The Principles of Peace ... during the Rebellion of 1798*, London, 1826, p. 105.

41 Cited in Dickson, op. cit., p. 268.

42 Gordon, op. cit., pp. 366–7.

43 Wheeler and Broadley, op. cit., p. 173.

44 John Jones, *An Impartial Narrative of ... Engagements ... during the Irish Rebellion of 1798*, Dublin, 1799, p. 42.

45 Extract from a Letter from a Gentleman in Ireland (B.M. Tracts relating to Ireland). Letter dated 1 August 1798.

46 ibid.

11 Collapse of United Irishmen

1 Letter of W. Wellesley Pole, Captain of Bally Fin Yeomanry, dated 24 August 1798. B.M. Add. MSS. 37308, f. 167.

2 ibid.

3 Ross (ed.), *Cornwallis Correspondence*, vol. ii, p. 355.

4 Maurice (ed.), *Diary of Sir John Moore*, vol. i, p. 311.

5 B.M. Add. MSS. 37308, 167.

6 Gordon, *History of the Rebellion*, p. 269.
7 Ross, op. cit., vol. ii, p. 369.
8 Jackson, *Narrative*, p. 21.
9 Diary of Captain Hodges, English Militia Officer, B.M. Add. MSS. 40166. Entry for 15 October 1798.
10 Sir Jonah Barrington, *Personal Sketches*, 2 vols., London, 1827, vol. i, p. 276.
11 MacNeven and Emmet, *Pieces of Irish History*, p. 189.
12 ibid., p. 196.
13 ibid., p. 189.
14 ibid., p. 221.
15 ibid.
16 Alexander, *Account of Rebellion in Kildare*, p. 95.
17 Ross, op. cit., vol. ii, p. 387.
18 ibid., p. 352.
19 ibid., p. 377.
20 Cited in Dickson, *Revolt in the North*, p. 121.
21 Tone (ed.), *Tone*, vol. ii, p. 511.
22 Cited in Dickson, op. cit., pp. 221–2.
23 ibid.
24 ibid., p. 135.
25 Lecky, *A History of Ireland in the Eighteenth Century*, vol. iv, p. 288. This work was first published in 1884.
26 Cited in Dickson, op. cit., pp. 222–4 and 227–31.
27 Hancock, *Principles of Peace*, p. 131.
28 ibid., p. 133.

12 The French Landing

1 Details of French decisions at this time from Edouard Guillon, *La France et l'Irlande Pendant La Révolution*, Paris, 1888, which is based on the French national archives. See particularly pp. 321ff.
2 Guillon, op. cit., p. 368.
3 ibid., p. 369.
4 L. O. Fontaine, *Notice Historique de la Descente des Français en Irlande*, Paris, 1801, p. 4. Fontaine was the third senior French officer in the expedition. Further details of the French arrival and subsequent events from *A Narrative of What Passed at Killala* (1801) by an eye-witness (i.e. the Bishop of Killala, J. Stock). The diary of another French officer who took part in the landing, Capitaine Jobit (*Analecta Hibernica*, no. 11, edited by Nuala Costello), is also factually interesting and largely substantiates other accounts, although it is animated by strong personal resentment against Humbert. The same edition of

Analecta Hibernica contains a diary covering the first ten days of the landing by a local Protestant clergyman.

5 Stock, *A Narrative of What Passed at Killala*, pp. 34–5.

6 ibid., p. 16.

7 Sir Herbert Taylor, *Impartial Relation of the Military Operations by an Officer*, Dublin, 1799, Appendix.

8 Stock, op. cit., p. 10.

9 Cited from *Dublin Journal*, 18 September 1798, in an article in the *Dublin Review*, vol. 121, no. 23.

10 Guillon, op. cit., p. 303.

11 Stock, op. cit., p. 96.

12 ibid., p. 103.

13 W. H. Maxwell, *History of the Irish Rebellion in 1798*, London, 1845, pp. 255–62, extracts from the Bishop of Killala's day-to-day diary.

14 Taylor, op. cit., p. 59.

15 ibid., p. 58.

16 ibid, p. 67.

17 Fontaine, op. cit., p. 34.

18 ibid., p. 36.

19 ibid., p. 37.

20 B.M. Add. MSS. 40166. Diary of Captain Hodges.

21 Fontaine, op. cit., pp. 41–2.

22 Maxwell, op. cit., p. 261.

23 Stock, op. cit., p. 145.

24 ibid., p. 163.

25 Sir Richard Musgrave, *Memoir of the Different Irish Rebellions*, Dublin, 1801, p. 480.

26 C. W. Vane (ed.), *Memoir and Correspondence of Viscount Castlereagh*, 12 vols., London, 1848–53, vol. 1, pp. 400–3, 406–9, Musgrave, op. cit., p. 464, Appendix XXI, 10 (letter of the Postmaster of Rutland Island written the day after the expedition arrived).

27 Musgrave, op. cit., p. 466.

28 ibid., p. 465.

29 Vane (ed.), op. cit., vol. i, p. 407. (A first-hand account by the Adjutant himself.)

30 ibid.

31 Ross (ed.), *Cornwallis Correspondence*, vol. iii, p. 338.

32 Details of the French fleet from Guillon, op. cit., p. 407. Sir John Warren in his dispatches quoted in the *Annual Register* for 1798 (Appendix, pp. 144–6) seems to have exaggerated the French gun strength.

33 Dispatches of Sir John Warren, *Annual Register*, 1798, Appendix, pp. 144–6.

34 Tone (ed.), *Tone*, vol. ii, p. 346. Commentary by the Editor. Tone's son,

seems to have got the account of his father's part in the action from returning French officers.

35 Historical Manuscripts Commission. Charlemont MSS., 2 vols., vol. ii, p. 337.

36 ibid.

37 An account by the bystander himself, Sir George Hill, given in a letter written the same day (see Lecky, *History of Ireland in the Eighteenth Century*, vol. v, p. 76n.). It seems more likely to be true than the story told by Tone's son that Hill viciously unmasked him while at breakfast with other French officers (Tone, op. cit., vol. ii, p. 348).

38 *State Trials*, XXVII, col. 616.

39 ibid., cols. 617–18.

40 ibid., col. 621.

41 ibid., col. 624.

42 Historical Manuscripts Commission. Dropmore MSS., vol. iv, p. 370.

43 ibid., p. 374.

44 *State Trials*, XXVII, col. 626.

45 Tone (ed.), op. cit., vol. ii, p. 370.

PART THREE

1 The Making of the Union

1 B.M. Add. MSS. 40166. Diary of Captain Hodges.

2 Leadbeater, *Leadbeater Papers*, p. 269.

3 ibid., p. 275.

4 B.M. Add. MSS. 40166. Diary of Captain Hodges.

5 ibid.

6 29 November 1798. Historical MSS. Commission. Laing MSS., vol. ii, p. 466.

7 Buckingham to Grenville, 11 March 1799. Historical MSS. Commission. Fortescue MSS., vol. iv, p. 497.

8 Historical MSS. Commission. Charlemont MSS., vol. ii, p. 348.

9 Lecky, *History of Ireland in the Eighteenth Century*, vol. v, p. 154.

10 Cited in McDowell, op. cit., p.244.

11 Author's italics. Quoted Lecky, op. cit., vol. v, p. 158.

12 ibid., pp. 148–9.

13 Charlemont to Hartley, 14 May 1799. Charlemont MSS., vol. ii, p. 351.

14 Lecky, op. cit., vol. v, p. 268.

15 ibid., pp. 415–16.

16 Duigenan to Castlereagh, 20 December 1798. Vane (ed.), *Castlereagh Correspondence*, vol. ii, p. 52.

17 Vane (ed.), op. cit., vol. ii, p. 48.

18 Castlereagh to Portland, 2 January 1798. Vane (ed.), op. cit., vol. ii, p. 81.

19 ibid., pp. 79, 328, 339.

20 Lecky, op. cit., vol. v, p. 202n.

21 Clare to Castlereagh, 16 October 1798. Vane (ed.), op. cit., vol. i, p. 393.

22 Cornwallis to Portland, 5 December 1798, ibid., vol. ii, p. 35.

23 Troy to Castlereagh, 24 December 1798, ibid., p. 61.

24 Lecky, op. cit., vol. v, p. 250.

25 ibid., p. 236.

26 Charlemont to Halliday, 25 January 1799. Charlemont MSS., vol. ii, p. 344.

27 ibid., p. 345.

28 Lecky, op. cit., vol. v, p. 351.

29 ibid., p. 298.

30 Moore to Castlereagh, 27 June 1799. Vane (ed.), op. cit., vol. ii, p. 343.

31 Cooke to Castlereagh, 18 September 1799, ibid., p. 403.

32 Vane (ed.), op. cit., vol. iii, p. 344.

33 Lecky, op. cit., vol. v, p. 288.

34 Vane (ed.), op. cit., vol. iii, p. 340.

35 ibid., p. 220.

36 Lecky, op. cit., vol. v, p. 237.

37 ibid., pp. 412–13.

2 *Robert Emmet's Fall and Rise*

1 Vane (ed.), *Castlereagh Correspondence*, vol. iii, pp. 366, 379, 381.

2 Lecky, *History of Ireland in the Eighteenth Century*, vol. v, p. 337.

3 Leon O'Broin, *The Unfortunate Mr Robert Emmet*, Dublin and London, 1958, p. 47.

4 ibid., p. 53.

5 ibid.

6 Madden, *The United Irishmen, Their Lives and Times*, 3rd series, vol. iii, p. 88.

7 ibid., p. 304.

8 ibid., pp. 97–8.

9 Details quoted from Thomas Emmet's diary by O'Broin, op. cit., pp. 56–7.

10 ibid.

11 Madden, op. cit., vol. iii, p. 304.

12 For this, and all other details of the failure, see the account which Emmet himself wrote for his brother on the eve of execution, but which was retained by the British authorities. Madden, op. cit., vol. iii, pp. 127–35.
13 ibid.
14 O'Broin, op. cit., p. 106.
15 Madden, op. cit., vol. iii, p. 132.
16 ibid., pp. 303–5.
17 ibid., pp. 312–16.
18 ibid., p. 134.
19 M. MacDonagh, *The Viceroy's Post Bag*, London, 1904, p. 413.
20 Madden, op. cit., vol. iii, p. 246.

3 The Failure of the Union

1 For earlier comparisons see above, p. 22.
2 Minutes before *Select Committee Inquiring into the Disturbances in Ireland*, 1824, p. 300 (5 June 1824).
3 Hansard, H.C. Debates, 3rd series, vol. 85, col. 753.
4 *Select Committee*, 1824, p. 126.
5 Cited in J. E. Pomfret, *The Struggle for the Land in Ireland*, Princeton, 1930, p. 8.
6 Kohl. Quoted P.S. O'Hegarty, *History of Ireland Under the Union*, London, 1952, p. 388.
7 Hansard, H.C. Debates, 3rd series, vol. 304, col. 1790.
8 De Latocnaye, *Promenade d'un Français dans l'Irlande*, p. 146.
9 *Select Committee*, 1824.
10 *Select Committee on State of Ireland*, 1825, p. 48.
11 R. D. Edwards and T. D. Williams, *The Great Famine*, Dublin, 1956, p. 127.
12 *Select Committee Inquiring into Disturbances in Ireland*, 1824. Minutes before House of Lords, p. 131.
13 R. B. O'Brien, *Thomas Drummond, Life and Letters*, London, 1889, p. 208.
14 Hansard, H.C. Debates, 3rd series, vol. 85, col. 751.
15 Select Committees of 1824, 1825; Devon Commission Report, 1845.
16 Minutes Before *Select Committee Inquiring Into Disturbances in Ireland* (5 June 1824), p. 361.
17 ibid., 17 June 1824, p. 437.
18 Edwards and Williams, op. cit., p. 252.
19 Hansard, H.C. Debates, 3rd series, vol. 85, cols. 1364–5.
20 ibid., col. 274.
21 ibid., col. 1363.
22 ibid., vol. 105, col. 1287.
23 ibid.

24 The best account of the famine is to be found in R. D. Edwards and T. D. Williams (eds.), *The Great Famine*. But it is a scholarly work not primarily concerned with narrative for its own sake. For the general reader there is also Cecil Woodham-Smith's *The Great Hunger*, in which good narrative and scholarship are combined.
25 Hansard, H.C. Debates, 3rd series, vol. 105, col. 300.
26 ibid., H.L. Debates, 3rd series, vol. 254, col. 1857.
27 ibid., H.C. Debates, 3rd Series, vol. 190, cols. 1357–8.
28 Angus Macintyre, *The Liberator*, London, 1965, p. 104.

4 Daniel O'Connell and Catholic Emancipation

1 John O'Connell (ed.), *The Life and Speeches of Daniel O'Connell*. Dublin, 1846, vol. i, pp. 23–4.
2 *The Nation*, 26 November 1844.
3 *The Nation*, 11 July 1846. Quoted by O'Hegarty, *History of Ireland under the Union*, p. 241.
4 9 September 1844. Quoted O'Hegarty, op. cit., p. 187.
5 Michael MacDonagh, *Daniel O'Connell and the Story of Catholic Emancipation*, London, 1929, p. 114.
6 ibid.
7 ibid., p. 115.
8 Michael Tierney (ed.), *Daniel O'Connell: Nine Centenary Essays*, Dublin, 1949, p. 133.
9 ibid.
10 James Reynolds, *The Catholic Emancipation Crisis in Ireland, 1823–9*, Yale, 1954, p. 96.
11 Tierney, op. cit., p. 138.
12 ibid., p. 122.
13 Reynolds, op. cit., pp. 141–2.
14 ibid., p. 140.
15 ibid., p. 148.
16 December 1824, ibid., p. 143.
17 ibid., p. 148.
18 ibid., p. 146.
19 ibid., p. 158.
20 ibid.
21 ibid.
22 ibid., p. 162.
23 MacDonagh, op. cit., p. 195.
24 ibid., p. 196.

5 *The Repeal Debate*

1 Hansard, H.C. Debates, 3rd series, vol. 22, col. 1093.
2 ibid., col. 1156.
3 ibid., col. 1178.
4 ibid., col. 1166.
5 ibid., col. 1188.
6 ibid., col. 1204.
7 T. W. Moody and J. C. Beckett (eds.), *Ulster Since 1800*, London, 1954, p. 34.
8 Hansard, H.C. Debates, 3rd series, vol. 22, col. 1204.
9 ibid., vol. 23, col. 246.
10 ibid., vol. 22, col. 1212.
11 ibid., col. 1195.
12 ibid., vol. 23, col. 70.
13 ibid., H.L. Debates, col. 303.
14 Angus Macintyre, *The Liberator*, London, 1965, pp. 164–5.
15 MacDonagh, *Daniel O'Connell and the Story of Catholic Emancipation*, p. 219.
16 ibid., p. 246.

6 *O'Connell and Davis*

1 MacDonagh, *O'Connell and the Story of Catholic Emancipation*, p. 250.
2 Sir James Graham, cited in Kevin Nowlan, *The Politics of Repeal*, London, 1965, p. 33.
3 Nowlan, op. cit., p. 51.
4 *The Nation*, 22 October 1842.
5 *The Nation*, 22 July 1842.
6 *The Nation*, 22 July 1843.
7 Charles Gavan Duffy, *Young Ireland*, London, 1880, pp. 373, 387–8.
8 Charles Gavan Duffy, *Thomas Davis: A Memoir*, London, 1890, p. 24.
9 D. O. Madden, *Ireland and Its Rulers*, pp. 247–51.
10 Duffy, *Davis*, p. 41.
11 Bolton King, *Mazzini*, London, 1902, p. 107.
12 An Address read before the Historical Society, Dublin, 26 June 1840.
13 Duffy, *Davis*, p. 84.
14 Quoted T. W. Rolleston (ed.), *Prose Writings of Thomas Davis*, London, 1889, p. 281.
15 Rolleston, op. cit., p. 194.
16 ibid., p. 160.
17 ibid., p. 162.

18 ibid., p. 155.
19 ibid., pp. 156–7.
20 ibid., p. 218.
21 ibid., p. 222.
22 *The Nation*, 22 October 1842.
23 ibid.
24 ibid., 25 March 1843.
25 ibid., 3 June 1843.
26 ibid., 17 June 1843.
27 ibid., 10 December 1842.
28 ibid., 25 March 1843.
29 ibid., 5 August 1843.
30 Duffy, *Davis*, p. 111.
31 ibid.
32 ibid., p. 114.

7 *'Monster Meetings'*

1 *The Nation*, 4 February 1843.
2 ibid., 19 November 1842.
3 ibid., 25 March 1843.
4 ibid., 22 April 1843.
5 ibid.
6 MacDonagh, *O'Connell and the Story of Catholic Emancipation*, p. 266.
7 *The Nation*, 27 May 1843.
8 Cited in Nowlan, *The Politics of Repeal*, p. 52.
9 ibid., p. 55.
10 *The Nation*, 3 June 1843.
11 ibid., 17 June 1843.
12 ibid.
13 ibid.
14 ibid., 8 July 1843.
15 ibid.
16 ibid., 22 July 1843.
17 ibid., 29 July 1843.
18 ibid., 22 July 1843.
19 ibid., 29 July 1843.
20 ibid., 5 August 1843.
21 ibid., 12 August 1843.
22 ibid., 19 August 1843.
23 ibid., 26 August 1843.
24 British Museum Catalogue, 1872, c. 1. (10), (Ballads).

25 *The Nation*, 19 August 1843.
26 ibid., 26 August 1843.
27 ibid., 30 September 1843.
28 ibid., 16 September 1843.
29 ibid., 23 September 1843.
30 ibid.
31 ibid., 7 October 1843.
32 ibid., 30 September 1843.

8 Biding Time After Clontarf

1 Duffy, *Young Ireland*, p. 371.
2 *The Nation*, 14 October 1843.
3 ibid., 2 December 1843.
4 ibid., 28 October 1843.
5 ibid., 11 November 1843.
6 ibid.
7 ibid.
8 ibid., 28 October 1844.
9 ibid.
10 ibid., 21 October 1843.
11 ibid.
12 ibid., 30 December 1843.
13 ibid., 17 February 1844, for attack on Catholics *not* resigning.
14 Duffy, *Young Ireland*, p. 519.
15 *The Nation*, 18 March 1848.
16 H.C. Debates, 3rd series, vol. 70, cols. 675–7.
17 *The Nation*, 30 December 1843.
18 ibid.
19 ibid., 17 February 1844.
20 ibid., 24 February 1844.
21 ibid., 2 March 1844.
22 ibid., 9 March 1844.
23 Duffy, *Thomas Davis: A Memoir*, p. 189.
24 *The Nation*, 2 March 1844.
25 ibid., 9 March 1844.
26 Clarke, *I.H.S.*, vol. iii, no. 9 (March 1942), p. 22.

9 O'Connell's Imprisonment and After

1 Duffy, *Thomas Davis: A Memoir*, p. 190.
2 *The Nation*. 9 March 1844.

3 ibid., 16 March 1844.
4 ibid., 23 March 1844.
5 ibid., 30 March 1844.
6 ibid., 6 April 1844.
7 ibid., 13 April 1844.
8 ibid., 1 June 1844.
9 ibid., 8 June 1844.
10 Duffy, op. cit., p. 230.
11 *The Nation*, 8, 22, 29 June 1844.
12 ibid., 8 June 1844.
13 ibid., 29 June 1844.
14 ibid.
15 ibid., 31 August 1844.
16 ibid.
17 ibid., 14 September 1844.
18 ibid.
19 Duffy, *Four Years of Irish History*, pp. 2, 22–3. Duffy sees no inconsistency in talking on the one hand of O'Connell's fading powers and yet attributing to him tactical skill and even genius 'to the last hour of his career' when accusing him of manoeuvring against Young Ireland (op. cit., pp. 120, 198). Modern historians have followed him in implying that by 1845 O'Connell had abandoned Repeal; e.g., Clarke, *I.H.S.*, vol. iii, no. 9, p. 22; Angus Macintyre, *The Liberator*, London, 1965, p. 277; Denis Gwynn, *Young Ireland and 1848*, Cork, 1949, p. 31. Gwynn describes O'Connell in 1844 as 'plainly worn out and weary of the burden of political leadership and agitation'. See also J. C. Beckett, *The Making of Modern Ireland*, London, 1966, p. 327.
20 W. J. O'Neill Daunt, *A Life Spent for Ireland*, London, 1869, p. 57.
21 ibid., p. 61.
22 *The Nation*, 14 September 1844.
23 ibid.
24 ibid., 20 July 1844.
25 W. J. Fitzpatrick, *Correspondence of O'Connell*, 2 vols., London, 1888, vol. ii, pp. 346–7.
26 *The Nation*, 14 September 1844.
27 ibid., 21 September 1844.
28 ibid.
29 Duffy, *Young Ireland*, p. 542.
30 Nowlan, *The Politics of Repeal*, p. 73.
31 ibid., p. 74.
32 ibid.
33 *The Nation*, 21 September 1844.
34 ibid., 28 September 1844.

35 ibid.
36 ibid.
37 ibid., 5 October 1844. For *Nation* optimism, 12 October 1844.
38 Fitzpatrick, op. cit., vol. ii, p. 331.
39 The letter is given in full in the Appendix to Fitzpatrick, op. cit., vol. ii, p. 434.
40 Duffy, *Thomas Davis: A Memoir*, pp. 249–50, 262.
41 ibid., p. 446.
42 Duffy, *Thomas Davis: A Memoir*, p. 244.
43 Duffy, *Young Ireland*, p. 578.
44 ibid., p. 589n.
45 ibid.
46 ibid.
47 *The Nation*, 30 November 1844.
48 ibid., 16 November 1844.

10 More 'Monster Meetings'

1 See, e.g., *The Nation*, 26 April, 3, 10, 24, 31 May, 7, 14 June, 2, 9 August, 27 September, 11, 18 October 1845.
2 ibid., 7 December 1844.
3 ibid., 14 December 1844.
4 ibid., 18 January 1845.
5 ibid., 29 March 1845.
6 Denis Gwynn, *Young Ireland and 1848*, Cork, 1949, p. 30.
7 *The Nation*, 29 March 1845.
8 ibid.
9 ibid., 26 April 1845.
10 ibid.
11 R. B. McDowell, *Public Opinion and Government Policy in Ireland, 1801–46*, London, 1952, p. 226.
12 *The Nation*, 26 April 1845.
13 Gwynn, op. cit., p. 34.
14 The criticism first came from an English Tory. Gwynn, op. cit., p. 41.
15 *The Nation*, 31 May 1845.
16 ibid.
17 ibid.
18 *The Pilot*, 28 May 1845.
19 *The Nation*, 31 May 1845.
20 ibid., 3 May 1845.
21 ibid.
22 ibid., 31 May 1845.
23 ibid.

24 ibid., 7 June 1845.
25 ibid., 29 March 1845.
26 ibid., 14 June 1845.
27 ibid.
28 ibid.
29 ibid., 12 July 1845.
30 ibid., 26 July 1845.
31 ibid., 2 August 1845.
32 ibid., 9 August 1845.
33 Duffy, *Young Ireland*, pp. 715ff.
34 Fitzpatrick, *Correspondence of O'Connell*, vol. ii, p. 363.
35 *The Nation*, 13 September 1845.
36 ibid., 20 September 1845.
37 ibid., 27 September 1845.
38 ibid.
39 ibid.
40 ibid.
41 ibid.
42 ibid., 4 October 1845.
43 ibid., 11 October 1845.
44 ibid.
45 ibid.
46 ibid., 18 October 1845.
47 ibid.
48 ibid., 15 November 1845.
49 ibid., 11 October 1845.
50 ibid., 25 October 1845.
51 ibid., 25 October 1845.
52 ibid.
53 ibid., 15 November 1845.

11 *Repeal, Famine and Young Ireland*

1 *The Nation*, 20 December 1845.
2 ibid.
3 ibid.
4 ibid.
5 See shipping columns of contemporary newspapers throughout the famine period *passim*, but particularly *The Nation*.
6 *The Nation*, 20 December 1845.
7 ibid.
8 Duffy, *Four Years of Irish History*, p. 116.

322

9 *The Nation*, 22 November 1845.
10 ibid.
11 Duffy, *Four Years of Irish History*, pp. 117–18.
12 ibid., p. 119.
13 *The Nation*, 31 January 1846.
14 ibid., 24 January 1846.
15 ibid., 14 February 1846.
16 ibid., 21 February 1846.
17 Duffy, *Four Years of Irish History*, pp. 10–11.
18 Duffy, *Four Years of Irish History*, p. 10.
19 *The Nation*, 21 February 1846.
20 ibid., 28 February 1846.
21 ibid., 24 January 1846.
22 ibid., 21 February 1846.
23 ibid.
24 ibid., 21 March 1846.
25 ibid., 4 April 1846.
26 ibid.
27 ibid., 16 May 1846.
28 ibid., 23 May 1846.
29 ibid., 30 May 1846.
30 ibid.
31 ibid., 13 June 1846.
32 ibid.
33 ibid.
34 ibid.
35 ibid., 20 June 1846.
36 ibid.
37 ibid.
38 ibid.
39 ibid., 27 June 1846.
40 ibid.
41 ibid.
42 ibid.
43 For this and all subsequent details of this part of the debate see *The Nation*, 18 July 1846.
44 ibid.
45 This and all subsequent details of this debate from *The Nation*, 1 August 1846.
46 Duffy, *Young Ireland*, p. 749.
47 ibid., p. 739.

12 The Irish Confederation

1 *The Nation*, 12 September 1846.
2 ibid., 29 August 1846.
3 ibid., 30 January 1847.
4 ibid., 26 December 1846.
5 ibid., 5 December 1846.
6 ibid., 7 November 1846.
7 ibid., 13 November 1847.
8 ibid., 20 February 1847.
9 ibid., 28 August 1847, 13 November 1847.
10 ibid., 6 November 1847.
11 ibid., 27 November 1847.
12 ibid., 17 July 1847.
13 *Irish Felon*, 1 July 1848, which contains a reprint of the letter Lalor wrote '... in the last week of January 1847 ... to a leading member of the Confederation'. See also Duffy, *Four Years of Irish History*, p. 474.
14 Duffy, op. cit., pp. 476–7.
15 Duffy, op. cit., p. 484.
16 *The Nation*.
17 *The Nation*, 1 January 1848.
18 Duffy, op. cit., pp. 487–8.
19 Duffy, op. cit., p. 494.
20 *United Irishman*, 12 February 1848.
21 ibid.
22 ibid., 15 March 1848.
23 *The Nation*, 5 February 1848.
24 Denis Gwynn, *Young Ireland and 1848*, Cork, 1949, p. 146.
25 Duffy, op. cit., pp. 504–5.
26 *The Nation*, 5 February 1848.
27 ibid.
28 ibid.
29 ibid., 18 September 1847.
30 ibid., 4 March 1848.
31 ibid.
32 Duffy, op. cit., p. 537.
33 ibid., p. 538.
34 ibid., p. 547.
35 ibid.
36 ibid., pp. 538–9.
37 *The Nation*, 11 March 1848.
38 *United Irishman*, 18 March 1848.
39 *The Nation*, 11 March 1848.

40 Cited in *United Irishman*, 11 March 1848.
41 ibid., 22 April 1848.
42 ibid., 8 April 1848. Quoted from the *Galway Vindicator*.
43 *The Nation*, 18 March 1848.
44 ibid., 11 March 1848.
45 ibid., 18 March 1848.
46 ibid.
47 Quoted, *United Irishman*, 29 April 1848.
48 ibid.
49 ibid.
50 *The Nation*, 15 April 1848; *United Irishman*, 29 April 1848.
51 *The Nation*, 25 March 1848.
52 ibid., 20 May 1848.
53 ibid.
54 Duffy, op. cit., p. 594.
55 ibid., pp. 595–6.
56 ibid., p. 597.
57 O'Brien's personal memorandum, quoted Gwynn, *Young Ireland*, p. 193.
58 *The Nation*, 27 May 1848.
59 *Irish Felon*, 24 June 1848.
60 Gwynn, op. cit., p. 193.
61 *Irish Felon*, 24 June 1848.
62 For this and the following details of Mitchel's imprisonment see Mitchel's own *Jail Journal*.
63 *The Irish Tribune*, 10 June 1848.
64 e.g. Gwynn, *Young Ireland*, p. 272.
65 Mitchel, *Jail Journal*, p. 53.
66 ibid., p. 124.
67 ibid., pp. 278, 284.

13 Smith O'Brien's 'Rising' 1848

1 *The Nation*, 15 April 1848.
2 Duffy, *Four Years of Irish History*, pp. 608–9.
3 ibid., p. 609.
4 Gwynn, *Young Ireland*, pp. 206–7, O'Brien's Memorandum.
5 Duffy, op. cit., pp. 617–18.
6 *The Nation*, 10 May 1848.
7 ibid.
8 ibid., 3 May 1848.
9 ibid., 10 May 1848.
10 *State Trials, Trial of Smith O'Brien*, vol. vii, cols. 877–8.
11 Gwynn, op. cit., p. 212.

12 ibid., pp. 212–13.
13 ibid., p. 213.
14 *The Irish Tribune*, 1 July 1848.
15 Letter from Joseph Brennan, a young man from Cork and a poet, *Irish Felon*, 8 July 1848.
16 *The Nation*, 17 June 1848.
17 ibid.
18 Duffy, op. cit., p. 624.
19 Duffy, op. cit., pp. 625–6.
20 Gwynn, op. cit., p. 228.
21 *State Trials, Trial of Smith O'Brien*, col. 110.
22 ibid., col. 111.
23 Gwynn, op. cit., p. 227.
24 *State Trials, Trial of Smith O'Brien*, col. 93.
25 ibid., Appendix A, col. 1096.
26 ibid., cols. 262 and 264.
27 Gwynn, op. cit., pp. 229–30, ibid.; Meagher's *Narrative*, p. 284; *State Trials, Trial of Smith O'Brien*, col. 264.
28 Verbatim quote by Maher in evidence, *State Trials, Trial of Smith O'Brien*, col. 264.
29 O'Brien's Memorandum, quoted Gwynn, op. cit., p. 230.
30 ibid., p. 282.
31 *State Trials, Trial of Smith O'Brien*, col. 97.
32 Meagher's *Narrative*, Gwynn, op. cit., p. 298.
33 ibid., p. 258. Also *Kilkenny Journal*, 29 July 1848.
34 Meagher's *Narrative*, Gwynn, op. cit., p. 280.
35 ibid., p. 286.
36 ibid., p. 288.
37 ibid.
38 *State Trials, Trial of Smith O'Brien*, col. 133.
39 Meagher's *Narrative*, Gwynn, op. cit., p. 289.
40 ibid., p. 290.
41 ibid., p. 291.
42 ibid., p. 292.
43 ibid., pp. 292–5.
44 O'Mahony's *Narrative*; see Michael Cavanagh, *Memoirs of Thomas Meagher*, New York, 1892, p. 273.
45 ibid., pp. 273, 275.
46 *State Trials, Trial of Smith O'Brien*, col. 138.
47 Meagher's *Narrative*, Gwynn, p. 304.
48 Michael Cavanagh, op. cit., p. 278.
49 O'Mahony's *Narrative*, Cavanagh, op. cit., p. 272; and Doheny, *Felon's Track*, p. 166.

50 *State Trials, Trial of Smith O'Brien*, col. 143.

51 ibid., col. 144.

52 Charles Kickham's *Narrative*, see Gwynn, op. cit., p. 316.

53 ibid., p. 233.

54 ibid., p. 316.

55 Cavanagh, op. cit., p. 258.

56 Magee's *Narrative*, Gwynn, op. cit., p. 320.

57 Kickham's *Narrative*, Gwynn, op. cit., p. 317.

58 ibid.

59 Duffy, op. cit., p. 664; Gwynn, op. cit., p. 253.

60 McManus's *Narrative*, Gwynn, op. cit., p. 312.

61 *State Trials, Trial of Smith O'Brien*, col. 162.

62 ibid., col. 163.

63 McManus's *Narrative*, Duffy, op. cit., p. 668.

64 ibid, p. 470.

65 *State Trials, Trial of W. S. O'Brien*, col. 72.

66 Father P. Fitzgerald, *Personal Recollections of the Insurrection at Ballingarry*, Dublin, 1862, p. 15.

67 McManus's *Narrative*, Gwynn, op. cit., p. 313.

68 McManus's *Narrative*, Duffy, op. cit., p. 683.

69 Fitzgerald, op. cit., p. 23.

70 *State Trials, Trial of Smith O'Brien*, col. 168.

71 ibid. Appendix A, col. 1089.

72 Duffy, op. cit., p. 686.

73 ibid., also *State Trials, Trial of Smith O'Brien*, col. 176–8.

74 *State Trials, Trial of Smith O'Brien*, cols. 180–83, 319.

75 ibid., cols. 170, 171.

76 ibid., col. 177.

77 Gwynn, op. cit., p. 319.

78 Fitzgerald, op. cit., p. 30.

79 *State Trials, Trial of Smith O'Brien*, Carrol's evidence, cols. 184–7.

80 McManus's *Narrative*, Duffy. op. cit., p. 688.

81 *Freeman's Journal*, 4 August 1848, cited *Kilkenny Journal*, 9 Augus 1848.

82 Gwynn, op. cit., p. 234.

83 Fitzgerald, op. cit., p. 26.

84 *Kilkenny Journal*, 9 August 1848.

85 *Longford Journal*, 12 August 1848.

86 *Kilkenny Moderator*, 20 August 1848.

87 *Kilkenny Journal*, 4 November 1848.

88 Michael Doheny, *Felon's Track*, Dublin, 1914, *passim*. Ryan, *Fenia Chief*, p. 42.

89 *Freeman's Journal*, 10 October 1848.

90 Cited *Longford Journal*, 21 October 1848.
91 ibid., 28 October 1848.
92 John Mitchel, *Jail Journal*, p. 300.
93 James Stephens, *Reminiscences, Weekly Freeman*, 3 November 1883, cited in Ryan, op. cit., p. 69.
94 Cecil Woodham-Smith, *The Great Hunger*, London, 1962, p. 417.
95 Cited in T. F. O'Sullivan, *The Young Irelanders*, Dublin 1945, p. 188.
96 R. G. Athearn, *Thomas Francis Meagher: An Irish Revolutionary in America*, Colorado, 1949, pp. 120–22.
97 ibid.
98 ibid.
99 ibid., pp. 137, 139.
100 ibid., p. 166.

14 The Corpse on the Dissecting Table

1 *Kilkenny Journal*, 19 August 1848.
2 *Dublin Evening Packet*, 27 July 1848.
3 *Kilkenny Moderator*, quoted in *Dublin Evening Packet*, 3 August 1848.
4 ibid.
5 See, e.g., *Freeman's Journal*, 'Evictions on Lord Clonmel's Estates', 11 September 1848.
6 *Freeman's Journal*, 15, 18, 19, 28 August 1848.
7 See description by the Reverend James Maher of Carlow, *Freeman's Journal*, 25 September 1848.
8 W. J. O'Neill Daunt, *Ireland and Her Agitators*, London, 1867, p. 230.
9 John Savage, *Fenian Heroes and Martyrs*, p. 333.
10 Marcus Bourke, John O'Leary: *A Study in Separation*, Tralee, 1967, pp. 18–19. *Freeman's Journal*, 11 November 1848.
11 Bourke, op. cit., pp. 25–6.
12 Frederick Lucas, *The Tablet*, cited in J. H. Whyte, *The Independent Irish Party* 1850–59, Oxford, 1958, p. 80.
13 Whyte, op. cit., pp. 71–81.
14 See P. J. Corish, 'Political Problems, 1860–1878', in *A History of Irish Catholicism*, vol. v.
15 Cited J. H. Whyte, 'Political Problems 1850–1860', in *A History of Irish Catholicism*, vol. v.
16 Whyte, *The Independent Irish Party*, p. 88.
17 ibid., p. 108.
18 ibid.
19 ibid.
20 ibid., p. 115.
21 ibid.

22 ibid., p. 120.
23 ibid.
24 W. J. O'Neill Daunt, op. cit., p. 242.
25 A. M. Sullivan, *New Ireland*, London, 1877, p. 247.

Index

British Government – *cont.*
continued influence during Grattan's
Parliament, 33–4
dismissal of Catholic magistrates, 205
early plans for Parliamentary Union
with Ireland, 152
fall of Pitt and Tories, 242
increasing hold by Crown patronage,
36, 37
passing of Catholic Relief Act (1793),
56
Pitt's plans for Union, 152, 153, 156,
157
prosecution of O'Connell for
conspiracy, 213
sedition charges against
Confederates, 267–8
Bruce, Rev. William, 52
Brugha, Cathal (Charles Burgess), 7
Bunclody, Newtownbarry, slaughter of
rebels at (1798), 120
Burgess, Charles (Brugha, Cathal), 7

CAMBRIDGE, Duke of, 247
Camden, Lord, Viceroy, and
Defenders' pikes, 68
Cane, Dr, sympathy with Smith
O'Brien, 277, 288
Carders, The, secret society, 25
Carickmacross, fighting between
Defenders and military, 58
Carlow, attempted rising at (1798),
101–3
Carnot, French Minister of War, 76
Carson, Sir Edward, 7
Cashel, County Tipperary, monster
meeting at, 240–1
Castlebar, battle of (1798), 'the races
of', 138
Castlebellingham, County Louth,
Tandy takes Defender oath at, 61
Castlereagh, Viscount—
and Catholic Emancipation, 157
letter to Pelham (1798), 106–7
Catholic Association—
and O'Connell elected at County
Clare (1828), 184–5
declared illegal, 183
founded by O'Connell, 182
O'Connel forms new, 183
Catholic Church, Irish—

ambivalent attitude to Irish
nationalism of, 293
political importance of, 292
Catholic Committee—
and condemnation of Defenders, 60
Keogh's leadership of, 51
Tone becomes official of, 54
Catholic Emancipation, 34–5
Bill passed (1829), 185–6
campaign for by O'Connell, 181–2
vague prospects of, 156–7
Catholic Relief Bill (1778), 35
Catholic Relief Bill (1793), 56, 57
Catholic Rent, penny a month, 182
Catholic Tablet, 296
Catholics, Irish—
active support by priests to
Repealers, 204–5
and Emancipation, 34–5
and Protestant division, 13
and the Great Rebellion (1641), 15,
16
and the militia, 106
and Ulster, 43–4
as landowners, 27
attitude to Union, 155–6
concession by Parliament to (1859),
297
effect of penal laws on, 19–20
legal humiliations, 42
'papered' by Orangemen, 71
Peel's measures to weaken
nationalist demand, 233–4
reduction in land ownership, 19
Relief Act (1793), 56–7
rights allowed under Catholic Relief
Bill, 35
rivalry with Protestants in North, 130
Charlemont, Earl, 30, 90
and Irish Constitution, 30
and Volunteers, 32
opposes Catholic political power,
35–6
opposes Union, 153, 157
Charles II, King, compromise with
Irish Protestants, 17
Childers, Erskine, 7
Clanrickarde, Earl of, joins Irish
National Society, 224
Clare, O'Connell, wins election (1829),
183–4